The Laws in the Pentateuch

THE LAWS IN THE
PENTATEUCH
and other studies

MARTIN NOTH

SCM PRESS LTD

Translated by D. R. Ap-Thomas from the German
Gesammelte Studien zum Alten Testament,
first published by Chr. Kaiser Verlag, Munich 1957,
second enlarged edition 1960.

Translation © Oliver & Boyd 1966

Noth, Martin
The laws in the Pentateuch and other studies.
1. Bible.O.T.——Criticism interpretation, etc.
I. Title   II. Gesammelte Studien zum Alten
Testament. *English*
221.6   BS1171.2

ISBN 0-334-00870-0

334 00870 0
First published in English 1966
by Oliver & Boyd Ltd

This edition published 1984 by
SCM Press Ltd
26–30 Tottenham Road, London N1 4BZ

Printed in Great Britain by
Richard Clay (The Chaucer Press) Ltd
Bungay, Suffolk

Contents

★   ★   ★

Introduction

by Norman W. Porteous

The translation into English of Professor Martin Noth's volume of collected essays should add greatly to the appreciation in the English-speaking world of the work of this very great Old Testament scholar. It is probably correct to regard Noth as Albrecht Alt's most distinguished disciple and to say that places him very close to one of the most fruitful influences upon the modern study of the Old Testament. This appears most clearly in the present volume in the long treatise entitled 'The Laws in the Pentateuch: their assumptions and meaning', which links Hebrew legislation right up to the time of Josiah in a living relationship to the continuing religious confederation of the tribes which bore the name of Israel, rather than to the monarchical system of government which did not correspond to the abiding reality of Israel. Even a prophet as late as Ezekiel in his vision of the future looked forward to something like a renewal of the tribal confederacy. According to Noth it was a clear sign of the loss of the vital sense of history that Judaism gradually transformed the Law into something independent of history and authoritative in its own right.

This fundamental insight of Noth's will be found as a controlling thought in a number of the other essays, for example in III which argues that obedience to the Law was regarded as a response to, not as an earning of grace; and in IV in which it is maintained that the ultimate significance of Jerusalem was its being the focal point of the ancient religious traditions of the confederacy rather than the royal capital of the nation.

Special attention may be drawn to the essay "God, King, and Nation in the Old Testament", which represents one of the most significant contributions on the German side to the debate about the nature of the kingship in Israel, joining battle, as it does, most effectively with the Scandinavian school of thought. That there was a unique controlling element in Israel's history is persuasively argued in this essay.

Of the remaining essays, II and VI are interesting examples of the way in which Noth turns to good account for our understanding of the Old Testament recent texts from Mari, while VII and VIII are notable contributions to the study of Apocalyptic and of the *Book of Daniel* in particular. Indeed none of the studies in this book should be overlooked as each contains penetrating insights such as are characteristic of all of Noth's work. As a supplement to the author's well-known *History of Israel* this book will be found invaluable. The publishers and the translator are to be congratulated on making it accessible to a wider circle of readers.

NEW COLLEGE,
EDINBURGH, 1966.

Foreword to the English Edition

The suggestion that I should publish a collection of my writings on the Old Testament came originally from Professor H. W. Wolff (Mainz), who gave me a great deal of valuable help in preparing this work.

In 1957 the first edition of this book was published in Germany. A second, enlarged edition was published in 1960.

The principal object in publishing this collection of studies has been, of course, to make available in convenient form those articles, essays, and lectures which were out of print or hard to find. This purpose is even more valid today than it was in 1957 —particularly outside Germany.

I would like to record my special thanks to all those who have helped in producing this English edition.

MARTIN NOTH

Jerusalem
  December 1965

Translator's Preface

Archaeologist, exegete, historian, orientalist, philosopher and preacher—in his writings on the Old Testament Professor Martin Noth has made significant contributions in the guise of each one, and the invitation to make this important collection of studies available to a still wider public by translating them into English could not be refused.

Professor Noth's German is not always easy, nor the length of his sentences and the qualifications of his phrases such as turn smoothly into a more matter-of-fact language such as English. A wholly literal translation—particularly in the more philosophizing sections—would be unbearable, and a compromise had to be worked out between lucidity and completeness. This has entailed some minor omissions and rewordings—a delicate task, but worth-while if thereby the author's argument can be more clearly followed.

The second German edition contains in an appendix several additional studies, separately listed and indexed. That inconvenience to the reader has been removed in the present translation.

It remains for me to thank the editorial staff of Messrs Oliver & Boyd for the improvements they have suggested while the work was in progress, and Dr. W. P. Hanson, now of the University of Exeter, for help given at one stage. Finally I must record my indebtedness to my wife and my daughter for aid with checking and proof-reading.

D. R. Ap-Thomas

German Title and place of first publication
of the Studies in this Book

I. *Die Gesetze im Pentateuch (Ihre Voraussetzungen und ihr Sinn)*. Schriften der Königsberger Gelehrten Gesellschaft. Geisteswissenschaftliche Klasse. 17. Jahr (1940) Heft 2. Max Niemeyer Verlag, Halle (Saale).

II. *Das alttestamentliche Bundschliessen im Lichte eines Mari-textes*. Annuaire de l'Institut de Philologie et d'Histoire Orientales et Slaves. Tome XIII (1953). Mélanges Isidore Lévy, pp. 433-444. Brussels 1955.

III. *"Die mit des Gesetzes Werken umgehen, die sind unter dem Fluch"*. In piam memoriam Alexander von Bulmerincq. Abhandlungen der Herder-Gesellschaft und des Herder-Instituts zu Riga. VI. Band Nr. 3 (1938) pp. 127-145. Ernst Plates, Riga.

IV. *Jerusalem und die israelitische Tradition*. Oudtestamentische Studïen. Deel VIII (1950), pp. 28-46. E. J. Brill, Leiden.

V. *Gott, König, Volk im Alten Testament (Eine methodologische Auseinandersetzung mit einer gegenwärtigen Forschungsrichtung)*. Zeitschrift für Theologie und Kirche, 47. Jahrgang (1950), pp. 157-191. Verlag J. C. B. Mohr, Tübingen.

VI. *Geschichte und Gotteswort im Alten Testament* (Rede gehalten bei der Jahresfeier der Rheinischen Friedrich-Wilhelms-Universität zu Bonn am 18. November 1949). Bonner Akademische Reden 3. Scherpe-Verlag, Krefeld.

VII. *Das Geschichtsverständnis der alttestamentlichen Apokalyptik*. Arbeitsgemeinschaft für Forschung des Landes Nordrhein-Westfalen. Geisteswissenschaften. Heft 21. Sitzung am 12. Oktober 1953 in Düsseldorf. Westdeutscher Verlag Köln und Opladen (1954).

VIII. *"Die Heiligen des Höchsten"*. Norsk teologisk tidskrift 56. Årg. (1955) 1.-2. Hefte. Festskrift til Professor Dr. Sigmund Mowinckel, pp. 146-161. Fabritius & Sönner, Oslo.

IX. *Amt und Berufung im Alten Testament* (Rektoratsrede an der Rheinischen Friedrich-Wilhelms-Universität zu Bonn 1958). Bonner Akademische Reden 19. Peter Hanstein Verlag, Bonn.

X. *David und Israel in 2. Samuel 7*. Mélanges Bibliques rédigés en l'honneur de André Robert. Travaux de l'Institut Catholique de Paris Nr. 4 (o.J. [1957]), pp. 122-130. Bloud & Gay, Paris.

XI. *Die Katastrophe von Jerusalem im Jahre 587 v. Chr. und ihre Bedeutung für Israel*. Revue d'histoire et de philosophie religieuses (1953), pp. 82-102. Strasbourg.

Bibliography and List of Abbreviations

ALT, A. *K.S. = Kleine Schriften zur Geschichte Israels.* 2 *vols.* Munich 1953-9.

A.N.E.T. = Ancient Near Eastern Texts relating to the Old Testament, ed. J. B. Pritchard. *2nd edn.* Princeton and London 1955.

A.O.T. = Altorientalische Texte zum Alten Testament, ed. H. Gressmann. *2nd edn.* Berlin and Leipzig 1926.

A.R.M. = *Archives royales de Mari,* Musée du Louvre, Département des antiquités orientales, Textes cunéiformes.

B.A.S.O.R. = Bulletin of the American Schools of Oriental Research.

Bei. *Z.A.W. =* Beihefte zur *Zeitschrift für die alttestamentliche Wissenschaft.* Giessen, later Berlin.

Bei. *H.Th. = Beiträge zur historischen Theologie,* Tübingen.

BENTZEN, A. *Daniel.* Hb. A.T. *2nd edn.* Tübingen 1952.
    King and Messiah, trans. E. W. Heaton. London 1955. Translation of *Messias-Moses redivivus-Menschensohn.* Zürich 1948.

BERTHOLET, A. *Hesekiel.* Hb. A.T. Tübingen 1936.

B.J.R.L. = *Bulletin of the John Rylands Library.*

B.W.A.N.T. = *Beiträge zur Wissenschaft von Alten und Neuen Testament.* Stuttgart.

CASPARI, W. *Die Samuelbücher.* Leipzig 1926.

ENGNELL, I. *Studies = Studies in Divine Kingship in the Ancient Near East.* Uppsala 1943.

Ev.Th. = Evangelische Theologie. Munich.

Festschrift für A. Bertholet = Festschrift für Alfred Bertholet zum 80. Geburtstag gewidmet, ed. W. Baumgartner, O. Eissfeldt, K. Elliger, and L. Rost. Tübingen 1950.

Hb. A.T. = Handbuch zum Alten Testament, ed. O. Eissfeldt. Tübingen.

HERRMANN, J. *Ezechiel.* Leipzig 1924.

J.B.L. = *Journal of Biblical Literature.*

JEPSEN, A. *Bundesbuch = Untersuchungen zum Bundesbuch.* Stuttgart 1927.

KNUDTZON, J. A. *Die El-Amarna-Tafeln.* Leipzig 1915.

KRAUS, H. J. *Gottesdienst in Israel.* Munich 1954.

MEISSNER, B. *Babylonien und Assyrien.* 2 *vols.* Heidelberg 1920, 1925.

MONTGOMERY, J. A. *The Book of Daniel.* Edinburgh 1927.

M.V.Ae.G. = Mitteilungen der vorderasiatisch-aegyptischen Gesellschaft.

NOTH, M. *History* = *History of Israel*. 2nd edn. London 1960. *Translation, rev.*
by P. R. Ackroyd, of *Die Geschichte Israels*. Göttingen 1950.
Pentateuch = *Überlieferungsgeschichte des Pentateuch*. Stuttgart 1948.
System der Stämme = *Das System der zwölf Stämme Israels*. B.W.A.N.T.
Stuttgart 1930.
Überl. Studien = *Überlieferungsgeschichtliche Studien* 1. Schriften der
Königsberger Gelehrten-Gesellschaft. Halle 1943.

O.T.S. = *Oudtestamentische Studiën*.

PROKSCH, O. *Jesaja* 1. Leipzig 1930.

RAD, G. VON. *Ges. Studien* = *Gesammelte Studien zum Alten Testament*. Munich
1958. Eng. tr. by Dr. E. W. Trueman Dicken, entitled *The Problem*
of the Hexateuch, and Other Essays, 1966.

ROST, L. *Thronnachfolge* = *Die Überlieferung von der Thronnachfolge Davids*.
B.W.A.N.T. Stuttgart 1926.

SCHAEDER, H. H. *Esra, der Schreiber*. Beiträge zur historischen Theologie Nr.
5. Tübingen 1930.

SMITH, W. R. *Lectures on the Religion of the Semites*. 3rd edn. London 1927.

STEUERNAGEL, K. *Das Deuteronomium übersetzt und erklärt*. 2nd edn. Göttingen
1923.

SUKENIK, E. L. *Megilloth Genuzoth*. 2 vols. Jerusalem 1948, 1950.
Osar ham-Meghilloth hag-Genuzoth she-bidhe ha-Unibhersitah ha-Ibhrith.
Jerusalem 1954.

T.G.I. = *Textbuch zur Geschichte Israels*, ed. K. Galling, E. Edel, and E. L.
Rapp. Tübingen 1950.

Th. Lz. = *Theologische Literaturzeitung*. Herrnhut.

T.W.Z.N.T. = *Theologisches Wörterbuch zum Neuen Testament*, ed. Kittel.

V.T. = *Vetus Testamentum*.

Z.A.W. = *Zeitschrift für die alttestamentliche Wissenschaft*. Giessen, later Berlin.

Z.D.M.G. = *Zeitschrift der deutschen morgenländischen Gesellschaft*. Leipzig.

Z.D.P.V. = *Zeitschrift des deutschen Palästinavereins*. Leipzig.

I

The Laws in the Pentateuch: Their Assumptions and Meaning

The following investigation has grown out of the detailed study of the presentation of the literary sources of the Old Testament. The form of the enquiry has been determined by considerations of the significance of a particular element within this motley complex of literary sources—the so-called legal sections of the Old Testament. In order to answer the questions posed, it has been necessary to cast the net rather widely; but the aim throughout has been to fix the actual place of the "law" within the history transmitted by the Old Testament. It may be briefly described, therefore, as a contribution to the exposition of the Old Testament.

Anyone acquainted with the theological literature of recent years will know to how marked a degree fundamental questions of interpretation have again come to the fore in general theological debate, and have taken on contemporary interest and significance. It will have been noticed how the question of the significance of "law" in the Old and New Testaments has become, either explicitly or implicitly, a central problem, and one which most frequently engenders a remarkable uncertainty and confusion of judgment. This happens not only where irrelevances impede the forming of a judgment, but also in appropriate contributions to the subject from the most varied theological schools. It is a timely task, therefore, to bring about a clarification in this matter of "law"; or, at least, to initiate a discussion of the matter, based on a rigorous expository study. So, it is hoped, the following investigation, which has as its object the ascertaining of the historical position by means of an unprejudiced exposition of the tradition, may further serve the essentially allied discussion of the theological question of "law".

This aim may indeed be helped by the fact that it has been confined to a definite, circumscribed task. It is urgently desirable,
furthermore, that the role of "law" in the New Testament,
too, should be exegetically investigated by those suitably
qualified.

It is no accident that the theological question of "law" has
again become important at the present time. Here too, as with
many other questions in contemporary discussions, those matters
have again come prominently to the fore which are really of
fundamental importance, and must continually be scrutinized
anew. And so, if theological ethics is to be more than merely a
subsidiary offshoot of philosophical ethics—which indeed it
often has been—it must take the Old and New Testament
manifestation of law as the foundation for its study.

1. The Subject of the Enquiry

Introduction

When the Old Testament canon, from about the fourth
century B.C. on, attained by degrees a fixed and final form, the
first of its three divisions—the Pentateuch—which had been the
first to reach canonical status and validity, gained the inclusive
title "the Law", though it is true that this title does not occur as a
superscription in the MS. transmission of the Old Testament,
whether in the original Hebrew, or in the versions. But when
several New Testament writings—quite apart from later
Rabbinic literature—already cite the Pentateuch as "the Law
(of Moses),"[1] and when, above all, the Greek prologue to the
translation into Greek of Ecclesiasticus (which dates from not
later than the second half of the second century B.C.), mentions
the threefold division of the Hebrew canon, and refers to the
first section simply as ὁ νόμος; then we may assume that from
the very beginning, within the Old Testament canon, the
Pentateuch would customarily be known as "the law". The
reason for this designation can only be the view that "law"

---

[1] The important passages are, in particular, those in which narrative sections
of the Pentateuch are cited as from "the law" *Gal.* IV.21, *I Cor.* XIV.34, also *Lk.*
XXIV.44, where the three divisions of the canon are mentioned.

comprised the central substance and principal content of the Pentateuch.[2]

The Pentateuch is the smallest in compass of the three divisions of the Old Testament canon; but, owing to its position at the beginning of the whole complex, as well as on account of its especially favoured role in the synagogal lessons, it was accounted the most important part of the Old Testament canon, and had a special significance. Consequently, the conception easily arose of the Old Testament as primarily law, i.e. it was considered that the legal portions of the Old Testament made up its real content, whereas the many and extensive other passages gave merely its historical framework and edificatory comment on it. These other passages were to be regarded as centring in the law as their real focus; and the religion of the Old Testament to all intents and purposes achieved its goal in the fulfilment of the law, while the God of the Old Testament was to be honoured primarily as donor and guardian of the law. A few passages in the New Testament already refer to the whole of the Old Testament as "the Law", since they quote passages from the two other divisions of the Old Testament canon as taken from "the Law".[3] When Paul speaks of the law, moreover, and discusses its meaning, he usually means the power to which man is subject within the spheres of faith and life that are covered by the Old Testament.

So it is no wonder that from the beginning of the Christian Church the equation "Old Testament = law" was very widespread, and remains current to the present day. In the church of the reformers the formula "Law and Gospel", as a description and short characterization of the Christian Bible, became and remains popular. Luther was deeply and con-

---

[2] Some, following J. Wellhausen and others, would identify "the law of your God, which is in your hand" (*Ezra* VII.14, also VII.25, 26), and "the law-book of Moses", which Ezra brought with him from Babylon to Jerusalem and made obligatory upon his newly organized post-exilic community (*Neh*. VIII.1ff.); with the Pentateuch in its present form (apart from some later glosses). If this were correct, the description of the Pentateuch as the law or law-book (of Moses) would go back to the middle of the fifth century B.C. Nevertheless, such an identification of the law-book of Ezra with the complete Pentateuch appears most unlikely.

[3] In *John* x.34 and xv. 25, passages from the *Psalms* are cited as from "the Law". In *I Cor*. XIV.21 a prophetic passage, and in *Rom*. III.19 a mixed citation from various prophetic and psalm passages, are described as a word "of the law". It remains uncertain to what the citation from "the Law" in *John* XII.34 refers.

tinuously engrossed with the definition of the concepts "Law and Gospel", and with their mutual relationship and biblical basis, regarding these themes as central to Christian theology. Nor did he simply equate "law" with the Old, and "gospel" with the New Testament, but found both entities in juxtaposition throughout the whole Bible; although, now and then, he did adopt that schematic association of the two concepts respectively with the two sections of the Christian Bible. It will be sufficient to refer to his *Preface to the Old Testament*, published for the first time in 1523, in the first part of the Old Testament in German, and reprinted in later editions of the complete German Bible. There we read:

> Know, then, that the Old Testament is a book of laws, which teaches what men are to do and not to do, and gives, besides, examples and stories of how these laws are kept or broken; just as the New Testament is a Gospel-book, or book of grace.

Nor is this statement essentially modified by the remark which follows, that

> in the Old Testament there are, beside the laws, certain promises and offers of grace by which the holy fathers and prophets under the law were kept, like us, under the faith of Christ.

Again, the remark leads on to the emphatic statement that

> the peculiar and chief teaching of the Old Testament is the teaching of laws, the showing of sin, and the furtherance of good.[4]

Luther was very ready to represent the Decalogue in *Exod.* xx.2-17 as the significant kernel of the Old Testament; this, indeed, was the only passage from the Old Testament that he incorporated in his brief summary of Christian instruction called the Short Catechism. And although he found in this very Decalogue a juxtaposition of gospel and law, it is still a passage from the Old Testament law which appears to him to express the essential content of the Old Testament. But it was not really until

---

[4] Texts in *Works of Martin Luther* (Philadelphia 1931-43) VOL. VI, p. 368; cf. also *Martin Luther, Vorreden zur Heiligen Schrift*, ed. W. Heinsius, Klassische Erbauungsschriften des Protestantismus No. 9, 1934, p. 2.

post-Reformation times that the evangelical churches properly began to speak of the conception "law and gospel" in the sense of the aforementioned simple equations. It remains the same today—particularly, once more, in controversies about the Christian Bible—even to a large degree in the field of theological literature.[5]

But, even on superficial observation, it now appears more than doubtful if the equation "Old Testament = law" can rightly stand, or that this view of the contents of the whole of the Old Testament (which accompanied its canonization) really corresponds to the facts. For on the one hand the Old Testament, with its agglomeration of the most disparate elements, is too many-sided ever to make it likely that its contents could be defined in such a short formula; furthermore, the literature of the Old Testament came into being over a period of approximately a millennium, so it must first be proved that throughout this lengthy period a manifestation so unique as "the law" remained at the focal point of that cultural milieu, which gave the Old Testament literature its character.

The legal sections, moreover, do not constitute such a large proportion of the Old Testament as this equation would suggest. Leaving aside the last two divisions of the Old Testament canon, from which law is virtually absent, even within the Pentateuch itself laws take up only about half of the whole; and taken all together, the Pentateuch is no law but, rather, a long narrative composition made up of varied elements, in which laws—albeit in fairly large amounts—have been inserted only at particular points. The arrangement of the Pentateuch thus makes law appear a subsidiary element, while it is the narrative strand that determines the structure of the work.

This state of affairs is too obvious to have been overlooked even by those who envisage the Old Testament as a "law-book", e.g. Luther. Whoever maintains in spite of this that the whole of the Old Testament is governed by the "spirit of the law" has to take the onus of proof upon himself. But, in any case, the question as to the actual place taken up by "law" within the Old Testament as a whole deserves to be thoroughly explored, not only

[5] Cf. E. Hirsch, *Das Alte Testament und die Predigt des Evangeliums*, Tübingen 1936, p. 76. See *Evangelische Theologie*, henceforth cited as *Ev. Th.*, XVI (1956), pp. 346ff., 349ff.; and *Evangelisches Kirchenlexikon*, VOL. I, Göttingen 1956.

with reference to the current conception of the meaning of the Old Testament law, but also simply on the ground that "law" *does* exist in the Old Testament, and that consequently the proper classification of this particular element within the whole is a task which scholars should undertake.

*　　*　　*

The problem of approach

A. It is quite doubtful whether we should speak of "the law" in the Old Testament at all, since on no view does "the law" appear as a unity. Any thorough investigation quickly shows that "the law" in the Old Testament, even from the most varied standpoints, is a very complex quantity. This well-known fact needs no more than a short recapitulation.

"Law" is present in a series of different *literary units*, in all manner of laws, law-books,[6] cultic ordinances, rituals, and short passages of the catechetical type.

Alongside the larger composite complexes of *Deuteronomy* (*Deut.* XII-XXVI) with its parenetic framework (*Deut.* I-XI, XXVII-XXX), and of the so-called Law of Holiness (*Lev.* XVII-XXVI),[7] we have the older and smaller law-book of the so-called Covenant Code (*Exod.* XX.23-XXIII.19). The collection of sacrificial rituals in *Lev.* I-VII, the group of cultic laws concerning purity in *Lev.* XI-XV, the ritual of the Passover and Maṣṣoth festivals in *Exod.* XII.1-20, 43-49, the ritual of the Day of Atonement in *Lev.* XVI,[8] directions for sacrifice in *Num.* XXVIII-XXIX and *Num.* XV, together with various smaller units of miscellaneous content in *Num.* V, VI, XIX, are all linked up with cultic life in the narrower or wider sense. The Decalogue in *Exod.* XX.2-17 (cf. *Deut.* V.6-21), the cultic instructions in *Exod.* XXXIV.11-26, the so-called curses in *Deut.* XXVII.15-26 form shorter "catechisms".

---

[6] Cf. P. Koschaker in the juridico-historical introduction to H. Ehelolf, *Ein altassyrisches Rechtsbuch*, Berlin 1922, pp. 12ff., for the differentiation between official "laws" put together and deriving their validity through legal enactment, and unofficial "law-books" composed on the basis of the judicial practice of jurists.

[7] In spite of the dissent of S. Kuchler, *Das Heiligkeitsgesetz* (Theol. Dissertation, Königsberg 1929), the "Law of Holiness" should be treated as a literary unit in the same way as is usual with the deuteronomic law, which is very similar to it.

[8] For the prehistory of this section cf. M. Löhr: *Das Ritual von Lev.* 16, Schriften des Königsberger Gelehrten Gessellschaft, Geisteswissenschaftliche Klasse, 2. Jahr, Heft 1, Berlin 1925.

All these were once independent units, subsisting in their own right, each having its own purpose and sphere of validity, and having been transmitted individually for its own sake in the first place.

With regard to the formulation of the individual legal passages, there are two main possibilities within the Old Testament. Firstly, the "casuistic" formulation introduces the protasis with an "If" or a "When", to specify the actual instance treated, and then in the apodosis gives the instructions for treating such a case (punishment, etc). Then secondly, there is the "apodictic" construction, which usually introduces a requirement with the singular form of address "Thou shalt (not)", but occasionally also with the plural "You shall (not)"; this form lays down its requirements without reference to an "If" or "But".

Both constructions occur within the literary units in either simple or modified form. They are frequently juxtaposed, or are even mixed up with one another, and refuse to be separated according to any slick category of law-giving, being found in close association in both sacred and profane law.

The type of formulation, however—at least for non-cultic law—may at least provide a clue to the origin of the individual precepts. It can be shown in detail[9] that the precepts formulated casuistically stand in close relationship, both in form and content, to the legal material available to us from the wide cultural area of the ancient Near East, as it has become so distinctively exemplified of recent years through the recovery of laws and law-books belonging to the great states of Mesopotamia and Asia Minor, and as it obviously was mediated through the Canaanite culture of the Palestinian city-states to the Israelite tribes.

The apodictic construction, on the contrary, appears to have been the normal pattern for the earliest legal matter of the Israelite tribes, and it was then taken up in the priestly Torah[10] in which the priests conveyed their information and advice. Subsequently Canaanite precepts and regulations governing both ordinary daily life and cultic matters were readily admitted. On this last point, it soon becomes clear that in the later develop-

[9] Cf. A. Alt, "Die Ursprünge des israelitischen Rechts", in *Kleine Schriften zur Geschichte des Volkes Israel* (henceforth cited as *K.S.*) VOL. I, Munich 1933, pp. 278ff.

[10] For their origin, form, and content, cf. J. Begrich, *Die priesterliche Tora*, Beiheft zur *Zeitschrift für die Alttestamentliche Wissenschaft*, henceforth cited as Bei: *Z.A.W.*, No. 66, Giessen 1936, pp. 63-88.

ment of Israelite law these different formulations, which had originally belonged to quite different realms, were used together interchangeably.

Very different dates too must be assigned to the different portions of Old Testament law. Apart from the short "catechisms", which can hardly be dated with any certainty, we possess, most probably from the time between the entry into Canaan and the establishment of the monarchy, the *Book of the Covenant*, and then, from the latest period of the monarchy, the *Book of Deuteronomy*, and probably too the *Holiness Code*. (=*Code of Holiness*.)[11]

The cultic laws in *Lev.* I-VII and XI-XV must also belong to the period of the monarchy,[12] while the passages *Exod.* XII.1-20, 43-9; *Lev.* XVI; *Num.* XXVIII-XXIX, XV, were without doubt first drawn up in the post-exilic community. Over and above this, most of these units have had their own particular literary prehistories, and each has taken up into itself all manner of older material in a more or less altered and revised form—a process which now can be elucidated in detail only in very few cases. So the components of "the law" in the Old Testament extend over a space of time amounting in any circumstances to more than five hundred years.

Finally the *content* of the law too is extremely diverse. In addition to the regulation of important regions of social life in the daily round, and general demands for participation in particular cultic actions, we find special directions for the fulfilment of particular sacrificial rites. Alongside the general prohibition of transgressions against the foundations of human

---

[11] The dating of the Code of Holiness is a particularly difficult problem, since grounds may plausibly be adduced for a pre-exilic as well as an exilic or post-exilic, a pre-deuteronomic as well as a post-deuteronomic attribution. The probability seems to be that the Code of Holiness should be brought down to about the time of *Deuteronomy*, with which it shares the closest affinities in its basic ideas, except that these are given a special priestly slant. In the matter of the unity of cult centres alone does the Code of Holiness appear to contradict *Deuteronomy*. The earliest possible date for the Code of Holiness would be the very end of the Judaean monarchy.

[12] These laws may well derive from the cult of the pre-exilic temple of Jerusalem. Against the most commonly accepted, post-exilic, origin is the fact that in them only priests and laity are reckoned with, and there is no concern with the minor clergy, the Levites, who in the post-exilic Temple cult come into such prominence. To this extent B. D. Eerdmans, in *Alttestamentliche Studien*, VOL. IV, Giessen 1912, esp. p. 5, may be correct.

community life, stand the various severe precepts against all participation in cultic activities for strange gods, in sorcery, etc., as well as detailed provisions about cultic purity and impurity.

All the points mentioned have been studied thoroughly with many assured results, in an extensive scholarly literature which takes into account the comparative material from the ancient East. Such work will naturally go on. These points show clearly how complicated the phenomenon of *"the* law" in the Old Testament is. All that permits "the law" in the tradition to appear (quite superficially) as a unity, is the circumstance that, on grounds to be discussed later, the individual elements of the law as a whole have at a later period been traced back to the activity of Moses as a historical person, and inserted for the most part into the narrative tradition about the sojourn of the Israelite tribes at Sinai, so that the legal sections lie close to one another in the Pentateuch. All scholarly work must, however, always take into account the results of the literary and material analysis of the legal portions.

On the other side it must not be overlooked that links in form and content between the individual parts of the Old Testament law appear just as clearly. The same precepts are met with in different literary units, the same materials are always reappearing. In the latest parts of the law there is scarcely a theme that was not already known to the oldest portions; and no subject of the oldest legislation ever becomes completely lost in the course of further legislative development. No instance appears of a particular legal point being judged in a fundamentally different fashion in different "laws"; and scarcely any material provision of any law is later waived, or has a contradictory provision set up against it.[13]

Nor can a clear separation into sacred and "worldly" law be carried out, just as no clear distinctions between cultic and "profane" circumstances existed for ancient thought; in most legal portions of the Old Testament these two spheres stand undifferentiated side by side. Individual precepts in the last resort may be of the most varied origin, having their roots partly in primitive legal provisions of the ancient Near Eastern civiliza-

[13] An exception to this point is furnished by the incisive teaching of the unity of the cult place first expressed in *Deut.* XII.13ff., which the other later and contemporary laws do not know.

tions, partly in customs and views of nomadic tribes, partly in the special circumstances and antecedents of Israelite prehistory; yet at the same time, through their common inclusion in the individual laws and law-books of the Old Testament, they have eventually grown together into a certain unity. Detailed examination certainly shows a historical development in the various branches of law along quite definitely established lines; but this simply shows once more the overall connection of the whole.

Considerably later portions of the law thus show themselves to be in literary dependence upon older ones, but in many cases individual sections are, quite independently of each other, expressions of the same legal material, differing according to their type and period, so that they are indirectly inter-connected. Within the Old Testament as a whole the "law" is in any case something apart, which, in spite of all inner divisions, appears as an entity of a peculiar type, and can and must be treated as one.

B. Face to face with this entity of the "law" the question arises not only as to its origin and development, but also as to its real nature, and the presuppositions for its existence. For it is not really self-evident that in a document of the faith, such as the Old Testament—a Holy Writ—there should stand laws which deal not only with cultic affairs but also with everyday social life. This question of origin has indeed often been raised and thoroughly discussed; yet the second question, concerning the grounds and circumstances of the very presence of the law within the Old Testament at all, has still hardly been discussed on the basis of the discoveries of the last half-century of general historical and juridico-historical studies. Granted that the literary and material analysis of the laws preserved in the Old Testament had to be the first and foremost task, we cannot for all that by-pass the more general question as to the basis of their existence and, therewith, their meaning within the framework of the whole.

It is unlikely that this question should be pointless, in regard to the Old Testament laws; much more probable is it that it should be of fundamental significance for their understanding. Other historical law-codes have had a definite disposition of affairs behind them, such as the ordered way of life of a people, or a political constitution; and solely within the framework of that particular disposition, to which they are tacitly or explicitly related, do they have a meaning or possess the claim to validity and authority which a "law", taken merely as a literary product, does not intrinsically possess. It is self-evident, too, that in these circumstances a law-code as a whole, just as in all its separate parts, can only be properly understood by reference to this given disposition of affairs.

Without more ado, we can presume that laws in the Old Testament are no different, since they are so definitely historically conditioned entities—as their links with the judicial history of the ancient Orient as a whole, and the fact of their belonging to Israelite juridical history (which can be reconstructed from them), abundantly prove. This circumstance of their being historically conditioned, however, forces the conclusion that the Old Testament laws, too, were once actually related to a prior datum such as we have envisaged; and so we can expect that these laws resist comprehension apart from this, and that, in spite of their divine Law-giver, originally these laws did not come into being as some sort of unrelated absolute entities which were to be treated as universally and completely valid, but rather —since they originated in a quite definite historical framework— they demand to be expounded and evaluated in terms of their own meaning.

There is another pointer in the same direction. The Old Testament laws are of a preponderantly negative content. Partly (and this applies particularly to the precepts with an apodictic formulation) they are prohibitions; partly (and pre-eminently in the casuistically formulated expressions, the curses, the group of "capital offences")[14] they lay particular activities under punishment, and thereby in practice really represent pro-hibitions. Furthermore (above all in the sections with a cultic content) we have all manner of directions for undertaking particular activities, without specifying the purpose of these activities.

On the other hand, the Old Testament law-codes nowhere show any intention of creating new legal systems themselves, or even framing new adaptations of a system already in

[14] For these, cf. A. Alt, "Die Ursprünge des israelitischen Rechts" 1934, in *K.S.*, VOL. I, pp. 307ff.

existence. Hence it becomes abundantly clear that, in the different spheres with which the Old Testament law-codes deal, the current existence of a system is presupposed, a system which the law-codes themselves have not sought to formulate, but whose dissolution and destruction they are called upon to prevent.

It appears necessary, therefore, to enquire into these circumstances under which the Old Testament law-codes came into existence, and by which their function was determined. It seems, as might be expected in a historically conditioned phenomenon, developing over a longish period, that the question must be given different answers at different times. We shall have to distinguish, in particular, between an *earlier* period up to the end of the independent states of Israel and Judah, and so to the factitive end of the Israelite nation, which is conventionally named the "pre-exilic period"; and a *later* period, in which, within the framework of the successive world powers, there was no more than a small community in and about Jerusalem, with a widely scattered diaspora—the so-called "post-exilic period".

2. THE PRACTICAL ASSUMPTIONS OF THE PRE-EXILIC LAWS

The political system and legislation

On the analogy of innumerable other law-codes in the world at large, it would be quite natural to presume (for the major part of the law-codes in the Old Testament) that a definite form of government provided the required precondition for their coming into existence—that is, that they were originally *state laws*. In the land where Israel dwelt we are acquainted with a whole range of governments. The monarchy of Saul was only a relatively short episode, and mainly turned upon the position of the king as leader of the Israelite tribal militia; consequently it was scarcely accompanied by the development of a fixed form of government. After it, in the tenth century B.C., came the state founded by David. Its core was formed by the monarchies of Judah in the south, of Israel in the north, and Jerusalem in the centre, all united in his own person; but there was also a whole system of variously dependent marginal states and provinces which were included.

After the death of Solomon, under whom this complicated system of government had already begun to break up, the union between the states of Judah and Israel was sundered; so that from now on the smaller kingdom of Judah (with the city of Jerusalem) and the larger kingdom of Israel existed separately side by side, until the latter was swept away by the Assyrians in 721 B.C., and the former by the Babylonians in 587, and their territories incorporated in the great empires. Consequently there are plenty of different forms of government available in the history of Israel which may be brought forward for consideration as a background for the Old Testament law-codes. Conversely it may be shown that many Old Testament law-codes came into being during the period when these forms of government flourished.

Deuteronomy was certainly composed during the so-called monarchic period, the *Holiness Code* probably also (see above, n. 11); and even behind the cultic laws of *Lev.* i-vii and xi-xv, which also probably came into existence during the monarchic period (see above, n. 12), the political system may stand as a background in so far as these laws probably had their origin in the Temple cult of Jerusalem—and the Temple in Jerusalem from its foundation until its destruction in 587 B.C. was a state sanctuary whose priests were royal officials, so that its ordinances could have been state laws. Apart from the short "catechisms", which are scarcely dateable, the idea of a system of government as a precondition fails only in the case of the (probably) pre-monarchic "Book of the Covenant", on the one hand, and the post-exilic cultic ordinances on the other. Furthermore, we still have the historical tradition in *II Kings* xxii, xxiii.1-3, 21-5 that the deuteronomic law[15] was put into force—apparently therefore as state law—by the Judaean king Josiah in the final third of the seventh century B.C.

There is a good deal to be said for the assumption that at least one series of Old Testament laws owes its existence and one-time validity to the institution of the monarchy. The kings of Judah and Israel used at that time to take upon themselves the role of law-giver, just as various other Oriental rulers did. The code

---

[15] The very old thesis, that the "law-book" of *II Kings* xxii-xxiii is to be sought in the original form of our present *Deuteronomy* has scarcely been seriously shaken by the various attacks upon it. Its correctness will be tacitly assumed in what follows.

of Hammurabi was introduced into the old Babylonian kingdom about 2000 B.C. by Hammurabi, the sixth king of the first dynasty of Babylon, who describes himself categorically as a law-giver in the introduction to the text of the laws.[16]

The Hittite law,[17] to which, however, no introduction has been preserved, probably goes back to a ruler of the new Hittite kingdom in the fourteenth or thirteenth century B.C.

We occasionally hear of Egyptian Pharaohs that they have given laws; although next to nothing has been preserved of Egyptian state laws.[18]

Yet in spite of many attempts, the Old Testament law-codes have not been satisfactorily expounded as state laws. This is scarcely accidental. Even after all that we know about the position of the monarchy on Israelite soil, the assumption that the existing law-codes were promulgated by kings arouses serious doubts. In spite of the relatively good and abundant tradition about the history of the Israelite monarchic period which we have in the Old Testament, we nowhere hear of the law-giving activity of the kings.[19] The monarchy was a relatively late institution in Israelite history; in spite of similar historical circumstances and the same level of culture, the neighbouring peoples attained the establishment of monarchy much earlier.[20] This is explained by the fact that amongst the Israelite tribes of the settled land another system had for the most part taken root, which held back the emergence of the monarchy, and of which more will be said later (see below, pp. 28ff.).[21] This in

[16] Cf. W. Eilers, *Die Gesetzesstele Chammurabis*, Der alte Orient, VOL. XXXI, Nos. 3-4, Leipzig 1932, pp. 12ff. For the dating, cf. M. Noth, *Die Welt des Alten Testaments*, 2nd edn., Berlin 1953, pp. 199, 214, 266.

[17] Cf. H. Zimmern and J. Friedrich, *Hethitische Gesetze aus dem Staatsarchiv von Boghazköi* (Der alte Orient, VOL. XXIII, 2, 1922).

[18] Cf. A. Erman and H. Ranke, *Aegypten und aegyptisches Leben im Altertum*, Tübingen 1923, pp. 157ff.

[19] Even in the incident in *II Kings* XXII-XXIII, King Josiah does not act as "law-giver"; the introduction of *Deuteronomy* at that time was a special case, whose legal preconditions will be discussed in detail below (see pp. 42ff).

[20] Cf. *Gen.* XXXVI.31-9; also *Num.* XX.14 for monarchy amongst the Edomites; *Num.* XXII.4ff.; *Judges* III.12ff., XI.12ff. [emended text] for it among the Moabites; *I Sam.* XI.1f. (cf. *II Sam.* X.1) for it among the Ammonites.

[21] The hostile attitude towards the introduction of the monarchy first appears in relatively late traditions (*Judges* VIII.22f. and especially in the later narrative of the election of Saul as king in *I Sam.* VII.2b-17, VIII.1-22a, X.18-25a, XII.1-25), but was probably as old as the monarchy itself and arose out of a clinging to the other, older system.

turn explains why, in the various forms of government which evolved on Israelite soil, the monarchy was here not so free to develop its functions as usually happens in monarchies.

We learn something about the legal position of the kings from the Old Testament. According to *I Sam.* XI.14*a*-15, Saul was made king by the acclamation of the army. His first appearance links up with the charismatic leadership of the period of the so-called Judges (cf. *I Sam.* XI.6, 7), and his elevation to be king means nothing much more than the extension of his leadership for his lifetime; even this was mainly on account of the outside pressure brought about by the Philistine power. Saul's monarchic role in fact included scarcely anything beyond the perpetual leadership of the army; and after his death Abner, the first officer of the army, who even during Saul's lifetime had been the sole office-bearer in the "state" (cf. *I Sam.* XX.25), was the one who "appointed" Eshbaal, the sole surviving son of Saul, to be King over the majority of the Israelite tribes (*II Sam.* II.8, 9). According to the tradition, David founded his kingship over the states of Judah and Israel upon negotiations between the king in person and the elders of the clans of the separate tribes (*II Sam.* II.4, V.3). Unfortunately we learn absolutely nothing about the content of the negotiations, but only of their practical outcome: that David was recognized as king, and "anointed".[22]

But we may well deduce from *I Kings* XII.3ff. that, in connection with the preliminaries leading up to such an agreement, certain conditions might be laid down by the elders, and perhaps even by David. Until its end in 587 B.C., the monarchy in Judah rested legally upon the compact with David mentioned in *II Sam.* V.3; for after David, thanks to his foresight and power, had once succeeded in getting one of his sons accepted as his successor, succession within the Davidic dynasty was maintained without interruption. Here the very momentum of the monarchy, once it was instituted, played the decisive part. In the state of Israel, on the other hand, the recollection of the one-time emergence of the kingship from the charismatic leadership remained alive; as a consequence, every now and then, upstarts were raised to

[22] Here we are dealing only with the kingship over the Israelite tribes united in the states of Judah and Israel. David's kingship over the city-state of Jerusalem or the Ammonites (cf. *II Sam.* XII.30) rests upon right of conquest; in these cases David adopted the rights of the "Canaanite" city-kings of Jerusalem and the Ammonite kings.

the throne in the same way as Saul—admittedly, on occasion, with the expressed concurrence of the "people", i.e. of its elders.

In Israel too, however, the principle of heredity did lead to the formation of dynasties just as had happened in the Solomonic succession.[23] Presumably no great change took place in the fundamental legal status of the individual kings after David; this status was determined by the concurrence of the elders as the spokesmen of the "people" at the elevation to the throne, whether this is explicitly mentioned or left implicit. Added to this there was another factor of much importance for a problem which will be treated later: the elevation of a person by the elders to be king originally had as its prerequisite a declaration of the divine will concerning the person who was to be the future king. This oracle, in practice, was communicated to the person summoned to rule by the mouth of a "seer" or "prophet".[24] This was what happened with Saul (*I Sam.* IX.26-X.1), and it was a "prophet" who informed the Davidic dynasty as a whole of the divine legitimation of its rule (*II Sam.* VII.8-17).[25]

In the same way, in the state of Israel, when new rulers and founders of new dynasties arose, "prophets" occasionally seized the initiative by uttering the oracle which led to the summoning of the king (*I Kings* XI.29ff., XVI.1; *II Kings* IX.1ff.). Kingship on Israelite soil appears therefore, from the very beginning and throughout its existence, to have been an institution not unconditioned or based simply on itself, but essentially subject to the will of God, as this revealed itself in the prophet's word,

[23] Cf. Alt, "Die Staatenbildung der Israeliten in Palästina", in *K.S.*, VOL. II, esp. pp. 65, 116ff.

[24] Elsewhere, too, the kings of the ancient Near East traced back their election to the will of the gods, particularly of the contemporary national god. Yet in general it was only later that the actual enthronement was visualized as a fulfilment of the divine will; in the cases above, God's decision (previously announced) led to elevation to the throne, and so exhibited a historically effective power.

[25] This "oracle" of the prophet Nathan which counts on an undiminished continuance of the Davidic kingdom probably arose in the time of David (vs. 13 is, however, secondary), at latest from the time of Solomon. As a sacral foundation for the overlordship of the Davidic dynasty in the state of Judah it undoubtedly had great significance, all the more so because the enthronement of both David and Solomon lacked the summons through a prophet's word. *I Sam.* XVI.1-13 is a secondary tradition which, in addition, belongs to the circle of Saul stories, not those of David; and the reference in Nathan's prophecy to a divine summons of David to be king "over my people Israel" is no historical testimony, but a *petitio principii*. By this means Nathan's prophecy replaces what was lacking in David's kingship, and that of his whole dynasty.

and to subsequent acknowledgement by the elders of the clans.[26]

Naturally the momentum of the existing monarchy, once instituted, procured for the king—particularly under powerful and ambitious rulers—all manner of rights, which in practice he simply appropriated. It was as leader of the militia of the twelve tribes that Saul was raised to be king, and the kings always had the right to call up the general levy of the tribes, to lead it, and to appoint its chief officers (*I Sam.* xiv.50; *II Sam.* viii.16, xx.23; *I Kings* iv.4).[27] They took over the property of anyone condemned to death, for the advantage of the royal estate (*I Kings* xxi.15)[28]; in particular cases they levied imposts on the free property-owners of the land (*II Kings* xv.20), and so on.[29] At will they distributed properties to their subjects (*I Kings* ii.42ff.). In the field of legal enactment the kings, or their mouth-pieces, took an active part, and so came into competition with an office pertaining from of old to the elders of the clans and villages. Probably the kings claimed only the right to decide cases brought before them as the highest court of appeal (cf. *II Sam.* xiv.2ff., xv.2ff.).[30] On the other hand, they would scarcely have had the

---

[26] *II Kings* xi.17, according to which, at the installation of David's descendant Joash on the throne of the state of Judah, after the discarding of Athaliah by the Jerusalem high priest Jehoiada, a covenant was concluded "between Yahweh, the king, and the people".

[27] The appointment of officers occurs also in the "King's Right" in *I Sam.* viii.11-17 as a right claimed by the kings (vs.12*a*). But the kings never had full liberty of action *vis-à-vis* the general levy. The national census (obviously put through by David in the interests of organizing the general levy) was regarded as an unwarranted interference in the relationship between Yahweh and the Israelite tribes, who owed their wellbeing to divine blessing (cf. *II Sam.* xxiv.1, 10ff.). The king's right to keep soldiers is the shoe on another foot; originally it has nothing to do with the king's authority over the Israelite tribes, but is derived from the historical influence of "Canaanite" petty kings on the institution of the monarchy in Israel—particularly in the case of David (cf. A. Alt., "Die Staatenbildung der Israeliten in Palästina", in *K.S.*, VOL. II, pp. 25ff., 36ff.).

[28] The overseer of the royal household and estates was one of the highest of the king's state officials (cf. *I Kings*, iv.6*a*, *et ser.*). The "King's Right" cf. *II Sam.* viii also speaks of the royal property and the possibility of its constant increase (vs. 14).

[29] A regular taxation of agricultural and horticultural produce and animal husbandry is mentioned as "King's Right" in *I Sam.* viii.15*a*, 17*a*. For the purpose of organizing this tribute, according to *I Kings* iv.7, v.2ff., the territory of the state was divided into districts, over which were overseers who in turn were subject to a supreme state official (*I Kings* iv.5*a*).

[30] In addition to this the king had a "chief justice" among his highest officials (*II Sam.* viii.16*b*, xx.24*b*; *I Kings* iv.3*b*). The "judges" of *Deut.* xvi.18-20, xvii.8-13, xix.15-21 were quite probably royal officials in whom the deuteronomic law recognized the judicial functions of "elders" (xix.11f., *et ser.*).

right, in theory or in practice, to conscript the free members of
the Israelite tribes for forced labour in a condition of bondage.
This would only have applied to the non-free population in the
territories of the former Canaanite city states.[31] So we can deduce
much the same as we learn from tradition about the legal
position of the kings. In the tradition we hear nothing about their
law-giving activities.

On the other hand, even the laws preserved in the Pentateuch
nowhere positively link up with the regulations for any one of
the patterns of a state which came into being on Israelite soil, or
indeed any other. Obviously, then, they do not presuppose
monarchy, or any particular form of government, as a necessary
state of affairs. In these law-codes the word "king" occurs only
in one single passage—in the so-called "law of the king" in
Deuteronomy (*Deut.* xvii.14-20); but it is clear that it occurs here
primarily because what underlay the law-code was *not* state regulations concerned with the institution of monarchy, but rather
another system on whose basis the then existing institution
of kingship is in fact criticized. In this "law of the king" it is not
the rights and duties of the monarchy which are specified, but
rather all manner of general limitations which are laid upon the
king's freedom of action; things are there prohibited to him
which had always belonged to the normal rights of a king in the
ancient East (the building up of a force of chariots, the accumula-
tion of a state treasury), and which were doubtless practised by
the kings of Judah and Israel. This unusual "king's right" is
mainly formulated in prohibitions; on the positive side there
is only the duty laid upon the king of punctually obeying
the deuteronomic law—which does not otherwise mention
him.

So it is not surprising that all attempts to explain this or that
Old Testament law-code as a "state law" have failed to carry
conviction. These attempts, naturally, have been undertaken
with particular reference to *Deuteronomy*. But *Deuteronomy*
according to its content is no state law; this is shown not only
by the inclusion of the "king's right", but also by the other

---

[31] The notice in *I Kings* ix.21f. deserves more credence on the grounds of inner
probability than does *I Kings* v.27ff. with its conspicuously high numbers. Before
the time of Solomon, David already had a director of forced labour (*II Sam.* xx.24a,
I Kings iv.6b).

elements of this law-book, as will be shown in detail on pp. 34ff.; and the role that Deuteronomy actually played in the sphere of Josiah's cultural and political measures in no way corresponded to its provisions or actual intentions (see below, pp. 48f.). On the score of content we could most easily consider the Book of the Covenant to be a state law, more especially the first part (*Exod.* XXI.1-XXII.16), with its casuistically formulated cases.

Caspari quite rightly recognized this with reference to the close relationships between this section and other ancient state laws, and also to the presence of material dealing with private property and with the person of the individual.[32] But for the Book of the Covenant *as a whole* this is not correct; in addition it is with great probability to be dated *before* the emergence of the first form of Israelite state organization under Saul.[33] The traits mentioned are adequately explained on the thesis that the casuistically formulated cases are derived from the world of Canaanite city-state culture in Palestine, so that in their *pre*-history they once upon a time did have validity within a state system.[34] But due to incorporation in the Book of the Covenant, and consequent combination with groups of legal enactments of different origins, their link with a state system became lost, and they were subjected to a different arrangement.[35]

Finally, it is probably no accident that in the tradition we hear not the slightest hint of a law-giving function of the Israelite and

[32] W. Caspari, "Heimat und soziale Wirkung des alttestamentlichen Bundesbuchs" in *Zeitschrift der deutschen morgenländischen Gesellschaft* (henceforth cited as *Z.D.M.G.*), N.F. VIII 1929, pp. 97-120, esp. pp. 104f.

[33] On the dating, cf., amongst others, A. Jepsen, *Untersuchungen zum Bundesbuch*, henceforth cited as *Bundesbuch* (Beiträge zur Wissenschaft von Alten und Neuen Testament, henceforth cited as B.W.A.N.T., III, No. 5, Stuttgart 1927), pp. 97ff.

[34] This is also Caspari's opinion (*Z.D.M.G.*, VIII, 1929). He traces the original form of the Book of the Covenant back to the "Amorite" state of King Sihon of Heshbon, though without being able to make this thesis really clear. Jepsen (*Bundesbuch*, pp. 71ff.) has given the scarcely correct name "The Law of the Hebrews" to the corpus of casuistically formulated legal precedents. But it is still best to seek its origin within the area of the old Palestinian city-states. The designation of the Book of the Covenant as the "programme of Jehu's revolution" (A. Menes, *Die vorexilischen Gesetze Israels* (Bei. *Z.A.W.* No. 50, Giessen, 1928, p. 43)) might be mentioned as a curiosity.

[35] The possibility that the other laws (such as the Code of Holiness or the collections of cultic regulations) might be state laws has, owing to their usual—but probably partially incorrect—post-exilic dating, never really been taken into consideration.

Jewish kings. The "laws" preserved in the Old Testament are
not in any case to be regarded as state laws; if there *were* state
laws promulgated by the kings, they are not to be found among
those laws preserved in the Old Testament; they have not been
handed down to us.

"Covenant" and Law

(a) *The community addressed in the Old Testament Laws.* The Old
Testament laws envisage throughout a particular community of
people resident on Palestinian soil,[36] whose distinguishing
feature consisted in the fact that "Yahweh the God of Israel"
was its God, a God whose connection with this community was
founded upon definite historical events of the past.[37]

That the common link with Yahweh was constitutive for the
community envisaged by the Old Testament law-codes is too
evident and too generally attested to need detailed proof. It is
sufficient to refer to one or two points. The decalogue in *Exod.*
xx is introduced and made binding by the sentence: "I, Yahweh,
am thy God";[38] the collection of cultic regulations in *Exod.*
xxxiv.11-26, in its original form,[39] twice has the solemn reference
to "Yahweh, the God of Israel"—first at the demand for attend-
ance thrice yearly at the sanctuary, and second at the offering of
the firstlings. Even the Book of the Covenant, the contents of
which give little occasion to refer to the close association with
Yahweh, mentions the name Yahweh outside its cultic section,[40]

[36] All laws preserved in the Pentateuch demonstrably presuppose settled
agricultural life, with the exception of the Decalogue in *Exod.* xx, where satisfactory
evidence for—or against—is lacking.

[37] This community is directly addressed only in the comparatively infrequent
clauses introduced by "You shall (not) . . ."; whereas the "Thou shalt (not) . . ."
formula, though occasionally doubtless having this collective reference, normally
means the individual; and the casuistically formulated objective clauses contain no
address at all.

[38] In this sentence the predicate cannot, in view of the sense, be *YHWH* (as for
example in Luther's translation) but must be *'ĕlōhĕkhā*. For a different view see
now W. Zimmerli, "Ich bin Jahweh", *Geschichte und Altes Testament, Festschrift
Albrecht Alt*, Tübingen 1953, pp. 179ff.

[39] On the literary and critical question in this passage, cf. now G. Beer, *Exodus*,
Handbuch zum Alten Testament, henceforth cited as Hb: A.T., Tübingen 1939,
pp. 159ff.

[40] On the constitutive elements out of which the present Book of the Covenant
has been put together, cf. particularly Jepsen, *Bundesbuch*, pp. 55ff.

in a passage which is noteworthy, because it is in an addition[41] made by the Israelite redactor to the borrowed corpus of casuistically formulated laws. He inserts here in an emphasized fashion the name Yahweh in place of the "gods", otherwise differently named in these laws.[42]

The most productive of examples are *Deuteronomy* and the *Holiness Code*. There is an emphatic reference to *one* Yahweh, whom to love is the prime commandment (*Deut.* vi.4ff.) at the beginning of that prologue to *Deuteronomy* which is shown (by the use of the second person singular) to be the oldest and probably original one, so that the whole corpus of law is filled with the idea of the close link with this God. *Deut.* XXIII.2-9 is the most important of all; here the questions concerning membership of the community envisaged by the law are discussed, and this community is described as *qĕhal YHWH*, "the community of Yahweh"[43]—a description first met with in *Mic.* II.5. It becomes quite clear here, that the law is addressed not to an imaginary recipient, but to a visible, clearly demarcated group defined by the close link with Yahweh.

The *Holiness Code*, however, has been given its name by modern scholars because in several of its sections the laws are based on constantly recurring stereotyped phrases, in which Yahweh himself makes his claims authoritative for those persons envisaged by the law: "You shall be holy, because I, Yahweh, your God, am holy" (*Lev.* XIX.2, XX.7, 26, XXI.6, 8); "I, Yahweh, am he that maketh you (them) holy" (*Lev.* XX.8, XXI.8, 15, 23, XXII.9, 16, 32); "For I am Yahweh (your God)" (*Lev.* XVIII.2, 4, *et ser.*). In the collections of cultic precepts, moreover, we are constantly told that all cultic practices take place "before Yahweh".

The link with Yahweh, in practice, meant for the community envisaged by the laws, separation from those inhabitants of Palestine who had no part in this association. In the Old Testament—due to a secondary extension of the originally more

---

[41] *Exod.* XXII.9-12 is demonstrably an addition, by an Israelite hand, to *Exod.* XXII.6-8; cf. Jepsen, *op. cit.*, pp. 38ff., 66ff.

[42] Since in *Exod.* XXII.8 *'elōhīm* as subject is supplied with a plural verb, we must take *'elōhīm* as a numerical plural elsewhere in the casuistically formulated laws of the Book of the Covenant.

[43] On the meaning of *qāhāl* cf. L. Rost, *Die Vorstufen von Kirche und Synagoge im Alten Testament*, B.W.A.N.T. IV, No. 24, Stuttgart 1938. *Qāhāl* originally meant "proclamation"; it occurs in the passages mentioned in *Mic.* and *Deut.* as a theological conception.

limited term "Canaan"—they are often called "Canaanites",[44] and within the circle of Israelite tribes for a long time they were regarded as "foreign" and different. Particularly in *Deuteronomy* and the Holiness Code the community addressed in the laws is emphatically distinguished from the "Canaanites", who are tied to "other gods". In the original form of the deuteronomic law the emphatic prohibition occurs at once, near the beginning, forbidding any relationships with "those peoples" and their cults (*Deut.* xii.29ff.); and the *qĕhal YHWH* are rigorously segregated even from those elements of the population who belonged not to the old stock of Canaanites, but to a later stratum of population related to the Israelite tribes, though not belonging to their inner circle (*Deut.* xxiii.4ff.). In the *Holiness Code* the "Yahweh statutes" are emphatically set in opposition to the habits customary in the "land of Canaan" (*Lev.* xviii.3ff.).[45]

The "tradition about the conquest" which was originally associated with cultic celebrations, and whose content forms the basis for part of the various literary strands of the Hexateuch narrative, kept alive among the Israelite tribes (who had been once upon a time led into this land by their God) the awareness of their own distinctiveness over against the older inhabitants of that land.[46] As G. von Rad, starting from the liturgical prayer *Deut.* xxvi.5-10*a*, has most recently shown,[47] this occupation tradition actually formed the festival legend for the so-called "Feast of Weeks"—that is, the chief harvest festival of agricultural Palestine. He has also shown that from its very nature this tradition could only have come into being at an encounter between older and later inhabitants on the level of cultic life, and that it arose out of the cultic tradition of the settled land.

At this very festival, however, the Israelite tribes recognised that they owed possession of their land to a historical happening brought about by their God—their settlement in Palestine; and

---

[44] Other passages know of a stereotyped catalogue of various tribal names—some still enigmatic—to describe them (cf. Fr. Böhl, *Kananäer und Hebräer*, Beiträge zur Wissenschaft vom Alten Testament No. 9, Leipzig 1911, pp. 63ff.

[45] In other laws the caution against the "Canaanites" is found mainly in literary additions of a secondary nature, as in *Exod.* xxxiv.11-13, and in the later postscript to the Book of the Covenant in *Exod.* xxiii.23f.

[46] *Deuteronomy*, which purports to have been delivered by Moses before the settlement, prefers to describe the Canaanites simply as "the inhabitants of the land".

[47] G. von Rad, *Das formgeschichtliche Problem des Hexateuchs* (translated in *The Problem of the Hexateuch*, Edinburgh and New York 1966).

further, that the fruits of this their land were to be ascribed to the blessing of this God, and not to the divinity formerly resident in it.

Through the opposition to the "Canaanites", who are always regarded as foreign, and through the linking up with cultic celebrations, the occupation tradition remained alive among the Israelite tribes, and prevented them from forgetting that they had migrated from elsewhere, and from considering themselves —as time passed, and as most other nations of history do— autochthonous in the land of their possession.

It is to this community, marked off by the occupation tradition, that the Old Testament laws address themselves.

This tradition, however, reaches still further back, and knows of a previous sojourn of the Israelite tribes in Egypt and their release from that land. In the liturgical prayer in *Deut.* xxvi.5ff., these events receive their most extensive treatment. The historical question, whether all the Israelite tribes later found united on Palestinian soil were ever really in Egypt or not,[48] may be left on one side. What here concerns us is simply that, due to this tradition held by them in common, the tribes later felt a common link, which differentiated them from the "Canaanites".

The laws in the Pentateuch refer repeatedly, however, to events of early history. This happens most frequently in *Deuteronomy* and the *Holiness Code*. In the framework of the law in *Deuteronomy*, particularly in the oldest prologue, which is composed in the second person singular, reference to this historical occurrence recurs frequently, following the emphatic warning against forgetting the God who led Israel out of Egypt (vi.12). But quite apart from this, in *Deuteronomy* we often find the ground for a particular law linked with the recollection of the delivery out of Egypt or the Israelites' bondage in that land (xiii.11, xv.15, xx.1, xxiv.18—in xiii.6, xxiii.5, xxiv.9 and xxv.17 the reference appears to be secondary).

Much the same is true in the *Holiness Code*; here reference to the Egyptian past is found in *Lev.* xviii.3, xix.34, xxv.42, 55, xxvi.45. In addition, it is repeatedly preserved in the stereotyped

---

[48] Particularly since the researches of C. Steuernagel, *Die Einwanderung der israelitischen Stämme in Kanaan*, Berlin 1901, it is quite generally recognized that only a few of the later Israelite tribes (probably the group of so-called Rachel tribes) had their residence for a period along the borders of Egypt.

formulas mentioned above (see p. 21): "For, I, Yahweh, am your God, who brought you up out of the land of Egypt" (*Lev.* xix.36, xxii.32f., xxv.38, xxvi.13). But the reference to the historical events in and around Egypt in the "festival calendars" of both the deuteronomic law and the *Holiness Code* goes beyond the more or less formal usage in the previously mentioned passages. Here, in differing stages, we come across the "historicization" of the three ancient Palestinian agricultural festivals— as they still show themselves to be in the Book of the Covenant.[49] The festivals evolve into historical memorial festivals for the perpetual remembrance of events and situations associated with the exodus from Egypt. This process of historicization appears in the two sets of laws in quite different guise, so that these show themselves entirely independent of one another, even though roughly contemporary; we see therefore that each of the two laws quite independently has in view the community which was fashioned by the occupation tradition with its memory of the sojourn in Egypt.

In *Deut.* xvi.1-8 the *pesaḥ-maṣṣoth* festival—that combination of the ancient pastoral custom of *pesaḥ*-sacrifice indigenous to the wilderness, with the *maṣṣoth* festival of the settled land, first mentioned in the Book of the Covenant (*Exod.* xxii.15*a*)— contains a twofold relationship to history; it is celebrated in the month of Abib, the month of the exodus from Egypt, and the *maṣṣoth* are explained as "bread of affliction" which were eaten during the hurried flight from Egypt.[50] On the other hand the Feast of Weeks (*Deut.* xvi.9-12, where only an indirect reference to the sojourn in Egypt is found), and the Feast of Tabernacles, do not yet receive any link with history[51] in *Deuteronomy*. In the

---

[49] In the Book of the Covenant the Maṣṣoth festival already has a historical explanation given for it (the month of Abib as the month of the exodus); but Jepsen (*Bundesbuch*, p. 10), is probably correct in regarding this explanation (*Exod.* xxiii.15*aβ*) as an addition (on the basis of *Deut.*).

[50] Generally the verses about the Maṣṣoth festival (vss. 3, 4, 8) in *Deut.* xvi are regarded as additions because they break the connection; in that case there remains the Passover festival in the original narrative of *Deut.*, linked with history by the selection of the exodus month Abib.

[51] According to H. J. Elhorst, "Die deuteronomischen Jahresfeste", (in *Zeitschrift für die alttestamentliche Wissenschaft*, henceforth cited as *Z.A.W.*, N.F. 1, 1924, pp. 136ff.), the sections concerning the Feasts of Weeks and of Tabernacles are also to be ascribed to the secondary stage in *Deut.* xvi, so that only the Passover with its historical *raison d'être* would remain, and the agricultural festivals of Palestine would be completely excluded.

Holiness Code, the *pesaḥ-maṣṣoth* festival and the Feast of Weeks pass without any historical *raison d'être* being ascribed; against this the Feast of Tabernacles, with its originally agricultural custom of living in "booths" (of twigs and branches) at the gathering of tree-fruit, is given a historical basis as a memorial festival of their forefathers' dwelling in huts (they had as a matter of fact been tents) after the exodus from Egypt (*Lev.* XXIII.43). In the remaining laws, where there is altogether less reflection and provision of "reasons", reference to the occupation tradition and the experiences in and around Egypt is found only as an exception. The most important is the introductory clause of the Decalogue (*Exod.* XX.2): "I, Yahweh, am thy God, who hath brought thee up out of Egypt". Apart from this, such references are absent in the "catechisms"[52] just as in the Book of the Covenant.[53] From the collections of cultic regulations we need mention only *Lev.* XI.45 and *Num.* XV.41.

We might assert, particularly if we take into account the position in *Deuteronomy* and the *Holiness Code*, that the Old Testament laws are addressed directly to that community whose forebears, according to the occupation tradition, were formerly brought up out of Egypt.

This community also bore a name of high antiquity—the name "Israel". Again it is *Deuteronomy* and the *Holiness Code* which most frequently use this name in address. The phrase, "Hear, O Israel", with which the oldest introductory address of *Deuteronomy* solemnly begins in *Deut.* VI.4, recurs again elsewhere in the introductory addresses (IV.1, V.1, IX.1), and may be found once even in the body of the law itself (XX.3). The name "Israel" appears in a few more or less stereotyped expressions which are found in *Deuteronomy*; they were not fashioned by the author of this law-code, but were handed down to him as already fixed expressions of the legal language. Frequently a law—particularly if it deals with a crime punishable by death—closes with the remark: "Thou shalt put away the evil from Israel" (XVII.12, XIX.13, XXII.22). In *Deut.* XXII.21 a certain crime is characterized as "a folly (*nĕbhālâ*) in Israel"; this formula

[52] In the passage *Exod.* XXXIV.11-26, which is closely parallel to the cultic section of the Book of the Covenant, the reference to Egypt in vs.18 is secondary, as it is in the corresponding verse *Exod.* XXIII.15 (see above, n. 49).

[53] The connection with the sojourn in Egypt is to be found only in the later additions in *Exod.* XXII.20, XXIII.9, 15 (cf. Jepsen, *Bundesbuch*, pp. 8ff.).

appears as a firmly established technical term from quite early on, and is found in the most varied parts of the Old Testament.[54] We should add also the expression; "this abomination (*tô'ēbhâ*) in Israel", which is used in *Deut.* XVII.4 to characterize a crime, and which (although only once used), gives the impression of a standard expression.[55]

In all these instances the law applies to one community—and to one only—whose regulations and institutions are protected by the law: the community, in short, which quite obviously and unmistakably went by the name "Israel". The same applies in connection with the occurrence of the name "Israel" outside these sterotyped expressions in the deuteronomic law (XVII.20, XVIII.1, 6, XXI.8, XXII.19, XXIII.18, XXIV.7, XXV.6, 7, 10).[56]

In the *Holiness Code* such formalized expressions are lacking; but here too the name "Israel" always describes the group to which the separate legal provisions apply (*Lev.* XVII.3, 5, 10ff., XX.2, XXII.15, 18, XXIII.42). The same holds good both for the older collections of cultic regulations (*Lev.* IV.13, VII.34, XV.31) and for the post-exilic legal sections (*Lev.* XVI.5ff.; *Num.* XV.26, 29, XVIII.5ff., XIX.9ff.). In the Book of the Covenant the name "Israel" is not found, any more than in the catechisms; in *Exod.* XXIV.23 alone do we come across the single solemn description of the God to whom the cultic action applies, as "Yahweh, the God of Israel".[57]

In these discussions about the way in which the community addressed in the Old Testament laws is marked out by the common link with Yahweh, by the demarcation from the "Canaanites", by the common tradition about the occupation which told of the ancestors' sojourn in Egypt, and by the name "Israel", it looks as if we are treating of such obvious matters that nothing of

---

[54] The passages are detailed in my *Das System der zwölf Stämme Israels*, henceforth cited as *System der Stämme*, B.W.A.N.T., IV, No. 1, Stuttgart 1930, pp. 104ff. The common phrase, "So is not done in Israel", which occurs not in the legal but in narrative passages of the Old Testament (references in Noth, *loc. cit.*) likewise refers to precepts applicable to the group of persons described as "Israel".

[55] The word *tô'ēbhâ* is a definite concept in a series of laws preserved in *Deuteronomy* (XVI.21-XVII.1, XVIII.10-12a, XXII.5, XXIII.18f, XXV.13-16).

[56] In *Deut.* XIII.12, XXI.21 "Israel" occurs in literary passages of a secondary nature.

[57] C. Steuernagel provides the statistics of the further occurrences of this suppression in the Old Testament in *Jahwe, der Gott Israels*, Festschrift für Wellhausen, Bei. *Z.A.W.* No. 27, Giessen 1914, pp. 331ff.

value would follow from their further study. Yet we must at least refer to these facts because they are of predominant importance for the investigation of the situation underlying the Old Testament laws. It appears, indeed, even from this standpoint to be impossible to place the Old Testament laws in any concrete relationship to any one of the historical forms of government on Israelite soil. For, with the possible exception of the short and evanescent episode of Saul's reign,[58] which certainly need not be considered as the background for the laws in the Old Testament[59], the sphere of the tribes to whom the above distinguishing marks applied never coincided even partially with the territory of any of the various states which emerged during the course of the Israelite monarchy. It was, at the same time, greater and less.

The particular path of David's rise to royal power had the consequence of dividing the Israelite tribes into two separate states, which under David and Solomon were indeed united in a personal union, but after the death of Solomon had each its own king, and went each its own way. Each of these states consequently included only a portion of the whole which was envisaged by the laws. But, on the other hand, they included more than the area of the Israelite tribes marked out by those distinguishing features, since a whole range of previously "Canaanite" city states and their territories belonged to their territory from David's day on.[60] The subject population of these former city states, however, in no wise became absorbed into the individual Israelite tribes, but remained as a separate element of the national population, alongside the tribes[61]; and it can scarcely be assumed that the consciousness of mutual foreign-ness

[58] Some doubt (probably unjust) has been felt whether the southern group of Israelite tribes ever belonged to Saul's kingdom; if not, Saul's kingdom would have been smaller than the unit envisaged in the laws.

[59] The character of Saul's monarchy, indicated above on p. 15, excludes the consideration of any law-giving activity on Saul's part.

[60] Evidence for this, apart from *II Sam.* xxiv.5-7, may be found in the division of the kingdom of Israel under Solomon into districts, according to *I Kings* iv.7-19; particulars for the kingdom of Judah are probably to be found in the list of Rehoboam's fortresses in *II Chron.* xi.5-10.

[61] According to *Judges* 1.21, 27-35 the individual tribes claimed, in theory, possession of the territory of the neighbouring city-states, but these were finally conquered not by the tribes but by the inclusive unit, i.e. the states which had meantime developed; in the divisions into districts, tribal areas and city-state territories appear distinctly separated from one another.

between these two elements disappeared—least of all on the Israelite side. Thus the community of people who are envisaged by the laws, and who were expressly differentiated from the "Canaanites" by the Yahwistic cult and tradition of the occupation, is in no way identical with the nation of the state of Judah, or of Israel, or of a (historically unreal) combination of the two states.

But the question then arises whether we know of any grouping in Israelite history which specifically included only the community of people envisaged in the laws. If not, we must either assume that the laws envisage a purely imaginary situation— and that could well be the explanation—or we must entirely give up the search for the situation behind the laws.

(b) *The sacral confederacy of the twelve tribes of Israel.* Undoubtedly a fixed constitution existed, which embraced the community of people indicated in the Old Testament law. It is permissible to draw some conclusions from the laws themselves, on the basis of the subjects they deal with, which would lead back directly to the reconstruction of such a government; but independently of this we are reasonably safe in concluding from other statements in the Old Testament that in the period between the occupation of Palestine by the Israelite tribes and the first attempt to form a state under Saul, a sacral union of the twelve Israelite tribes was formed, whose focal point was a central sanctuary with a cult practised in common by the tribes. This arrangement was due to the traditional twelve-tribe system; it is simply the list of members of this union.[62]

Here we have an institution for which there are many historical parallels. Something corresponding probably existed among some of the neighbouring peoples; but comparison may be made particularly with the "amphictyonies" in ancient Greece, and their parallels on Italian soil. In all these cases we are dealing with institutions which reach back into the period before the emergence of statehood amongst these peoples. Details concerning the organization of the Israelite twelve-tribe confederacy are unfortunately not preserved in the tradition, but it certainly had a fixed form, and conducted its affairs

[62] For substantiation and all matters of detail I refer to my *System der Stämme*.

according to regular rites and according to prescribed forms of conduct. The confederacy exhibited those characteristics which, on pages 20ff. above, we found that the Old Testament laws themselves suggested as their own background.

The link with Yahweh was provided by the common cult, whose visible centre was apparently the "Ark of Yahweh".[63] From this common cult, as from the limitation of the membership of the league to the twelve tribes of Israel as laid down by the traditional tribal system, resulted the isolation over against the "Canaanites".[64] The tradition of the occupation which preserved the account of the sojourn of their forebears in Egypt also deals with the same circle of twelve tribes.[65] The name "Israel" appears in the Old Testament narrative as the inclusive term for the group of these same twelve tribes.[66] We have here a completely self-contained and fixed nexus of tradition, whose origin lies in the historical appearance of that league of the twelve tribes of Israel.

Now, clearly, this institution was neither replaced nor removed by the states later brought into being on the territory occupied by the people of Israel.[67] These states cannot in any way form a substitute, if only because their extent did not coincide at all with the limits of the old tribal league.[68] But neither did the regulations and functions of the state consciously displace that older institution. During the period of the monarchy the Old Testament, with its one-sided interest in the persons of the kings and a few "prophetic" figures, tells us nothing about it, though

[63] At the close of the period of the Judges it stood in the temple at Shiloh; whether it had always been there, or where it had stood earlier, we no longer know.

[64] We are not concerned here whether, or how far, any individual tribes were composed of ethnographically disparate elements, but merely whether they felt themselves linked with the other tribes, and so distinct from the "Canaanite ethos" rooted in the city-state culture with its cultic and social life.

[65] The historical circumstances (see p. 23, n. 48) play no decisive role here; the tribes have simply adopted for themselves (or their forebears) a particular historical tradition.

[66] The tribal founders, secondarily derived from the names of the tribes in the personifying traditions, were given "Israel" as their father; and this "Israel" is later identified with the traditional figure of Jacob, as has happened in the stories of the change of name in *Gen.* XXXII.29, XXXV.10.

[67] On this point I believe my thesis in *System der Stämme* can and must be carried further.

[68] The kingdom of Saul, which appears to have corresponded roughly to the old tribal league (but cf. p. 27, n. 58) was too short-lived to displace or oust from memory an old hallowed arrangement like the sacral tribal league.

references to the consequences of certain factors indirectly confirm its continuance. We may recall in this connection the role played by the sanctuary in Jerusalem during the period of the monarchy. By the transfer of the "Ark of Yahweh" to Jerusalem, the Temple there took over the role of the old "amphictyonic" central sanctuary; only *then*, when it had actually performed this function in the monarchic period, does the significance of the Temple at this time[69] become really comprehensible—particularly in its expectations for the future during the following period.[70]

The fact that the Temple stood in Jerusalem, the Davidic capital, could scarcely commend it to the Israelite tribes; this city was, and remained, a "Canaanite" city, with which the tribes had no connection—least of all a cultic one. The Temple built by Solomon, however unique a phenomenon it might be in type and equipment, could hardly forge bonds strong enough to bind the Israelite tribes to itself merely as the representative sanctuary, so as to displace the older—and therefore, cultically speaking, more important—sanctuaries of the country. Less still would the fact that it was a royal sanctuary, built by Solomon within the bounds of his palace complex to the north of the old city of Jerusalem, assure it recognition on the part of all the Israelite tribes. For when the northern and eastern tribes— following a traditional tendency (cf. *II Sam*. xx.1)—finally forsook the Davidic hegemony in Jerusalem (*I Kings* xII.16), they would have rejected also the Davidic sanctuary in Jerusalem; and their first king, Jeroboam, would have been spared the worry that his subjects might still "go up to offer sacrifices in the house of the Lord at Jerusalem" (*I Kings* xII.27). Yet we gather from a casual comment in *Jer*. xLI.5 that even centuries later the Temple in Jerusalem received honour amongst these tribes, and that after its destruction by Nebuchadnezzar in 587 B.C. men from Shechem, Shilo, and Samaria—that is, from places with once famous and important sanctuaries—had come

[69] Even if one were to set aside in this connection the words of the Jerusalemite Isaiah (*Isa*. vIII.18, xIV.32) as being a biased witness, we may call to mind *Amos* 1.2, and cf. my "Jerusalem and the Israelite Tradition" (below, pp. 132ff.).

[70] Apart from the special messianic expectations linked to the Davidic dynasty note Deutero-Isaiah's proclamation of Yahweh's return to Jerusalem (*Isa*. LII.7ff.) or the thought of Haggai that the rebuilding of the Temple in Jerusalem was the prerequisite for the commencement of the Last Age (*Hag*. 1.7ff., II.2ff.).

up to present, with the customary indications of mourning (on account of the destruction of the Temple), sacrificial gifts[71] to the holy places. And when, under Cyrus, the rebuilding of the Temple was put under way, these very tribes sought to have a part in the task (*Ezra* IV.2).

Dynastic loyalty towards the Davidic line on the part of the tribes of Judah would never have given such preponderant weight to the royal sanctuary as we find, since Jerusalem the capital, with its establishment, always retained its special position in the state of Judah,[72] and remained something foreign to the other tribes. The Temple at Jerusalem seems to have played a double role: it was a state sanctuary belonging to the Davidic dynasty, but at the same time, through the presence of the "Ark of Yahweh" in its Holy of Holies, it was the "amphictyonic" central sanctuary for the whole of the Israelite tribes. This fact alone explains the meaning which it had for the Israelite tribes during the monarchy, and later. It was therefore a very shrewd move on David's part to fetch up the "Ark of Yahweh" to Jerusalem; thereby he gave his chosen capital an appearance and a significance for his own day—and for the future—which went far beyond the political role of Jerusalem.

We do not mean that this significance of Jerusalem lay merely in the relationship to the ancient tradition of the Israelite tribes about a long-past history brought about by means of the "Ark of Yahweh". Such a tradition is quickly forgotten, unless it stands in a concrete relationship to the life and activity of the present. The gradual transformation which the rise of state ordinances necessarily brought about in the circumstances of everyday life, and people's outlook, would certainly have driven the twelve-tribe confederacy and the "Ark of Yahweh" out of mind, in a very short time, had not the "Ark of Yahweh" remained the central point for the tribes, and held them together in spite of their division

---

[71] That the men were bringing only "meal-offerings" and incense could be explained on the ground that the most important sacrifices—the burnt offerings—would no longer be ritually celebrated after the destruction of the Temple and altar of burnt sacrifice; so that only the "meal-offerings" simply set up in holy places, and the apotropaic burning of incense were looked upon as possible. The "temple of Yahweh" in *Jer.* XLI.5 can only mean Jerusalem.

[72] Cf. A. Alt, "Die Staatenbildung der Israeliten in Palästina," in *K.S.*, VOL. II, pp. 116ff.

into separate states, and in spite of their union with former "Canaanite" elements in these states. It did this not simply as a shadowy "idea" or "ideal", but inevitably in the fixed form of a continuing institution with regulated and lasting functions, which embraced[73] the whole of the tribes, and distinguished them from the "Canaanites". We must therefore conclude that under the monarchy the sacral twelve-tribe confederacy continued in its old form, and lived on with its own functions.[74]

A similar conclusion may be drawn from the complicated history of the name "Israel".[75] It is a strongly attested fact that this name, which originally[76] served as a designation for the sacral confederacy as a whole, continued throughout the monarchy in its old significance. This would hardly have happened had it not also retained a concrete relationship to a real and visible contemporary entity, particularly since the same name "Israel" by this time had a second, very precise, meaning.

For as David was made king in Hebron over the state of Judah, the state comprising the other tribes, then under the leadership of Ishbaal, is described as "Israel"; the name was retained by this state even when it elected David to be its king also.[77] Furthermore it retained this name when it separated again from the Davidic dynasty after Solomon's death, and formed a kingdom of its own with Jeroboam as its first king. With the claim of uniting the main part of the ancient Israelite tribes under its own leadership, this state from the first took over the old common name, which remained attached to this state even when the claim had long since fallen into the background, and the state of "Israel" had annexed the territories of numerous "Canaanite" city-states. This political use of the name "Israel"

---

[73] It is therefore largely immaterial how far the individual tribes—several of which scarcely had any separate existence, even in the period of the Judges—continued to be significant historical entities. What matters is that their membership of the twelve-tribe confederacy was maintained at least formally.

[74] This was all the more possible, since the twelve-tribe confederacy already in the time of the Judges lay outside the political sphere, and left the very freest hand for the political activity of the tribes.

[75] A section of this history is provided in the full and thorough investigation by L. Rost, *Israel bei den Propheten*, B.W.A.N.T., IV, No. 19, Stuttgart 1937.

[76] The original meaning and reference of the name "Israel" is not known for certain; we know only the above-mentioned oldest extant meaning of the word.

[77] David was officially "king of Israel and Judah" from then on, as he is repeatedly called in the Old Testament narrative.

was only discontinued when the Assyrians put an end to the state in the second half of the eighth century B.C.[78]

The name "Israel" was used with precise reference as a description of a state which had endured with little change in size for nearly 300 years. It cannot be supposed, therefore, that the name "Israel", used in a different way in "religious speech", would have established itself if this "religious" "Israel" belonged merely to an ever further receding past, which, the farther it receded, existed more and more only in the world of memory and "idea". It must rather have been a tangible entity alongside the state of Israel, with its own actual functions; if so, it could only have been the continuing institution which had borne the name "Israel" in the pre-monarchic period. Here too we arrive at the same conclusion as when we were considering the significance of the Temple of Jerusalem.

But obviously it is this institution—the sacral twelve-tribe confederacy—which fits the situation pre-supposed by the pre-exilic laws of the Old Testament. In the case of the Book of the Covenant, the probability of its composition in pre-exilic times makes it unlikely that any other background need be considered for it.[79] In the case of *Deuteronomy* and the *Holiness Code*, however, the details given above on pp. 20ff. show that they envisage the twelve-tribe confederacy as it existed before the form of state in force in their own day.[80] In both these law-codes—as indeed in all the law-codes of the Old Testament—the name "Judah" (the

[78] That the name "Israel" in its older meaning is only seldom found before the fall of the state of Israel is due to the extant narratives of this period—both legends about and sayings of the prophets—having preponderantly the history of the state as their subject. But naturally the use of "Israel" in the older sense, which is richly attested from the time of Isaiah on, did not begin in the eighth century, but links up with a never-broken tradition. The political use of "Israel" ceased in 721 B.C.; for the Assyrians no longer used this name after their annexation of the state of Israel.

[79] Cf. my *System der Stämme*, pp. 97ff. A direct link between the Book of the Covenant and the twelve tribe confederacy is found in the use of the title *nāśī'* in *Exod.* XXII.27 (cf. *System der Stämme* pp. 97 f., 151ff.). It may be supposed that the section of the Book of the Covenant, in which this title appears—"the religious and moral prohibitions of the Book of the Covenant"—(cf. Jepsen, *Bundesbuch*, pp. 87ff.), was from the start one of the compilations of the "Amphictyonic law" current in the twelve-tribe confederacy, to which several collections of laws current in the circle of the twelve-tribe confederacy were united to form the existing Book of the Covenant.

[80] Apart from the state of Judah, we must consider also the Assyrian provinces established on the territory of the former state of Israel, and in which at least remnants of the old tribal confederacy lived on (cf. *Jer.* XLI.5).

name of the only independent state surviving at the time of their composition) is completely lacking; this is a further sign that the commonly occurring name "Israel" here means, not the state of Israel (since the state of Judah would have had to be mentioned along with it), but the more inclusive unit, the sacral twelve-tribe confederacy. There is nowhere in the laws any explicit mention of this institution and its functions, nor is its founding or maintenance demanded or portrayed in any detail; for the Old Testament law-codes no more served to set up the constitution of the sacred confederacy than state laws first establish a state; as was only to be expected, they take it for granted.

Once it is recognized that the pre-exilic laws in the Pentateuch envisage the sacral institution as their accepted background, then all manner of peculiarities in their content become understandable. Attention has been drawn to the fact that many specific demands had proved impracticable—and in this respect *Deuteronomy* may stand as a model,[81] since it is particularly true of that book.

Some of these demands seem to belong to an unreal and indeed unrealizable situation, and point to the "ideological character" of the whole legislation.[82] But it is inappropriate to use the measuring-stick of state laws to judge by, and uphold that judgment on the ground that the law-giver "has quite often disregarded the realities of life in actual nations or states",[83] for no political system was before the law-giver's eyes. It is natural that the ordering of a sacral confederacy should at many points stand in conflict with state-sense; that its demands often and perhaps sharply contradict state interests and necessities; that the state structure, with its massive weight of power, should then hinder the carrying out of such demands, and that from the state's point of view they would be declared "ideological".

The existence of political institutions over and above the surviving tribal confederacy under the Israelite monarchy doubtless strongly restricted the confederacy's chances of life.[84]

---

[81] Cf. G. Hölscher, "Komposition und Ursprung des Deuteronomiums", in *Z.A.W.*, XL (1922), pp. 161-255, esp. 227ff.

[82] Hölscher, *op. cit.*, p. 228.

[83] Hölscher, *op. cit.*, p. 227: "Sich gar oft von jeder Rücksichtnahme auf die Realitäten eines bestehenden Volks und Staatsleben entfernt habe".

[84] The opposite case, which occurs with the role played by *Deuteronomy* under King Josiah, is dealt with more fully below, pp. 34ff.

But, even if this be so, the intention of the law-giver cannot be measured by the usual requirements of state regulations, if one is to judge realistically.[85] Since the editor of *Deuteronomy* in several important points has expressly kept in mind the practical consequences of his far-reaching demand for the unity of the cult place (cf. *Deut.* xii.20ff., xiv.24ff.), it is not at all likely that he would be otherwise completely unconcerned as to whether his "ideological" demands were realizable or not. So far as the sacral twelve-tribe confederacy bound to Yahweh was concerned, the uncompromisingly strong prohibition against apostasy from Yahweh to "other gods", and incitement to such apostasy (*Deut.* xiii.2ff.), was not at all impracticable, however unenforceable such a law was for the *states* of Israel or Judah, to which "Canaanites" (who had their own cults) also belonged. But the law was not intended to apply to these "Canaanites".

For reasons of state, the regulations on matters of warfare in *Deut.* xx.1-20 (grounds for non-participation in a campaign, the "banning" of booty, etc.), and the requirements concerning the cleanliness of military camps in *Deut.* xxiii, were either ignored or regarded with indifference; they concerned the conception of the "Holy War"[86] and the "Holy Camp" (expressly in *Deut.* xxiii.15). "Holy" war is not waged by a state, as such, but by a sacral confederacy; so that for the latter such regulations are not "ideological".[87]

The regulation in *Deut.* xv.1ff. concerning the remission of debts to be observed every seven years, which is based on the essential equality of standing of all individuals within the community at large, and so seeks constantly to re-establish this equality, were certainly not in place in the "Canaanite" city states with their association of an aristocracy and a bond lower class. In the confederacy of Israelite tribes, on the other hand, the condition was presupposed. That such a regulation is not just "ideological" is shown by the historical instances of a

[85] The requirements complained of were no more "unfulfillable" than the requirement of the single cult place, which according to *II Kings* xxii.23 was actually once carried out.

[86] Cf. Fr. Schwally, *Semitische Kriegsaltertümer*, VOL. I: *Der heilige Krieg im alten Israel*, 1901, esp. pp. 59ff.; and G. von Rad, *Der heilige Krieg im alten Israel* (Abhandlungen zur Theologie des Alten und Neuen Testaments No. 20, Zürich 1951).

[87] In principle the laws about the sabbatical year and the year of jubilee in *Lev.* xxv should also be compared.

general remission of debts. Indeed, history appears to show a more or less regular repetition of such a general remission, throughout the ancient East. In Mesopotamia at the time of the old Babylonian kingdom "the year", or, "the month" appears to recur "in which the king broke the tablets (i.e. the records of debt)".[88] The "law of the king" in *Deut.* XVII.14-20 alone should be reckoned as truly "ideological". It is so, not because its requirements are not conceived in the interests of the state system, nor because they were completely unrealizable, but because here the regulation goes outside the sphere of the sacral tribal confederacy's system over into other territory. In other words, prescriptions are made for a monarchy which did not exist under the confederacy, and the monarchy did not have to accept them.[89]

Only in so far as the Davidic king—that is really what is meant here—belonged as a Judaean to the sacral twelve-tribe confederacy, would he understand these laws to apply to himself, but even then it would mean apply to him as a Judaean, not as king. Only the resuscitation of the different regulations, owing to the historical situation which had developed, can explain why *Deuteronomy* broke bounds and—uniquely among Old Testament law-codes—took over a special law concerning the king into its series of enactments.

In conclusion, we may say that the pre-exilic law-codes in the Pentateuch—none of which can be shown to be state-law—although they show different points of view, clearly refer to a definite situation; and this situation existed not only in recollection or in "idea", but was actually current in the confederacy of the twelve Israelite tribes which, with its own functions, survived in the period of the monarchy.

(c) *The Sinai covenant tradition.* The Old Testament laws have been handed down with the claim to be of divine origin.[90] The sacral twelve-tribe confederacy is assumed by the pre-exilic laws,

---

[88] References are given by J. B. Alexander in *Journal of Biblical Literature*, LVII (1938), pp. 75-9.

[89] Following on what was said above, pp. 15ff., such prescriptions would have their place in the discussions between the king and the elders of the people.

[90] Also where, as in the beginning of the Decalogue (*Exod.* xx.2, 3, [5, 6]) or in the formulae of the Code of Holiness cited above, on p. 21, we do not have God speaking in the first person (*Deuteronomy* sets itself out as a speech of Moses) this essential claim is without doubt present.

and is represented as a divinely willed institution; so the question arises, what was the foundation for its assumption that these laws were linked with Yahweh in this way? For this connection with Yahweh was constitutive; it made the "Ark of Yahweh" the confederacy's visible centre, and gave rise to what was for *itself* at least the real distinction from the "Canaanites" who lived in the immediate neighbourhood in Palestine, and from other nations.

The answer to be given to this question, according to the Old Testament, is clearly that the tradition of the covenant made at Sinai[91] provided the basis in history for that relationship which in the Old Testament is indicated by the frequently attested formula prefixed to many individual declarations: "Yahweh the god of Israel, and Israel the people of Yahweh".[92] It is not here a matter of what historical precursors may lie behind this "Sinai tradition" and have given occasion for the formation of this tradition complex,[93] but merely that, as tradition, it has supplied the main foundation of the twelve-tribe confederacy. Now this "Sinai tradition" formed the nucleus of a portion of the narrative of the Hexateuch,[94] and was originally a self-contained and independent element of the tradition. Partially following S. Mowinckel,[95] G. von Rad[96] has recently shown that this tradition once stood as a festival legend at the centre of a regularly observed cultic festival, probably the one celebrated (according to *Deut.* XXXI.10ff.) every seven years as the making of the covenant in connection with the great autumn festival.

It cannot be doubted that this celebration goes back into the period before the formation of the state; therefore it arose and was observed within the framework of the only external form of

[91] K. Galling, *Die Erwählungstraditionen Israels*, Bei. *Z.A.W.* No. 48, Giessen 1928, has shown that the narratives of pre-Sinaitic covenants in competition with the Sinai covenant are traditio-historically secondary to it.

[92] In these formulae the name "Israel" is naturally to be understood in the sense indicated above, pp. 20ff., 32ff.

[93] It cannot be doubted that a historical experience lies behind this tradition; but it is very difficult to seize on what is historical in this experience, which underlies the subsequently moulded narrative tradition. Still, our concern is not with the experience itself, but merely with the tradition about it.

[94] Of the different literary strata in the available traditions about the experiences at Sinai in *Exod.* XIX-XXIV, not one provides the original form of the Sinai tradition; they are all rather off-shoots from the original tradition, formulated from the point of view of a larger literary connection.

[95] S. Mowinckel, *Le Décalogue, Études d'histoire et de philosophie religieuses* No. 16, Paris 1927.   [96] G. von Rad, *Problem of the Hexateuch* (1966), pp. 11ff.

organization then existing among the Israelite people—the
sacral confederacy of the twelve tribes—and within this framework it survived into the monarchy. Consequently the twelve-
tribe confederacy traced back its relationship with Yahweh, and
so its own existence, to the unique experience of a covenant made
between Yahweh and Israel,[97] and so to a personal entry into a
relationship between God and people, described by an image
taken from a form of human judicial agreement called a covenant.[98] Different methods of concluding a covenant among men
have served as models for the different strata of the tradition concerning the conclusion of the covenant at Sinai in *Exod.* xxiv.[99]

In the Old Testament tradition the conceptions "covenant"
and "law" are closely connected. According to *Deut.* xxxi.11,
the festival of covenant-making mentioned above featured a
solemn reading of "the law" "before all Israel". On the basis of
various indications in the Old Testament tradition, von Rad
(*op. cit.*, pp. 18ff., 23ff.) has sought to reconstruct the source of
this festival, and quite rightly ascribes an important place to the
reading of the law which, according to *Deut.* xxxi.11, formed the
main content of the festival.[100] Supporting evidence lies in the fact
that the Old Testament not only includes most of the laws within
the limits of the parts narrating the events at Sinai, but beyond
that has linked all preserved legal sections to the person of Moses,
who takes a central place in the Sinai narrative.[101]

The Old Testament has consequently dated practically all
laws too early, and compressed into a single act, or at least into

[97] For details of the view that the historical events underlying the narrative
of *Joshua* xxiv were probably of decisive importance for the historical founding of
the sacral twelve-tribe confederacy in consequence of the experience on Sinai,
reference may be made to my *System der Stämme*, pp. 66ff., 133ff.

[98] It need not be doubted that the conception "covenant" in this derived, non-
literal use has partly altered in meaning. Consequently, "covenant" is here to be
interpreted on the basis of the presuppositions mentioned—and not *vice versa*. Here
"covenant" does not mean simply a legal arrangement between equal partners,
but only the establishment of a secure and lasting relationship.

[99] For details see below, pp. 39ff.; and pp. 108ff. "O.T. covenant-making in the
light of one of the Mari Texts".

[100] Whether the texts adduced by von Rad, *Hexateuch, op. cit.*, pp. 20ff. provide a
sufficient basis to allow definite laws to be singled out as those which were read
on this occasion, seems to me doubtful. Even apparent references to the introduction
of the Decalogue ("I, Yahweh, am thy God"), in *Ps.* l.7, lxxxi.11, would go back,
in common with the Decalogue, to a liturgical formula spoken on this occasion.

[101] Outside the framework of the Sinai narrative, the most noteworthy section
is *Deuteronomy* which Moses is supposed to have delivered shortly before his death.

a short space of time, what in reality came into being during the course of a long history of successive laws and law-books. The tradition has thus quite rightly expressed the actual connection of "covenant" and "law"; it has merely brought together into a single act what took a long time before it developed into this permanent state of affairs as a consequence of that act. It has quite correctly expressed the historical dependence of the laws, which are not traced back to the creation, for example.

It is especially important in this connection that the Old Testament quite clearly associates the conceptions of "covenant" and "law" with one another in a definite relationship. The mediation of this relationship is certainly made more difficult by the fact that the literary analysis of the Sinai narrative of *Exod.* XIX-XXIV is throughout difficult, and the definitive unravelling of the original strands of narrative which have been brought together in this section appears to be almost impossible.[102] Apart from that, however, it appears quite clear that the old strata of narrative in *Exod.* XIX-XXIV[103] precede or supersede the conclusion of the covenant, or—in other words—the proclamation of laws. In the remarkable passage (*Exod.* XXIV.9-11), which is fairly unanimously regarded as the oldest form of the tradition concerning the act of covenant-making, in spite of other divergences in the literary analyses of *Exod.* XIX-XXIV,[104] the preface to the making of the covenant is represented in the form of a common covenant meal between the parties to the covenant.[105]

[102] The attempt at a literary analysis by W. Rudolph, *Der Aufbau von Exodus* 19-34, Bei. *Z.A.W.* No. 66, 1936, pp. 41-48, in its opposition to the different earlier attempts only shows how difficult literary investigation in this section is. Particularly questionable is the association of the cycles of tradition (which must in any case be separated from one another) in *Exod.* XIX-XXIV with the prevalent narrative strata in the rest of the Hexateuch, particularly those in *Genesis* and the first part of *Exodus.* If we ask in what relationship the legal sections in *Exod.* XIX-XXXIV stand to the narrative strata, it appears virtually impossible to tell whether and how far they have been inserted into any particular narrative cycle from its beginning; or, if not, when they were incorporated into an existing narrative.

[103] Under this heading I include the traditional material which is left after taking out the easily separable post-exilic narrative tradition (P). This latter will be dealt with more fully on pp. 91ff.

[104] Rudolph (*Der Aufbau von Exodus* 19-34 p. 44) also recognizes here a "primitive saga" taken over by his Yahwist from an older tradition.

[105] For covenant meals between human parties cf. *Exod.* XXVI.30, XXXI.54; *Joshua* IX.14; *II Sam.* III.20. J. Pedersen, *Der Eid bei den Semiten, Studien z. Gesch. u. ..ultur d. Islam. Orients*, Heft 3, Strassburg 1914, pp. 24ff. offers parallels to the covenant meal from Arab tradition.

Moses ascends into the mountain of God with "seventy of the elders of Israel", and there they take part in a meal. Neither in this passage, nor in sections attributable to similar strands of the narrative, is anything mentioned about laws which might have been given in connection with the making of the covenant. This therefore appears as a basic act that establishes a relationship which did not necessarily, or at least not immediately, require the definition of its consequences in the form of legal requirement, but had a content and a possibility of existence even without this. At the same time, at least indirectly, the "covenant" and the state of affairs it established are prefaced to all the laws which can be admitted into this framework. In the later representation of the preliminaries to the making of the covenant in *Exod.* xxiv.3-8, at whose centre stands the covenant sacrifice and the sprinkling of the blood of the sacrifice[106] on both parties,[107] legal demands already play a significant role. Even before the covenant sacrifice is offered on an altar specifically built for the purpose, Moses delivers "all the words of Yahweh" (i.e. the legal requirements now to be observed) to the people, and when the people have declared themselves willing to observe them, writes them down in a book.

All the same, it is not (as might later appear) that the "law" is put before the "covenant", since this first announcement—acceptance and recording of the law—belongs merely to the preparations for making the covenant, just as does the erection of the altar. The narrative concerning the actual act of concluding the covenant first comes in vss. 5-8. Here the covenant sacrifice stands first, and the repeated reading of the law which now follows, and the solemn engagement of the people to honour their law, both occur while the sprinkling with blood is being carried out; in fact, between the sprinkling of the blood on the altar and on the people. Throughout this section "covenant" and "law" are very closely interwoven; so much so, indeed, that the law is continually being drawn into the framework of the situation established through the "covenant".

Consequently we may recall in this connection the words of

---

[106] On covenant sacrifices amongst the Arabs, cf. Pedersen, *op. cit.*, p. 27.

[107] The divine party to the covenant is represented there by means of the altar which is erected. The Israelite tribes are symbolized in turn by the "maṣṣeboth" set up around the altar; but the blood is sprinkled on the people themselves.

the introduction to the Decalogue. Here the introductory formula: "I, Yahweh, am thy God" (*Exod.* xx.2) indicates the relationship between God and people which has been brought about by the conclusion of the "covenant"; and the preliminary reference to the "covenant" as the fundamental factor is then followed by the "law" in the various provisions of the Decalogue as a sort of consequence. In similar fashion in *Deut.* vi.4, preceding the deuteronomic law at the beginning of the oldest and probably original preface, we find the sentence, "Hear, O Israel, Yahweh our God is one Yahweh". Here again we have a reference to the relationship of the people to the *one* God which has been brought about by the "covenant"; following this declaration we have abiding by this God made into a duty in the preface, and this duty is to be carried out by observing each individual provision embodied in the corpus of law.

So, according to the Old Testament, the laws apply within the framework of a specified situation established by means of the "covenant"; and this situation attained its fixed form in the sacral confederacy of the twelve Israelite tribes.

(d) *The enacting of the covenant under Josiah.* One question still needs special attention: in what way are we to envisage the role of the deuteronomic law in the kingdom of Judah under King Josiah?

In this instance the law appears to stand in the closest connection with the national order, so that the results gained in the discussion up to now would be at least partly lost. The assumption that the law-book found, according to *II Kings* xxii, xxiii, in the Temple at Jerusalem towards the end of the seventh century B.C., refers to the Old Testament book of *Deuteronomy*, or at least to an early form of this law-book, is an old one which, since de Wette's *Dissertatio critica* of 1805, has achieved almost universal acceptance. Even recent attempts to dispute it have not really shaken its hold. The casting of this law as an address by Moses must in any case be designated secondary, since it must have been composed in a settled country and be considerably later than Moses. So it has often been maintained that this deuteronomic law-code was put together expressly in the interests of certain cult-political measures, which were to be instituted in the kingdom of Judah. Its "discovery" in the

Temple, therefore, was a show, staged with more or less ingenuousness, intended to prove to the people and possibly even to the king himself the antiquity (and therefore also the sanctity) of this law. If this is true, then *Deuteronomy* is indeed to be construed as a state law-code intended to be put into operation.

This particular form of the old theory which identified the law-book of Josiah with *Deuteronomy*, however—quite independently of the considerations to be advanced below—proves to be incorrect. It is, above all, to the investigations of Th. Oestreicher[108] that we owe the recognition that in *II Kings* xxii, xxiii the account of the finding of the law (xxii.3-xxiii.3, 21-25) is to be sharply distinguished from the annalistic account of the measures taken by Josiah in the cult-political sphere (xxiii.4-20). The separate acta of the so-called reform of King Josiah, which are recorded in chronological order in the annalistic account— more especially the step-by-step elimination of all Assyrian cults from Jerusalem and from the kingdom of Judah—resulted naturally from Josiah's political disengagement from the over-lordship of Assyria, which was now sinking to its downfall. It therefore needed no newly found law-book for its motivation, and in fact the law-book found in the Temple did not provide its impetus. The influence of the finding of the (deuteronomic) law was first effectively felt during the course of the "reformation" which was already under way, especially with regard to the abolition of the ancient local sanctuaries in the country (*II Kings* xxiii.8).

The situation must be envisaged as follows: the discovery of the law in the Temple—of whose historicity there can be no question, since the account of the discovery exhibits a very dependable source composed within the actual lifetime of Josiah—took place during the process of cleaning up the cult; further progress in this was then influenced by the law, particularly with regard to the far-reaching centralization in the Temple at Jerusalem of the cult as it existed throughout the kingdom of Judah. But in these circumstances, the supposition that *Deuteronomy* was composed *ad hoc* on behalf of the cult-political "reformation", which was to be put through by King Josiah, loses any real basis; and we

---

[108] Th. Oestreicher, *Das deuteronomische Grundgesetz*, Beitr. z. Ford. christl. Theol. No. 27, 4, Gütersloh 1923. Not all the theses in this book are to be accepted, but the statements of Oestreicher cited above are without doubt correct.

need not strain the significance of *Deuteronomy* against its own obvious intention by representing it as a composition intended to be introduced as state legislation. Probably it already existed before Josiah's day, was deposited[109] in the Temple in a sacred place, and finally found there, under Josiah.

Yet *Deuteronomy*, although not so intended, does appear to have attained the status of state law in the kingdom of Judah, through the king. But even that is not strictly accurate. According to *II Kings* XXIII.1-3, *Deuteronomy* was put into operation by means of a "covenant" concluded in the Temple at Jerusalem; and "the elders of Jerusalem and Judah" were gathered together for this ceremony, "the men of Judah and the inhabitants of Jerusalem" being present there in addition. The king, standing in the place specified for him in the Temple,[110] read out the discovered law-book to the gathering, and concluded the ceremony of making the covenant "before Yahweh", and "the people"—i.e. probably the elders, as their spokesmen, "entered into the covenant". We must try to interpret these statements correctly, for they are susceptible of several different interpretations. It is particularly necessary to find the correct answer to the question, who are the parties to the covenant, between whom the covenant is here concluded—a point not clear in the text. That we are concerned with a covenant between king and people—as might appear at first sight, and as is often assumed—is just as uncertain as the assumption that the term "covenant" figures here so loosely, that it merely describes a directive issued by the king which the "people" were bound to obey.

The closest parallel to *II Kings* XXIII.1-3, however, is to be found in *Joshua* XXIV.25—although slightly differently formulated. There Joshua makes a covenant "for the people", and lays down for them a constitution and rule. In this whole context, the narrative of *Exod.* XXIV.3-8 (which has been treated in more detail

---

[109] The preservation of laws and other documents in sanctuaries has been frequently attested as customary in various spheres of the ancient east, references in A. Jirku, *Altorientalischer Kommentar zum Alten Testament*, Leipzig 1923, pp. 184ff. That a law was deposited in the state sanctuary of Jerusalem naturally does not mean that it was rated a state law; rather, the Temple at Jerusalem here functions simply as a plain sanctuary, or also as the amphictyonic central shrine of the Israelite tribes.

[110] The description of this stance ("by the pillar") is textually uncertain and exegetically obscure; the same expression occurs in a corresponding connection again in *II Kings* XI.14.

above, p. 39ff.) should be compared. It is not stated in *Joshua* xxiv, either, between whom the "covenant" is concluded in Shechem; yet no one doubts that it was neither a covenant between Joshua and the Israelite tribes, nor a directive issued by Joshua for the people, but a covenant between God and people, and that the rule laid down by Joshua was regarded as given by God within the framework of the covenant relationship. In *Joshua* xxiv, in the opinion of the narrator, Joshua played the same part as Moses in the narrative of *Exod.* xxiv.3-8—i.e. he staged an act of covenant-making with all that it entailed—even though nothing, in this instance, is actually said about the act itself. It is obvious that Josiah's covenant is to be interpreted in the same way; consequently it must be a covenant between God and people.[111] The role of the King was to bring about the actual conclusion of the covenant.

Considered in the light of contemporary literature also, the author of *II Kings* xxiii.1-3 must be understood as implying a covenant between God and people. *Deuteronomy* and the deuteronomic literature recognize the covenant conception only in the relationship between God and the people or their ancestors; and since the account of finding the law-book in *II Kings* xxii-xxiii is linked with this literature not only in material but also in style,[112] the editor is to be understood in the same sense when he speaks simply of a covenant, and does not expressly and explicitly give his account a different connotation. The prophet Jeremiah in his authentic oracles[113] also used the covenant conception only with regard to the relationship between God and people.[114]

It seems to me certain, then, that in *II Kings* xxiii.1-3 we have an instance of concluding a covenant between God and people. Furthermore it can scarcely be doubted that the account of the finding of the law-book, since it was composed during Josiah's

---

[111] That the conclusion of the covenant took place in the Temple cannot be advanced as an argument; for even the conclusion of covenants having secular contents often took place in sanctuaries.

[112] The long clause *II Kings* xxiii.3 is typically deuteronomic in formulation.

[113] In Baruch's account of Jeremiah in *Jer.* xxxiv.8ff. there occurs a "covenant" between king and people.

[114] Most especially we think of *Jer.* xi.1ff. Were the references here to Josiah's covenant in particular, as is often assumed, then this would have been expressly understood by Jeremiah as a covenant between God and people. But the relationship of *Jer.* xi to the narratives underlying *II Kings* xxii-xxiii is more than questionable.

lifetime[115] and seems to be very well informed about its course, even in detail, also provides a dependable statement on this point. So then through the agency of Josiah, *Deuteronomy*, which had been discovered in the Temple, was made operative by the conclusion of a "covenant" between God and people; that is, not by an act of state, but by a sacral ceremony.[116]

This covenant therefore was simply a renewal or re-confirmation of the Sinai covenant, which basically still stood. This was inevitable with a covenant through which the deuteronomic law was solemnly to be made operative; for this law-code is presented as the work and speech of Moses not only in its ancillary sections, but in the very body of its legislation[117], and so in its very wording claims to belong to the group of laws directly issuing from the Sinai covenant.[118] Anyone who wished to put this law into circulation must necessarily pay heed to this real connection, and so bring the Sinai covenant to mind. From *II Kings* XXIII.1-3, it would appear that this is what Josiah actually did; and this draws our attention to the festival of the "renewal of the covenant" which is alluded to in *Deut.* XXXI.10ff., and which appears to have been regularly celebrated.

If our view is correct, then the introduction of the deuteronomic law under Josiah took place under those circumstances to which the law belonged, on its own showing. By the time of Josiah the sacral twelve-tribe confederacy had been severely reduced from its ancient condition, following the downfall of the kingdom of Israel and the deportation of its upper class by the Assyrians more than a century earlier. But since the confederacy must *ex hypothesi* have formed the basis of the covenant

[115] We must conclude from this that Josiah's end came about in quite a different way from that indicated by the prophetess Huldah in *II Kings* XXII.9ff. See my *Überlieferungsgeschichtliche Studien I*, (henceforth cited as *Überl: Studien*), Schriften der Königsberger Gelehrten-Gesellschaft, 18. Jahr, Heft 2, Halle 1943, pp. 86, 92ff.

[116] The "before Yahweh" in *II Kings* XXII.3 means that the concluding of the covenant was completed as a cultic celebration in the Temple.

[117] Cf. especially the "I" in *Deut.* XVIII.15ff.

[118] The present position of the law within the framework of the narrative of the Hexateuch is not to be considered as a genuine tradition, and the body of the law itself contains nothing which tells, according to the editor's way of thinking, against the original direct connection with the making of the covenant at Sinai. But already the oldest preface probably separates the law from the experiences on Sinai (cf. especially VIII.2ff.) and transposes its publication to the end of the wandering in the wilderness. But through the person of Moses as the supposed compiler, *Deuteronomy* is closely linked with the Sinai covenant.

transaction in the Temple of Jerusalem, this weakening was not vital, so long as it did survive with its functions—as it seems to have done. In another direction, however, the circumstances attending the historical role played by *Deuteronomy* at that time are complicated.

The next question to be asked is how the behaviour of the king at the introduction of the law should be judged? Looked at from without, at this ceremony he adopted the same attitude as Moses in *Exod.* xxiv and Joshua in *Joshua* xxiv. But Josiah can hardly be considered a charismatic leader of the Israelite tribes, as Moses and Joshua had been; the less so since, in contrast with the monarchy in the former state of Israel, the Davidic monarchy in Judah had never been considered in theory to be a continuation of the old charismatic leadership (see above, pp. 15ff.). However, it was scarcely a matter of basic importance *who* took the initiative and made the preparations for such a covenant transaction; on the testimony of its own content, this covenant was executed according to some holy ritual as a transaction between God and people. Josiah's position was in any case legitimated by the fact that as a descendant of David he belonged to the Israelite tribe of Judah, and so to one of the subdivisions of the twelve-tribe confederacy; to use the deuteronomic phrase (see above, pp.21 ff.), he was therefore a member of the *qĕhal Yahweh* (the congregation of Yahweh). In this circle he was singled out by his position; he was the leading member of the *qĕhal Yahweh*, and as such could take the initiative. In addition, he was the occupier and master of the Temple at Jerusalem, which fulfilled the role of the "amphictyonic" central sanctuary; and consequently he was the most suitable person to undertake the introduction of a sacred transaction which was to be settled in this Temple. At this point there now occurs a revival of various regulations which marks the covenant-making under Josiah, and which made the introduction of the deuteronomic law an event fraught with dissension and problems.

The difficulty was not that it was the King who took these matters in hand, but rather that according to *II Kings* xxiii.1, he gathered "the elders of Judah and Jerusalem"—that is, the spokesmen of the people of his kingdom[119]—and thereby declared

[119] The discovery and introduction of *Deut.* took place before Josiah had commenced the annexation of Assyrian provinces formed from the territory of the

the people of this kingdom to be the party in covenant with Yahweh—which it could in no wise be.[120] Further it was particularly inappropriate that the King should treat *Deuteronomy* as state law and make it the foundation for political measures on cultic matters, although it had come into being not as state law, but as a covenant between God and people. For the steps which Josiah proceeded to take at the instigation of *Deuteronomy*, in particular the abolition of the local cult-places in the country in favour of the single sanctuary in Jerusalem, followed the line of all his cultic-cum-political activities. These took their rise in the political position which he had taken up at the beginning, and in the main they continued along the same lines,[121] as is recorded indeed in the official notice belonging to the royal annals in *II Kings* XXIII.4-20, where no distinction is drawn between political and cultic.

Perhaps it was just the lot of the deuteronomic law to be discovered in the Temple at the very moment when repairs undertaken by the King (particularly with reference to the cult) were being put in hand; so it was quite natural that the execution of some of the requirements of this law[122] was immediately combined with that work. The real intentions of the law consequently

---

former state of Israel; the abolition of the local sanctuaries was first undertaken in the old state of Judah "between Geba and Beersheba" (cf. *II Kings* XXIII.8*a*) and only then extended step by step to the province of Samaria (cf. vs. 15, 19). The "elders of Judah and Jerusalem" represented therefore the two elements of the ancient state of Judah.

[120] Even if Josiah had wished to allow the Judaeans to serve, in virtue of being the only members of the ancient confederacy of the twelve tribes which still lived under their own government, the inhabitants of Jerusalem, at least, are out of place in this connection.

[121] How far the king was justified in actively interfering with the sacral law of the cultic activity is a separate question. In the Temple at Jerusalem, and in the city-state of Jerusalem as a whole, it was naturally he who wielded authority, even with regard to measures introduced by his royal predecessors in the land of Judah (cf. *II Kings* XXIII.5). Apart from this, the monarchy in the states of Israel and Judah would scarcely have possessed this right from the beginning. In the state of Judah this may perhaps have changed after the events of 701 B.C.

[122] In the extract from the annals in *II Kings* XXIII.43ff. there is a reference to the results of *Deuteronomy* only in the matter of the centralization of the complete Yahweh cult at the Temple in Jerusalem (vss. 8*aβ*, 15, 19) and its consequences (vss. 8*aα*, 9; to which belongs also the new type of passover festival mentioned at the end of the account of the finding of the law). We should also include the abolition of the various foreign cults which had earlier found a footing here (vss. 10, 13f.; cf. *Deut.* XII.29ff.). Apart from this, we hear nothing of any practical results of Josiah's activity arising from the *Deuteronomic* law.

recede into the background, although it was intended (in partial continuation of older regulations) to give a new vitalized life,[123] adapted to the changed historical circumstances, to the association of Israelite tribes as party to Yahweh's covenant. For though it was very advantageous for the swift and thorough execution of certain of the requirements of this law-code that the King put his authority and the powers at his disposal in the state of Judah behind it, the whole of the law-code could hardly be turned around for the sake of the state, since it was not intended to be a state law-code at all. After the unfortunate death of Josiah it is clear that his whole work of "reform" came to nought. Naturally, this was mainly because the political circumstances under which it had been embarked upon rapidly underwent a complete change; but in so far as it concerned the execution of the deuteronomic requirements, the failure was also due to the fact that these had no adequate foundation.

The fate of the deuteronomic law-code under Josiah was that it was henceforth treated, quite against the actual sense of its contents, as a state law-code, the implementation of which became the task of conscientious monarchs. This is indicated by the so-called deuteronomic redaction of the *Book of Kings*, with its obvious references to the deuteronomic law, and the close relationship between its language and this law-code. It is not irrelevant that, in its judgment upon the individual kings of Judah and Israel, the requirement of the single sanctuary (*Deut.* XII.13ff.)—which probably became established in the written tradition for the first time during the seventh century B.C.—was made the critical yardstick even for those kings whose reigns long antedated it. This requirement links up directly with the fact that the sacral confederacy of the twelve tribes had from the very first had one central sanctuary; but, more particularly, the realization of this requirement was sought by the kings with all the powers of state at their disposal.

This is the situation against which to view the role played by *Deuteronomy* under Josiah, which for a time gave this law-code a position of note in history, and ensured for it a deep influence extending even beyond the period of its currency as state law. At the same time, however, it is the fault of this situation that,

---

[123] Cf. A. Causse: *Du groupe ethnique à la communauté religieuse*, Paris 1937, pp. 114ff.

by neglecting both the contents as a whole and the range of ideas on which the law-code was based, one single requirement (which, with its immediate sequel, had perhaps been actually carried out under Josiah), was regarded as the real content of the whole code.

(e) *The content of the Old Testament law-codes.* Their content shows that the pre-exilic Old Testament law codes presuppose a situation based upon the covenant between God and nation. It is not possible to reduce this content to a short formula, and we must guard against forcing the mass of laws into externally imposed categories. For the content of Old Testament law-codes is both varied and colourful, and even within the separate sections of law the different walks of life and activity appear in kaleidoscopic array as objects of legal regulation. Even the old, and still much used, common differentiation between cultic and non-cultic (ethical or social) provisions cannot be made consistently, since the Old Testament law-codes took their origin in a milieu where no sharp distinction was drawn between the cultic and the non-cultic sphere of activity, but where every side of life had its links with cultic celebrations. It is mainly in some of the short collections of a catechetical nature that we find a comparatively limited content.

In the interest of a general orientation, however, we can draw up at least a rough classification of laws in so far as—by comparison with other ancient Oriental law-codes which have come to light—we can seek to distinguish between what is peculiar to the Old Testament in the wide realm of law, and what the Old Testament has in common with other law-codes amongst its nearer or more distant neighbours.

Since all sides of life are represented in the Old Testament laws, including normal everyday life, which was linked up with the whole ambit of ancient Oriental culture through multitudinous relationships, we find a whole series of laws which regulate the relationship of man to man (protection of life, physical capabilities, property, considerations about unbiased judgments, etc.), and also the position of the individual within the basic patterns of human society (marriage, family, including the *patria potestas*, etc.). All these occur in considerable quantity in the law-codes and law-books of the ancient East. In the Book of the Covenant, in particular, this category of law is strongly present, and we find a strong literary affinity between a portion of these legal provisions and the ancient Oriental state law-codes, except that of necessity in some cases the provisions have been modified to suit the outward circumstances and cultural level of the Israelite tribes. Here we shall deal only with particular points in the ordinary daily life of the Israelite tribes, and the social structure of the ancient East in general, as expressed at various times and in various places—this social structure being simply a particular manifestation of those prescriptive necessities laid down in the very ordering of the created world. There is nothing particularly characteristic of the Old Testament law-codes here.[124]

The same is true of a basic system of cultic requirements, which likewise is not peculiar to the Old Testament laws. This is of course due to the fact that we are here dealing partly with the adoption of very ancient cultic traditions of a Palestinian civilization much earlier than the Israelite settlement (sanctuaries, the three great agricultural and horticultural festivals, various details of the sacrificial system)[125]; partly, too, we are dealing with the continuation of cultic customs which prevailed among the nomadic tribes of the steppe and desert, and possibly still do (particular types of sacrifice, like the "Passover" sacrifice).[126] Briefly, the Old Testament cultic regulations are here directly connected with cultic customs which were widespread throughout the whole ancient Near East, in various forms dictated by the specific cultural milieu and historical circumstances; and these customs in turn are but a particular form of the systematization of the intercourse between God and man, which has been customary throughout religious history, and—as we must suppose—grew out of primeval man's conception of the sphere of the divine, and man's relationship to it.

The fact that Israel belonged historically to the world of the ancient Near East, and also of course to the universal realm of

---

[124] Martin Luther comes to a similar conclusion when he describes the law of Moses as *der Juden Sachsenspiegel* ("the Jews' Saxon law-code"), i.e. a particular embodiment of general regulations underlying the concrete provisions of law throughout the world.

[125] Cf. R. Dussaud, *Les origines cananéennes du sacrifice israélite*, Paris 1921.

[126] Cf. especially the complex of cultic institutions as they are treated in the classic work of W. R. Smith, *Lectures on the Religion of the Semites*, 3rd edn. London 1927.

human activity in general, explains why we find amongst the Israelite tribes some basic regulations concerning daily life and cultic activity which are quite unconnected with the particular Old Testament type of belief about God. This basic nucleus of legal requirements merely provides us with an individual form of a universally occurring element of human laws. The laws in the Old Testament are universal and fundamental, and cover every conceivable field of human activity. But many of the regulations—and their consequences—obviously do not set before us the really essential part of the Old Testament laws; most of them could indeed have stood, with scarcely any change of form, in any other human law-code.

The vital element in the content of the Old Testament laws must be what is peculiar to them alone—that is to say, those provisions in the field of daily life or cultic activity which show something beyond those other universal ordinances, and which cannot simply be derived directly from the basic regulations. It appears to me that we can grasp this peculiar factor under one consistent viewpoint: they are provisions which seek to ensure the exclusive nature of the relationship between God and people, between Yahweh and the Israelite tribes, or (in other words) which guard against a defection in any form from the sole God, who is thought of as the partner to the covenant. The history of religions by and large knows nothing of this concept of "defection", because it is solely a consequence of a strict requirement of restriction to a single God.

This brings us back to the constitutive foundation of the sacral confederacy of the twelve tribes of Israel, based on the Sinai tradition with the covenant at Sinai. Any defection, with its consequent definite disbanding of the existing covenant relationship, would be regarded now not only as a possible giving up of the cult belonging to the single God, but also as a simultaneous adoption of the cultic honouring of other gods or divine beings; for the restriction to the one God was from the first linked to the unconditional requirement of strict exclusiveness in this worship of a single God. Furthermore, since the Old Testament laws originated in a world where worship and cult permeated all walks of life, this basic requirement of exclusive worship of one God gave rise to consequences which extended into the farthest reaches of their activity. So because the Old Testament laws not only contain the fundamental prohibition of any apostasy, but also keep in mind every possibility of an actual manifestation of any such apostasy, they include a great many separate provisions dealing with apostasy. It is evident in this connection, however, that the law-codes in the Old Testament are based on an attitude which already existed, and were not themselves the first advocates of it, because the restriction to the one God is not made the subject of legal provisions[127]; rather, in countless laws we find the merely negative prohibition against breaking up the accepted state of affairs.

A basic general prohibition of cultic worship of "other gods" is never of common occurrence in the law-codes of the Old Testament. The most common and most comprehensive formulation is in the familiar Decalogue (*Exod.* xx.3); apart from that, it is found in a quite general form in the list of "capital crimes" which finds a place in the complex of the Book of the Covenant (*Exod.* xxii.19).[128] In a broader sense, the deutero-nomic requirement of the unity of the cult places also deals with the same theme (*Deut.* xii.13ff.); for it is based on the idea that the unity of God (cf. the emphatic expression at the beginning of the oldest introductory speech, *Deut.* vi.4) would be visibly expressed in this unity of the cult places, and that the purity of the cultic activity could best be ensured at this single cult centre, and guarded from any influences from foreign cults and cultic practices.

Where, however, the legal provisions deal with specific details, they are not orientated towards any general conception of an ideal with regard to worship and cult, or what might be regarded as therefore cultically legitimate or illegitimate; rather, they are framed against the specific manifestations of foreign cults and their consequences with which the Israelite tribes came into immediate contact—in other words, the whole gamut of manifestations included in the Old Testament under the description "Canaanite". Even the deuteronomic requirement of the unity of the cult places is not based on any specific ideal—

---

[127] It is however referred to in substantiations of individual laws such as *Deuteronomy* particularly favours; and it naturally plays a considerable role in the framework of *Deuteronomy* too, where an interest in matters far beyond the scope of the laws is found.

[128] For the original form of this law, which has been secondarily altered in the text, cf. A. Alt, *Die Ursprünge des isr. Rechts*, in *K.S.*, VOL. I, p. 311, n. 2.

for, in so far as it is not a matter of a locally restricted deity, it is really quite immaterial where, and in how many places, any specific cult is practised. No, apart from an association with the ancient central cult place of the twelve-tribe confederacy, it is a matter of opposition to the multiplicity of "Canaanite" sanctuaries in the land, with their multiplicity of deities worshipped there.

The rejection of all images, in the catechism of *Exod*: xx. 4*aα* and 4*aβ*-7, and of *Exod*. xxxiv.17, and also in the Holiness Code (*Lev*. xix.4, xxvi.1), is to be explained much less from an original "spirituality of the conception of God"[129] than as a prohibition against adopting[130] or imitating "Canaanite" practices which envisaged, by the representation of deities, the attribution of divine "power" to the images, and thereby in both appearance and practice implied human authority over this "power".

From the same standpoint, Old Testament laws forbid arrangements and practices which are in themselves neutral, just because they are in practice closely related to the "Canaanite cults". As examples, in *Deuteronomy* (xvi.22) and the Holiness Code (*Lev*. xxvi.1) the erection of *maṣṣēbhôth* is forbidden. These were stones erected at sanctuaries, and originally at least considered to be the dwelling-places of the purely local deities, but which the Israelite tribes had at first regarded as memorials of theophanies, etc. (cf. *Gen*. xxviii.18, 22, xxxv.14, 20—all E).[131]

---

[129] The primitive sanctuary, the "Ark of Yahweh", thought of as the throne of God (cf. *Jer*. iii. 16f.) implies an anthropomorphic conception of God. Of later date are the reflection on the total difference between all representable creatures and the being of God (*Deut*. iv.15ff.) and the mocking reference to the lifelessness of a fashioned image (*Isa*. xliv.9ff. etc.).

[130] Obbink (in *Z.A.W.*, N.F. vi 1929, pp. 264ff.) may be right in his assertion that the prohibition against images did not envisage images of Yahweh, since the idea of making representations of Yahweh had not entered the thoughts of the Israelite tribes; the prohibition referred rather to "Canaanite" cult images, which might be erected in Yahweh sanctuaries. In *Lev*. xxvi.1, the prohibition of images is set in immediate proximity to a prohibition of "idols". Elsewhere, however, the prohibition of images appears in quite general form, and so excludes images of Yahweh, too. Cf. W. Zimmerli, "Das zweite Gebot", in *Festschrift für A. Bertholet*, ed. W. Baumgartner *et al.*, Tübingen 1950, pp. 550-63.

[131] The *maṣṣēbhôth* play a harmless part at covenant enactment ceremonies also, *Joshua* xxiv.26*b*, 27 (though here actually the technical term *maṣṣēbhâ* is not used of the stone which is set up), serving as a "witness to the completed covenant enactment", i.e., as a memorial. In *Exod*. xxiv.4 it has a symbolic significance (see above, n. 106).

Later they were disallowed by the law-codes as too closely involved with the cultic arrangements and customs of the "Canaanites", so that we find the deuteronomistic literature prone to speak of "the *maṣṣēbhôth* of the Canaanites" (*Exod.* XXIII.24, XXXIV.13; *Deut.* XII.3).

Much the same is true of the prohibition against adopting the customary local mourning rites which we find in the Holiness Code (*Lev.* XIX.28)[132] as well as in a provision of the deuteronomic code (XIV.1) which is shown by the plural form of address to be a later expansion. These mourning rites were certainly in their original form regarded as apotropaic practices connected with the soul of the dead, but were understood by the Israelite tribes simply as conventional expressions of grief—just like the tearing of the garments, which belongs in the same context, and which was clearly not prohibited. But these practices were forbidden by law because, amongst the "Canaanites" and in general amongst the peoples of the ancient East, they were linked up with the cult of the dead, which was liable to make a breach in the strict exclusiveness of the Israelite tribes' worship of God.

On this last point we find that the consequences of this basic requirement of exclusiveness in the relationship of the Israelite tribes to their God had already bitten really deeply into daily life and custom. Throughout the settled region of Palestine, and indeed the lands of eastern civilization as a whole, the cult of the great universal mother goddess had played a significant role from earliest times. The figure of this ancient Mediterranean and Oriental mother goddess, whose worship has tentatively been traced back to a matriarchal order of society, was of great practical significance for faith and cult, since she was regarded as authoress of life, and of both human and agricultural fecundity.[133] So the more the cult of this deity spread and was intensively practised[134] in the area known to the Old Testament

---

[132] In *Lev.* XXI.1-6 the priests are specifically forbidden any participation in mournings for the dead—with a few exceptions—because there must still have lingered on therein a cultic element which was reckoned to be incompatible with the Yahweh cult.

[133] The name "Astarte" (see below) occurs in *Deut.* VII.13, XXVIII.4, 18, 51 simply as a designation for the lambing of the flocks.

[134] Evidence of this is provided by the figurines of the mother-goddess found at all scenes of excavation and in all ancient strata of excavation (cf. E. Pilz, "Die weiblichen Gottheiten Kanaans", in *Zeitschrift des deutschen Palästina-Vereins* (henceforth cited as Z.D.P.V.), XLVII (1924), pp. 129ff.

(where she was usually known by the name of Astarte) the more did its adoption become an ever-present temptation to the Israelite tribes, and consequently all the more decisively do the Old Testament law-codes forbid not only its practice, but also the adoption of all arrangements and customs which characterized or were bound up with it.

Amongst these may be reckoned in particular the celebration of the "sacred marriage", which was the imitation of the fructifying union between the mother goddess and a male deity. This "sacred marriage" celebrated as a sacral action at the sanctuaries led in practice to a widespread promiscuity in the circles of adherents to this cult.[135] In the complete rejection of this whole cult which is found in the law-codes of the Old Testament, the retention at the sanctuaries of "sacred" persons of both sexes, whose special duty was the performance of this "sacred marriage", is specifically forbidden (*Deut.* XXIII.18f.). So was everything else which in practice militated against the purity and sanctity of marriage.

J. Hempel has quite correctly pointed out[136] that the Old Testament law-codes differ strikingly from other known Oriental law-codes by their unusual severity in this field. In particular they do not leave the requital for trespasses in this field to the private initiative of the wronged person, as was customary, but make it a matter for the whole community, so declaring it to be a matter of vital public interest. The reason lies not so much in a concern to keep the social basis of the clan, the family, and marriage, pure—though this was also present of course amongst the Israelite tribes—but rather in their opposition as a matter of principle to the "Canaanites" and their cults, in particular the cult of the great mother goddess, whose effects even down into the realm of daily life are tracked down by the Old Testament law-codes, and rejected for the Israelite tribes.[137] Here too it is quite clearly shown that the Old Testament law-codes are not satisfied with general, basic prohibitions, but lay

---

[135] As an example, the prophet *Hosea* (IV.13.) treats these cultic celebrations in the light of the actual state of affairs (adultery and whoredom).

[136] J. Hempel, "Gottesgedanke und Rechtsgestaltung in Altisrael" (*Zeitschr. f. syst. Theol.* VIII 1930-31), pp. 377ff.

[137] The "laws of chastity" in *Lev.* XVIII are expressly and in detail formulated from the point of view of opposition to the "Canaanites" (and Egyptians). Cf. vss. 3 and 24-30; also XX.22-24.

down in detail the rejection of foreign manners, and in particular foreign cults.

It is here too, in connection with the rejection of foreign cults, that the apparently so abstruse regulations about clean and unclean animals belong. The normal Hebrew technical terms for cultic cleanness and uncleanness, i.e. cultically permitted and cultically forbidden, are used throughout. The animals declared unclean are not rejected on hygienic or other practical grounds, but because they are animals which were revered or sacrificed in various other cults in the areas occupied by Israelite tribes. Consequently they were forbidden for cultic slaughter and even for food,[138] because every possible connection with foreign cults was to be avoided.[139]

Even apart from this, certain animals are declared cultically unclean because they were regarded by the Israelite tribes and their contemporaries as demonic beings or as hosts to demonic powers, so that contact with them was regarded as a meddling with a separate superhuman sphere irreconcilable with the exclusive cult of Yahweh. The Old Testament tradition itself shows that this was the meaning of the regulations concerning clean and unclean beasts. We have two Old Testament law-codes which give lists of edible and non-edible animals; they largely correspond, although apparently independent of one another from the literary standpoint. In *Deuteronomy* a list of clean and unclean beasts has been appended to a short law, which forbids the eating "of anything abominable" (xiv.3, 4-21aα). The list was probably added later as a suitable exposition of the summary prohibition. But in vs. 21aγ[140] this short law is expressly

---

[138] In the period before the so-called secularization of slaughtering, as enacted in *Deut.* xii.20ff., which still indeed preserved a certain cultic element, every slaughtering of an animal was to be reckoned as a sacrificial act (cf. also *I Sam.* xiv.32ff.), with the exception, understandably, of game killed in hunting (cf. *Deut.* xii.22). Consequently animals which might not be sacrificed were forbidden as food.

[139] In a corresponding situation Paul in *I Cor.* viii.4ff. took up an independent position, but still allowed the Old Testament regulation for such a case to have validity for the "weak".

[140] In vs. 21aβ, partaking of the "abomination" is allowed to the *gēr*—which must in this case mean someone who does not belong to the circle of the Israelite tribes, i.e. the "Canaanite" citizens of the state of Israel and Judah—and to the "foreigner", not of course because something less good would do for such people, but because for them the tie with Yahweh and consequent basis for this conception of a cultic "abomination" simply did not exist.

based on the statement: "For thou art a nation holy unto Yahweh thy God", i.e. a people whose exclusive relationship to Yahweh and to his cult forbade the sacrifice and consumption of such animals as had a place in foreign cults. Similarly the other lists of clean and unclean animals in *Lev.* xi are rounded off with a specific motivation, which strictly applies only to the last clause concerning small cattle (vss. 41ff.), but in fact should certainly be applied to the whole of the list:

> For I, Yahweh, am your God, and you shall keep yourselves holy and be holy, for I am holy; and you shall not make yourselves cultically unclean (with all small animals that creep on the earth); for I am Yahweh who brought you out from the land of Egypt to be your God. So shall you be holy, for I am holy. (Cf. also *Lev.* xx.25.)

In some instances[141] proof is still available that the animals forbidden in the Old Testament law-codes as unclean did in fact play some role in the foreign cults bordering on the Israelite tribes. We may single out as an example the well-known fact that swine, or more correctly the wild pig, might not be sacrificed or eaten (*Deut.* xiv.8; *Lev.* xi.7.). In the cult-mythological texts of Ras Shamra from the first half of the fourteenth century B.C. eight boars* (*h n z r*) appear in one place in the train of the god Al'iyan Ba'al, clearly being animals sacred to him.[142]

Furthermore we have the mention, in the additions to the book of *Deutero-Isaiah*, of sacrifices of the blood of swine or boars (*Isa.* LXVI.3), and of eating the flesh of swine or boars (LXV.4, LXVI.17) in connection with accounts of illegal cult practices amongst the post-exilic community. In addition too there are the various remarks of later Greek authors of the Hellenistic and Roman periods about the spread of the cultic role of the boar in Syria and the neighbouring regions.[143]

[141] Our knowledge of the different cults in the areas fringing on Israel is much too sparse (based largely on details preserved by accident) for it to be possible to provide similar proof in all other instances.

[142] In the text I*A B COL. v z.9 (cf. Ch. Virolleaud in *Syria*, xv, 1934, pp. 325, 327, Pl. XL)—Bauer's enumeration, A*V, 9 (cf. H. Bauer, *Die alphabetischen Keilschriften von Ras Schamra*, Kleine Texte für Vorlesungen und Übungen, No. 168, 1936, p. 40). Now also in C. H. Gordon, *Ugaritic Manual*, Analecta Orientalia, VOL. XXXV, Rome 1955, Text 67, v. 9; translation in C. H. Gordon, *Ugaritic Literature*, Rome 1949, p. 41.

[143] To be found in W. R. Smith, *Lectures on the Religion of the Semites*, 1927, pp. 290; W. W. Graf Baudissin, *Adonis und Esmun*, Leipzig 1911, pp. 144ff.

* Doubts have since been thrown on the meaning of *h n z r*.

Apart from the report of Lucian of Samosata in *De dea Syria*
LIV, which tells us that in certain cities of Syria the boar was
regarded as sacred and—on that account—was not sacrificed or
eaten in other parts of Syria,[144] the boar played a particularly
important role in the Phoenician Adonis myth[145] associated with
the cult of the mother goddess; Antiphanes commented[146] that
in Syria the boar was sacred to Astarte, i.e. the mother goddess.
John of Lydia[147] tells us that on the island of Cyprus, with its
long and close cultural connection with Phoenicia, wild pigs
were sacrificed to Aphrodite—clearly an ancient Astarte. This
association of swine with the cults of the great mother goddess in
the areas fringing on Israel[148] sufficiently explains its rejection
in the Old Testament law-codes in the light of what has been
said above (pp. 54ff.).

Not all animals which were sacrificed elsewhere are, however,
declared unclean in the Old Testament; neither the ox nor the
sheep nor the goat. These beasts were everywhere used in the
sacrificial cult in lands possessing pastoral and agricultural
economies: they therefore represent such widely distributed
materials of sacrifice that they had no special links with any cult
in particular; consequently their use implied no recognition of
any specific cult, and was permitted—even prescribed—in
the Old Testament law-codes, which indeed recognise and
require on their own side a sacrificial cult as such. Only those
animals were declared "unclean", and therefore not to be
sacrificed or eaten, which were especially associated with
particular foreign cults, or with all manner of forbidden super-
stitious ideas and their corresponding celebrations.

So then the enumeration of "unclean" beasts has, quite
simply, developed out of practical requirements, to provide a

[144] Cf. now C. Clemen, *Lukians Schrift über die syrische Göttin*, Der alte Orient,
VOL. XXXVII, Nos. 3-4, 1938, p. 26.

[145] References in full in Baudissin, *op. cit.*, pp. 142ff.

[146] This statement by Antiphanes (fourth century B.C.) is preserved in Athenaeus
(third century B.C.) III.49; cf. W. R. Smith, *op. cit.*, p. 291.

[147] Early sixth century A.D. Baudissin, *op. cit.*, p. 144, n. 3 cites evidence to show
that swine were sacrificed to Aphrodite among the Greeks also. Behind this wide
diffusion there probably lies a tradition deriving from the cult of the early primitive
Mediterranean and Oriental mother-goddess.

[148] Although the evidence for the connection of the boar or swine with the
Astarte cult is considerably later than the O.T. and the law-codes under consideration, it can scarcely be doubted that it concerns early, possibly quite primitive
cultic customs; for in cultic matters man is normally very conservative.

specifically formulated prohibition against taking part in cultic practices for "other gods". In the lists preserved in *Deut.* xiv and *Lev.* xi the clean and unclean beasts are not all individually specified, but are arranged together in groups according to some external distinguishing feature,[149] so that they are all squeezed into a single scheme that now creates the impression that it is these external distinguishing marks which qualify or disqualify any particular animal as material for sacrifice. Nevertheless, it is certain that this classification has arisen solely out of the human tendency towards simplification and classification, so that the distinguishing features thus singled out have nothing in the slightest to do with the core of the matter.

Just as in the treatment of clean and unclean beasts, so in other points too it could be shown that what is unique and peculiar in the content of the Old Testament law-codes is directed towards the exclusiveness of the connection between God and people, which is the foundation of the "covenant", and consequently of the arrangements built up thereon within the framework of the sacral confederacy of the twelve tribes of Israel. Furthermore, with its claim to exclusiveness it forbids apostasy from the legitimate cult of the twelve-tribe confederacy. This state of affairs would appear still clearer, perhaps, were we better informed in the tradition about the historical milieu within which the Israelite tribes lived, and about their cult and life. But the essential facts seem to me to be plain enough; and it would be well worth while to expound the Old Testament laws thoroughly one by one from the standpoint that, to the extent that they are not simply examples in an individual dress, or expression of basic regulations of the social and religious life of the ancient Near East or of humanity in general, they consistently have the aim of protecting the sacral regulation of the twelve-tribe confederacy and its foundation, and warding off its breaking up in innumerable specific instances. Here we can follow up this matter in detail only so far as to show conclusively, from samples of the content of the Old Testament laws, how little they

[149] It is the chewing of the cud and the forking of the hoof which play a role for mammals. In some instances it is demonstrable that the zoological connection has not been correctly fixed. This circumstance, together with the fact that the grouping is certainly only used as a convenient aid and not intended as a survey of the animal world, makes it impossible for us to attribute specific animals to one or other group, where they are not expressly named.

could have been intended as state law, and how inappropriate they would be for those (always larger) areas with a completely "Canaanite" population, which were included in the states actually established by the Israelite people; and also how they quite definitely centre on a cultic or "theological" standpoint, and take the existing institution of the sacral confederacy of the twelve tribes of Israel as their accepted background.

3. The Validity of "The Law" during the Transition Period

The end of the old order

The ancient order of the twelve-tribe confederacy, which formed the basis for the pre-exilic law-codes of the Old Testament, broke down completely during the historical catastrophes which, between the second half of the eighth century B.C. and the beginning of the sixth, broke over the Israelite people and the various political states. The decisive factors in this breakdown were not, however, the external ones. The fall of the Northern Kingdom in which the majority of the ancient tribes of Israel lived, and the exile of its upper class by the Assyrians in the eighth century, had neither in principle nor in practice laid open the way for the cessation of the sacral tribal confederacy, for this was comparatively independent of political arrangements (see above, pp. 29ff.). The ancient Israelite tribes still survived as a remnant in the four Assyrian provinces into which the state of Israel had been partitioned by the Assyrians. Likewise, after the destruction of the state of Judah by Nebuchadnezzar in 587 B.C. and the double deportation of the Judaean upper class in 598 and 587 B.C., the surviving remnant could have considered themselves the bearers of the ancient tradition, and indeed did so; and they would have maintained the ancient order even after the balance of the tribes had been to a considerable extent destroyed.

The numerical strength of the population played no decisive role in this matter. Even the transfer of a new, foreign, upper class into the four Assyrian provinces in 733 and 721 B.C. provided no real hindrance, because for a long time the Israelite tribes who belonged to the sacral confederacy had lived in political organisations that included other elements beside themselves.[150] More decisive proved the destruction of the Temple in Jerusalem by Nebuchadnezzar in 587 B.C., because it concerned the visible centre of the twelve-tribe confederacy. Even though the holy place remained and cultic practices were still continued there, and even though theoretically a general participation of the tribes in those cultic activities could have followed, apparently the cult as once instituted at this place could no longer be practised in its entirety.[151] At all events, so much of the accustomed external framework was now lacking that contemporary opinion—which naturally took into account not so much the essence of the matter as the accustomed forms— remained doubtful whether any continuation of the ancient institution was still possible.

The collapse of the external political situation and the misfortune that befell the visible centre-point terminated what had been a long drawn-out process of attrition; but more important were the inner conflicts which now brought the old establishment to an end. After the two deportations of 598 and 587 B.C., those who remained behind in the territory of the former state of Judah not only regarded themselves as the legitimate owners of the land[152] (*Ezek.* XI.15,[153] XXXIII.24), but also felt themselves to be the sole[154] heirs of the ancient tradition. They saw in themselves the only remaining posterity of Abraham (*Ezek.* XXXIII.24), and by regarding the deportees as "far from Yahweh" (*Ezek.* XI.15), obviously laid claim themselves to be near Yahweh, since indeed the ancient holy place remained in their midst and they still dwelt in the land that Yahweh had once promised and given to their ancestors. But this claim was as decidedly disputed, since in the circle of the exiled aristocracy the remnant of institutions

---

[150] The Babylonians settled no new upper class on the territory belonging to the state of Judah, and introduced merely a provisional government.

[151] This would have been so at least if the suggestion put forward in n. 71 above were correct.

[152] This was the easier for them, since the deported aristocracy was there not replaced by a new one.

[153] The doubt cast on the "authenticity" of *Ezek.* XI.14-21 is, in my opinion, unfounded. But even should it not stem from Ezekiel, it may still be used in this context as the expression of an opinion from the time of the Babylonian exile.

[154] Possibly the residuary remnant were of the same opinion in this matter as the remnant of the lower classes among the Israelite tribes, similarly left in the land of the former state of Israel.

and people in the land were reckoned as nothing more than a pitiful survival of what had been; it was within their *own* ranks that they saw the heirs of the ancient tradition, and the starting-point for a future restoration, even though, due to the lack of a sanctuary, the ancient institution which had formed the framework of this tradition could no longer be kept alive.

Prophetic utterances could be quoted in support of this. After the first deportation in 597, Jeremiah had already had the vision of the two baskets of figs (*Jer.* xxiv), whose interpretation declared those remaining in the land to be completely rotten and doomed to destruction. On the other hand, to the exiles is promised continuing divine favour, a future return, and the renewal of the old relationship between God and people. At this same period Ezekiel's judgment about the remnant (*Ezek.* xi.1-12, xxxiii.23-9)[155], and probably about the exiles (*Ezek.* xi. 14-21)[156], was similar. These two-pronged judgments are simply an indication that the ancient institution which had hitherto been the vehicle of the tradition has indeed come to an end, and is dead.[157] For the uncertainty expressed could only have existed when there no longer remained any visible indication of where the old order lived on. So long as a sacral institution (such as the twelve-tribe confederacy had become) still functioned, its existence did not depend on the worth or otherwise of the men supporting it; it was only after its *démise* that men began to reflect on who was worthy or unworthy to be considered guardians of the good old tradition. That such considerations were current at the time when the Jewish state had been obliterated is a symptom that by now the twelve-tribe confederacy had really ceased to exist, or to be manifest after its old manner in particular functions—in short that it now existed only in the memory of the past.

[155] There is much to be said for the increasingly accepted supposition that Ezekiel delivered his oracles against Judah and Jerusalem, even if not all his prophecies, in Judah itself and not in Babylonia.

[156] If this passage comes from Ezekiel himself, the prophet will have spoken it in Babylonia, presumably therefore at a second stage of his activity, because it can never have been other than a voice out of the Babylonian exile (cf. A. Bertholet, *Hesekiel*, Hb. A.T. vol. xiii, 1936), pp. 40ff.).

[157] The prophetic passages mentioned date mostly from the time shortly before the fall of Jerusalem and Judah; but even after the first deportation, and in anticipation of the imminent and final end, these prophets already speak as if the actual end had come about.

Apart from the outward events which occasioned it, the end was brought about by the removal of the foundation upon which the old institution of the sacral twelve-tribe confederacy had rested—the covenant relationship between God and nation; and for this the content of classical pre-exilic prophecy was in the first degree decisive. For the prophets of the sixth and seventh centuries, when we consider their various menacing and reproving pronouncements as a whole, not only announced all manner of imminent hard blows of fortune which should bring to nought the whole people of Israel and all that they had accomplished —their political statehood, their cultic existence, their social order; they had not only prophesied those future events which actually came about; but they knew themselves to be called as God's messengers to expound God's judgment on the people of Israel. This judgment would mark the end of the old relationship between God and people in the misfortunes which were to befall the whole complex of peoples and states in Syria and Palestine (cf. *Amos* I-II) in connection with those vast historical movements which overran the whole of the ancient East. Since the people of Israel had not maintained the loyalty required by the establishment of the covenant, nor upheld the exclusive worship of one single God with all its consequences, therefore the announcement of the covenant relationship which had accompanied its establishment would now find its divine repudiation in large-scale historical catastrophes, and at the same time the covenant would from now on be cancelled by God.

Hosea regarded the transgression of the covenant relationship by the Israelite tribes as having started as early as their settlement in Palestine (*Hos.* VI.7, VIII.1). Consequently he proclaimed the dissolution of the relationship between God and people: "You are not my people, and I am no longer [your God]" (1.9). Similarly, Isaiah in the early part of his ministry had declared, "[Yahweh] has rejected his people" (II.6).[158] Similarly too Jeremiah, shortly before the collapse of the Judaean kingdom, had announced irretrievable ruin over the state of Judah and the city of Jerusalem, consequent upon the rupture of the covenant made with the forefathers (*Jer.* XI.1-13); and his well-known saying about the future new covenant explicitly assumed that the covenant made with the fathers at the exodus from Egypt

[158] On the text of this passage cf. O. Procksch, *Jesaia I*, 1930, pp. 63ff.

was now at an end (*Jer.* XXXI.32). In the same way the announcement of a future (new) covenant by Ezekiel assumed the giving
up of the old covenant (*Ezek.* XVI.59-63, XXXVII.26-8).[159]

Little heed may have been paid to the prophets in their own
day, and consequently little credence given to their declaration
that the covenant relationship between God and people was
breaking up, or indeed dissolved; furthermore this declaration
may have had no influence on those arrangements, existing
within the framework of the relationship, which continued
undisturbed for a while. Yet the events attending the fall of the
state of Judah, with which, after the earlier fall of the state of
Israel, the last visible vestiges of the old order collapsed, later
justified the prognostications of the prophets in so striking a
fashion, that the bases of these prognostications of theirs
acquired validity, along with their pronouncements on the disintegration of the covenant relationship. Few had listened to the
prophets at first, when they had claimed that their words would
be regarded as an important "sign" for "future days" (cf. *Isa.*
XXX.8). Events at the beginning of the sixth century, however,
seemed to justify them. For in view of the destruction of
Jerusalem, it could scarcely be doubted any longer that the
catastrophe announced by the prophets had in fact occurred.

If the prophetic pronouncement was thus borne out by the
actual course of events, then clearly the covenant between God
and people was now ended; and the destruction of the "amphictyonic" covenant sanctuary, with the subsequent dispersion of
sections of the Israelite tribes, could but strengthen the conviction
that God himself had pronounced sentence on the old covenant
in the unmistakable speech of historical events, and had himself
brought about its end. I cannot therefore doubt that the sacral
union of the Israelite tribes now ceased to function because its
basis had been taken away, although it could in fact have been
kept in existence, even under more difficult internal circumstances.

Thereby, however, the necessary condition was lost which had
previously kept the laws effective; they had now no further claim
to validity, since their basis had gone. They had therefore to be

---

[159] *Jer.* XXII.9; *Ezek.* XLIV.7, which speak of the breaking of the covenant, are
"unauthentic"; the passage *Ezek.* XVI.59ff. mentioned above also may perhaps not
come from Ezekiel.

considered as placed *ultra vires* unless some fresh basis for their claim to be kept could be given. Thus there began a totally new stage in the history of the law within the Old Testament.

The survival of the law within the framework of future expectation.

After the historical catastrophes at the beginning of the sixth century B.C., the link with the life and customs of the past did not just disappear among the Jews, whether we mean those deported to Babylon or those left behind—though with the latter we can speak only of probability, since tradition tells us scarcely anything about them.[160] This link survived through the "future expectation." Although the old covenant might have broken down, yet the prophets had also foretold that God would some day establish a "new covenant" (*Jer.* xxxi.31ff.; *Ezek.* xxxvii.26ff.) which in some unspecified way would correspond to the old covenant. This would then once more validate the statement: "Yahweh, Israel's God; Israel, Yahweh's people". If a law-code had been valid within the context of the old covenant, it would be equally valid within the context of the new (*Jer.* xxxi.33; *Ezek.*xxxvi.27). Admittedly nothing is said in these passages of the content of this new law-code, merely that God will bring about the prerequisites for the observation of the law.

After 587 B.C., however, much stronger than the hope of a new covenant and a new law, i.e. a new order, was the expectation that the old order would be restored; it only remained doubtful how retrospective such a restoration would prove, and whether it would simply reverse the catastrophe of the Judaean kingdom, or would not indeed cover the whole sequence of misfortunes which the people of Israel had suffered during recent centuries. The prophets opposed this expectation, which sprang to life immediately after the first deportation from Judah, both amongst the deportees and those who remained behind; they dubbed it

---

[160] There is no tradition which tells us anything about the upper-class deportees carried off by the Assyrians from the kingdom of Israel, which is probably a sign that all ties with home and past in their case had snapped, whereas the lower class who remained behind remained members of the twelve-tribe confederacy. The Jews who fled to Egypt (cf. *Jer.* xliii.1ff.) also leave absolutely no trace in the tradition. For the time after 587 B.C. we are confined to the remnant left in Palestine, and to those who were deported to Babylon.

"false prophecy" (cf. *Jer.* XXVIII.1ff., XXIX.1ff.; *Ezek.* XIII.1-16). Their opposition, however, was confined to the denial that this expectation would be fulfilled in the near future; for they themselves fostered and announced similar expectations in various degrees and in various forms (cf. the separate passages put together in *Jer.* XXX-XXXI and *Ezek.* XXXIV-XXXVII), and so contributed to the dissemination and keeping alive of the hope in a future restoration.

It is understandable that amongst those who harboured and cherished this hope and retained the tie with the past, this tie would be expressed in everyday habits. The traditional way of life would be retained, or, in other words, "the law" (which had regulated the affairs of daily life) would still be observed, although it had now lost the basis of its validity—at least, the requirements of the old law-code were by now only partially applicable in practice. The deportees had no chance legitimately to practise their cult, and even on the site of the Temple at Jerusalem an organized cult clearly existed no longer to the old extent, so that the ancient cultic regulations and provisions now hung in the air. Only the observance of particular requirements from the old law linked together the Jews of the dispersion, amongst themselves and with those who remained in the homeland, now that a common cultic praxis failed. Likewise it made visible the separation from those "nations" who were not bound by the same tradition.

According to the *Book of Ezekiel*, it was the observance of the command to rest on the Sabbath—which remarkably enough appears too in the short compendium of the most important divine requirements in the Decalogue (*Exod.* xx.8)—that now served among the deportees as a token of the continuation of the traditions of the Israelite tribes (*Ezek.* xx.11ff., xxii.8, xxiii.38), and so found itself transposed to the central point of the old law-code. In *Ezek.* xx.12, 20 the Sabbath is actually depicted as the (distinguishing) mark of the relationship between God and those who acknowledge him. As a consequence, it gained such importance that its introduction was later connected with the creation of the world (*Gen.* II.2f.).

Along with this distinguishing mark most scholars would include the retention of the law of circumcision, which may be found among the old laws in *Lev.* XII.3, and which was later carried back to Abraham (*Gen.* XVII.9ff.). The provision about shedding blood in non-cultic slaughtering, which is enjoined in *Deut.* XII.23ff., may come from the same circle; it was later carried back to a regulation made by God for Noah after the flood (*Gen.* IX.1ff.). The observances mentioned were suited to be "signs" or confessional expressions, for the reason that they were in fact peculiar, more or less, to the tribes of Israel; this was true of circumcision, at least for those deported to Babylon, since the peoples of ancient Mesopotamia, in contrast to most peoples of Syria and Palestine, appear not to have known the circumcision rite. So certain elements of the ancient law retained importance and significance as distinctive marks, which they had not possessed during the time that the actual circumstances which called for the laws were in force.

After the cessation of the old order, this clinging to laws whose validity was really in abeyance had no meaning, except in connection with the confident expectation of a restoration looming in the immediate future. The same is true of the concentration on certain provisions, in view of the impossibility of fulfilling more than a part of these laws. For these people their own times had the character of a dwindling period of transition; the actual end of the old order was not regarded as final and decisive, but was understood in the sense of a temporary suspension. Consequently, in theory and in practice, the validity of the old law was allowed to stand, especially as the character of the present as a passing epoch was emphasized, and the claim for the restitution of the former era was registered. This certainly meant that the declarations of classical prophecy, interpreting what had happened as a sealing of the end of the covenant between God and people, were not accepted in full earnestness or with complete finality. The *prophetic* expectation of a "new covenant" with a new law would indeed have accorded with these declarations, because this expectation presupposes the final character of the events which had taken place. However, the heralding by Jeremiah and Ezekiel of a new covenant seems to have played no special role in later times; it faded before the hope of a speedy restitution of the old order.

The so-called Future Programme in *Ezek.* XL-XLVIII provides us with an extensive document concerned with uniting the validity of the old law with the hope of an immediate, complete restoration. Probably this section does not go back to Ezekiel himself,[161] but in view of its content and its position as an appendix to the *Book of Ezekiel* (the traditional prophet of the exile) it must have arisen amongst those deported to Babylon. That is the important point. We have here a compendium and a new formulation of the most important cult ordinances for the Temple at Jerusalem. The ordinances handed down from the pre-exilic Temple, partly as laid down in older law-codes and partly as actually in use,[162] are taken as a starting point. At the time of this projected scheme the Temple at Jerusalem was in ruins, and a regulated cult was not possible there in full; the whole project was a programme for the future, and in *Ezek.* XL.1-4 it is introduced as a vision whose scene is the future Temple and its ordinances. Moreover this compendium of cultic ordinances and provisions for the Temple of the future—as in this context it must be—appears in the context of a wider vision of the imminent restoration of Israel. The validity of the law and the expectation of the return of the ancient order of things consequently appear here closely and appropriately bound up together.

It is interesting to note which elements in the old order appear to the editor of this "visionary" programme to be significant for the concept of the restoration. He does not speak of a new constitution of the defunct kingdoms of Israel and Judah, nor of any return of the idealized Davidic government (as the Messianic expectation of the pre-exilic and earliest post-exilic prophets would have it) but speaks only of the restoration of the nation of twelve tribes. This restoration, however, is spoken of in such an emphatic way that the individual dwelling-places of each of the twelve tribes is indicated (*Ezek.* XLVII.13-XLVIII.29). The previous political ordinances play a role in this picture of the

[161] There are various grounds for denying this project to Ezekiel, even if we overlook the fact that Ezekiel's expectation of a new covenant (XXXVII.26) entails the provision of a new law and not a new formulation of old legal provisions. It appears to me particularly important that the role allotted to the envisaged "princes" in the future programme (cf. esp. XLV.7, 9ff.) is scarcely consistent with Ezekiel's messianic expectation, at whose centre stands the figure of a new David (*Ezek.* XXXIV.23f., XXXVII.22ff.); though the prophet can hardly have intended him to have had the unassuming role foreshadowed for the "prince" in the author's "programme for the future".

[162] The separation of the priests from the minor clergy or Levites first appears in legal formulation in *Ezek.* XL-XLVIII (XLIV.9ff.), but that is only the explicit recognition of a practice actually operative in the pre-exilic Temple, according to *II Kings* XXIII.9.

future only to the extent that a "prince" is foreseen; but he is scarcely delineated as a ruler over the twelve-tribe nation, he is merely charged with the outward care of the central sanctuary, and looks after the cult practices to be observed there. It is in this connection that he is accorded a place of honour in the sanctuary (*Ezek.* XLIV.3, XLV. 17, 22ff., XLVI.1ff., XLVIII.22).

So we see that the old national and political order comes into the picture of the future only at that point where it was once most closely interwoven with the sacral institution of the twelve-tribe confederacy—in the Temple at Jerusalem, which was at the same time a national sanctuary and amphictyonic central shrine of the tribes. The picture of the future, cast in the form of a vision in *Ezek.* XL-XLVIII, appears as something final and definitive, bound up with wondrous changes in the face of nature, as, for example, in the passage about the eschatological Temple spring and the wondrous river fed from it (*Ezek.* XLVII.1-12). Through this eschatological aspect the significance and inclusive character of the expectation of the future as here formulated are strongly emphasized.

In view of the importance which the picture of the future thus gained, it may appear striking that the basis upon which the old order had rested in the last resort, and upon which consequently the restored order would have to rest, is scarcely reflected at all in *Ezek.* XL-XLVIII. The term "covenant" occurs a single time only in the whole section, and there with reference to the former covenant which had been broken by disloyalty and apostasy (XLIV.7). Thus there is no more than an indirect suggestion that the new order will exhibit a renewed assurance of covenant relationship. The vision of the re-entry of Yahweh into the future Temple (XLIII.1-9) naturally implies also the restoration of the old relationship between God and people, which shall not again be dimmed. The force of tradition has therefore clearly preserved this assumption of the covenant relationship in *Ezek.* XL-XLVIII, though it is not strongly emphasized by the editor. It is all the more remarkable that all constitutive elements of the earlier order of affairs here reappear once again in their proper form; the twelve Israelite tribes will be present in future not simply by virtue of a more or less forced and artificially upheld tradition, but once again as living entities. The single Yahweh sanctuary will be in their midst, not only figuratively but spatially, too, in the centre; and then there are the laws and ordinances which were once valid within this ordered whole.[163]

From *Ezek.* XL-XLVIII we see very clearly how the ancient sacral order, even though it had in practice already come to an end, is projected into the future in very specific form; furthermore, in the view taken of this future, the old laws are regarded as fundamentally valid.

Practical necessities

For a while the old pre-exilic laws still continued to be treated as binding, even after the dissolution of the old order, because the present was treated simply as a time of transition to a renewal or restoration of the old; but this position could not be maintained indefinitely, since it gradually became evident that the times were not transitional. So as time passed, the new circumstances took upon themselves more and more the character of a definitely new order; whereas the previous view of affairs, which reappears once again in *Ezek.* XL-XLVIII in a glimpse of the return to the old order expected in the near future, lost ground in time and faded out. For the "new covenant" as the renewed basis of the law did not immediately become a reality; it remained as the message of individual prophetic announcements, which never seem to have played any great role in the faith of the succeeding period; at most it represented a hope for that more distant future, whose outcome was not capable of strict forecast.

Nor did the restoration of the old order follow, which would have been the basis for a renewed validity of the old laws. For what Cyrus did for the Temple of Jerusalem, after his conquest of Babylon in the year 538 B.C. by which he took over the Neo-Babylonian Empire, was in fact by no means that restoration of the old order which had been hoped for after the happenings of 587 B.C., either amongst those left behind in the land or even more by those deported to Babylon. It is only a later secondary tradition which would openly explain the events of that time

---

[163] The fact that for the editor of *Ezek.* XL-XLVIII the specific elements of the former sacral order appear so plainly and certainly, without his expressly referring to its "theological" basis, appears to me to suggest that in his time the visible and ancient institution with its actual functions was still a living memory, and that its actual end lay not so far in the past, and that it therefore probably existed and functioned until the end of the kingdom of Judah (see above, pp. 29ff.).

as the repair of those losses and damages which had been suffered during the former historical catastrophes.

After the whole Neo-Babylonian Empire (including Palestine) had fallen into his power, Cyrus adopted towards Palestine that thoroughly positive attitude towards the old suppressed cultures of conquered peoples which marked both him and his Achaemenid successors.[164] In the context of this basic attitude he issued a permit, whose wording is preserved in its original "Imperial Aramaic" in *Ezra* VI.3-5. In this document he arranged for the rebuilding of the Jerusalem Temple on its ancient holy site,[165] and the return of the costly Temple vessels taken by Nebuchadnezzar as booty after the conquest of Jerusalem in 587 B.C. As a consequence, a beginning was actually made with the rebuilding, and the possibility emerged of a renewed concentration around the Temple cult, now once more to be practised in a more worthy context and a broader setting. But of a restoration of the old order, in the sense in which it had been expected and hoped for, there is not the slightest indication. For the actual destruction of the Temple in 587 B.C. was the only act to be reversed in the long drama of the downfall of the ancient people of Israel and their institutions. There was not even an immediate return of the Judaean upper class, who had been deported to Babylon at that time,[166] and who had claimed to qualify above all others as heirs of the old traditions. And though in the following decades various groups of deportees appear to have returned again to the land of their fathers,[167] there was never that general festive gathering of all dispersed persons to reverse the previous deportation, which had played so large a role in the hopes for the future.

In spite of this, however, it was not in the last resort so much a

---

[164] Cf. esp. E. Meyer, *Die Entstehung des Judenthums*, Halle 1896, pp. 19ff.; R. Kittel, *Gesch. d. Volkes Israel*, VOL. III, Pt. 1, 1927, pp. 283ff., 290.

[165] The question is, whether the expression in vs. 3—"the site where sacrifice was made and fire-offering presented"—should be referred to the past or the present; if to the past, the continuation of the cult at the site of the ruined Temple would be expressly declared.

[166] The Chronicler, who in *Ezra* 1.2-4 (cf. *II Chron.* XXXVI.23) reproduces his own form of the permission of Cyrus, was the first who, apparently of his own accord, added the command for the return of all deportees. By doing this he gave to it the implication of a thorough restoration of the ancient order (which goes beyond historical reality), and strongly stresses this point by introducing the long list in *Ezra* II.

[167] In the tradition indeed we hear only of the group which returned with Ezra in the middle of the 5th century (*Ezra* VII.13, VIII.1ff.).

matter of the actual external events as of the interpretation which they permitted. Once God's judgment on the old order and the dissolution of the old covenant relationship had come about in only too palpable historical catastrophes. Many important events resulting from these catastrophes now took place under the early Persian monarchs; but in almost pointed contrast to the former time, the scattered remnants of the ancient people of Israel now experienced comparatively little of the events of general history. The connection between those events which they did experience, and which were important for them—the permission to rebuild the Temple and the gradual return of separate groups of deportees—and those earlier events, in which the divine abolition of the old order had been perceived, was not readily apparent, so that no one really discerned in the march of events the great "reversal" which was to quash the judgment and bring back the old order.

The more this return of the old order was envisaged in detail (as was done by the author of *Ezek.* XL-XLVIII), the clearer it became that what had taken place under Cyrus, however heartening in spite of its limitations, could never serve as the fulfilment of their cherished hope. To what a limited extent his contemporaries themselves saw in Cyrus's edict the decisive turn in events, or even the start to a new time, is shown by the fact that no one in Jerusalem plucked up enough energy or will to carry out Cyrus's command to rebuild the Jerusalem Temple. And as long as the exiles, who had the chief interest in executing the edict, did not themselves set to work, the Persian officials apparently took no steps to see that the imperial command was obeyed. The rousing speeches of the prophets Haggai and Zechariah twenty years later were needed before the people could be induced to undertake the work of rebuilding the Temple. These speeches were full of an urgent, messianic, future expectation, requiring the building of the Temple as the prerequisite for the arrival of the eschatological age which would bring about the restoration of the old relationship with God (*Hag.* 1.2ff.; *Zech.* VI.13; *Ezra* VI.14). In consequence of their efforts, the new Temple was ready for consecration in 515 B.C. But even while the rebuilding of the Temple was in progress there were those who expressed doubt about the usefulness of the work, as clearly no grand new era was imminent, in view of its meanness; it was clear that very little was being undertaken in connection with a grand new era (cf. *Hag.* II.2ff.).

However, the messianic expectation of Haggai and Zechariah was not fulfilled, as quickly and unquestionably became evident, since this expectation—a remarkable occurrence in the history of messianic pronouncements—was directly linked to a contemporary historical person, the governor Zerubbabel (cf. *Hag.* II.23; *Zech.* VI.11ff. [emended text]). Even those older expectations of a restoration of the old order, as finally expressed in *Ezek.* XL-XLVIII, had to be more and more regarded as not to be fulfilled. Under Cyrus a new beginning had apparently been made, but it just did not turn out to be the prelude to a fulfilment of these expectations.

It is certainly no accident that, after Haggai and Zechariah, we find no other proponents of the messianic hope,[168] and pronouncements about the future, in the style of *Ezek.* XL-XLVIII, cannot be traced in the succeeding period. So when the hope of a restitution of the old order within a foreseeable time had to be given up, a basis for the continued validity of the old pre-exilic laws shrank more and more.

And yet the old laws could not be dispensed with in practice just yet, however slender the grounds for the continuation or renewal of their validity. After the re-erection of the Jerusalem Temple and the recommencement of cultic observances in it, it was self-evident that not only would the cultic practices be continued which had been observed on the holy site during the time the Temple edifice had lain in ruins, but that the traditions of Solomon's Temple would be revived and the cultic regulations (written records of which still existed) reintroduced.[169] For a

[168] In place of the messianic hope which envisaged the return of a bygone state of affairs, and looked towards an (idealized) Davidic dynasty, an eschatological expectation of the "end" now takes a more and more prominent place in the history of prophecy. It proclaimed not the repetition of a historical manifestation, but rather the end of the present historical scene and its dissolution by means of an eschatological event.

[169] The prophet Malachi presupposes their validity in the first half of the 5th century B.C., when he speaks of "God's covenant with Levi" (for the use of the word "covenant" in this context cf. below, p. 94), which was being disregarded and broken on all sides by the priests, according to the utterance of the prophet (*Mal.* II.4ff., III.3). The continuation of any pre-exilic Old Testament literature presupposes the rescue of written records of the old laws and other literature at the time of the fall of Jerusalem, whether they were kept in Jerusalem or taken along by those deported.

fixed form of cultic observance is a natural necessity, and innovations in an area of the cult upon which the time-hallowed order depended so much would not as a rule be welcome. So the cultic provisions of the old pre-exilic laws regained their previous validity in the new Temple cult at Jerusalem, which was regarded simply as a restoration of the ancient cult after the period of enforced interruption. In the new Temple the outward observances of the old cult were simply re-adopted on the basis of tradition—and without any reference to practical justification. In this way the ancient pre-exilic laws now found to some extent their necessary basis.

In addition, however, the non-cultic regulations of the old laws, which preserved various ritual customs or dealt with general occurrences of daily life, were regarded as still operative. For many years, ever since the break-up of the old order, men had held on to them in expectation of a coming restoration, so that force of habit prolonged their validity even when that expectation gradually faded more and more.[170] Practical considerations, which appeared important after 587 B.C., also continued to apply. Now, as before, the laws were indispensable for those scattered in the Dispersion who wished to keep up their link with past traditions, but who could not take any direct part in the newly established Temple cult at Jerusalem; only by observing these laws could they demonstrate their mutual solidarity and communal differentiation in relation to the world around them (see above, pp. 66ff.). Consequently the old laws remained in force, or—like the ancient cultic provisions— were put into force once more after the rebuilding of the Temple, although any real basis for them was more than ever lacking.

In addition to these considerations there appeared a quite accidental reason for the continued validity of the ancient laws: the imperial Persian Government, according to the dependable witness of tradition, showed an interest in the maintenance of the "Law" among the post-exilic community whose nucleus in Jerusalem lay within its dominion, as did most sections of the Dispersion.

The flow of events was as follows: in the year 458 B.C., under

---

[170] *Mal.* iii.7ff. presupposes the validity for his own time of the divine statutes "from the days of your fathers".

Artaxerxes I, a certain Ezra, belonging to the group of Jews who had been deported to Babylon, was sent by the Persians on an official mission to Jerusalem to undertake duties connected with the "Law". The title borne by Ezra in this office is preserved for us in its official "imperial Aramaic" form in *Ezra* VII.12, 21, in the context of an official document.[171] It consisted in fact of two parts[172]: the description "the priest" denoted Ezra's position within the post-exilic community, while the description "the secretary of the law of the God of Heaven" depicted the commission assigned him by the Persian Government. The imperial Aramaic term *sāphar*, translated "secretary", was a technical term used in Persian diplomatic language,[173] and the expression "the God of Heaven" also clearly has its origin in the language of Persian officialdom,[174] whether it is being used as an expression so general as to be colourless, or to convey Iranian religious conceptions. No doubt can remain, therefore, that the description "scribe of the law of the God of heaven" was a title for Ezra coined by the Persians.[175] Consequently Ezra came to Jerusalem as an expert[176] on an official government mission to put in order the affairs of "the law of the God of heaven", or, as his accompanying official letter put it (*Ezra* VII.14), "to inquire concerning [the province of] Judah and Jerusalem, according to the law of thy God which is in thine hand".

In the execution of this special commission Ezra assigned renewed validity to the "law (of God)" in Jerusalem among the post-exilic community, according to *Neh*. VIII.9. So even if we do not exactly know what this "law which was in the hand of

[171] In *Ezra* VII.6, 11, this title appears in Hebrew—imperfectly in part—in different paraphrastic renderings.

[172] H. H. Schaeder, *Esra der Schreiber*, 1930, pp. 39ff.

[173] Cf. H. H. Schaeder, *op. cit.*, pp. 39 ff. It was the mechanical turning of this Imperial Aramaic technical term *sāphar* into the Hebrew *sōphēr* which first made Ezra into the "scribe"="literary scholar" of the later tradition.

[174] Under the influence of this same official Aramaic of the Persian empire "the God of Heaven" appears also in the papyri from Elephantine (see below, p. 76, n. 178). It appears there not only in official (30:2, 27f.; 32:3f.), but also in more or less private writings (38: 2ff.; 40: 1).

[175] The word for law (*dt*) here is probably a Persian loanword (cf. most recently W. von Soden, in *Z.A.*, N.F. x, 1938, pp. 181-183). In that case all elements of this title of Ezra were of Persian origin, either in actual speech or by derivation.

[176] He is officially denoted by the title "Priest".

Ezra" included,[177] we may at least clearly deduce from the tradition that the Persian Government was interested in the law of the community which centred on Jerusalem, and that it took measures to ensure the validity of this law. A similar case has come to light in the papyri from the Jewish military colony on the island of Elephantine[178] in the Nile. In Cowley's Pap. No. 21 from the fifth year of Darius II (419 B.C.) the leader of this military colony is informed by a certain Hananiah of the contents of an order sent by King Darius II to the Egyptian satrap Arsam, commanding the proper celebration of the feast of Passover and Unleavened Bread[179] from the 15th to the 21st of the month Nisan.[180] This shows the interest taken by the Persian Government even in a detail of Old Testament law.

The Persian Government, however, was scarcely concerned about the contents of the Old Testament community's laws as such; their interest must depend on other considerations. With regard to the military colony on the island of Elephantine, and in neighbouring Aswân on Egypt's southern border, Persia's interest could only be the security of this strategically important military post. The steps outlined clearly had this aim, and must have been intended to ensure the maintenance of order within this military colony, and its external stability, in the face of some

[177] Neither the view that this "Law" consisted of the complete Pentateuch in its present form (see above, p. 3, n. 2), nor the theory that it concerned the so-called "Priestly code" (i.e. the laws which it is presumed were at some period incorporated into the narrative stratum called P) is well founded. These laws form no proper unity, nor is it likely that they were ever united into a literary whole before their association in the present Pentateuch. We simply do not know what this "law in the hand of Ezra" was, and can only guess that it was a collection of laws preserved from pre-exilic times, with perhaps a few newly formulated bits added. Cf. my *History of Israel*, 2nd edn., p. 355, London 1960 (henceforth cited as *History*).

[178] Cf. the edition of A. Cowley: *Aramaic Papyri of the fifth century B.C.*, Oxford 1923, whose enumeration is followed above; see also *Textbuch zur Geschichte Israels*, ed. K. Galling *et al.* (henceforth cited as *T.G.I.*), 1950, p. 73; and *Ancient Near Eastern Texts relating to the Old Testament*, ed. J. B. Pritchard (henceforth cited as *A.N.E.T.*) 2nd edn., 1955, p. 491; a German translation may be found in *Altorientalische Texte zum Alten Testament*, ed. H. Gressmann (henceforth cited as *A.O.T.*), 2nd edn., 1926, p. 453.

[179] In the badly preserved papyrus the actual words "passover" and "unleavened bread" are unfortunately missing, but in view of the date given (see following note) no other festival can be intended.

[180] These dates are first specified in the Holiness Code, *Lev.* XXIII.5-8.

threat[181] whose nature is unfortunately unknown to us. The
Persian officials' belief that an official guarantee of the un-
hindered execution of Old Testament legal requirements[182]
would be conducive to this end, can only have been derived
from those of the military colony who also formed a religious
community—otherwise they would have known nothing about
such internal affairs.[183] Darius II's permit is therefore a practical
expression of the fundamental attitude of the Achaemenids
towards ancient traditional cults in their Empire.[184]

This precedent from Elephantine is important, because it
sets in the right light the official despatch of Ezra to Jerusalem
in the matter of "the law of the God of heaven" a full generation
later. The Persian Government's interest in all that spelled
"law" for the Old Testament community at home and abroad
was clearly the same as in the instance of the intervention in a
matter of the "law" in Elephantine. Even the territory occupied
by the community grouped around Jerusalem[185] was from a
military point of view not unimportant for the Persians, since
it lay near the route to Egypt, an important Persian possession
which was constantly threatened and occasionally even lost.
Various archaeological finds have shown that not very far from
Jerusalem the Persians built various installations for the defence
of the last stages of the route from Asia to Egypt. Grain stores of
the fifth to fourth centuries B.C., that is from the period of Persian
domination, have been found in the ruined sites of Tel Jemme in
the Wadi Ghazze to the south of the border fortress of Gaza.
These were obviously intended to supply the Persian troops

[181] First and foremost we might think of the enmity against the cult of this
military colony displayed by the surrounding Egyptians (cf. particularly Pap.
No. 30: *A.N.E.T.*, p. 492; *A.O.T.*, pp. 450ff.).

[182] How far pre-exilic Old Testament laws were regarded as binding among the
Elephantine community, and how this came about, has not yet found a satisfying
answer—particularly in view of their very "un-lawful" cult of three divinities.

[183] Hananiah the sender of Pap. Eleph. No. 21 (cf. Pap. No. 38: 7ff.) may indeed
have been the spokesman for the community before the Persian officials in this
supposed affair.

[184] The especial interest of the Persians in this Jewish military colony, which was
of such importance to them, is still further underlined by the fact that on one
occasion their temple in Elephantine was spared by Cambyses when he destroyed
the temple of the Egyptian gods, according to Pap. Eleph. No. 30: 13ff.—*A.N.E.T.*,
p. 492; *A.O.T.*, pp. 450ff.

[185] *Neh.* III.1-32 allows us to deduce the bounds of their territory with considerable exactitude as being confined to the Judaean highlands in a wide sweep around
Jerusalem.

before they started out on their march through the Sinai desert towards Egypt.[186] Still further south in the Wadi Ghazze there has come to light the grave of a Persian who was apparently an officer stationed there, and which dates from the last third of the fifth century B.C.[187] It may be granted that the territory belonging to the Jewish community did not lie across this important line of communication from the centre of the Persian empire to Egypt, but only in the hinterland of the final station on Asiatic soil, up on the somewhat out-of-the-way Jewish highlands; but it was near enough at this particular point to make it understandable that the Persian officials were strictly charged with the duty of ensuring peace and order in this territory. It is certainly this consideration that explains the Persian interest in the internal affairs of the Jewish community.

The various oracles of Malachi show us that prior to Ezra's appearance in Jerusalem on his officially promoted mission, the condition of affairs among the community there had not been properly consolidated, and various tensions existed. There was considerable uncertainty as to what should be done in conditions which—in spite of the re-establishment of the Temple—were still rather chaotic. The distinctiveness of Malachi's oracles compared with others in the Old Testament lies in the fact that here questions concerning practical behaviour are discussed in argument and counter-argument *within the Jerusalem community*. There were members of the Dispersion living in Babylon who had the ear of the Persian authorities,[188] and who also, like Malachi in Jerusalem, represented the concern for preserving the connection between the community of the Old Testament and its historical past, and maintaining the line of demarcation between themselves and the "gentiles", who now shared with them the political unity of the Persian Empire. Consequently they wished to have the laws preserved from pre-exilic times made binding again, and if we are right in our reconstruction of the situation it is conceivable that it caused them to draw the attention of officials to the unsatisfactory conditions in and around Jerusalem. They might also have suggested that a firm

---

[186] Cf. Flinders Petrie: *Gerar* (Brit. Sch. of Arch. in Egypt, VOL. XLIII, 1928, Pl. XIII), and further, K. Galling, in *Palästinajahrbuch*, XXXIV (1918), pp. 78ff.

[187] Cf. Flinders Petrie, *Beth Pelet I* (Brit. Sch. of Arch. in Egypt, VOL. XLVIII, 1930, Pll. XLIV-XLVI); and, for its date, J. H. Iliffe in *Q.D.A.P.* IV (1935), pp. 182ff.

[188] That this was possible is most clearly indicated by *Nehemiah II.*1ff.

re-establishment of the community living there (and, indeed, of the Dispersion as a whole) on the basis of the surviving laws, would guarantee that peace and order which the Persian Empire needed at this militarily sensitive spot. So it was that Ezra was sent officially as "the priest and scribe of the law of the God of heaven".[189]

The validity of the traditional law in the post-exilic community was now finally and firmly established by Ezra.[190] Naturally the co-operation of the Persian authorities did not mean that these laws now acquired validity as Persian laws of the realm; the Persians simply followed their normal recognition of the regulations proper to the traditional cults of their subject peoples, and in their own interest supported tendencies apparent among the Old Testament community and helped them to final victory. The obligation to keep the traditional laws was in the last resort not imposed by the Persian state, but fulfilled voluntarily by the community or its elders (*Neh.* VIII.13). Of course, the influence of the Persian Government from without, along with the tendencies and constraints within the community itself, undoubtedly helped considerably to ensure that the laws which rested on old traditions remained valid or were put into force once more.

The basis on which the laws rested in the last resort was not in fact re-established, because the conditions which had given

[189] A similar case, which however has basically nothing to do with the question of the validity of the law, concerns Nehemiah. The Persians were disturbed by dissensions in the province of Samaria which apparently arose from opposition between the sections of the population who had long been resident in a subdistrict of the province which had once formed part of the territory of Judah on the one hand, and the gradually returning Diaspora Jews on the other. In order to put an end to this, Judah was constituted an independent province and put under the governorship of Nehemiah, who was personally known to the Persian king, and by this official appointment the long-disputed rebuilding of the walls of Jerusalem was carried through. This desire to remove tensions among one of the subject peoples, who in themselves were unimportant from the Persians' point of view, can be attributed only to their interest in peace and order in the southern part of Palestine.

[190] Things did not at first go too smoothly. Even though Nehemiah had become governor and had completed the work of rebuilding the walls of Jerusalem, he tells us in his memoirs how he still had to assert his authority in order to put into operation the laws whose validity had been reasserted by Ezra (*Neh.* XIII.10-31), including cases in which Ezra, whose terms of authority were not so wide as his, had found difficulty. (For the relationship of Ezra and Nehemiah cf. my *History of Israel*, pp. 318ff.)

validity to the laws in ancient Israel had long since disappeared. Actually the primary relationship of affairs and regulations became more and more reversed. Whereas it was originally the relationship of God and man depicted as a "covenant" which had constituted the ancient sacral confederacy of the tribes, and whereas it had been the presence of this institution which had provided the necessary prerequisite for the validation of the old laws, it was now the acknowledgement and observance of the law by the individuals which constituted the community—for whoever undertook to keep the law joined the community[191]; and the presence of this community appeared to be a sign that the covenant relationship between God and people still existed.

It is customary to speak of the "individualism" which arose during exilic and post-exilic times in place of an earlier "collectivism", and often we tend to see an element of progress in this change. The reason for this was the transfer of the decisive emphasis from *divine* activity to the behaviour of individual *mortals*—which is a decline from the original basis of the faith. Even if it were possible for the institution of the cult in Jerusalem to be the basic foundation of life for the community living within the confines of Judaea, yet for the large, scattered, and ever more important Dispersion it was not. For them participation in the cult—apart from possible pilgrimages to Jerusalem—was impossible; individual subjection to the requirements of the law formed the decisive requirement, and also the bond which held together all these individuals. And so by virtue of this reversal in the actual relationship, the fiction gained ground that, in this form adopted by the law, the post-exilic community with its Dispersion had become the successor of ancient Israel, so that although the outward appearance had been much reduced by historical catastrophe, fundamentally the old relationship to God had not been abrogated. Consequently the content of the classical pre-exilic prophets' message was not retained in its extreme depth and uncompromising finality. Nor, in the time of Ezra and Nehemiah, had the expectation been given up that God would once again bring about the restoration of ancient Israel; the contemporary community therefore was not only the inheritor of old tradition, but at the same time formed the

---

[191] It was this principle which first created the conditions for the inclusion of "proselytes" of other nationalities in the community.

historical actuality on to which the restoration of Israel (looked for in the future) and the gathering together of the dispersed would at some time be able to join.

Consequently the contemporary situation was not to be regarded as final. Admittedly this expectation was now very strongly applied only to external circumstances; and the question of a re-establishment of the old relationship between God and people—at least in the manner in which it was referred to in *Ezek.* XL-XLVIII, in the vision of the return of the "Glory of Yahweh" into the future Temple (*Ezek.* XLIII.1-9)—from now on seems to have retreated quite into the background. The consciousness of living in a transition period still remained, in view of the contemporary expectation for the future, so the obligation to keep the law would continue at least until the restoration, and this would once again provide the complete justification of its validity.

Support for this reconstruction of the situation is most clearly provided by the long prayer which, according to *Neh.* IX, was spoken before the assembled community in connection with the introduction of the law brought by Ezra. Its present form is certainly due to the editor of the Chronistic work; but even if it does not give the authentic words of Ezra,[192] and even though there be no historical basis for this tradition, it is still significant as a witness for the time soon after Ezra.[193]

The first noteworthy feature of this prayer is the unrestricted and unqualified view that the post-exilic community formed the direct continuation of the twelve tribes of ancient Israel. The major portion of the prayer consists of a historical retrospect, in which the forefathers of the contemporary community were simply identified with the twelve tribes of former times, and all their ancient traditions attributed to the "Fathers" of the community. The prayer begins with a reference to Abraham (vss. 7f.),[194] and then recapitulates (vss. 9-25) the main points

---

[192] H. H. Schaeder, *Esra der Schreiber*, pp. 64ff. also deals with *Neh.* IX in a detailed way—though from a different point of view—and accepts this passage as an actual utterance of Ezra with a documentary value; but in view of the interrelationship of traditions in the *Book of Ezra*, this is impossible.

[193] The groundwork of the Chronistic work to which *Neh.* IX may belong is probably to be placed about 400 B.C. (A different view was expressed in my *Überl: Studien*, pp. 150-155).

[194] For the "covenant" with Abraham mentioned here, see above, p. 37, n. 91.

of the conquest as well as of the Sinai tradition, in the mutually interconnected form adopted by the ancient writers of the Hexateuch, always attributing them to "our Fathers".

Following this comes, in similar vein, a short summary of the contents of the tradition about the period of the so-called Judges (vss. 26-9).[195] Then, after remarking that even in times of greatest catastrophe God had not completely rejected their ancestors, nor snapped the thread of Israel's history (vss. 30b-31), the writer plunges into a lament about the present, a time of humiliation and poverty which had lasted—and this is historically correct—"from the times of the Assyrian kings down to our own day" (vs. 32). This lament brought before God implicitly includes the petition for a future restoration, and the hope that it will be realized. It regards the present as a time of waiting between the past and a future that will correspond to that past.

On the other hand it is noteworthy that the most important aspect of the historical circumstances under review is taken to be the outward one; the suppliants, we are told, are now "slaves", and that, moreover, in the land once given by God to their ancestors as a free possession (vs. 36). Furthermore, the kings of a foreign empire lord it over their persons, their possessions, and the yield of their land (vs. 37). In remarkable contrast to *Ezek.* XL-XLVIII, the condition of political humiliation and the lack of external prosperity are here regarded as the most important features of the existing distress, whose coming removal is awaited.

The real crux, the question of the connection between all this and God, is not seriously considered. It is true that in the retrospect of past history the disobedience of the fathers, the transgression of the law and the commandments are quite frequently mentioned (vss. 16, 17a, 18, 26, 29, 34.); but God looked on this in long-suffering and mercy, and if he did occasionally punish, yet in his graciousness he did not bring about a complete destruction (vss. 17b, 19-21, 27b, 28b, 30.). But the prayer contents itself with this interpretation not only with respect to ancient times among the twelve tribes of Israel, but also more

---

[195] This section in particular shows the closest connection with the deuteronomic literature, especially the deuteronomic framework of the *Book of Judges* (cf. the following note).

emphatically with regard to the great historical catastrophes which in fact had brought that ancient Israel to an end.

In the matter of the relationship between God and people the prayer finds no break in the history; indeed at this juncture it uses a strongly deuteronomistic expression about the God "who keeps covenant and loyalty" (vs. 32, cf. *Deut.* vii.9, 12; *I Kings* viii.23),[196] and so indirectly indicates that the "covenant" was not in doubt. Consequently the validity of "the law" is no longer a problem; rather, its validity right down into the present is regarded as self-evident. To such a degree has the appreciation of the decisive significance of ancient Israel's downfall evaporated; and in consequence the future expectation is no longer, as in *Ezek.* xl-xlviii, directed towards the fundamentally important prelude of the restoration of the ancient twelve tribes, but towards the more tangible renewal of political independence. It is now apparent how far this prayer has moved in some respects away from the old, fundamental tenets of Old Testament faith; that is what makes it a document characteristic of its period.[197]

We find these fundamental matters still more definitely in another document, where they are however only indirectly touched upon; this is in the so-called Priestly strand of the Penta-teuchal narrative, which is probably somewhat older than the Chronistic Work and belongs to the fifth century B.C. In language and viewpoint it[198] is closely related to the post-exilic redaction of the cultic laws, and to this extent has a direct bearing on the matter of the law. Although it is a narrative about the far distant

---

[196] This expression is frequently used by the editor of the Chronistic work (cf. *II Chron.* vi.14; *Neh.* i. 5); and G. v. Rad, *Das Geschichtsbild des chronistischen Werkes*, B.W.A.N.T., iv, No. 3, Stuttgart 1930), has shown that he generally aligns himself with *Deuteronomy* and the deuteronomic literature.

[197] The prayer in *Ezra* ix.6-15, which was also composed by the Chronicler, gives us a similar but less detailed document. There is a reference here too to the "days of the Fathers" (vs. 7), to the present state of "slavery" (vs. 9), and to the still valid, but often transgressed, commandments (vss. 10, 14).

[198] Contrary to the usual view, P is in my opinion to be considered a purely narrative source which originally contained no laws, but aimed at providing a description of the arrangements and ordinances at Sinai, for which the pre-Sinaitic history with its various covenants and associated introduction of precultic ordinances merely supplied a general introduction. The "priestly laws", literally speaking, were inserted at a secondary stage, and it is quite questionable whether—apart from *Lev.* xvi—they had ever been included in the separate P narrative. Their stylistic and material relationship to the P narrative arises from similarity of milieu. (Cf. my *Überlieferungsgeschichte des Pentateuch*, henceforth cited as *Pentateuch*, 1948, pp. 7ff., 250.

past, it shows by its manner that it regards its own time as a temporary period of transition. What is remarkable about this narrative is that, in contradistinction to the older narrative strands of the Hexateuch, it paints its picture of the past quite consciously from the point of view and attitude of its own time— the post-exilic period. Its main theme is the description of the setting up of the cult, and the regulation of the life of the Israelite tribes as laid down by the proceedings on Sinai.

This ordinance is regarded by the editor quite openly as the right and proper arrangement not only for the past, but for always. The P narrative depicts this ordinance as if it were based on the arrangements of its own day; the post-exilic Temple serves as a pattern for the building of the tent sanctuary in the wilderness, the contemporary organization of cult personnel is applied to the Sinai period, and so on. Yet it is not the real contemporary situation that reappears in the picture of the Sinai ordinance, for neither the Ark in the sanctuary nor the twelve tribes of Israel— both of which play an important role in P's narrative of Sinai— were any longer known at that day. That is, it is an idealized present that appears in the description of the Sinai ordinance, or more correctly—since P would scarcely concern himself with an idle play about an unreal and unrealizable ideal—it is a hope and an expectation for the future, which has induced the editor of P to depict the "correct" ordinance of past times, and so also a future which God will bring to pass. For it would be scarcely credible that the compiler of P, who so admittedly starts off from the arrangements of his own day (in contradistinction to the older narratives in the Hexateuch), would speak in such detail of ordinances such as the division of Israel into twelve tribes—which by his day had been completely destroyed by the vicissitudes of history—unless his whole delineation had had in his view a direct meaning for his own time.

This contemporary significance could subsist only in the expectation—not to say the promise—of a restoration of the proper state of affairs. So, in contrast to the remarks of the Chronicler, the emphasis is laid not upon the return of political independence, but on the ancient sacral state of affairs. On this point the esoteric, priestly narrative of P[199] has preserved what

---

[199] For an analysis of the character of P cf. especially G. von Rad, *Die Priesterschrift im Hexateuch*, B.W.A.N.T., IV, No. 13, 1934, pp. 186ff.

was essential in the presuppositions of Old Testament faith. Unexpressed in its description, there dwells latent the expectation of a future restoration of the ancient sacral ordinance, which had been merely temporarily discontinued. But even here we are concerned with the external factors of this ordinance, which could link up directly to the cult already existing in the post-exilic Temple, as it appears so clearly in the background throughout P; whereas the more important matter of a restoration of the relationship to God is clearly not dealt with, because for the editor of P this relationship did not appear to have been decisively destroyed or interrupted.

4. "THE LAW" AS AN ABSOLUTE ENTITY DURING THE LATE PERIOD

The circumstances

In the section above, on the so-called "Transitional Period", we noticed a remarkable complexity and uncertainty of judgment with regard to the validity of "the Law"[200]; and this contrasts with the quite clear and definite conception of the basis and meaning of the various laws in pre-exilic times. At the same time, there is already clearly evident the tendency to take up and develop this question. Some of the authors mentioned in the preceding section must be discussed again in what follows, which deals with the final chapter in the history of the validity of the Law in the Old Testament; because in other passages in their works—unperturbed by earlier views—they represent the last stage in this history.

The variety of views in the transitional period shows that the old definite, clear situation had disappeared. In course of time, however, even the expectation of a restoration of the essential elements (which could have brought about once more the requisite basis for the laws) was bound to disappear. Had this expectation not arisen directly after the downfall of the old order, and had the occurrences of Cyrus's time not given the impression of being this event (or at least the beginning of it), and had the topical messianic expectation of the prophets Haggai

---

[200] When the various laws had become entities in the tradition, the conception of them all together as forming *the* Law grew up.

and Zechariah (not)been realized, then the expectation of a restoration could not conceivably have remained alive indefinitely. Then the possibility of attaching the validity of the law to it also failed. As will always happen under such circumstances, since the expected turn of fortune did not eventuate, people became accustomed to the state of affairs that had developed during the course of historical events, accepted it as customary, and reckoned with it as the now normal reality.[201]

In addition to the political organization of the province of Judah within the framework of the vast Persian Empire, which was set up in the time of Nehemiah, there was also the regular cult, re-established in Jerusalem at the rebuilding of the Temple, in which ancient traditional ordinances were interspersed with newly formulated and developed ones. To this cult belong particularly the Pentateuchal laws. These to a large extent governed and regulated not only cultic life in its widest sense, but also the everyday life of the community in Palestine and in the Dispersion. By virtue of the power of inertia, the surviving laws remained valid and binding simply on account of their practical indispensability (see above, pp. 73ff.). After periods of domestic strife and disorder they would be put back into force, although they did not correspond to circumstances, nor had any basis in the contemporary situation, as they had had in pre-exilic times. Nor could it be said of them that they were being introduced *ad hoc* during a period of transition to an expected renewal of the appropriate situation.

Consequently there follows a third and last stage in the position and justification of these laws. "The law" became an *absolute entity*, valid without respect to precedent, time, or history; based on itself, binding simply because it existed as law, because it was of divine origin and authority. Viewed in this way it was no longer possible to restrict the validity of the law to any particular circle of people, since it no longer presupposed any community of people *brought together* in a particular way, to which it could be tied. It was no longer tied to anything; even if in fact this law

---

[201] It was not that the directing of the glance toward the future, to what God would one day do again in the future, had been given up. And it was not any longer an expectation of a state of affairs restored in this way or that, but rather of a new world under the universal rule of God. The law applied to this present world, whether the future world would also have a law was another matter. In this way, expectation for the future and the validity of the law became two separate issues.

was applied only amongst one particular group of people in the world, that could only be considered as a—perhaps temporary—historical accident, and certainly not, as in pre-exilic times, a law made to fit certain specific circumstances. The law became a power in its own right. If it did in fact stand in a historical relationship to a particular human community—the post-exilic community at home and in dispersion—the old, obvious relationship was now reversed; it was not now this community which formed the prerequisite for the being and application of the law, but rather it was the law, as the unprecedented primary entity, which fashioned this community, which was nothing but the union of those people who submitted to the law on all points. When this community preserved and maintained the ancient narrative tradition of the history of Israel along with it, it was understood as a collection of historical examples of the attitude of man to the law and its consequences.[202] So when the edifice of the old establishment collapsed, the law which had formed a single pillar in the framework of the whole was the only part which finally remained erect. It then became the centre column and stay of a new edifice erected on the ruins of the old.

Evidence for this development is plentiful in the later Old Testament literature. One characteristic is a fondness for referring to *the* law, *the* commandments, *the* precepts; and for speaking of "keeping" and "observing" them—or of transgressing them. This has the effect of making the law as the totality of commandments appear as a complete, firm entity, whose overall validity cannot be doubted. Of course, this attitude is already to be found in *Deuteronomy* and in the deuteronomic redaction of the old historical tradition, where expressions such as "keeping the law, the commandments of God" or the similar "walking in the paths of God" are among the most obvious and common features of the deuteronomic and deuteronomistic style.[203] But the deuteronomic law addresses the "congregation of Yahweh"—i.e. the confederacy of the twelve tribes of Israel—so directly, and the deuteronomistic redaction of the historical tradition so obviously deals only with the ancient history of the Israelite

---

[202] New narratives from the late period, like the Daniel legends in *Dan.* II-VII, quite expressly have the aim of providing examples of correct fulfilment of the law.

[203] Cf. the collection of deuteronomic and deuteronomistic expressions in the Hexateuch in H. Holzinger, *Einleitung in den Hexateuch*, Leipzig 1893, pp. 284ff.

people, that here the reference is still undoubtedly to the validity
of "the law, the commandments of God" within the actual
context set by the ancient people of the twelve tribes. In addition,
the expression "the law of Moses", quite frequently used in the
deuteronomic literature, indicates the correct historical association of the law and its application. This applies also in the late
historical writing of the Chronistic work, where the same
expressions are freely used; but the Chronistic work can be
proved to be strongly under the influence of the deuteronomic
literature,[204] so it has not the same value as an independent
witness. On the other hand, in very late psalms—for example in
the so-called Wisdom psalms, and in other parts of the wisdom
literature which belong to the latest sections of the Old Testament—we find general references to *the* law, and *the* commandments.

It is no coincidence that in *Ps.* 1, which was prefaced as a sort
of motto to the complete collection of psalms, probably in the
second century B.C., praise is accorded "the man" who delights
in "the law of Yahweh", and in this law meditates "day and
night". This expression is found in a deuteronomistic passage
in *Joshua* 1.8, and shows how the law has there become not simply
a controller of behaviour as founded on belief, but itself a
foundation of belief which should be regarded as an object of
continuous meditation. In this way it attained a value which did
not in fact belong to it originally.

The same is true in the Wisdom poem *Ps.* xix.8-15, in whose
first part the perfection, excellence, and goodness of the law of
Yahweh are praised. Here too the law appears as an independent
power, of divine origin and authority, about which expressions
in almost hymnic style can be framed, such as occur elsewhere
in hymns to God himself. The law of Yahweh is described in a
succession of six or eight[205] synonymous expressions; and already,
in discussing it, a special festal terminology of a cultic sort has
been developed. This is particularly evident in the long alphabetic acrostic poem *Ps.* cxix, in each of whose twenty-two eight-
line strophes eight synonyms are used for the concept law, so

---

[204] See above, p. 83, n. 196; and my *Überl. Studien*, pp. 133ff., 166ff.
[205] In the original text of vs. 11 it appears possible that two other synonyms once
stood at the beginning of the lines, but have fallen out owing to later textual
corruption. Cf. KBH³, *ad loc.*

that the whole of this elaborate poem rings the praises of "the law". On account of its international connections the Old Testament Wisdom literature was slow to represent any peculiarly Old Testament belief, but in late sections we do find the law of Yahweh, when it is mentioned as the norm of behaviour, appearing as a firm, independent, self-standing entity.[206]

From some indications in the Chronistic work we may gather that in later times "the law of (Yahweh)" became not only an object of personal meditation, but also a subject to be taught to the people by priests, and in particular by the Levites. This links up with an ancient task of the priests, which was to provide the laity with information and advice in matters of cultic, ritual, and daily life (cf. *Deut.* xxxiii.10; *Hos.* iv.6). The new element was that the firm, fixed, written body of "the law" now served not only as the foundation, but also as the subject of the teaching; moreover this teaching was systematic, and not merely given in reply to queries and on cultic occasions.

In *II Chron.* xv.3 the oracle attributed to a prophet of the time of Asa, King of Judah, contains the following words indicating the foundations of the faith: the "true God", the "law", and— between the other two—the "teaching priest".[207] In this short summary the mention of "the law" is as significant as that of priestly instruction, since really the subject in this context could only be the law itself.

Apart from this passage it is mainly the Levites to whom the role of teachers of the law is assigned. In *II Chron.* xvii.7-9 we are told that Jehoshaphat, King of Judah, once despatched five of his higher state officials, eight Levites,[208] and two priests to the cities of Judah, so that they might teach the people out of "the book of the law of Yahweh". Here the editor of the Chronistic work, as often, has clearly applied the conditions of his own day to the scene he is describing. Such a passage should be evaluated with reference to post-exilic times; royal commissions and the participation of royal officials fall out, as an editorial adaptation

[206] Further details may be found in J. Fichtner, *Die altorientalische Weisheit in ihrer israelitisch-jüdischen Ausprägung*, Bei. *Z.A.W.*, No. 62, 1933, 81ff., 113.

[207] Cod. Vat. omits this last expression. Even if this represents quite by itself the original text of the lxx, the lack in the lxx would be traceable to a *Homoioarkton* and would be of no consequence for the Hebrew text.

[208] The last of the Levitical names included is certainly a dittograph, and should be omitted.

to the period under consideration, leaving us with the teaching of the law "in the cities of Judah" (i.e. in the towns of Palestine which belonged to the post-exilic community) by Levites and certain priests.[209]

Similarly in *Neh.* VIII.5-8 the same editor portrays how, on introducing the law which he has brought with him from Babylon, Ezra reads it out to the community assembled in Jerusalem, and how a number of Levites—whose names are given—then expound[210] to the people the law or "reading" (i.e. the portion read out). However remarkable this statement may appear to be in its context, since Ezra himself could have explained the law he read to the audience as easily as could the Levites—and since he was the sole responsible agent in this affair, he would be the obvious choice—yet for this very reason we may the more confidently deduce from this passage that for the editor of the Chronistic work the teaching and expounding Levites were closely associated with the concept of the law.[211]

Finally we must mention *II Chron.* XXXV.3, where, in a narrative about Josiah which has nothing to do with teaching the law, and in an obviously stereotyped expression, the "Levites who teach all Israel" are spoken of.[212] In view of what we have just said, the reference is again without doubt to the teaching of the law; this activity seems to the editor to be so closely associated with the position of the Levites that he refers to it even in a passage where he is recording something quite different about them.

This teaching of the law by the Levites was probably one of the roots of synagogal worship, whose beginnings are so wrapped in mystery, but in which the reading and exposition of "the law"[213]

---

[209] *II Chron.* XIX.8ff. may also be mentioned. We are told here that Jehoshaphat appointed Levites and priests, among others, to the office of judge; but the Chronicler then immediately goes on to remark that during the carrying out of this assignment the teaching of "law, commandment, statutes and judgments" was to become the task of these Levites and priests.

[210] This word which occurs twice in this context literally means "make understandable", and so here means interpret something which was in a fixed written form.

[211] So we are not justified in removing the remarkableness of this passage by excisions from the text, such as removing vs. 7 and changing the plurals of vs. 8 into singulars (as e.g. G. Hölscher in Kautzsch, *Die Heilige Schrift*, 4th edn., *ad loc.*).

[212] The word mentioned in n. 210 is used here also.

[213] In the synagogue service the Pentateuch, as we have it, very soon provided "the law", and this was read out in separate portions (see above, p. 3).

played a central role. This all shows how during the later period the law became the basis not only of behaviour as determined by the relationship to God, but of that very relationship itself. It shows, further, how the law became freed from its historical presuppositions which now no longer existed, and was placed on its own feet. It had become a "separate entity".

The two concepts of "covenant" and "law" had always been closely related to one another; their sundering was of great significance in the separation of the law from its historical background. In *Pss.* i, xix b and cxix, whose theme is very particularly "the law", the word "covenant" nowhere occurs, which is especially remarkable in *Ps.* cxix with its wealth of words. But in these didactic psalms which seek to put the meaning of "the law" in the correct light, there is no single reference even indirectly to the covenant. Elsewhere in the *Psalms* the covenant is repeatedly mentioned; God is praised as the one who "keeps covenant", or he is petititioned—in laments—"to remember his covenant"; mention is made of those "who keep his covenant" or "do not remain true to his covenant"; but in these cases there is no mention at all of the law.[214] "Covenant" and "law" appear here as permanent concepts of religious speech that occur most frequently in fixed formulae, but whose real connection with one another is no longer apparent.

The same is true of the latest, post-exilic, strand of narrative in the Pentateuch, the "priestly" narrative already mentioned (P). The case is the more striking here because the central theme of this narrative is the event which took place at Sinai, in which (historically speaking) the connection between covenant and law had its roots, and in which the association was made clearly enough apparent in the older strands of narrative. P knows the concept "covenant" well enough. According to it, God "established" a "covenant"[215] with Noah and his descendants after the Flood, that such a judgment would never occur again (*Gen.* ix.8-17). The covenant with Abraham, according to P, also

[214] Only in *Ps.* l.16 and lxxviii.10 do "covenant" and "law" (or "statutes") appear together in poetic parallelism. H. J. Kraus, "Freude an Gottes Gesetz", in *Ev. Th.*, x (1950-51), pp. 337-351, cf. esp., pp. 340ff., interprets this fact differently.

[215] P no longer uses the old technical term for "making a covenant", but different verbs which exclude the (metaphorically related) conception of the covenant between God and people.

contains the promise that Abraham shall have numerous descendants whose future possession of Palestine is declared (*Gen.* xvii.2ff.). The concept "covenant" certainly survives in these instances, but only as a decorative feature of the narrative which serves to give to a divine promise a solemn form[216]; it might without any real loss be omitted from the passage in question.[217]

In P's Sinai narrative, on the other hand, which can be easily and certainly separated out in the section *Exod.* xixff. on literary-critical grounds,[218] the word "covenant" never occurs, and even any incident which might represent an act of covenant-making is completely lacking. After the arrival of the Israelites at Mount Sinai (*Exod.* xix.1), the appearance of the "divine glory" on the holy mountain follows immediately, and thereafter the call of Moses up to the mount (*Exod.* xxiv.15*b*-18), followed immediately by the detailed divine instructions to Moses about the ordinances he is to give to the people concerning cultic and everyday life. The communication and carrying out of these ordinances take up the main part not only of the Sinai pericope, but of P's whole narrative. These ordinances have as their only prerequisite here the divine will, and they are simply imparted, at a definite historical time, and in the framework of a definite historical situation, both fixed by old and immovable tradition. The validity of the ordinances, moreover, appears to be no longer governed by a historical act of institution expressed in a relationship between God and people, which took place on a specific occasion in history.

Looking at it in this way, therefore, the editor of P could never have conceived of any cessation of this relationship happening within history, for it would have resulted in the removal of the proper basis for the ordinances set forth by him. At this late period the ancient ordinances and laws remained for all practical purposes in force, even though their prerequisites no longer

---

[216] The early tradition (*Gen.* xv.9ff.) already knew of a "covenant" between God and Abraham as an anticipation of the Sinai covenant; here too it contained a promise. The history of Abraham in particular was already regarded in Israel in early times as a model of the fundamental events which led to the emergence of the people of Israel.

[217] The statute about circumcision (*Gen.* xvii.10ff.) is in P only loosely connected with the Abrahamic covenant.

[218] Cf. O. Eissfeldt, *Hexateuch-Synopse*, 1922, pp. 146*ff.; and my *Pentateuch*, p. 18.

survived; but P's conception reflects the post-exilic view that
they had never been tied to such prerequisites, but had been
"separate entities" from the beginning.[219]

The reverse of thus making "the law" an absolute, and
separating the concepts of "covenant" and "law" from one
another was, quite naturally, that in the late Old Testament
literature the word "covenant" (used in the figurative sense of
the relationship between God and people) was emptied of all
its meaning, and lost its special reference to the Sinai covenant.
The older tradition had used the concept "covenant" in this
figurative sense only of the solitary act consummated at Sinai,
and of its forshadowing by Abraham (see above, p. 92, n. 216),
and its later renewals such as the covenant at Shechem and
with Josiah (see above, pp. 42ff.). But later times used the concept "covenant" in a very watered-down sense for all manner of
rules about the relationship between God and people.

That is why the P narrative mentions a covenant with Noah
(see above, p. 91) as well as the old traditional covenant with
Abraham. The later literature uses more frequently the idea of
a covenant of God with David, the terms of which are supposed
to be given in the ancient oracle of Nathan in *II Sam.* VII.8ff.
concerning the continuation of the Davidic dynasty. In direct
dependence on this passage the late psalm, *Ps.* LXXXIX speaks of
the covenant with David (vss. 4, 29, 35, 40). The equally late[220]
"last words of David" in *II Sam.* XXIII.1-7 also show acquaintance
with the same concept (vs. 5). *The Book of Chronicles* mentions
the Davidic covenant (*II Chron.* XIII.5, XXI.7),[221] again with a
clear reference to *II Sam.* VII; and similarly also *Ps.* CXXXII.12.[222]

---

[219] The unexpressed expectation behind the P narrative of a future restoration
(see above, pp. 83ff.) linked up therefore not with the relationship between God
and people, but with the external condition of the sanctuary and the people of the
twelve tribes.

[220] Cf. S. Mowinckel in *Z.A.W.*, N.F. IV (1927), pp. 30-58.

[221] Remarkably enough the mention of the Davidic covenant in *II Chron.* XXI.7
is an addition by the Chronicler in a passage which otherwise follows the wording
of *II Kings* VIII.19.

[222] *Jer.* XXXIII.21 with its mention of the Davidic covenant stands in a secondary
passage; in *Ezek.* XVII.13, 14 the "covenant" with someone of David's lineage
appears to be of uncertain meaning; *Isa.* LV.3 speaks of a future covenant on the
grounds of the promise to David. Cf. L. Rost: "Sinaibund und Davidsbund," in
Theologische Literaturzeitung (henceforth cited as *Th. Lz.*), LXXII (1947) pp. 129ff., and
H. J. Kraus: "Gottesdienst in Israel," *Beiträge zu Evangelische Theologie* No. 19,
Munich 1954, pp. 77ff.

The concept appears still fainter in the representation given of the "covenant with Levi", which could not be linked up with any ancient tradition. Its content is envisaged to be merely the entrusting of their office to the Levites as the only legitimate servants of the cult. This representation occurs in *Num.* xxv.12, 13 in a later addition to the P narrative, and again in *Mal.* 11.4, 5, 8; *Neh.* xiii.29, and *Dan.* xi.22.[223]

According to *Ezra* x.3 the regulation of mixed marriages by Ezra was put through in the form of a covenant enactment, and in the later section of the *Book of Proverbs* marriage appears as a "divine covenant" (*Prov.* 11.17). But wherever the reference is to Sinai, the concept "covenant" appears in such an attenuated and distorted form that it could simply be equated with the law given on Sinai, or even with the tables on which the law was written. In the introductory speech using the plural form of address, *Deuteronomy* already speaks of the "tables of the covenant" (*Deut.* ix.9, 11, 15) which Moses had received on Sinai. Although this may be taken as an abbreviated form of expression meaning the law which was given in the context of the covenant relationship, and written on tablets, yet *II Chron.* vi.11 speaks directly of the "covenant of Yahweh" which was found in the holy land[224]; here the concept "covenant" has lost all implication of an act of covenant-making, and at most preserves a hazy conception of the old traditional relationship of covenant and law, which identified the validity of the law with the existence of the covenant relationship; it completely ignores the real circumstances (see above, pp. 39ff.).

A similar weakening in the later literature may be demonstrated with regard to the concept of "election", although this concept never had such a firm connection with the covenant. Yet together with the concept of the covenant it did express more emphatically the fact of divine activity. Ancient tradition had expressed the first steps toward election in its own way, without using the concept itself (cf. *Gen.* xii.1-3). Later *Deuteronomy* in its basic form traced back the experience at Sinai to a divine "election" (*Deut.* vii.6), and spoke in stereotyped phrases of the "election" of the central sanctuary for the "congregation of

---

[223] The "covenant with Levi" also appears in *Jer.* xxxiii.21 (see previous note).
[224] This links up with the tradition, first found in *Deut.* x.4ff., that the tablets inscribed with the law were laid in the sacred Ark.

Yahweh" founded through the covenant (*Deut.* XII.14, etc.)
Later still the divine "election" was applied to all manner of
objects. Secondary passages in *Deuteronomy* and in the deuteronomistic history acknowledge the "election" of King David
(*I Kings* XI.34); there is an "election" of the tribe of Levi to the
priestly office (*Deut.* XVIII.5, XXI.5).[225] In addition to the election
of the central sanctuary there is an "election" of the city of
Jerusalem (*I Kings* XI.13, etc.). The Chronicler speaks of an
election of David (*I Chron.* XXVIII.4; *II Chron.* VI.6), of an election of Solomon (*I Chron.* XXVIII.5, 6, XXIX.1), of an election of
the city of Jerusalem (*II Chron.* VI.6, 34, 38, XII.13, XXXIII.7),
of an election of priests and Levites (*II Chron.* XXIX.11) and
of an election of the Jerusalem Temple *building* (*II Chron.*
VII.16).

This loose and hazy way of using earlier definite concepts is a
symptom that they no longer meant much for this late period,
and no longer possessed any decisive context, but were simply
carried on as traditional material bereft of their full meaning, so
that they were no longer vital for the understanding of the law
and its force which was so much in the forefront. This simply
means that in the late period the law was no longer tied up with
historical considerations, but stood upon its own feet as an
independent entity.

Consequences

This attainment by "the law", in the late period, of independence and paramountcy brought with it a series of important
consequences which fully appear only in post-canonical literature, though their roots go back into the period of late canonical
literature.

We have already mentioned (pp. 79ff.) that the setting free
of the law from the context of a pre-ordained pre-existent system
of society brought about a momentous swing of emphasis from
divine activity to individual human behaviour. According to the
old order of things, behind the laws stood the institutions whose
origin was traced back in the basic Sinai narrative to the free
initiative of God; and the response of man within these institutions to the laws in force was to be thought of simply as a kind of

[225] These verses are secondary insertions.

answer to the preceding divine activity. But now in the relationship between God and man the behaviour of the individual man,
in view of the unfettered force of the law, became decisive; as for
God, apart from the fact that he retained the first word as giver
and upholder of the law, he really had nothing else to do but
react to the behaviour of man according to the standard laid
down by the law.

The old social order traced back its institution in history to the
hand of God, and consequently man's position in it had been
determined and fixed by this circumscribed and visible historical
phenomenon. According to one of the relevant laws, man's
actions were nothing more than the mere activation of the
arrangement pre-determined by God in this historical manifestation. God's constant activity in history had been for man
an ever-present underlying assumption of his being and doing
in his relationships at large. At a later period man, as a being
solely determined by the creation of God, was faced by the timeless law, no longer attached to any historical manifestation.
How should he behave with regard to it? Was he prepared, by
subjecting himself to the law, to join that secondary social
edifice which included all those who recognized "the law" as
obligatory?

In ancient times the divine initiative was the decisive step
towards the completion of an act of covenant-making; the
community as a whole, or their representatives, then had the
task of ratifying this covenant relationship and fulfilling their
obligation to a law which now became applicable under the
conditions of the covenant. According to the ancient Sinai
tradition, this is what happened there; in essentials it happened
too, naturally, at the ceremonies of covenant-making which were
merely the renewal of the Sinai covenant, e.g. the Shechem
covenant of *Josh.* XXIV.2ff., 25ff., and Josiah's covenant in
II Kings XXIII.1ff. In the days of Ezra also it was once more
the whole community who, through their spokesman (*Neh.*
VIII.13ff.), undertook to observe a divine law laid before them
on a historical occasion; this same law was soon afterwards, at
Nehemiah's order (*Neh.* x.1ff.), made the object of a written
obligation undertaken by the appointed representatives.

In *Is.* LVI.1-8, however, we have a late oracle which was
probably composed after the time of Ezra and Nehemiah, and

which begins with a summons to observe the law; surprisingly enough this summons expressly refers to the "strangers [foreigners] who wish to adhere to Yahweh" (vss. 3, 6), and speaks of those who "choose" what "is the will" of God, and "apprehend" the law of God[226] (vss. 4, 6), and by doing so gain a place in the Temple at Jerusalem and in the post-exilic community.

In the later literature expressions frequently occur which indicate the personal and emotional liking or dislike of men for "the law", and therefore illustrate an attitude which is completely inappropriate with regard to a law as such, which is either in force or not in force. This clearly shows how human behaviour has lost its centre of balance. Those "whose delight is in the law of Yahweh" are mentioned in *Ps.* 1.2; while in *Ps.* cxix we meet expressions such as "delight in thy law" (vs. 70), "thy law is my delight" (vss. 77, 92, 174), "how I love thy law" (vss. 97, 163). A probably secondary passage in *Lev.* xxvi.43 speaks of those "who abhorred my statutes," whereas *Ps.* xix praises the law because it "restores the soul" (vs. 8), "rejoicing the heart" (vs. 9). In these and similar cases the phrases show how "the law" had become something *which man evaluates for himself*; and a personal attitude towards the law is expected of every man. On the other hand a man must then bear the consequences of his attitude.

One further consequence follows: with the abolition of an antecedent social ordinance founded by God, the *individual* is now noticed by the law. Originally the "thou" which occurs in the laws meant either the whole of the Israelite tribes or the individual in the context of this whole. The address in the Decalogue of *Exod.* xx is typical; in the preface, "I, Yahweh, am thy God, that brought thee up out of Egypt" (vs. 2), that the whole people is addressed is as clear as that the subsequent "Thou shalt not . . ." clauses can only refer to the individual, who has already been characterized in the preface as a member of the whole community. Furthermore in a case where there had been a transgression of a legal regulation (normally by an individual), it was the whole community that was responsible for the requital

---

[226] The word "covenant" is again used in the sense of "law" here (see above, pp. 93ff.). The keeping of the sabbath is mentioned in vss. 2, 4, 6 as an important element in the law (see above, p. 66, for this).

and expiation of the crime. *Deuteronomy* already has the stereo-typed formula "Thou (Israel) shalt put away the evil (com-mitted by some individual) from the midst of thee" (XIII.6, XVII.7, etc.). The whole society was thus responsible for a trespass originating with an individual, and had to bear its consequences —a good example being the law concerning the expiation for murder committed by an unknown person (*Deut.* XXI.1-9). The new situation in later times, in which the human attitude to the law had become decisive, made it necessary that the individual himself should begin to be responsible for keeping its require-ments. So in practice the responsibility of the whole society for the actions of the individual fell into abeyance.

The presence in the law of passages based on this sense of corporate responsibility which no longer applied gave rise in the later period to the problem of interpreting and applying "the law". The law had developed historically in separate parts, but was now regarded as a timeless entity with no history; although composed of multifarious elements, each with its historical basis, it now passed as a unity. Consequently it could only be fitted into its new situation by force, and the disparities of its various parts could be concealed only by a consciously harmonizing exposition which interpreted the whole—necessarily in a forced and artificial way—according to the new orientation. In the Old Testament itself this process is scarcely discernible, since in the Pentateuch we have only the traditional wording of the old laws and of a few post-exilic ones—with at most a few harmonizing additions here and there—but no exposition. The harmonizing exposition of the law became in later times one of the chief exercises of rabbinic learning.

Of greater practical importance and more fruitful consequence was the fact that by making the law into an absolute, and trans-ferring the emphasis from the divine activity to human response and behaviour, the concepts of *reward and punishment* were com-bined with the law. These alternative consequences of keeping, or not keeping, the provisions of the law were unknown in ancient times, and rightly so; for the double concept of reward *and* punishment has nothing at all to do with the realm of law. As is customary with other laws, so ancient laws (particularly those with a "juridical formulation") envisaged fixed punish-ments for particular transgressions which violated the order protected by law; and the corporate unit was responsible for carrying out the appropriate punishments, and so maintaining the proper order. These punishments were intended to "remove the evil from Israel", as *Deuteronomy* frequently puts it, so that by slaying the transgressor, for example, the corporate unit could free itself of the evil deed committed and make up for the damage done by some form of compensation, thereby annulling the transgression.[227] If the corporate body neglected to impose the punishment required by law, then the *status quo*—i.e. the "covenant" relationship between God and people—changed; and that was enough to ensure that the requirement was enforced.

The thought of a reward for submission to the law's requirements was as little known to ancient Israel as it is today, when laws derive their force from a given constitution. The incorporation of an individual into an existing order without his choice would at once bring about his subjection to the laws applying within that order; so that if the individual rendered obedience to these laws it was not a service to be rewarded, but merely an obligation inherent in the situation. The idea of a reward which might be *earned* by the fulfilment of the law's requirements only arose with the dissociation of the "the law" from a pre-ordained order, independent of the individual, and basing its authority on the timeless and changeless will of God; so that the theoretical possibility of man's acceptance or rejection was left open. Under these circumstances the tie between the individual and any social order whose validity depended on specific laws broke down; the individual stood without any mediator over against the will of God, which was revealed in "the law"; he had the apparent right of free choice between observing and rejecting it, and this immediately attracted to itself the idea of a corresponding recompense.

Of course mankind is so prone to the idea that to avoid a false step is to do something good and so deserve a reward, that it is no cause for wonder that even in pre-exilic legal passages allusions are found to divine recompense showing itself in reward *and*

---

[227] The *lex talionis* of *Exod.* xxi.23b-25 ("a life for a life, an eye for an eye", *etc*)— which should not be mistaken for a rule governing the relationship of man to man, but refers only to the administration of justice—reduces this idea of compensation to a formula as simple as it is drastic.

punishment; yet in the older parts of the Old Testament law-codes we find no more than hints.

In the solemn conclusions of *Deuteronomy* (*Deut.* XXVIII) and of the Holiness Code (*Lev.* XXVI), God's blessing on those who keep the laws, and his curse on those who do not are indeed mentioned, and the results of this blessing or curse are described in more or less detail. But it can easily be shown[228] that in these conclusions the emphasis is on the threatened curse, to which the promised blessing provides nothing more than a formal counter-part. There are exact parallels to these conclusions in laws and legal documents throughout the ancient Orient—probably even some actual prototypes; and everywhere the curse at the end of a regulation is to ensure punishment if it is transgressed, thereby guaranteeing its continued observance. The blessing merely pre-sumes the continuance of what is thought to be the normal con-dition, and is demonstrably nothing but a secondary appendage to the curse. Consequently in these cases the blessing is usually noticeably shorter than the curse—as in *Deut.* XXVIII and *Lev.* XXVI.

In the laws of the Old Testament—particularly in *Deuter-onomy*[229]—the divine blessing is a gift present before the law and its fulfilment, and therefore independent of them.[230] By the fulfilment of the law divine blessing is assured, but it cannot be earned. These concluding clauses in *Deuteronomy* and the Holi-ness Code speak only indirectly and figuratively of reward, and this is true also of other parts of those laws. The introduction in the second person singular appears to speak (in *Deut.* VII.7-11) of a dual recompense, where it says that God will keep covenant and loyalty with those who "keep his commandments", but "repays them that hate him" (vss. 9, 10).[231] Yet this passage begins with a reference to the free "election" of the people by

[228] Further details may be found in the article on pp. 118-131.

[229] Cf. especially G. v. Rad, *Das Gottesvolk im Deuteronomium*, B.W.A.N.T., III, No. 11, 1929, pp. 39ff.

[230] Cf. the section *Deut.* VII.12ff., in the original introduction to the law. The protasis in vs. 12a shows itself to be a secondary addition by its sudden change to the plural and its sundering of originally related clauses (the *wĕšāmartā* of vs. 11 and the *wĕšāmar* of vs. 12b clearly refer to one another. Vs. 12a makes divine blessing conditional upon the fulfilment of the law.

[231] K. Steuernagel, *Das Deuteronomium übersetzt und erklärt*, 2nd edn. 1923, p. 79, regards vss. 10 and 11 as additions since the following exposition has no reference to them; in that case the apparent reference to a dual recompense would disappear from this passage. There seem to me however to be insufficient grounds for deleting these words.

God, and to their love and loyalty in consequence of his promise (vss. 7, 8). It is therefore implied that by "keeping the commandments" the divine gifts already promised are kept in force, though not thereby earned (cf. *Deut*. IX.1-7 where not the "righteousness" of the people, but rather the preceding divine promises, form the basis for God's beneficent dealing with his people). The references to divine blessing as a consequence of fulfilling the law, which may be found in the body of the law-code (*Deut.* XV.10, XVI.20, etc.) must therefore be understood in the same sense. Such blessing is not brought about by fulfilling the law, but is simply assured thereby.

God's blessing as a reward earned by fulfilling the law appears first in secondary passages of *Deuteronomy*. A significant case is provided by the obvious insertion (*Deut.* VII.12a; see above, p. 100, n. 230); in a passage which mentions that, as God keeps covenant and loyalty, so should the people keep the law, there has been inserted immediately before this reference to God's behaviour the clause: "as a reward that ye hearken to and keep these judgments". This shows that the deuteronomic law still presupposed the ancient attitude, since the avowed thought of a reward first shows itself in these additions. For a consistent theory, which carried through the two alternatives of reward and punishment, depending upon the attitude shown towards "the law", could only be formulated when the law had shaken free from the historical setting which had supplied its validity, and appeared as an absolute entity over against the individual, who could recognize it and decide his own reaction to it himself, and no longer feel subjected to it because he was a mere cog in a pre-existing machine. Now the individual could feel that in "keeping the commandments" he was performing good works and earning a reward from God.

This theory of "individual requital" may be traced not only in the additions to the deuteronomic law, but frequently also in the deuteronomistic redaction of the ancient historical traditions[232] in the time when the ancient order had ceased. It arose and spread very rapidly, and appears in a greatly developed form in exilic times[233] in two sections of the *Book of*

---

[232] The dogma of retribution is basic to the interpretation given in the deuteronomistic framework of the Books of *Judges* and *Kings*.

[233] This dating appears probable even if Ezekiel is not the author.

Ezekiel[234] (XVIII, XXXIII.1-20) where it is expressed and worked out in detail. In opposition to the tenor of a current proverb (*Ezek.* XVIII.2),[235] the author unfolds how each individual earns his reward or punishment[236] from God according to his own behaviour with regard to the law,[237] without reference to any connection with a historical order existing independently of himself.

This idea of a dual requital is particularly frequent in late psalms. *Psalm* I takes the "law of Yahweh" as its main subject, and divides the company of the "righteous" from that of the "unrighteous",[238] according to their attitude to the law, assigning to each group its "earned" fate. In *Ps.* XCIV God is addressed as judge (vs. 2); he pronounces judicial decisions (vs. 10), and exercises retribution (vs. 23).[239] The psalm then speaks again of the law of God (vs. 12), and in detail of the "righteous" and "unrighteous" whom God rewards or punishes. Doubtless therefore the standing epithets "righteous" and "unrighteous" have an implicit reference to "the law", and are to be understood in the sense of supporters and enemies of the law even in those psalms which do not explicitly mention it. This applies, for example, in the late alphabetic acrostic *Ps.* XXXVII, whose

---

[234] Whether these two sections and the passage *Ezek.* III.16b-21, which is related in subject, are to be attributed to the prophet Ezekiel seems to me doubtful on account of the considerable difference between them and the content of Ezekiel's other prophetic oracles. Even the oracle *Ezek.* XIV.12-20, which is comparable in content, does not derive with certainty from Ezekiel, since it looks like a later explanation of *Ezek.* XIV.21-23. The unfortunate interposition of ch. XVIII between chs. XVII and XIX, which clearly belong together in subject-matter, remains striking.

[235] "The fathers have eaten sour grapes, and the children's teeth are set on edge". This proverb, which seems to have expressed the view that the fate of the individual was bound up with that of his society, is already quoted in *Jer.* XXXI.29, where its applicability is not denied (as in Ezekiel) with regard to the present, but only for "those days", i.e. a new time in which the present historical ties will be removed.

[236] Reward and punishment are here described as "life" and "death", respectively.

[237] The "statutes" of God are mentioned (XVIII.9, 21, XXXIII.15); and in XVIII.6ff. some examples of these statutes are given.

[238] The Hebrew *rāšā'* is usually translated by "godless" and, in contradistinction to *ṣaddîq*, "upright", originally denoted those who were found guilty in a court of law.

[239] *Hēšîbh*, "recompense", lit. "give back", indicates the reaction which corresponds to and follows another's action; it is therefore a good term to express the correspondence between human activity and divine reward or punishment.

broadly handled theme is the success of the "righteous" and the evil fate of the "unrighteous"; and again in *Ps.* xcii, where the merited fate of the "unrighteous" (vss. 8ff.) and the "righteous" (vss. 13ff.) are contrasted.

In the *Book of Job* the author conveys in the speeches of Job's friends the doctrine of dual requital which was current in his day, although he himself (in the speeches put in the mouth of Job) disputes its correctness on the basis of his own experience of life and faith. Although no direct reference is made to the law in these speeches, the expressions "righteous" and "unrighteous" undoubtedly envisage the law. This orientation was so unmistakable in later times that there was no longer need of any direct mention of "the law" to explain the words "righteous" and "unrighteous". In the last speech of the friends as recorded in *Job* xxii, their questions result in an undisguised formulation of the doctrine of dual requital; although the friends, with a certain caution, only gradually reveal their final goal.

The spread of this idea of a dual divine requital orientated towards the law and linked with the individual human being shows definitely how "the law" in the later period had freed itself from the pre-existent order of society to which the individual belonged willy-nilly. It had now become an absolute entity which faced every individual with the same directness. In the process of this development it became possible for each individual to see in the fulfilment of the law—understood as a definite unit, literarily fixed in extent and verbal form—an embodiment of what was pleasing to God, and, for practical purposes, he could "exhaust" his religion in it.

5. CONCLUSION

In the light of tradition the line of development actually undergone by the law in the Old Testament must appear inapt. It began with the incorporation of the separate, historically determined laws within the context of an existing sacral social order—the ancient confederacy of the twelve tribes of Israel. Next followed the provisional linking together of the traditional laws, with the expectation of an immediate restoration of the past order. This led to the continuing validity of the law, which was now regarded strictly as a unity, and an unconditional and

timeless entity of divine provenance. In this way the discussion
returns to where it began; "the law" as an independent entity
was so central in the late post-exilic community, at home and in
the Dispersion abroad, that it came to be regarded as the main
feature of the Pentateuch, into whose narrative its component
parts had been inserted. Indeed it gave to the whole of this
literary complex the designation "the law", and even the whole
of the Old Testament canon could be regarded as "the law" on
account of its first and most important section, the Pentateuch—
a conception which has continued even down to the present day.
But we have shown that this conception represents a view of the
meaning of the law which only appeared incidentally along with
the canonisation of the Old Testament; for originally the laws in
the Old Testament presupposed a particular state of affairs, as
laws normally do in human history. Furthermore, within this
context the laws were dependent on the continuing existence and
validity of that particular ordering of society.

In the New Testament, the controversy with contemporary
Judaism came to a head in the matter of the canonical Holy Writ
of the Old Testament, as maintained by the Jews. It was therefore proper to take a good look at this Holy Writ in the contemporary rabbinic exegesis, where it was understood as law
whose fulfilment enabled the individual to earn a reward from
God. But the New Testament sayings[240] which are directed to
the contemporary evaluation of the Old Testament canon
naturally cannot tell us anything about the proper understanding
of the different elements in the Old Testament tradition itself.

These sayings are a witness to the legalistic conception of the
whole Old Testament in the period following the formation of
the Old Testament canon. This legalistic conception of the Old
Testament is not called in question by the continuing presence
of future and eschatological expectations among the post-exilic
community, which were also based on the Old Testament; for
although this expectation concerning a nearer or more remote
future might continue as a living subject of faith, yet it was

---

[240] In dealing with New Testament sayings about the Old Testament we must
separate those instances where the controversy is with contemporary Judaism on
the basis of their ("Jewish") understanding of the Old Testament, from those
instances in which the Old Testament is adduced in its real sense from the point of
view of the story of God's dealings with man. The former occurs particularly in
Paul, whereas the latter is found more in the synoptic tradition.

scarcely a decisive factor in their day-to-day life, which was regulated by the Old Testament viewed as law. Nor was the legalistic interpretation of the Old Testament affected when the law temporarily regained its position in the social order, as appears to have happened in the second half of the *Book of Daniel*; it is probably no accident that, in this latest portion of the Old Testament which we can accurately date, the visions of chs. VII-XII, the old relationships reappear once more—even though formulated in a new way, and perhaps only suggested.

The long interval of rest and the lack of any decisive events had led to the stabilization of the law as an absolute entity, and to the separation of the life regulated by the conception of the Old Testament as law from the future and eschatological expectations. Yet the historical background of the second half of the *Book of Daniel* was the disturbed and turbulent time of Antiochus IV's attack on the Jerusalem Temple-cult, and the future and eschatological expectations once more became highly relevant at one stroke during the subsequent Maccabaean rising (cf. the explicit mention of the imminent "End Time" in *Dan.* XI.40). Here the word "covenant" is perhaps no longer used in its original sense of an act of covenant-making, nor for the covenant relationship based thereon; yet it is surprising that it does not, as elsewhere in the late period, indicate the law simply, but is applied to the community in and around Jerusalem— clearly as bearer and guardian of the covenant relationship with God (*Dan.* IX.27, XI.22, 28, 30, 32); that is, it again implies a visible institution. And the oracular saying in *Dan.* IX.24-7, which is admittedly so difficult to understand, speaks not only of a fulfilment of the ancient promises, but also of the coming of an "eternal righteousness" (vs. 24)—presumably the complete fulfilment of the law. However, like the tense eschatological expectation of the Danielic visions, this inclusion of the law here once more in a definite (future) situation had to recede again into the background, when the fulfilment of the expectation failed to appear. This episode clearly had no lasting effect on the legalistic interpretation of the Old Testament.

The interpretation of the Old Testament as law cannot offer a real understanding of the Old Testament, although it was the result of a longish development in which the law stepped ever more strongly and exclusively into the foreground. Most of the

Old Testament, and particularly those portions whose contents are of importance, is of an earlier period; and the majority of the most significant Old Testament laws still belong to the period when the old conditions prevailed, or at all events to the "period of transition" soon after the downfall of that ancient order. Consequently even for the specifically legal parts, the overall interpretation of the Old Testament as law cannot be the viewpoint of an authoritative exegesis; the majority of these parts are to be interpreted rather from the position of that ancient situation. The casting of "the law" into bold relief as an absolute entity with no history resulted in a new evaluation of the material handed down in the laws, which came to be regarded as a large unit, and finally resulted in a new conception of the body of Old Testament literature as a whole. This new interpretation first appears in the latest sections of the Old Testament, and then more fully in the post-canonical rabbinical literature; but since it denotes a falling away from the real ancient foundation of faith and life, it cannot form the basis for a proper and complete interpretation of the Old Testament, nor for a satisfactory exegesis of most of the laws in the Old Testament. For an explanation of the laws, we must pay particular regard to the old sacral situation which provided their background.

The gradual making absolute of "the law" must be looked upon as a false track, which led to consequences which led right away from the authentic foundation of faith, which in the pre-exilic writings had formed the subject of the tradition, the ordinances, and the testimonies. But this significant process must certainly be regarded as typical, and we can see that the Old Testament story can serve also as a pattern for characteristic and ever-recurring lapses in human history. It is the fate of human institutions which arise out of definite historical situations to decline in the course of history. But the ordinances and statutes, which had had their place in the context of those institutions, obstinately maintain their existence and, after their real basis has disappeared, take on a worth of their own which they had never possessed and which is not their due. Then do men worship dead ordinances and statutes, and regard it as a particular service and a work worthy of reward that they preserve what has been handed down merely because it has been handed down, and allow their lives to be governed by such fossilized laws. So that

when in the New Testament the controversy with the Old
Testament law comes to a head, it is not only a former Judaism
which is confronted, but something which meets us in human
history everywhere and always, then and now. So the history of
Old Testament law possesses a significance more general than
the narrow context of its actual circle of experience.

II

Old Testament Covenant-making in the light of a Text from Mari

Almost as soon as the content of the Mari texts became known it was noticed that there were striking resemblances between them and the Old Testament. It is not easy to explain the apparent connection between those "West Semites" who appear from about the nineteenth century B.C. in the territories of Mari and Babylon, and play a not inconsiderable role as founders and rulers of states, and the Israelite tribes who only very much later emerge into the light of history. In what follows I shall concentrate on one detail which itself points to this connection between the Mari texts and the Old Testament, bringing with it the possibility that the Mari texts may supply something towards the explanation of an Old Testament institution and its associated speech formula. The phenomena need, however, to be examined on a wider basis.

Mari text II.37[1] refers to the making of a covenant, the actual passage reading:

> ⁶a-na ḫa-a-ri-im ḳa-ta-li-im ⁷bi-ri-it Ḫa-na^meš ù I-da-ma-ra-az ⁸me-ra-na-am ù ḫa-az-za-am iš-šu-ni-im-ma ⁹be-li ap-la-aḫ-ma-a me-ra-na-am ¹⁰ù ḫa-az-za-am ù-ul ad-di-in ¹¹ [ḫa]-a-ra-am TUR a-ta-ni-im ¹²a-na-ku ú-š[a]-aḳ-ti-il ¹³[s]a-li-ma-am bi-ri-it Ḫa-na^meš ¹⁴ù- I-da-ma-ra-az aš-ku-[u]n.

> For "ass-slaying" between the Hana people and Idamaraz one brought a young animal and lettuce[2]; I feared my lord and permitted no young animal or lettuce. An ass, offspring

---

[1] *Archives royales de Mari II*, Musée de Louvre, Département des Antiquités Orientales, Textes cunéiformes, VOL. XXIII, ed. by Ch.-F. Jean 1941; and *Archives royales de Mari II: Lettres diverses*, ed. by Ch.-F. Jean, 1950, pp. 82f.

[2] The translation "young animal and lettuce" follows W. F. Albright in *A.N.E.T.*, p. 482b, and G. E. Mendenhall in *Bulletin of the American Schools of Oriental Research* (henceforth cited as *B.A.S.O.R.*) CXXXIII (1954), pp. 26ff.

of a she-ass I myself caused to be killed; an agreement between the Hana people and Idamaraz I brought about.

This passage occurs in a letter in which the royal functionary Ibal-ila communicates various items of information to King Zimrilim. It deals with the relationship between the two groups, the Hana people and the people of the region of Idamaraz, who both belonged to the administrative territory of Mari. In order to stabilize this relationship—whose conditions and circumstances there is no need to follow up here—an agreement, a "covenant" between the two partners is brought about by the royal deputy. In this connection the expression "ass-slaying" occurs as an obviously fixed technical term, having the meaning "covenant-making". G. Dossin has dealt with this expression, both elements of which are non-Akkadian, in a survey of the contents of the Mari texts.[3] It rests on a particular form of the art of making a covenant, in which the essential thing was the sacral slaying of an ass. This form was undoubtedly brought in by the governing class in Mari on the basis of traditions preserved by them at the time when they settled in Mesopotamia; and the non-Akkadian expression continued to be used for it, even though it did not fit in with the rules of Akkadian syntax.[4]

This slaying of an ass as an essential part of the act of covenant-making recalls information in the Old Testament concerning covenant-making, e.g. *Gen.* xv.9, 10, 17, and *Jer.* xxxiv.18, 19. The ass was certainly the riding animal and beast of burden before the Mari folk became sedentary, for they were not yet acquainted with the domesticated camel for riding or carrying loads. The ass was for them clearly an animal which might be sacrificed, and was indeed a particularly valuable sacrificial animal, more valuable than any other animal of the flocks; consequently on important occasions they "slew an ass", in the same way as the Arab tribes later made their camel offering. In the Old Testament the ass was an animal which could not be sacrificed, for it was "unclean"; maybe the declaration that the ass as well as the camel were "unclean"[5] is to be traced directly

---

[3] G. Dossin in *Syria*, xix (1938), pp. 108ff.

[4] On the construction *ana ḥayarim ḳatālim* cf. W. von Soden, *Grundriss der akkadischen Grammatik*, Rome 1952, para 150h.

[5] This may be concluded from the summarizing and systematizing regulations in *Lev.* xi.3ff. and *Deut.* xiv.4ff.

to some important role which ass and camel played in foreign cults[6] in the countries bordering on Israel. In any event, the word *ḥayarum* corresponds to the Ugaritic *'r*, to the Old Testament *'ayir*, and the Arabic *'air^{un}*, and means an adult male ass, not an ass-foal. This has been proved for the Old Testament *'ayir* by L. Koehler,[7] and doubtless applies also to the use of the same word in the other Semitic dialects.[8]

Mari text II.37 shows that "to slay an ass" had become a traditional expression for "to make a covenant". For however difficult it may be to make out the meaning of lines 8-10, they clearly indicate that the partners between whom the covenant was to be enacted brought along objects which were to play some part in enacting the covenant.[9] Consequently it was the intention to complete the covenant in some manner perhaps customary for both partners, or at least one of them. In this instance the making of the covenant was not to take the form of the sacrificial slaughter of an ass,[10] but the royal deputy did not permit an alternative method of making a covenant on behalf of his lord. Thus he brings about the "slaying of an ass"—i.e. the accomplishment of the covenant instrument in whose final act the "slaying of an ass" still followed literally.

If (as we may deduce from the non-Akkadian formula "ass-slaying") this was the old traditional method of enacting a covenant by the people who belonged to the ruling class in Mari, then King Zimrilim must clearly have laid stress on the maintenance throughout his domain of the covenant-making customs which he himself had received from his ancestors. In this connection Ibal-ila remarks that he caused a *ḥayarum TUR atānim*

---

[6] Cf. above, pp. 55ff. The provision in *Exod.* XIII.13a at least assumes that the ass may not be sacrificed, but also that its firstborn "belongs to Yahweh". This statement may preserve an old custom in which the firstborn of the ass was sacrificed as one of the important animals in the possession of man.

[7] L. Koehler, *Kleine Lichter: Fünfzig Bibelstellen erklärt* 1945, pp. 52ff.

[8] The rendering "ass foal" (also by Ch.-F. Jean, "*ânon*", in the translation of the passage from the Mari texts here discussed) rests on a misunderstanding of the expression T U R *atanim* (line 11 in this text, and frequently) which is now to be discussed.

[9] G. E. Mendenhall, in *B.A.S.O.R.*, CXXXIII (1954), adduces interesting and important material on the part to be played by "young animal and lettuce"—if we are to translate thus.

[10] The word *meranum* does not allow us to deduce with any certainty what species of "young animal" is intended. Ch.F. Jean translates by "puppy" (*loc. cit.*). Probably nothing more is meant than that a young ass is not in question.

to be "slain" to complete the act of covenant-making. W. F. Albright has already drawn attention to exactly the same expression occurring in the Old Testament in *Zech.* IX.9 *'ayir ben-'āthōnôth.*[11] Accordingly most people have thought of an "ass foal", but almost certainly *Zech.* IX.9[12] and the Mari texts are not concerned with an "ass foal", but with an adult male ass only. The words *TUR atānim* and *ben-'āthōnôth* must rather mean an ass of pure breed, as against a hybrid which was not born of a she-ass, but was a cross between a jackass and a mare—a mule, which was apparently known in Mesopotamia from very early times.[13] The mule could presumably be called *ḥayarum = 'yr* in the wider sense, so that where it was desired to specify beyond doubt a pure-blooded ass then the expression *TUR atānim = bn 'tnwt* was added. It is obvious why no hybrid, but only an "irreproachable" animal should serve for such a sacral act as the making of a covenant.

The "slaying of an ass" at the making of a covenant (as depicted by the Mari texts) is related to a method of enacting a covenant which was known to the Old Testament, with the exception that in the Old Testament it was a matter not of an ass, but of other animals which alone might be sacrificed in this sacral act. It is this method of completing a covenant ceremony which is usually taken to explain the remarkable use of the verb *kārath* in the expression *kārath běrîth* (lit. "to cut up a covenant", i.e. to "cut up" an animal for the purpose of making a covenant). We must probably postulate an involved prehistory for this strange form of expression. Occasionally the verb *kārath* is used alone with the meaning "to make a covenant", as in *I Sam.* XXII.8, and *I Sam.* XI.2, where however the full expression occurs in the preceding verse. It occurs also in *I Sam.* XX.16, where indeed a corruption in the text is usually suspected, though on doubtful grounds. It appears very questionable whether in these instances we should presume an ellipse, so that the word *běrîth* is to be mentally supplied after it, or whether there is not here, rather, a particularly ancient and original expression, because the simple *kārath* represents very closely the meaning of the *ḥayaram ḳatālum* of the Mari texts, except that the animal "cut

---

[11] W. F. Albright, in *A.N.E.T.*, p. 482*b*, n. 6.
[12] Cf. L. Koehler, *Kleine Lichter*, pp. 52ff.
[13] Cf. B. Meissner, *Babylonien und Assyrien*, VOL. I, 1920, p. 219.

up" at the covenant-making ceremony is not mentioned. Consequently it is difficult not to believe in a connection between the Old Testament *kārath běrîth* and the formula *ḥayaram ḳatālum birît* X *ù* Y (Mari II.37, lines 6ff.).

The origin of the word *běrîth* is so far unexplained. At present the tendency is to suppose a derivation from the root BRH "to eat", *běrîth* being understood as the bond brought about by a common eating.[14] Apart from the objection that this assumption is a little far-fetched, the fact that we then have in the expression *kārath běrîth* the combination of two totally different methods of accomplishing a covenant—the "cutting up" of an animal, on the one hand, and on the other a common meal (cf. *Gen.* XXI.54; *Exod.* XXIV.11—tells against it. The theoretically unobjectionable possibility that the word *běrîth* derives from a root BRH is inadequate argument in favour of this thesis. If there exists an actual historical connection between *birît* in the Mari formula and the Old Testament *běrîth*, then we must assume a complicated series of intermediate stages; and this necessity does militate against the assumption of such a connection.

At all events, the Old Testament expression *kārath běrîth* is not the result of a simple semasiological and phraseological development; there is nothing in what we find in the Old Testament against a supposition that the word *běrîth* had its origin in this very expression *kārath běrîth*. It would then be necessary to assume that the preposition *birît* (between) attained independence in an adverbial sense. This assumption is made easier by the circumstance that in *birît* we have a preposition which has developed out of a prepositional expression, *ina birît* . . ., going back to a noun *birîtum* (intervening space),[15] and that in Akkadian also the adverbial use is possible—*birît birît* (in two).[16] It would therefore be possible to suppose the existence of something after the following form of expression: *ḥayaram ḳatālum birît* (to slay an ass in between). Then the *birît* would take on substantival meaning in the sense "a between", "a mediation", so that it would now become necessary to introduce the parties to the covenant by means of a separate preposition, so that there arose

[14] So, most recently, L. Koehler in *L.V.T.L.* (1953) p. 152; "Problems in the study of the language of the Old Testament", in *Journal of Semitic Studies*, 1 (1956), pp. 4ff.

[15] Cf. W. von Soden, *op. cit.*, 115q.

[16] Cf. C. Bezold, *Babylonisch-assyrisches Glossar*, 1926, p. 92b.

(the Hebrew) *kārath bĕrîth* bên . . . ûbhên (*II Kings* xi.17, etc.).[17]
Finally *bĕrîth* then became the usual word for covenant, even
outside the expression *kārath bĕrîth*, and could be used in connection with other verbs independently.

There is another concept in the Mari texts which is in many
ways linked up with the "slaying of an ass", and which supports
the idea of a relationship with the language of the Old Testament. That is the word *salīmum* (reconciliation, agreement). In
the Mari text mentioned above Ibal-ila formulates the result of
his "ass slaying" in the words *salīmam birīt Ḥana^{meš} ù Idamaraz
aškun* (l. 13). We may compare the clause of the letter of Bannum
to Zimrilim in a passage quoted by G. Dossin[18]: *hayaram ša
salīmim kutul-ma* (slay an ass of agreement)! There are certain
uses of the word *šālôm* in the Old Testament which may very
obviously be compared. The formula *salīmam birīt . . . ù . . .* is
very similar to the Old Testament *šālôm bên . . ûbhên . . .* (*Judges*
iv.17; *I Sam.* vii.14; *I Kings* v.26[19]). Likewise the phrase *hayaram
ša salīmim katālum* reminds one immediately of the Old Testament
kārath bĕrîth šālôm (*Ezek.* xxxiv.25, xxxvii.26). But most particularly the expression *salīmam . . . aškun* corresponds very closely
to the Old Testament phrase *'āśá šālôm*; this phrase occurs in
Isa. xxvii.5, and especially in *Josh.* ix.51 where it stands in
immediate association with *kārath bĕrîth*. In root and meaning
the Old Testament *šālôm* certainly expresses the Akkadian
šalāmu/šulmu; it is possible that *salīmum* also entered into the
make-up of the Old Testament *šālôm* at the same time, along the
path of the historical relationships between the "West Semites"
of Mesopotamia and the Israelite tribes. This seems likely, in
view of material found in the Old Testament, since the idiom
'āśá šālôm—even if perhaps not so much the use of the word in the
expressions *šalôm bên . . . ûbhên*, and *bĕrîth šālôm*—can only be
explained with difficulty and in a forced fashion on the basis of
šālôm's original equivalence to *šalāmu* (wholeness, welfare,
prosperity). Added to this we now have the formula of the Mari
texts, which at least sets us the task of testing the use of *šālôm* in
the Old Testament to see whether *salīmum* does not lie at the base

[17] We would thus have a pleonastic expression, which would however no longer
be felt as such owing to the change in meaning of the word *birīt/bĕrîth*.

[18] Dossin, in *Syria*, xix (1938), p. 109.

[19] It is noteworthy that this passage is immediately followed by a clause with
kārath bĕrîth.

of some uses of this word. This task is too complex to be undertaken here, but some idea of it is to be found in the foregoing
statement of the case.[20]

Finally the Mari texts throw light on what is meant by *běrîth*
as a concept in the Old Testament, and on the development of
this concept—quite apart from the possibility of a philological
connection between *běrîth* and *birīt*. In his stimulating and
thorough investigation of the meaning of *běrîth*, J. Begrich[21]
raised the question whether originally a transaction between
equal partners was implied, or whether it was the granting of a
special relationship by a superior to an inferior. He decided in
favour of the latter, and declared the concept of an agreement
with a mutual relationship between contracting partners of an
equal rank to be a secondary intrusion. Begrich adduced a considerable amount of important material from the Old Testament
for his thesis, consisting mainly of numerous examples of
covenants made between men.

The question does arise, however, whether this point of view
is not too one-sided and simple. A ceremony of covenant-making,
as primitive and really ancient even on historical grounds as the
one expressed in *Gen.* xxxi.44-55 in two conflated literary
variants,[22] directly and intentionally stresses the mutual nature
of the agreement between two parties standing on the same level.
It may be more likely, therefore, that in Israel from very early
on there existed different types of covenant-making alongside
one another, for all of which the formula *kārath běrîth* served. This
view is supported by the Mari texts where we find covenant-
making acts of various kinds, including in particular a third type
such as is found in our text ii.37. Here a high official, the royal
deputy, causes "an ass to be slain" "*between*" the two parties to
the agreement. Here therefore there is a third party present, who
mediates the covenant and is thereby named as the subject of
the covenant-making, he enacts the covenant between X and Y.

---

[20] The difficult passage Num. xxv.12b also needs to be tested from the standpoint given above.

[21] J. Begrich, "Berit. Ein Beitrag zur Erfassung einer alttestamentlichen
Denkform", in *Z.A.W.*, N.F. xix (1944), pp. 1-11.

[22] It may be wondered whether the occurrence in this context of the covenant-
making formula without any preposition (vs. 44a, "We desire to make a covenant,
and thou") is to be regarded as particula rl y original (cf. above, pp. 111f.).
Cf. also *Gen.* xxi.27, 32; *I Sam.* xxiii.18; *I Kings* v.26.

In addition, Mari provides a case in which one party "slays an ass" with another, e.g. the text given by Dossin[23]; *it-ti Ḳar-ni-lim* *imērḫa-a-ra-am aḳ-tu-ul*. In this case, instead of the preposition *birīt* with *ḫayaram ḳatālum* we have the preposition *itti* which corresponds to *'ēth* (or *'im*), which is frequently found in the Old Testament with *kārath bĕrîth*.[24]

The possibility that a third person might "enact a covenant" between two others occurs also quite clearly in the Old Testament, so that Begrich's alternative breaks down. But it must be admitted that in the Old Testament this possibility is perhaps only evidenced in connection with the transfer of the covenant idea to the relationship between God and nation. In such circumstances as these the role of the covenant mediator can no longer be described as that of a "superior". But surely such a transference presupposes that in the purely human realm covenant-making was practised between two parties through the medium of a third.

The clearest formulation of this in a relevant Old Testament passage is *II Kings* xi.17. The wording now runs as follows: "The priest Jehoiada made the covenant between Yahweh and the King and the people that they would be a people of Yahweh (and between the king and the people)". The words in parenthesis, which appear to have been omitted in one branch of the Septuagint tradition, and which are lacking from the parallel passage in *II Chron.* xxiii.16, are usually deleted as an accidental repetition. In that case we are being told that after the assassination of Queen Athaliah, during whose rule in Jerusalem an illegitimate Baal cult had been introduced (cf. vs. 18), the covenant between God and people was renewed by the Jerusalem high priest Jehoiada, and the King as master of the temple in Jerusalem is expressly named together with the people as a party to the covenant. In any case Jehoiada appears in the role of a third party who "enacts a covenant" between others.

It appears doubtful, however, whether the words in paren-

[23] Dossin, in *Syria*, xix (1938), p. 108.

[24] G. Dossin, *op. cit.*, p. 109, gives extracts from a text which also deals with the slaying of "an ass of agreement" "with" another—except that the construction here is more extended, and the "with" (*itti*) occurs not directly in the covenant-making formula itself but only in a following independent sentence.

thesis are really to be regarded as an addition,[25] and not rather as describing a factor of the original situation, so that the mention of God's name and the remark about Israel's position as the people of Yahweh are to be regarded as later glosses, arising from the idea that a covenant enacted by a priest would have to be a divine covenant. In that case the sentence would originally have run: "The priest Jehoiada enacted the covenant between King and people". The point of the transaction would therefore be that after the rule of the foreign Athaliah, Jerusalem and Judah bound themselves again to the dynasty of David, which had once succeeded to sovereignty over Judah by an act of covenant (*II Sam.* v.3). The context of the narrative in *II Kings* XI seems to me to tell in favour of this interpretation. If this is so, we would have an example of the enacting of a covenant on a purely human level through the mediation of a third party, corresponding to the reference in Mari text II.37.

A definite transference to the relationship between God and people occurs in *Joshua* XXIV.25: "Joshua made a covenant for the people". According to Begrich[26] the construction found here (*kārath běrîth lĕ*) belongs to the interpretation of the covenant as the guarantee of a relationship to an inferior by a superior. On this view we would have to suppose that in this fairly early passage (*Joshua* XXIV.25) we have an inappropriate use of a formula, since it could not really refer to any covenant "guaranteed" to the people by Joshua. It is more probable that Joshua as "third party" here mediates a covenant between God and people. We must therefore assume that in describing a covenant through a third party it was possible to use the expression "to make a covenant between X and Y" (*II Kings* XI.17), or "to make a covenant for X and Y". In *Joshua* XXIV.25 the requisite "for Yahweh and the people" was abbreviated, because the transference of the covenant conception to the relationship between God and people no longer permitted the full formula, since Yahweh could not be mentioned as just one partner alongside another. A still greater change has been made in the formula

---

[25] If the expanded form of *II Kings* XI.17 lay before the Chronicler and the Septuagint translator, as seems probable, it will be at once realized that the words in parenthesis above would be omitted as a repetition. In that case no witness to the original wording of *II Kings* XI.17 may be deduced from *Chronicles* or the *Septuagint*.

[26] Begrich, in *Z.A.W.*, N.F. XIX (1944), pp. 3, 5.

which occurs in the considerably later passage *II Kings* XXIII.3, where King Josiah as "third party" mediates a covenant between God and people. Here it is said, simply, "He made the covenant before Yahweh", i.e. in the sanctuary as the place of the divine presence, and at the end we are told simply that "the people assented to the covenant"[27] and thus accepted the provisions of the divine law. Here therefore, although a definite type of covenant-making may lurk in the background, any suggestion that God would be a contracting party is excluded in the formula.[28]

Finally we may still ask whether the various types of making a covenant can be brought into a relationship of dependence one upon the other. Since in the Mari texts we find the making of a covenant by one party "with" another party of equal rank, we must presume the possibility of such covenant-making *along with* others from the very earliest days of the Old Testament. But the negotiation of a covenant by means of a third party presumably remains an antecedent possibility. If we are correct in postulating a connection between the *birīt* of the Mari texts and the Old Testament *běrîth*, it is quite probable that the phraseology of covenant-making in the Old Testament has been determined by the mediation of a third party, because the *birīt* occurs in Mari text II.37 in direct connection with an act of covenant-making negotiated by a third party. It will be recalled that Begrich argued for the originality of the covenant as a guarantee on the part of a superior of a relationship to an inferior, but the evidence shows only that this was customary. The question is still open whether the covenant may not in some way go back to the role of a "superior official" in bringing about a covenant between two other parties. The "higher official" may have exerted a patron's function in the interests of the two other parties, but eventually he could guarantee his patronage to one of the other parties in the form of a solemn act of covenant-making.

[27] The Old Testament expression, usually translated as above, would probably originally have had a more concrete signification within the context of some definite ceremony of covenant making.

[28] Other Old Testament expressions also are to be considered in the light of this last passage, e.g. *Deut.* XXVIII.69, where (according to the context) Moses as "third party" "makes a covenant" between God and people. Cf. further H. W. Wolff "Jahwe als Bundesvermittler", in *Vetus Testamentum*, VI (1956), pp. 316-20.

III

"For all who rely on works of the law are under a curse"

The words in the title are those with which Paul (in *Gal.* III.10) describes the position of those who seek to be righteous before God by fulfilling the requirements of the law—that Old Testament law of which *Deut.* IV. 8 says that the whole world cannot show its like; Paul also quotes *Deut.* XXVII.26 in confirmation, following very nearly the Septuagint text: "Cursed be every man who does not abide by all things written in the book of the law, and do them".

In its original context this quotation is the last of a series[1] of twelve curses (*Deut.* XXVII.15-26), which all begin "cursed be...", and with this formula lay various transgressions under an unspecified curse. Alt is right when he comments[2] that here we are dealing with transgressions which would normally take place in secret, and would therefore seldom figure in the realm of human jurisdiction; consequently transgressors, who would scarcely be reached by human law, were to be punished by a curse[3] which would be solemnly pronounced on regular occasions, and which would undoubtedly take effect on those who came within its scope.[4] These twelve curses, therefore,

---

[1] This saying appears to have been appended to the rest simply in order to bring the number of sayings up to the intended twelve (cf. Alt, "Die Ursprünge des israelitischen Rechts," in *K.S.*, VOL. I, p. 313).　　[2] *Op. cit.*, p. 314.

[3] Cf. Hempel, *Z.D.M.G.*, LXXIX (1925), pp. 20ff., esp. pp. 26ff.

[4] The context in which these curses now stand is secondary. The usually accepted connection of these sayings with a (regularly occurring) solemn ceremony in or near Shechem cannot be substantiated anywhere, since the verses *Deut.* XXVII.11-13, although they show a connection with Shechem, can hardly by their reference to blessings *and* curses give the original introduction to vss. 14ff., quite apart from vss. 1-8 with their special content. However, the instruction accompanying some of the curses that "the people" should confirm them with their "Amen" shows that it does deal with the groundwork of a cultic, judicial act of probably regular recurrence.

which have no parallel anywhere else in the Old Testament, appear to deal with rather special cases. For elsewhere, as a general rule, particular punishments are envisaged for particular transgressions, and these punishments are inflicted on those found guilty by the competent court without any curse being pronounced over them.

The question arises whether Paul has not wrongly appealed to the passages he quotes from *Deuteronomy* in support of his judgment on the law in general. In one not unimportant particular he has altered his citation of one passage from the form it has in the Septuagint (which was doubtless the text he used) as well as in the original Hebrew. Whereas these two speak of "this Torah", clearly meaning the section of twelve curses, Paul speaks of "the book of the law" as such, meaning the whole Old Testament law.

In this way he has broadly generalized what was a statement of specific, limited, application. It is moreover noteworthy that the Old Testament itself does not appear to share Paul's judgment upon the law, for from the law it apparently opens out the perspectives, "blessing *and* curse", i.e. *either* blessing *or* curse, according as the individual or the group fulfils or does not fulfil the requirements of the law. Thus, with reference to the deuteronomic law immediately following, *Deut.* xi.26-28 offers the people a choice of "blessing and curse"; and *Deut.* xxx.19, referring back to the same law, sets forth this choice once more in a particularly solemn form.

What has been briefly indicated in these two passages in the deuteronomic framework then appears to be given its full expression in the great concluding chapter of the deuteronomic law concerning blessing and curse (*Deut.* xxviii).[5] This has its exact counterpart in the concluding chapter of the so-called "Holiness Code" (*Lev.* xxvi). At the conclusion of the two corpuses of law contained in the Old Testament[6] we find precise

---

[5] This chapter certainly belongs to the original deuteronomic law, and not to any sections successively added to the law. The "Holiness Code", which has no added sections and yet contains a concluding chapter of blessings and curses, supports this. Originally *Deut.* xxviii.1ff. directly followed xxvi.16-19 (or, more accurately, xxvi.16, 17*aba*, 18*a*).

[6] The differentiation between law and statute book (cf. Koschaker, "Quellenkritische Untersuchungen zu den 'altassyrischen Gesetzen'," *M.V.Ae.G.* xxvi, No. 3, 1921, pp. 79ff.) cannot, without due regard to the circumstances, be applied to the constituent parts of Old Testament law, at least not in such a simple and

details concerning the content of the blessing and of the curse which will follow the observance or non-observance of the preceding legal requirements. In what follows, instead of looking at the content of blessing and curse,[7] let us rather seek out the real relationship of blessing and curse, according to the stress laid on the one or the other, let us begin with *Deut.* XXVIII.

In *Deut.* XXVIII.1-68, we are struck by the external inequality between the comparatively short section on the blessing (vss.1-14), and the significantly more extensive details about the curse (vss. 15-68). However, the existing form of the chapter differs from the original; commentators are agreed that the section which follows the clear conclusion in vss. 45ff., and which introduces the terror of hostile attack and siege, and the dispersal of the people (vss. 47-68), has been added later in order to explain the historical events at the fall of the Judaean kingdom at the beginning of the sixth century as the express working of the curse attendant on a failure to fulfil the laws. Yet even after the removal of this addition the blessing and the curse sections remain remarkably dissimilar, which is the more striking in that they each begin in exactly the same way, even to the actual form of words. After an introductory phrase setting out the circumstances (vss. 1*a* = 15*a*)[8] and a general announcement of blessings or curses (vs. 2*a* = 15*b*)[9] there follows the formula of blessing or cursing which was probably not composed *ad hoc*, but had come down to the editor in this solemn

---

schematic way as is done by Jirku, *Das Weltliche Recht im Alten Testament*, 1927, pp. 13ff., since in Israel a state chamber as law-giver first appears late on, and even then is only secondary and exceptional. The earliest possible law-book (or "mirror of the law"), in the sense of a private collection of applicable or actually used law without any rigid systematization or finality about it, is the Book of the Covenant in *Exod.* XXI-XXIII. In *Deuteronomy* and the Holiness Code, on the contrary, in spite of all the dependence upon previously formulated legal matter of various kinds, there is at least the intention to create a law which was to be brought into being and into force by an act of legislation. *Deuteronomy* at least—even if only in a secondary form—was actually elevated under Josiah to be the state law of Judah. These two books would be the first which I should regard as "law-books" in the narrow sense. The so-called priestly laws with their mainly cultic and ritual content stand in a separate category.

[7] Here we might compare, among others, Hempel in *Z.D.M.G.*, LXXIX (1925), pp. 51ff.

[8] Vs. 1*b* is an addition according to XXVI.19.

[9] Vs.2*b* is a deuteronomistic formula added later.

fixed[10] form, and had originally served as the formula for pronouncing a blessing or a curse on an individual, and not on the whole nation:

> Blessed (cursed) shall you be in the city,
> blessed (cursed) shall you be in the field.
> Blessed (cursed) shall be your basket and your baking trough.
>
> . . . . . .
>
> Blessed (cursed) shall you be when you come in,
> and blessed (cursed) shall you be when you go out.
>
> (*Deut.* XXVIII.3, 5, 6 and 16, 17, 19)[11]

Further on, both sections diverge widely in both form and content, and we may ask[12] whether we should regard as original only those parts which contain corresponding sections of blessing and curse, and regard all else as later expansion. This assumption apparently commends itself by its results, but the actual circumstances of the tradition tell against it. The material which follows directly in the blessing section really gives a much stronger impression of being secondary than does the continuation of the curse section, with its extremely specific content. Even the frequent use of quite customary deuteronomistic expressions (vss. 8b, 9, 10, 11b, 13b, 14) permits doubt as to the originality of the section vss. 7-14. Furthermore a comparison of vss. 12b, 13a with vss. 43, 44 shows that the first part has very probably been added later on the same pattern. The change in the relationship of the established full citizens to the sojourners dwelling in the land, who had no landed property and were therefore normally weaker economically in general, appears in vss. 43, 44 in an appropriate context amongst the curses.

The same expressions appear in vss. 12b, 13a, where however they refer to the sojourning of foreign peoples; but in this way

---

[10] The fixed form of these expressions shows itself not only in the prefixed "blessed/cursed", which is invariably stressed, but most especially in the fixed rhythmical arrangement of the phrases (double trimeter).

[11] Vs. 4=vs. 18 appears to me to be secondary. For one thing, these phrases occur at different points within the fixed curse formula. Then again rhythmical arrangement is lacking in them, and the long succession of subjects dependent on "blessed/cursed be" disrupts the connection of the remaining terse phrases. They have clearly been interpolated in accordance with *Deut.* VII.13. Possibly a parallel double trimeter has later fallen out in vss. 5, 17.

[12] See Steuernagel, *Das Deuteronomium übersetzt und erklärt*, p. 150.

the content of these expressions, which can be quite specifically and practically introduced in the curse section, is generalized and attenuated.[13] Vss. 12b, 13a together with the dependent clause vss. 13b, 14 therefore may be regarded as secondary. What still remains of the section (vss. 7a, 8a, 11a, 12a) could therefore have been an original explanation of the blessings. However, the fact that vs. 7 has an exact verbal counterpart in vs. 29 in the curse section tells against the originality.

No one can now maintain that everything which now stands in the curse section in vss. 20-46 belongs to the original form. Without entering upon details here, I would regard vss. 20b (with Yahweh in the first person), 21b, 29, 34, 36, 37, and perhaps also vss. 38-41, as later additions. We might also wonder whether the sentence beginning with the words: "Yahweh strike thee with . . ." (vss. 22, 27, 28, 35) once formed a complete series of curses, and so in their original form were grouped more closely than now. Be that as it may, however, the number of the original curses with quite specific content—and almost invariably with very unusual and varied formulations, which are always concerned with the destruction of life and prosperity in one way or another, remains large enough to justify the claim that the emphasis in *Deut.* xxviii lies quite one-sidedly upon the section of curses. One almost gets the impression that the section of blessings at the beginning of the chapter is more a formal counterpart to the section of curses, introduced for the sake of balancing blessings and curses.[14] Occasionally in the section of blessings the stereotyped blessing formula was originally followed by a quite short and general expression.

Deut. xxviii has reasonably close parallels in the Code of Hammurabi; owing to the influence which this renowned code had for a long period throughout the Near East, it cannot be doubted that the custom, attested for the Old Testament by *Deut.* xxviii and *Lev.* xxvi, that a law should end with blessing and curse had its pattern in the Code of Hammurabi. This

[13] Should not the sentence xv.6, which stands in the secondary passage *Deut.* xv.4-6, really be dependent primarily on *Deut.* xxviii.12b, 13a? In view of vs. 8 it would merely mean that a different word was being used for "borrowing" and "lending". The sentence is not properly motivated by the context in *Deut.* xv, so that the thought comes near to being a borrowing.

[14] Blessing and curse are mentioned successively often enough; cf. merely *Gen.* xii.3; xxvii.29; *Num.* xxii.6; *Jer.* xvii.5, 7.

contains fairly extensive sub-sections where Hammurabi[15] sets himself up expressly and in detail as a law-giver, and as a powerful and ideal king. But at the end Hammurabi pronounces blessing and curse—with particular reference to his successors on the throne. He utters a blessing upon those who maintain his law unaltered, and a curse upon those who despise, alter, or abolish it. The blessing is compactly formulated at the beginning in a few short words, including a conditional prefatory sentence which is almost identical with the wording of the conditional sentence prefaced to the beginning of the curse. There is also a short concluding sentence which explains the content of the blessing to be a long reign in righteousness; whereas in the curse a long series of strophes follows on the prefatory sentence, in each of which one particular divinity is summoned to fulfil the curse with those means at his disposal. So here we have before us a remarkably close parallel to the construction of *Deut.* XXVIII; and again it happens that the curse is really drawn right into the foreground, whereas the prefixed blessing appears here too as merely a formal counterpart to it.

Attention is paid to the rhythmical and strophic form of parts of the Code of Hammurabi in the translation by T. J. Meek, *A.N.E.T.*, pp. 163 ff.

But the frame can easily be extended still more. In the same way that Hammurabi's law was to be secured by the speaking or writing of effective curses, even at a time when the King himself could no longer himself watch over it, other legal ordinances and directives also were protected against alteration by a closing curse attached to the end of the document in question. We shall here refer to two categories of legal matters only. In international treaties, divinities who stood above the parties to the treaty and outlasted the treaty-making rulers were involved as guarantors, so that they could avert breaches of the treaty by implementing the curses included in the treaty document. This phenomenon is known especially from the treaties made by the new Hittite kingdom with a series of neighbouring states. They are important mainly because both blessing and curse are expressed

---

[15] The treaties in Akkadian have been published in E. F. Weidner: *Politische Dokumente aus Kleinasien, die Staatsverträge in Akkadischer Sprache aus dem Archiv von Boghazköi (Boghazköi Studien 8 and 9)* 1923; those in Hittite in J. Friedrich: *Staatsverträge des Hatti-Reiches in hethischer Sprache*; I, in *M.V.Ae.G.* XXXI, No. 1 (1926); and II in *M.V.Ae.G.*, XXXIV, No. 1 (1930).

in them at the end, in such a way that again the curse receives greater prominence. Here the curse usually precedes the blessing, which is unusual, and can only mean that the emphasis is to be laid on the curse.[16] In the two treaties between Subbiluliuma and Mattinaza of Mitanni,[17] the prefixed curse section is again considerably more extensive, and with a more specifically defined content, than the following section of blessing. In other treatises, admittedly, the two sections are mostly built up parallel, so that the section on cursing is then only emphasized by being placed first, as in the following treaties: Subbiluliuma with Tette of Nuhašše[18]; Subiluliuma with Aziru of Amurru[19]; Muršiliš with Duppi-Tešup of Amurru[20]; Muršiliš with Targašnalliš of Ḫappalla[21]; Muršiliš with Manapa-Dattaš[22]; Muwattalliš with Alakšanduš of Wiluša[23]; and finally also in the famous treaty of Hattušil with Ramses II.[24] In these treaties, therefore, the tendency to place blessing and curse formally in parallel has gained a strong hold, and the stressing of the curse is expressed only in the order of the two sections.[25]

In contrast to this group of documents we shall now briefly

[16] From this standpoint it is worth noting that in certain treaties (e.g. in the treaties between Muršilliš and Kupanta-dKAL [M.V.Ae.G., xxxi (1926), pp. 106ff.], Muwattalliš and Alakšanduš [M.V.Ae.G., xxxiv (1930), pp. 50ff.], and Suppiluliumaš and Ḫukkanaš [op. cit., pp. 106ff.]) even at the end of some sections the putative violator is threatened with the "oaths" (i.e. curses), which are then to "pursue him ceaselessly".

[17] Weidner: Politische Dokumente aus Kleinasien, pp. 2ff. (Rs. 59-69 curse; Rs. 70-75 blessing), and pp. 36ff. (Rs. 25-34 curse; Rs. 35-39 blessing; Rs. 44-53 curse; Rs. 53-59 blessing).

[18] Weidner, op. cit., pp. 58ff. (Col. iv.48-52 curse; 53-57 blessing).

[19] Weidner, op. cit., pp. 70ff. (Rs. 12-16 curse; Rs. 17-20 blessing).

[20] Friedrich, in M.V.Ae.G., xxxi (1926), pp. 4ff. (§20 curse; §21 blessing).

[21] Friedrich, op. cit., pp. 52ff. (§15 curse; §16 blessing—both sections preserved only very imperfectly).

[22] Friedrich, in M.V.Ae.G., xxiv (1930), pp. 4ff. (§19 curse; §20 blessing).

[23] Friedrich, op. cit., pp. 50ff. (§21 curse and blessing).

[24] Cf. G. Roeder: "Aegypter und Hethiter", Der alte Orient, vol. xx, Leipzig 1919, p. 44 (§25 curse; §26 blessing). This ending of the treaty is preserved only in the hieroglyphic edition, which represents the translation of the text of the treaty laid down by the Hittite king and sent to Egypt. On the "thousand gods" mentioned here cf. Friedrich, in M.V.Ae.G., xxxi, 1926, p. 69 (Rs. 55).

[25] For a much later period reference would be made to the treaty of the Assyrian King Esarhaddon with King Baal of Tyre (translation in D.D. Luckenbill: Ancient Records of Assyria and Babylonia, vol. ii, 1927, §§586ff.). Here there is a curse expressed even before the framing of the provisions of the treaty; but since the beginning of the whole treaty has not been preserved the question remains whether or not the curse was preceded by some sort of short blessing formula.

mention another group which invariably contain a series of curses at the end, under whose protection the ordinances laid down in the documents were placed. These are those of the so-called *kudurri*[26] ("boundary stones") which appear in Babylonia at the Cassite period, and are official deeds which lay down ownership rights over a particular transferred property, and set any future dispute or violation of this right to ownership under the curse of certain gods specified by name.

Here also the curse (as elsewhere the blessing and curse) is introduced by a conditional prefatory sentence. In all these instances the point of the particular emphasis in the curse is easily discernible. At the conclusion of all these legal documents interest centres naturally not on those who will keep the provisions enjoined therein, but on those who would transgress, alter, or reject them, and who therefore are subject to the working of the curse—especially where no mere human judge is either available or able to prosecute. The legal ordinance may be of three sorts; it may refer to a law-code promulgated by a king for his country, or some perfectly legitimate law for regulating questions of property ownership, or even an international treaty concluded between two qualified parties on the basis of a specific mutual relationship. Such an agreement will naturally be based on the supposition that this ordinance will be kept. The idea that the party who keeps the ordinance should be specifically rewarded, and that such a reward should previously be promised him, is in the nature of things quite alien, for he will do only what he is bound to do in virtue of an existing ordinance independent of himself.

It was only later experience of the possibility of violation and transgression of an ordinance guarded by a final curse of this kind

[26] Cf. the *kudurri* texts translated by Peiser in *Keilinschriftliche Bibliothek*, VOL. III, Pt. I, 1892, pp. 154ff., 174ff., and VOL. IV, 1896, pp. 56ff. L. W. King, *Babylonian Boundary-Stones*, London 1912, was not available to me. The Assyrian loan documents are of a special kind (cf. Otto Weber, *Die Literatur der Babylonier und Assyrer*, 1907, pp. 245ff.). In these, instead of a curse at the end, we find a short blessing (cf. *Keilinschriftliche Bibliothek*, VOL. IV, pp. 142ff., lines 68-70, also pp. 64ff., Rs. 11ff.); but that is clearly a secondary development.

On the significance of the *kudurri* and the content and construction of their inscriptions, cf. Fr. H. Steinmetzer: "*Uber den Grundbesitz in Babylonien zur Kassitenzeit nach den sogenannten Grenzensteinen dargestellt*", in *Der alte Orient*, VOL. XIX, Nos. 1-2, 1919, pp. 10ff. (On the curse formula, see pp. 22f.) The *kudurru*-text of the Kassite king Melišipak translated in *A.O.T.*, pp. 431-3, forms an exception to the rule, since here a short blessing formula is prefixed to the expressed curse.

which then brought about in many instances the thought of providing for the future maintenance of the ordinance by means of a blessing. But the constitution of the blessings in the examples adduced shows plainly their purely subsidiary and formal significance, and considerations of content equally support this opinion. An ordinance of this kind is no neutral matter allowing a free choice between accepting or not accepting, and then simply retailing the consequences of each course of action; it starts essentially from the positive requirement of fulfilment, without the necessity of offering a reward for this fulfilment.

If we may now return to *Deut.* xxviii, we shall easily see that in spite of the special circumstances the essential case is closely analogous. Here too the blessing appears as a purely formal counterpart to the curse, a fact which corresponds entirely to the circumstances of the case. The deuteronomic law, like every other law in the Old Testament, proceeds from Yahweh himself as law-giver, and is legitimately founded on the basis of the relationship subsisting between God and people, in so far as Yahweh as lord of his property must be recognized as their law-giver. Consequently the law must require the fulfilling of its provisions. Whoever keeps the law does no more than his duty, and can make no claim to a reward.[27] In fact the blessing contained in *Deut.* xxviii (apparently intended in respect of future fulfilment of the law) was already present before the law, for it rests on a previously given divine promise. Even the law itself (*Deut.* xii-xxvi), which has not much reason to refer to such matters, in its original form occasionally speaks of the "blessing of Yahweh" which will fall to the lot of Israel as of something to be taken for granted (xii.15, xvi.17). Or, in a clause which is not conditional but temporal, and with reference to the conquest, it may likewise speak of a situation free of any proviso in these words: "when Yahweh thy God shall bless thee" (xiv.24, xv.14, xvi.10, 15).[28]

In a piece of liturgical agenda attached to the law in *Deut.* xxvi, reference is made to the blessing promised to the fathers in connection with the territorial promise (xxvi.15) which there-

---

[27] Cf. also the words of Jesus in *Luke* xvii.7-10.

[28] So also in the secondary passages xii.7, xv.4, 6. Occasionally the fulfilling of an individual provision is motivated by the divine blessing which is being kept in view (as xiv.29, xv.10, 18, xxiii.21, xxiv.19). In these cases we would then be dealing with an actual inconsistency (cf. also xxx.16).

fore long antedates the law. On occasion these matters are naturally expressed more clearly in sections of the framework, which are so closely related to the deuteronomic law that they may be taken into consideration unhesitatingly in fixing our understanding of its basic ideas. We may note the importance of the passage VII.12*b*, 13, 14 which is in the singular.[29] After reading in vs. 6 of the free choice of the people, we then come to a section telling us that Yahweh has already sworn a covenant to the fathers, that he will keep this oath and therefore that he intends to bless the people with life and riches beyond all other peoples. And so the blessing announced here is plainly and exclusively brought into connection with the promise of long ago, without reference to the law which was given only afterwards.[30]

Amongst the sections of the framework in the plural[31] relevant here, the most important is XXVIII.69-XXIX.28, with its particular train of thought.[32] Here the fact of the covenant is described throughout as the constituted whole within whose framework the deuteronomic law fits (XXVIII.69),[33] and the keeping of the covenant is commanded. Then in the section XXIX.9-20 the concepts covenant and curse[34] are brought into a close relationship, as indeed—in *Gen.* xv.9ff. and *Jer.* xxxiv.18ff.—the outward form of a covenant-making ceremony follows the model of a cursing rite. The alternative therefore is either the continuation of the covenant inaugurated by Yahweh, together with the

[29] The introductory sentence VII.12 in the plural is certainly secondary. If we follow Steuernagel, *Das Deuteronomium*, in taking the stereotyped vss. 10 and 11 as additions, too, then the rest of the passage follows on vs. 9 very well.

[30] Of the sections of the framework in the singular we might also adduce II.7, where, looking back to the time previous to the decreeing of the deuteronomic law, the divine blessing is mentioned.

[31] Cf. also I.11 where the blessing is traced in a quite general way from a past divine promise.

[32] The following passages are secondary in this context: vss. 4, 5 (Yahweh, in the first person), vss. 6, 7 ("we"), vss. 10*a* ii, *b*-12 (singular); and probably also the concluding passage, vss. 21-8, where, in distinction from the preceding one, direct reference is made to the historical situation during the Exile.

[33] In XXVIII.69 the making of a covenant appears to be so necessary a prerequisite of a law that here, with reference to the historical situation asserted in *Deut.* I.1ff., the making of a covenant "in the land of Moab" is postulated, although only as a supplement to the covenant made "on Horeb".

[34] In XXIX.20 we have mention of "the *covenant-curse* inscribed in this book of the law" (according to the original text). The word *'ālā*, which occurs elsewhere in the book only in XXX.7, is used in this section.

keeping of the law based on that circumstance, or the activation of the curse on account of the violation of the covenant brought about by the transgression of the law. As we would expect, there is here no mention of any blessing.

We may briefly summarize the arrangement of material to be found in the *Book of Deuteronomy* as follows. At the beginning we have the promise of Yahweh, made to "the fathers" and covering the occupation of the promised land and the divine blessing therein. In the course of its realization we come to the making of the covenant between God and people at Sinai at whose conclusion that law was delivered[35] whose observance Yahweh (as the legitimate law-giver) must demand as the self-evident sequel to mutual loyalty to the covenant. The content of the law is intended to ensure first and foremost loyalty to God in every walk of life. Transgression of the law—even though it be in only one particular[36]—implies a forsaking of covenant-loyalty,[37] and consequently covenant-breaking and defection; and for all defections the curse attached to the law comes into operation, executed by Yahweh himself. The blessing which is also pronounced in *Deut.* XXVIII for fulfilling the law can then basically have only the negative implication that non-transgression of the law permits Yahweh's ordained order, and therewith also his promised blessing, to operate.

One last consideration will show that for *Deuteronomy* fulfilment and non-fulfilment, blessing and curse, are not both on the same level—nor, from the point of view of the law, are they two open possibilities offered for man's selection. In all probability, *Deuteronomy* in its basic form was composed during the seventh century. At this time, however—and this was certainly the opinion of its author—the threatened curse had already begun to appear as an actual reality. Since the middle of the eighth century the Israelite people's territory had been reduced to a comparatively small part of that which they had held as

---

[35] The final words of the actual law in *Deut.* XXVI.16-19, refer—although they do not actually use the term—to the covenant with which the law is linked. The covenant in mind is probably that of Sinai originally; the connection of *Deuteronomy* with another historical situation in 1.1ff. must really be secondary.

[36] The trespass of an individual against a provision of the law must be visited with his expulsion from the community (cf. *Deut.* XIII.6, etc.); otherwise such an incident would mean the breaking of the covenant between God and people.

[37] Constancy is an element in the concept of loyalty (*ḥesedh*), which will not deviate from its obligations on any single point.

Yahweh's covenant-partners since the time of the Judges.[38] In addition the message of the eighth-century prophets had certainly shaken their careless self-confidence. It was just this simple continuance of the regular relationship between God and people that the prophets questioned and disputed as against the popular view. Would the author of *Deuteronomy* be unaware of this? Certainly not. Consequently the blessing is for him already something unreal, but the curse a reality which in his own day had already appeared.[39] The impression made by *Deuteronomy* when it was found at the time of King Josiah agrees with this. The other material in *II Kings* XXII.11ff. clearly shows that at that time no one doubted that the curse was in operation, which was threatened for the disloyalty of transgressing the law. In spite of the earnestness and zeal with which King Josiah addressed himself to the matter, the message of the prophetess Huldah (vss. 16ff.) does not consider the possibility that the curse might be changed into blessing by any future fulfilment of the law. An act of keeping the law, which is an obvious duty, can never undo a transgression. The law has been transgressed, so now the curse will become reality in divine judgment. There is no human possibility of changing the position. That is the knowledge that the discovery of *Deuteronomy*, according to *II Kings* XXII, brought with it.

If we glance now at the chapter of blessing and curse which concludes the Holiness Code (*Lev.* XXVI) we notice at once the similarity of construction with *Deut.* XXVIII. Here also in conjunction with a conditional prefatory sentence (vs. 3) we have first a comparatively short section of blessing (vss. 4-13), then a considerably longer section of curses, which is divided into a series of subdivisions at whose head the conditional introductory sentence is each time repeated (vss. 14, 18, 23, 27). The curse section ends here—unparalleled in *Deut.* XXVIII—with a suggestion that in spite of Yahweh's impending judgment on the breaking of the covenant, the people will not be cast away even

---

[38] The confederacy of the twelve Israelite tribes probably came into existence on Palestinian soil, and this was probably also where the covenant relationship founded at Sinai was extended to include all the tribes, cf. my *System der Stämme*, pp. 65ff.

[39] The section *Deut.* XXVIII.47-68, which includes an express reference to the events at the close of the kingdom of Judah in the curse, must be secondary, but represents throughout the thought of the curse section.

in this case, but that he will be mindful still of his covenant.[40] The basic circumstances are also the same as in *Deut.* xxviii. The Sinai covenant (vs. 46) is taken for granted; for those who break it by transgressing the law (so vs. 15, in the sentence leading up to the curse-section) a curse is threatened which signified "vengeance for the (breaking of the) covenant" (vs. 25). And it is in this light that we are to understand vss. 9, 11-13[41]: if the law was kept, the covenant relationship between God and people would continue. But the differences between *Deut.* xxviii and *Lev.* xxvi are just as clear. Whereas in *Deut.* xxviii we still have real blessings and curses,[42] *Lev.* xxvi deviates from the usage customary throughout the Near East, and deals with words of promise and of threatening, which in addition are essentially *vaticinia ex eventu*, in *Lev.* xxvi Yahweh speaks in the first person.

What we could conclude about *Deut.* xxviii from the historical situation at the time of composition—that the curse was not merely a possibility but an actual reality—is given direct expression in *Lev.* xxvi. Along with that, the subdividing of the curse section in *Lev.* xxvi is not altogether a stylistic partition but a chronological arrangement, as may clearly be seen from the formulations in vss. 18, 23, 27. Here a survey of events that have really happened is given, up to and including the downfall of the kingdom of Judah and the deportation to Babylonia, which then forms a history of the divine judgment visited on the violation of the covenant and transgression of the law.[43]

Here too all the stress is laid on the judgment which has been threatened and has meanwhile become fact. The fulfilling of the law even according to *Lev.* xxvi would not have actually brought

---

[40] Towards the end of *Lev.* xxvi there are later expansions. General opinion is correct in so regarding vss. 34, 35. This is of no further importance here; but the fact is important that in vss. 39ff. also everything is not original. A. Bertholet, *Leviticus*, 1901, p. 93, in agreement with B. Baentsch, *Das Heiligkeitsgesetz*, 1893, considers that the whole passage (vss. 39-43) is secondary; while Baentsch himself in his commentary (*Exodus-Leviticus-Numeri*), 1903, p. 436) regards only vss. 41*b*-43 as an addition. This is however the important passage, for here confession of sin and repentance is secondarily made a motive for the restoration of the covenant.

[41] Vs. 10 is an addition which destroys the connection.

[42] The verbal forms in the main clauses are here to be taken as jussives, cf. the jussive in vss. 8, 21 (36); indubitable imperfect forms are found in the primary text only in vss. 25, 43.

[43] *Lev.* xxvi comes from the exilic period, as is shown by the close linguistic affinity with the *Book of Ezekiel* (cf. thereon Baentsch in his commentary, p. 431).

about the blessing, but would only have permitted covenant and blessing to continue.

According to the Old Testament passages with which we have dealt, the law is not therefore an unconditioned and vaguely existing mass with regard to which two possibilities were equally available—fulfilment and non-fulfilment, good works and bad ones, reward and punishment, blessing and curse. The law, rather, presupposes the view which calls the Old Testament the covenant between God and people, which was established by Yahweh on his own initiative and which is bound up with the promise freely made by Yahweh. On the basis of this law, which can and does demand fulfilment, there is no place for the idea of good, meritorious works and a reward which may be earned thereby; the blessing is not earned, but freely promised. On the basis of this law there is only one possibility for man of having his own independent activity: that is transgression, defection, followed by curse and judgment. And so, indeed, "all those who rely on the works of the law are under a curse". But in *Deut.* xxviii and *Lev.* xxvi the position is that defection and curse are no longer merely possibility, they are already the reality.

Only the formal contrasting of blessing and curse in *Deut.* xxviii and *Lev.* xxvi, and the similarly formal association of the words blessing and curse in passages such as *Deut.* xi.26-28, xxx.19, could later give rise to the view that there were positive and negative performances of the law, and that these attitudes could be reckoned up against one another as from a neutral centre point, and add up to a store of good or evil works. In the development of this view Ezekiel's teaching about individual retribution naturally played a part; but the bases of this teaching deserve a separate investigation.

IV

Jerusalem and the Israelite Tradition

The Old Testament keeps us well informed about the external events in the story of Jerusalem within the frame of Israelite history. However many individual questions may remain unanswered we are not faced with any serious problem in this respect. The most remarkable feature of this story of events is that, unlike many other Bronze Age cities situated on the Judaean and Samaritan hills, on which the tribes of Israel had principally settled, Jerusalem in spite of its position in this west Jordanian highland plays no definite role in Israelite history until very late. The account of the occupation and the stories about the period of the Judges contain only the short and historically not quite dependable notice about the struggle of the Judaeans against a certain Adonibezek, who is never described as king, and whose relationship to Jerusalem (according to the account in *Judges* 1.5-8) consists in being brought to Jerusalem and dying there, after having been vanquished and mutilated by the Judaeans, who then captured and burnt the city. On this basis, *Joshua* x makes this Adonibezek into "King of Jerusalem".[1]

If any warlike disagreement of any sort between the city-state of Jerusalem and the neighbouring Judaeans to the south underlies this narrative, then it can have been no more than an episode without further consequence. The theoretical tribal geography of the pre-monarchic period assigned Jerusalem to the "sphere of interest" of the tribe of Benjamin (*Joshua* xv.8, xviii.16). But we are expressly told in *Judges* 1.21 that Benjamin was unable to

---

[1] Cf. my *Das Buch Josua* (Hb. A.T.) 1938, pp. 35ff.; 2nd edn., 1953, pp. 6off. Jerusalem has been included in the list of conquered Canaanite cities in *Joshua* xII.10 only on account of *Joshua* x. There is no separate tradition behind this notice.

capture this city.[2] Consequently Jerusalem remained a city-state apart, with no connections with the Israelite tribes in the land. For the Israelites it was a "foreign city" in which no one willingly tarried overnight, but pressed on so as to reach some place in Israelite tribal territory if unexpectedly caught by darkness while travelling in that area (*Judges* XIX.11, 12). It was on account of this lack of connection with any tribal territory of Israel's that Jerusalem so appealed to David as a royal capital.

These are the reasons why the name Jerusalem nowhere appears in the Pentateuch, although it is probably envisaged in the phrase "King Melchizedek of Salem" in *Gen.* XIV.18-20. Whatever may be our judgment on *Gen.* XIV, it can scarcely be said that we have here an old section of some specifically Israelite tradition. The absence of Jerusalem from the Pentateuch is noteworthy from two directions. On the one hand, it confirms that the substance of the Pentateuchal narrative was in essentials given its definitive form in the premonarchic period, and that its literary fixation made no considerable changes in its substance.[3]

Jerusalem is not at all deeply rooted in the ancient tradition of Israel. In view of the role which it was called upon to play later on in the history of Israel, this is a point of real importance. Jerusalem has no connection with the fundamental traditions of the Israelite tribal confederacy upon which its existence, its understanding of itself, and its faith rested. As far as we can see,[4] Jerusalem did not appear either in the grand theme of the promise of possession of the land to the fathers, or in the theme of the fulfilment of the promise in the occupation by the Israelite tribes. Up to the end of the pre-monarchic period, Jerusalem signified absolutely nothing for the tribes of Israel, their faith, or their life.

On the other hand, if we hold that *Ps.* CXXXVII expresses in an extreme form the longing of the pious for Jerusalem and their

---

[2] Cf. *Joshua* xv.63, a secondary attribution of the attempt on Jerusalem to the Judaeans instead of the Benjaminites. The appearance of Jerusalem in the Benjaminite list of cities (*Joshua* XVIII.28) rests on associations from a much older time.

[3] Elsewhere Jerusalem plays a role—and indirectly and unmentioned, at that—only in the account of the Brazen Serpent (*Num.* XXI.4b-9). See my *Pentateuch*, pp. 133ff. But both on literary and traditio-historical grounds this account is secondary and late, so that it provides no argument against the points made above.

[4] This limitation must be inserted since the accounts of the Occupation from J and E are not preserved. But in view of the historical course of events it is difficult to suppose that Jerusalem did figure there.

close inner ties with this city, then it is clear that in the course of four eventful centuries a decided change in the estimation of Jerusalem had taken place in Israel. It is at once obvious that the change goes back to the work of David, who did two things for Jerusalem. He made it his royal capital and seat of government, specifically because it had had no relation with the Israelite tribes hitherto and was therefore completely neutral between his two states of Judah and Israel; furthermore it stood geographically between the two states. From here he ruled his ever-growing and ramifying kingdom. In addition he transferred the Ark of Yahweh to his city, with the intention of giving the sanctuary in Jerusalem real significance for the Israelite tribes. The Ark would never have been transferred to Jerusalem, nor would Jerusalem ever have come to possess any cultic significance for the tribes of Israel, had not this city—which had hitherto stood quite outside the Israelite tradition—been made the "city of David". Nor would this have happened had David, for the sake of this city and apparently on his own authority, not undertaken the transfer of the Ark from considerations of political astuteness. For we cannot conceive that David had any object other than to provide a link with the cultic life of the Israelite tribes for this, his royal seat, still in the eyes of Israel a city without any tradition.

In this way David hoped to link Jerusalem to the tradition of Israel, and possibly to lift the Ark completely out of the realm of any jealousy between the states of Judah and Israel. It was—and this deserves to be clearly emphasized—an astute royal manœuvre of very questionable legitimacy; David certainly had cultic rights and duties as King of the city of Jerusalem and successor to the rights of previous kings of the city, but in the cultic life of the Israelite tribes, as king over the states of Judah and Israel, he possessed no *ex officio* functions. However, by transferring the Ark to his capital and setting it up in the sanctuary, he insinuated himself into the cultic traditions of Israel, in so far as they concerned the cultic activity which was performed before the Ark. And this was how the transferred Israelite cult of the Ark became blended with the political arrangements of the Davidic monarchy in Jerusalem, as comes so plainly into view in the plan of Solomon's city, with its Temple incorporated in the complex of the royal palace buildings, so that this cult was repeatedly entangled in a disastrous way with the twists and turns of political history. This was how the royal city Jerusalem became a prominent cultic centre for the tribes of Israel.

If the legitimacy of David's transfer of the Ark to Jerusalem is doubtful, his imposing personality, which was recognized by all the tribes of Israel, silenced any doubts about it; and the tribes very soon acquiesced in a state of affairs in which the shrine of the Ark was situated within the royal sanctuary of David and his dynasty in Jerusalem. If this move endowed Jerusalem with that significance in Israel which it retained until the end of Israelite history, then we must ask what it was that attached the tribes of Israel to the city. Was it the institution of the Davidic monarchy, to which Jerusalem owed its rise and everything which followed from that? Or was it rather the presence in the sanctuary at Jerusalem of the Ark, which represented a factor which soon (irrespective of the political attitude of the kingdom) became important enough to assure the significance of Jerusalem for the tribes of Israel? This question seems to be of paramount consequence in considering the problem of the position of the monarchy in Israel. There do exist points of contact in the Old Testament tradition for a decision on this question. Let us now consider it.

During the days of David and Solomon the relationship between Ark and monarchy was possibly so directly alive that for them they obviously belonged together. An attempt may have been made to find a basis for David's moves regarding Jerusalem *vis-à-vis* the Israelite tradition. A sort of "court theology" may have explained that Yahweh had in fact chosen David as the one entrusted to act on his behalf, and that he had chosen Jerusalem not only as the royal capital, but also as the "divine capital"—that is, as the place of the chief sanctuary. In this way David's work would be legitimated even with respect to the transfer of the Ark. As it happens, the expression of the divine "election of David *and* Jerusalem" first occurs in the Old Testament in the deuteronomist (*I Kings* VIII.16 [LXX] = *II Chron.* VI.6; *I Kings* XI.13, 32). The formulation may be deuteronomistic, and here we have a piece of deuteronomistic theology in content too. We must, however, assume that this was also the official attitude of the Davidic and Solomonic monarchy, and the deuteronomist (who had at least indirect access to the annals of the Judaean kings) would in the above passage be linking up with the ancient official tradition.[5]

After the death of Solomon, Jerusalem still remained the capital of the Davidic line, and its sanctuary the shrine of the Ark; but most of the tribes had forsaken the Davidic dynasty, and had no connection with the Jerusalem monarchy of the Davidic line. This monarchy carried indeed the promise of continuity (*II Sam.* VII), and this promise doubtless meant the government of David in its whole extent. But this promise was handed down in Judaean circles, and it is unlikely that the other tribes would share this promise, which included (after the death of Solomon) the expectation of a restoration of Davidic rule.

What was the attitude, then, of these other tribes towards the sanctuary of the Ark in Jerusalem? Were the conditions of the reigns of David and Solomon still binding for them—conditions which had lasted a mere two generations, and from which they had cut themselves off? And could the royal sanctuary in Jerusalem, which had no ancient Israelite traditions, signify anything for them? Unfortunately we possess only very scanty traditions from tribal circles in Israel; but at least we do still have the prophetic narratives concerning Ahijah of Shiloh in *I Kings* XI.29-39, XII.1-20, 26-31, XIV.1-18, which touch on this problem. Their "North Israelite" character is shown not only by their subject, which is the appearance of a prophet who lives in Shiloh before the Israelite King Jeroboam I, but also by the way in which (in XII.1ff.) the blame for the schism of the state of Israel is laid solely on the behaviour of the Davidic Rehoboam, so that the behaviour of the tribes of Israel at the gathering at Shechem is justified.

This narrative shows Jeroboam clearly believing that his subjects will continue to go up to the "house of Yahweh in Jerusalem", so that eventually they might once more be drawn back under the political hegemony of the Davidic dynasty; as a consequence, the narrative shows Jeroboam setting up his own royal sanctuaries in competition with Jerusalem (XII.26ff.). But

[5] In *Ps.* CXXXII we have a link between the divine oath to David and the recognition that Yahweh had "chosen Zion" as his "dwelling place", his "resting-place for ever". This may be a reference to the official view which lies behind the psalm. I shall not deal in more detail with this psalm, since it is dealt with more fully by H. J. Kraus in *Die Königsherrschaft Gottes im Alten Testament*, Bei. H.Th. 13, 1951.

this action is viewed as disobedience and apostasy on the part of Jeroboam (xiv.8), and as a ground for the divine judgment upon him and his house (xiv.10ff.). In its reference to the downfall of Jeroboam's house—for the narrative has clearly been composed after the end of his dynasty—it therefore condemns the cultic schism of the tribes of Israel from Jerusalem, whereas it regards the political detachment from the Davidic monarchy as legitimate and justified. We may suppose that it reproduces an attitude towards the Jerusalem question which was prevalent, though not perhaps universally.

Here for the first time we come across a clear division between the political and the cultic sides of this question, between the role of Jerusalem as the capital city of the Davidic line and as the city of the sanctuary of the Ark. David's action in bringing the Ark into the royal sanctuary in Jerusalem had met with approval, quite independently of approval for the Davidic rule. Although the possibility of a return of Israel to be ruled by the Davidic line is perhaps mentioned only as a groundless fear of Jeroboam (xii.27), yet in xi.36 mention is made of a dispensation of favour by Yahweh to the Davidic monarchy, for whose sake *one* tribe (meaning Benjamin) would remain "that David my servant may always have a lamp before me in Jerusalem".[6] This allusion is far from clear. David shall always have a *nîr* before Yahweh in Jerusalem. The word *nîr* is generally equated with *nēr* (lamp), but the well-known word *nēr* is simply not there, and further, no sense is yielded by the meaning "lamp". For there scarcely can have been an "*eternal* lamp" either in the sanctuary or even in the homes of Israel. K. Galling[7] suggests that a light streaming out of a house was understood as a sign that the family living in it still existed and had not died out; but I cannot help feeling that this is too forced to be true. The Old Testament does have the word *nîr* in the sense of "new break", "newly broken-up piece of ground", used in a figurative sense of "new beginning" in *Jer.* iv.3; *Hos.* x.12.[8] Is it not simplest to take this word—which is there—in the same sense in *I Kings* xi.36 also? In this case we should translate it: "Whereby my servant David shall have

---

[6] In *I Kings* xi.32-35 we clearly have a deuteronomistic expansion; a deuteronomistic addition may also occur in vs. 36*b* ii.

[7] *Z.D.P.V.*, xlvi (1923), pp. 33ff.

[8] In *Prov.* xiii.23 the word occurs in a very obscure connection.

(the possibility of) a 'new break' (new beginning) for ever before me in Jerusalem".[9]

Whatever be the truth, the Ahijah narrative at all events reckons that the Davidic monarchy still had a chance in Jerusalem. But this is an extremely vague notion to be regarded as providing the basis for justifying the continuance of the tribe of Benjamin under the rule of the Davidic dynasty. The Ahijah narrative in fact concentrates on condemning any rejection of the cultic importance of Jerusalem.

The tradition attached to the Ark, which is now transferred to Jerusalem, is shown by this move to be clearly very important; and matters may have developed in this direction farther among the tribes of Israel without our knowing anything more specific about it.[10]

The stream of Judaean tradition flows more fully in the Old Testament. Judah remained politically united with Jerusalem under the rule of the Davidic dynasty after the death of Solomon; the royal capital Jerusalem remained juridically the personal possession of the Davidic line, *alongside* the state territory of Judah. If one wished to describe the realm of the Davidic rulers accurately, one had to name Jerusalem *and* Judah in sequence.[11]

The Judaeans had to consider therefore what Jerusalem meant; for even for them it could not be immaterial whether the cultic significance of the Jerusalem sanctuary should merely be part

---

[9] The deuteronomist has later taken over the expression of the *nîr* from the Ahijah narrative (*I Kings* xv.4; *II Kings* viii.19. *Ps.* cxxxii. appears to favour the customary equation of *nîr* and *nēr*, where *nēr* is found with reference to the future of the Davidic dynasty. But we may ask whether here too *nîr* in the above sense did not stand, which would not fit in badly with the *'aṣmîaḥ* in the parallel first half-verse.

[10] When we read in *Jer.* xli.5 that people from different places in the Ephraimite highland came to offer sacrifice in "the house of Yahweh" even after the fall of Jerusalem in 587 B.C., that can only mean the shrine of the Yahweh sanctuary, which presupposes a tradition of pilgrimages to Jerusalem from the areas of the tribes who had made up the previous state of Israel, which had never been quite eradicated, and was therefore a continuing recognition of the cultic significance of the Jerusalem sanctuary.

[11] This occurs in *Isa.* i.1, ii.1, iii.1, 8, v.3, and very frequently in *Jeremiah*, but also elsewhere. Occasionally we find the special expression "the neighbourhood of Jerusalem (*měsabbê yerûšālayim* or *sěbhîbhôth yěrûšālayim*). This may refer to the territory belonging to the city-state of Jerusalem (cf. *II Kings* xxiii.5). In *Jer.* xvii.26, xxxii.44, xxiii.13, along with "the cities of Judah" and the "neighbourhood of Jerusalem", the "land of Benjamin" is also mentioned, i.e. that small portion of the territory of Israel which remained to the Davidic dynasty.

of the role of Jerusalem as the capital, now that the Ark had found a sanctuary there. This question cannot be answered in favour of Jerusalem's independent cultic significance simply because the rule of David and Solomon came to an end; for in Judah, even more than in Israel, the promise made to David concerning the possibility of a restoration of that rulership might have given food for thought, and the cultic role of Jerusalem could have been understood as a surviving portion of the Davidic monarchy. We are not left with mere surmises, however, since we have the evidence preserved in the Old Testament.

The great majority of references to Jerusalem in the Judaean traditions of the period of the monarchy refer only to the historical Jerusalem of that particular period, whether giving some item of information about the reigns of Judaean kings, or a threat of one of the eighth- or seventh-century prophets addressed to the contemporary population of Jerusalem and Judah. But we do find expressions which allow us to see something of the fundamental significance attributed to Jerusalem. These are found in the writings of the prophets, especially those of the eighth century, so that they can be dated and have a tolerably well-established origin. First there are the well-known messianic oracles: the "rebuilding of the tabernacle of David" (*Amos* IX.IIff.); the renewal of "the throne and monarchy of David" (*Isa.* IX.6); the new "shoot out of the stock" of David's ancestry (*Isa.* XI.I); the future ruler "of the tribe of Ephrath" (*Mic.* V.I); the "righteous Branch" which shall arise for David, i.e. for the Davidic dynasty (*Jer.* XXIII.5); the returning "servant of God, David" (*Ezek.* XXXIV.23f., XXXVII.24). These passages need merely to be called to mind to establish the remarkable fact that neither Jerusalem nor Zion is named in them.

To indicate any particular spot we have only the incidental reference to the Bethlehemite tribe Ephrath (*Mic.* V.I; cf. *Isa.* XI.I). The only exception is the messianic oracle of *Zech.* IX.9ff., which looks forward to the entry of the messianic king into Jerusalem. But in all probability this last passage is of late, post-exilic origin, and may therefore be left out of consideration here.[12] The pre-exilic prophets do not speak of Jerusalem in messianic oracles. It is however difficult to suppose that, when they

---

[12] For the late dating of the passage cf. K. Elliger: *Das Buch der zwölf kleinen Propheten*, VOL. II, 2nd edn. 1951, p. 140.

announced a future Davidic kingdom, they would not immediately think of Jerusalem as the future royal city. Would the
corruption of the Davidic monarchy of their time, and its capital,
have made the thought of a messianic-royal Jerusalem more
difficult? That is improbable. Isaiah had indeed announced that
this city, which had become so evil, would one day be purified by
the divine judgment, and would once more become a "city of
righteousness", a "faithful city" (1.21-26). We must deduce that
to have Jerusalem as the capital of the messianic kingdom was not
so essential for the prophets that they felt obliged to mention it;
in other words, for them the link between the Davidic monarchy
and Jerusalem was something which existed, but was not actually
essential. For Isaiah Jerusalem was the city which David had
once besieged (and captured) and which, for the fulfilment of the
divine judgment, would again be besieged (xxix.1ff.).[13] As a
native of Jerusalem himself, he thus indicates his awareness of
the historical steps by which Jerusalem became the royal capital.

This obviously low estimate of Jerusalem as a royal capital is
all the more remarkable when contrasted with the reputation of
the city as the shrine of the divine presence—the sanctuary and
the Ark. Amos speaks of the voice of Yahweh which roars
terrifyingly from Zion, and goes forth out of Jerusalem (1.2).[14]
For Isaiah Yahweh is the one "which dwelleth in mount Zion"
(viii.18), "whose fire is in Zion, and his furnace in Jerusalem"
(xxxi.9). This passage may refer to the sanctuary as a place of
sacrifice, possibly also as a shrine of the self-revealing divine
presence (cf. Gen. xv.17).[15] The prophets refer only to their own
day, but Jerusalem will still play a central role as a divine city in
the future. Admittedly Micah uttered that strong denunciation
which regards Jerusalem not as the royal capital but as the shrine
of the sanctuary, since it names "Zion", "Jerusalem", and
"mount of the (Temple) house" one after the other (iii.12); it
may be that Micah saw no future for Jerusalem even as a cult
centre. Isaiah, on the other hand, speaks of the foundation-stone
on Zion (xxviii.16) which Yahweh would lay, and so envisages
(in the image of a new building) not a future monarchy and a

---

[13] For the interpretation of ḤNH in vs. 1 cf. O. Procksch, *Jesaja* 1, 1930, p. 371;
against B. Duhm, *Das Buch Jesaja*, 4th edn., 1922.
[14] There is no cogent reason for denying this passage to Amos; cf. T. H.
Robinson in Robinson and Horst, *Die zwölf kleinen Propheten*, Hb. A.T., 1954.
[15] Cf. Procksch, *Jesaja* 1.

new state structure, but *a people of God in the city of God*. According to *Isa.* II.2f. and *Mic.* IV.1f.[16] Zion, Jerusalem, "the mount of the house of Yahweh", shall become not the government centre of an empire, but the pilgrim shrine of the nations, who shall seek and receive right instruction here. Finally[17] Jeremiah foresees the restored tribes of the former state of Israel some day making pilgrimage "to Zion, to Yahweh" (xxxi.6), and thus thinks of Jerusalem not as a seat of monarchy, but as a cultic shrine of the divine presence.

Consequently the position in classical prophecy appears quite clear and straightforward. In so far as Jerusalem has any specific significance in prophecy, and is not simply included in the whole condemnation under the judgment of God, it is *the shrine of Yahweh's sanctuary*, and will sustain this role into the future. We should not ask how this role was thought of in the context of the messianic kingdom, for the two concepts were simply not brought into relationship with each other.

The question is, however, not unimportant. For the tribes of Israel as well as for the Judaeans the holy shrine of Jerusalem had during the monarchy attained a significance which had its own importance, independent of the political circumstances of the Davidic monarchy from which it had arisen. The Jerusalem cult-shrine possessed no Israelite tradition of its own, therefore this significance can only have come from the sanctuary of the Ark which was placed there. This allows and even demands an appraisive deduction concerning the great importance of the Ark for all Israel in pre-monarchic days, for it was clearly unique. Only a cult object with an established and unique tradition would have helped a non-Israelite Jerusalem to attain to such an important cultic role that soon it no longer needed the support of the monarchy.

The little that tradition tells us of the history of the Ark in pre-monarchic days supports this. There are short, isolated, and historically rather unreliable mentions of the Ark in the narrative sources of the Pentateuch (*Num.* x.33ff., xiv.44); and it appears in the aetiological story about the crossing of the Jordan as part

---

[16] The question of the source of this prophetic oracle may here be left open; it appears to me to be in any case a pre-exilic prophecy, and therefore from either *Isaiah* or *Micah*.

[17] *Zeph.* III.14ff. and III.16ff. might also be adduced; but the authenticity of these passages appears to me to be at least dubious.

of the narrative of the occupation in the book of Joshua (*Joshua* III, IV).[18] In both of these the pan-Israel function of the Ark is taken for granted. Then in *Judges* XX.27 we meet it as the shrine of the divine presence at a juncture in the affairs of the confederacy of all the Israelite tribes; finally (and most particularly) we have *I Sam.* IV-VI, where it again represents the presence of the God of Israel (IV. 4-8). The hypothesis has been put forward in various forms that an "ark" was part of the furnishings of any sanctuary in settled Palestine, so that there may have been many of them; yet even though the wording of the passages might allow this interpretation, it appears to me that the significance of "*the* Ark" for Jerusalem excludes this possibility. This significance can be understood only if the Ark had been *the* central covenant sanctuary before David's day, with a considerable portion of the cultic tradition of Israel as a whole attached to it, and when the Ark was transferred to Jerusalem its influence continued to operate from there.

David's action in transferring the Ark to Jerusalem was possible because, so far as we can gather from a few indications in the tradition, it had previously changed its home at various times. The cultic centre of the Israelite tribal confederacy was the movable Ark, which as a cult object may well have begun as a nomadic shrine; it was not a specific local sanctuary. In Jerusalem things were different: the tradition of locally fixed cult centres, current in the settled land, carried the day against the probably pre-Palestinian tradition of the Ark. Even though the sanctuary in Jerusalem became a cultic centre for the tribes on account of the presence of the Ark, this shrine itself became more and more a central holy place, gaining as such an importance of its own. At one time "the Ark was called by the name of Yahweh Sabaoth that sitteth upon the cherubim" (*II Sam.* VI.2), Yahweh Sabaoth became he "which dwelleth in Mount Zion" (*Isa.* VIII.18). The "mountain of the house" (of the temple) (*Mic.* III.12), the "mountain of Yahweh's house" (*Isa.* II.2; *Mic.* IV.1), the "mountain of Yahweh" (*Isa.* II.3; *Mic.* IV.2), now becomes important. Zion becomes "the holy mountain of Yahweh" (cf. *Isa.* LXVI.20, and *Isa.* XXVII.13). The holiness of this mountain then becomes independent of the Ark, which had

[18] In *Joshua* VI the Ark has been introduced as a consequence of its role in *Joshua* III, IV.

once conferred on it such singular holiness in the eyes of Israel.

After the catastrophe of 587 B.C., therefore, after the termination of Jerusalem's role as the Davidic capital, after the destruction of Solomon's Temple, and even after the disappearance of
the Ark (which most probably fell victim to the same holocaust
which laid low all Solomon's city in *Jer.* xxxix.8) it became
possible for Jerusalem with its "holy mountain" to remain a
focal point for those Israelites who held fast to the ancient
traditions at home or in the Diaspora. It is very significant that
the Ark is not even mentioned in the records of the experiences
of 587 B.C., and no word of complaint about its loss is to be found
anywhere, not even in the *Book of Lamentations*. Clearly it had
long since relinquished its function as a cultic focus to the holy
shrine in Jerusalem, a cult place with a fixed geographical
situation. It was with the holiness of this shrine that the whole
later development of the cultic community in Jerusalem linked
itself in the post-exilic period.

We might finally ask whether this elevation of Jerusalem to be
the cultic centre of the Israelite tribes by the transfer of the Ark
took place without any opposition. It had commenced indeed
with a sovereign act of King David. The later Samaritan schism,
and its precursor in the strife at the time of the re-building of the
Temple during the first years of the Persian period, make it
possible to deduce that opposition to the pretensions of Jerusalem
was never completely stifled. Understandably the Old Testament tradition, having been put into shape in Jerusalem, has not
left many recognizable traces of this.

The main question here is the intention of the original
deuteronomic law with respect to the cult places. Josiah, and
consequently the deuteronomic writer, understood *Deuteronomy*
in a Jerusalemite sense; whoever deposited this lawbook in the
sanctuary in Jerusalem, so that it could be found there in the days
of Josiah, clearly envisaged Jerusalem as the single cult place
demanded by this law. This understanding of the law consequently goes back a very long way; but if, as has often been
suggested, the material of the deuteronomic law is of north
Israelite provenance,[19] then the question remains open whether
the author, with his well-known phrase "the place which
Yahweh shall choose to cause his name to dwell" (*Deut.* xiv.23,

[19] Cf. A. Alt, "Die Heimat des Deuteronomiums", in *K.S.*, vol. ii, pp. 250-75

etc.) is avoiding a direct reference to Jerusalem on account of the Mosaic setting, or whether he has intentionally left the selection of the single cult place open, and has therefore actually decided against Jerusalem. It is, however, probable that Jerusalem was accepted in view of the deuteronomic requirement of cultic unity. The formula uses the conception of "dwelling" (ŠKN), which appears to be at home in the cult theology of Jerusalem (cf. *I Kings* VIII.12, 13 and *Isa.* VIII.18), and perhaps too the expression about the "election" of the cult place goes back to a Jerusalem tradition. However this may be, the practical consequences of the deuteronomic law grew out of understanding the requirement of cultic unity with reference to Jerusalem; and by understanding it in this way, *Deuteronomy* added considerably to the advancement of the unique significance for Israel of the cult place of Jerusalem.

V

God, King, and Nation in the Old Testament

That the Old Testament itself is and must remain the foundation for the understanding of the Old Testament is a datum to be retained under all circumstances. Even if one is convinced that the subject concerned extends beyond the Old Testament and over into the New, this conviction can only be justified if we allow both Old and New Testaments to speak for themselves. To such treatment both Testaments have an undoubted claim, as bodies of material which have been handed down to us.

The understanding of the Old Testament is bound up with the historicity of this literary complex—so much is clear. It is also clear that what causes the problems in any preoccupation with its understanding lies, at least partly, just in the fact of this historicity. It is perhaps correct to say that the main characteristic of contemporary scholarly research on the Old Testament is the way in which the fundamental questions of understanding rear up again and again. The great historico-critical work on the Old Testament had to be built up out of the very material itself; it made mighty strides in philological study, and laid the literary-critical and historical basis for a scientific exegesis. But beyond the establishment of the reading of some word, there arise deeper questions of "meaning", which are not immediately answered by philological discoveries, and which come to light when it becomes a matter not of taking cognizance of a historical circumstance, but of the applicability of some word.

Is a real understanding in this deeper sense possible? We must remember that the Old Testament came into being in a sphere of human history remote from our own in both time and space; furthermore it belongs to a world which had a mental approach very different from our own. In order for us to attain a complete "understanding", is it necessary for us to enter into these other ways of looking at things and modes of thought so that we can no longer be our real selves? This question has been considered by Henry J. Cadbury in an article in *Interpretation*.[1] This journal deals specifically with questions of *understanding* the Bible, the Old as well as the New Testament. Cadbury would regard as legitimate the scholar's scientific attempt to feel his way into the world of the Old and New Testament, but sees a "danger" in the adoption of such a mental approach when it becomes a matter of more than observation by a scientific investigator.

He has been answered by G. Ernest Wright in the same volume[2]; Wright points out that uninterrupted Christian tradition links us with the world of the Bible, and that what stands in the Bible is not tied to any particular historical mental approach, which is in any case always changing; a mental approach correct for any particular century is no more eternally valid than one of previous centuries or millennia. He maintains, therefore, that it is essential for us to comprehend what has been expressed by people having different thought-patterns from our own. Whether this is entirely possible may for the present be left aside. The possibility of transposing oneself into the mental approach and mode of thought of someone else is the precondition for any understanding between men, though the understander does not have to give up his own identity. This possibility rests, therefore, on the existence of a basic community of thought between man and man, lying deeper than the variable mental approaches and modes of thought; and this is true also of understandings which extend over a long period of time. But we must take the trouble to think ourselves into the world of others.

Consequently a task for Old Testament scholarship remains, which is not only of academic interest but also of real contemporary importance; this is to illuminate, as far as possible, the spiritual world in which the Old Testament writings came into being and took their form. From many sources we nowadays have a knowledge of the ancient East as a whole, and we know that the Old Testament grew out of this background. At the same time it has also become clear that, in spite of this, comparatively little is established in detail, since the ancient Orient

---

[1] "The peril of archaizing ourselves," in *Interpretation*, III (1949), pp. 331ff.
[2] "The peril of archaizing ourselves," *op. cit.*, pp. 450ff.

covered such a vast area and such vast lengths of time that the place of the Old Testament within it needs to be more precisely fixed before the real connections between the Old Testament and the ancient Near East can be precisely studied. It may be true that there were viewpoints and attitudes common to the whole ancient Near East, which we may expect to find presupposed in the Old Testament, but this should not be taken for granted. Our knowledge of the ancient Near East is nowadays so rich in detail that it is scarcely justifiable any longer to use the expression "ancient Oriental" without closer definition, nor to regard everything belonging to the ancient Orient as belonging to the historical and mental background of the Old Testament.

It is not easy to ascertain the mental concepts and pre-suppositions of a world remote from our own, because in the nature of things these have not been handed down in so many words. They underlie what is said or written or pictured, but are not specified or formulated nor even thought of as anything remarkable, since they applied quite normally within their own world, and only become notable and non-universal in another world which has its own different presuppositions. Consequently these presuppositions can be deduced and scientifically compre-hended only on the basis of studying the many expressions of the attitude to life. Since they cannot be determined exactly and simply, in the way that the facts concerning some single event may be established on the basis of a surviving tradition, we need the sort of scientifically controlled intuition which is indispens-able in all scientific work that aims at opening up new experi-ences. Where it can be applied here, it plays a special role in sorting out, from among the great diversity of manifestations, the essential element in the unspoken though fundamental attitudes and concepts. There is a very real danger of a subjective and unacceptable viewpoint. Any view expressed must prove its correctness by demonstrating that it makes a large number of recorded occurrences more understandable, and shows them in a convincing new light.

In the following pages we shall seek to study more closely this intuitive picture of the spiritual background of the ancient East and of the Old Testament, which is beginning to play such a role in present-day study. It is a phenomenon worth studying for its own sake, but it also raises some essential points of discussion, both on the relationship of the Old Testament to the religio-historical world of the ancient East, and on the proper exegesis of the Old Testament itself. This viewpoint is especially prevalent amongst British and Scandinavian scholars. It is associated (particularly in Scandinavia) with the rejection of literary-critical work on the Old Testament. That is no accident. As a whole it marks a reaction against a method of treatment which has at times been rather one-sided; so this new line of research is important and worth attention even on that account. For without questioning the necessity of literary-critical work, we must admit that some critics in the past have viewed the Old Testament too much through the eyes of a literary age, and in a rather too strongly intellectualistic spirit. Perhaps we have not reckoned sufficiently with the depths of human life as they are worked out in attitude and thought. Of course, insight into the limitation of literary-critical study is not a recent discovery; and there have been reactions to literary-critical study for some time. It takes its place in the larger context of a development in research which has been going on for a long time.

In 1933 there appeared in England under the title *Myth and Ritual* a collective work edited by Professor S. H. Hooke, who himself supplied the first essay, called "The Myth and Ritual Pattern of the Ancient East"; other scholars then dealt with the theme "Myth and Ritual" with reference to various areas of the ancient East. In 1935 another collective work (under the same editorship) appeared bearing the title *The Labyrinth: Further Studies in the Relation Between Myth and Ritual in the Ancient World*. This contained loosely connected contributions by various British scholars, again bearing on the theme "Myth and Ritual"; the editor's own article was on "The Myth and Ritual Pattern in Jewish and Christian Apocalyptic". In 1938 S. H. Hooke published his Schweich Lectures for 1935 on the subject *The Origins of Early Semitic Ritual*.

The titles mentioned indicate what was intended. After demonstrating the obvious fact that supposedly effective cultic activity existed over the whole of the ancient Near East, they further maintain that myth belonged to this cultic activity, and grew out of it in the form of liturgy until it attained its full development, so that cult and myth decisively affected the whole of life, attitude, and thought—which again is scarcely disputed;

but then these authors would argue for the existence over the whole of the ancient Near East of a "myth and ritual pattern" with a comparatively limited content. The essential element, according to them, was the annually repeated renewal of life which was cultically enacted at the New Year; in fact it centred on all the myth and ritual of the so-called dying and rising god. Now it has long been recognized that this cult was widely known in the ancient Near East, and that it carried exceptional significance for life and thought there. In so far as it united the annual cultically activated renewal of life with the thought of an ever repeated re-creation of the world, it formed an essential element of what is often called the "cyclic thinking" of the ancient Orient, which saw the march of events as a continuous recurrence of the same happenings. We shall need to study more closely the way in which the dying and rising was performed in the cultic New Year celebration of the renewal of life; for with it is bound up the cultically enacted rite of the "holy marriage" (ἱερὸς γάμος), by means of which the fertility and blessing of the newly created world were activated. The widespread character and significance of this rite has also been known from several sources for a considerable time.

What distinguishes the Myth and Ritual School is that basically it derives the whole cultic and mythical activity of the ancient Near East from this single New Year festival with its various celebrations, and maintains that individual cultic rites hived off secondarily from this larger complete complex and developed into independent cultic festivals on their own. As the fundamental feature, it further follows that they suppose a fixed cult-mythical "pattern" which was the same all over the ancient Near Eastern world, and that throughout the varied regions of this area this pattern did not produce any real variation of development; so that even in later historical times it is still to be met with complete with its main features, except that at last a certain "disintegration" set in at many points. Israel too shared this common Oriental heritage; it was here[3] that the great prophetic movement of the eighth century B.C. for the first time brought about a break in the close connection with the religio-historical world round about, and showed Israel new and individual paths.

[3] *The Origins of Early Semitic Ritual*, London 1938, p. 9.

What distinguishes the Myth and Ritual School finally and especially is that they attribute a central and decisive role to the king in cultic activities. The king in his person was the embodiment of the whole of his realm, and at the same time, God. In the cultic rite of the New Year festival he himself—identified with the dying and rising god—accomplished the universal renewal of life and, in the celebration of the "sacred marriage", he brought about life and fertility for the new season each year. He was at the same time the priest in person, and the godhead at work in the cult. The annual dying and rising of the god-king may on these occasions have been enacted in various forms, ranging from the original actual slaying of the former king, through all manner of symbolically represented actions of the king, on to the appearance of various substitutes for him.[4] Basically it was of course a matter of the dying and revival of the god-king himself. The "sacred marriage" was consummated by the god-king with the supposedly equally divine priestly queen. Consequently this divine kingship formed the actual underlying basis of life as a whole; and this significance of the divine kingship in connection with the annual renewal of life was the same over the whole of the ancient Near East,[5] including Israel.

This conception of the Myth and Ritual School has been taken up by a series of Scandinavian scholars and further developed, particularly with respect to the divine kingship. Since it is not my intention to review the literature produced but rather to discuss a particular religio-historical view, it will be sufficient for the moment to name only a few important publications. In the *Uppsala Universitets Årsskrift* for 1941 the religious historian Geo Widengren published a study on "Psalm 110 and the sacral kingship in Israel", in which the Jerusalemite kingship of the Davidic dynasty is discussed in the light of the divine king ideology, on the basis of the pre-Israelite traditions of Jerusalem.[6]

In 1943 the Uppsala Old Testament scholar Ivan Engnell brought out his detailed *Studies in Divine Kingship in the Ancient Near East*. Bringing forward a most abundant assortment of

---

[4] Details are given by S. H. Hooke, *op. cit.*, pp. 10ff.

[5] Cf. A. R. Johnson, "The role of the king in the Jerusalem cultus", in *The Labyrinth*, ed. S. H. Hooke, 1935, pp. 71-111.

[6] "Psalm 110 och det sakrala kungadömet i Israel", Cf. *id.*, *Sakrales Königtum im Alten Testament und im Judentum*, 1955, and the reference in *Ev. Th.* XVI (1956), p. 345, n. 30.

texts, he seeks to demonstrate conclusively that divine kingship
in cult-mythical affairs and actions had as great a significance
throughout the whole of the ancient Near East as was envisaged
by the Myth and Ritual School itself. Engnell deals in detail
with kingship in Egypt and Mesopotamia, and studies most
particularly the divine-king ideology in the Canaanite area
(Syria and Palestine). In accordance with the present position
of scholarly research he draws particularly on the newly found
texts of Ras Shamra (ancient Ugarit), as did S. H. Hooke[7]; these
texts at present form the only extensive original source-
documents for religious history from Syria and Palestine, and
belong to the period shortly before the occupation of Palestine
by the Israelite tribes (fourteenth century B.C.). They are without
doubt very important, but unfortunately they are of considerable difficulty and uncertainty, and in spite of all the endeavours of scholars they remain still unclarified in countless
details.

Engnell has, however, devoted a great measure of personal
research to them in order to press them into the service of his
divine kingship scheme. When he wrote his *Studies in Divine
Kingship* the publication of the second tablet of the so-called
k-r-t text from Ras Shamra was unknown to him. This tablet,
which is of paramount importance for his theory, features a
certain personage named *"K r t"*, and Engnell allotted a
separate study to it,[8] although the text is unfortunately preserved
only in a very fragmentary condition. Engnell has supplied an
important contribution to the elucidation of the Ras Shamra
texts as a whole.

In this present connection we are not specially concerned with
the Ras Shamra texts, nor indeed with any direct manifestations
of ancient Oriental religious history, but only with the Old
Testament; basically, of course, the Old Testament is the target
towards which the forementioned works have been directed. The
English contributions to the theme Myth and Ritual were all
intended to lead to a new understanding of the Old Testament;
Engnell too has the Old Testament in mind in his investigations. His *Studies in Divine Kingship* offers a comprehensive preliminary to a new understanding of important elements in the

---

[7] Cf. *The Origins of Early Semitic Ritual*, pp. 28ff.
[8] "The text IIK from Ras Shamra," in *Horae Soederblomianae*, 1 (1944), pp. 1ff.

content of the Old Testament from the standpoint of the divine king ideology.

Engnell has also promised us an investigation of his own to help to establish in detail that the ancient Near Eastern divine king ideology was of decisive importance for the Old Testament, and has given a short summary of the consequences for the Old Testament of the results of his study.[9] This indicates that they will be extraordinarily far-reaching. The idea of a divine king, we are told, had a central significance in Israel and in the Old Testament as well, which only the late secondary redaction of the Old Testament canon in Jerusalem has concealed, though many traces of it are still clearly discernible. This idea first shaped the original traditions about the early and prehistoric periods, and thereafter of course the traditions about the Davidic monarchy which continued its life in the high-priesthood of Jerusalem.

The divine king is supposed to have had special relationships with the dying and rising fertility god, and consequently was always represented as the life-giving bringer of good fortune, i.e. a messiah. Messianism was therefore the central *motif* of the whole of the Old Testament. The divine king ideology remains most clearly visible in the Psalter. All the psalms are to be cultically understood, i.e. from the standpoint of the divine king ritual; consequently all the psalms are pre-exilic.[10] Since the king was understood in the ritual as a dying and rising god, the laments in the Psalter were to be applied to the king in connection with the situation during the annual New Year ritual (which was carried out in detail) when he was handed over into the power of death, from which he later revived and annually came forth, bringing with him new life. Consequently a psalm like the well-known *Ps.* xxii is to be regarded as a royal psalm, and—in view of the fundamentally "messianic" character of the monarchy— Engnell and others have drawn conclusions for the Old Testa-

---

[9] *Studies in Divine Kingship in the Ancient Near East*, henceforth cited as *Studies*, Uppsala 1943, pp. 174-7.

[10] *Ps.* cxxxvii, which alone is definitely to be dated with certainty, forms the single exception. Engnell (*op. cit.*, p. 176, n. 2) declares it to be the only psalm which is not pre-exilic, i.e. therefore the latest psalm. So, on the contrary, the defendants of the generally post-exilic origin of the psalms (except *Ps.* cxxxvii) had to take it as the oldest psalm (cf. B. Duhm, *Die Psalmen: Kurzer Handcommentar zum alten Testament*, ed. by K. Marti, 1899, p. xix).

ment from this general picture of the ancient Near Eastern divine king ideology.

In a study of the Servant of the Lord in Deutero-Isaiah,[11] Engnell has understood this figure as "messianic", and emphatically declared this to be the only possible way to understand it: the "divine servant" can only be the divine king of David's house, and what is different about Deutero-Isaiah's Servant Songs is that in them the divine king who incorporates the whole within himself appears mainly as doing penance and suffering—on the analogy of the dying and rising god Tammuz—though at the same time he finally triumphs. This conviction that the "messianic" proclamation is the essential and central element in Old Testament prophecy is to be seen also in the background of Engnell's study of the call of Isaiah,[12] which provides a detailed exegesis of *Isa.* VI.

Harald Riesenfeld, in an interesting study closely linked with work on the divine king ideology, has sought to show that the celebrated vision of Ezekiel about the resurrection of the dead bones (*Ezek.* XXXVII) is to be explained from the New Year ritual with the dramatically represented dying and rising of the divine king.[13] The consequences of this interpretation extend right down into the New Testament, as is shown by the same author's widely ranging book on the transfiguration of Jesus.[14] The interpretations of this school have influenced a circle much wider than that of the actual advocates of the ancient Near Eastern and Old Testament divine king ideology. As an example there is the monograph by Aage Bentzen, *Messias—Moses Redivivus— Menschensohn*[15] (*Abhandlungen zur Theologie des Alten and Neuen Testament*, No. 17), 1948. Bentzen maintains all reserve *vis-à-vis* the theories of the Uppsala school, but yet goes along with them quite a way; he links the psalms with the King—even the psalms

[11] This article first appeared in the *Svensk Exegetisk Årsbok*, X (1945), pp. 31-65, and then in a translation bearing the title "The 'Ebed Yahweh Songs and the suffering Messiah in *Deutero-Isaiah*, in *Bulletin of the John Rylands Library*, XXXI (1948), pp. 3-42.

[12] I. Engnell, *The Call of Isaiah*, Uppsala 1949.

[13] H. Riesenfeld: *The Resurrection in Ezekiel* XXXVII *and in the Dura-Europos Paintings*, Uppsala 1948.

[14] H. Riesenfeld, *Jésus Transfiguré* (Acta Seminarii Neotestamentici Uppsaliensis XVI), 1947.

[15] Abhandlungen zur Theologie des Alten und Neuen Testament, No. 17, Zürich 1948; Eng. trans. *King and Messiah*, tr. by E. W. Heaton, 1955.

of lamentation—and he accepts the "messianic" interpretation of Deutero-Isaiah's Servant of the Lord, and even Engnell's argument that the king in his cult-ritual activity as corporate representative of the community is identified with "Primeval-man".[16] Bentzen's half-way position has something rather ambivalent and imprecise about it.

It may strike some readers that in this school concepts, which historical criticism and, in particular, literary criticism had rendered at least problematic, suddenly reappear almost as if to be taken for granted; for example we have the stressing of "messianism" as a central feature throughout the Old Testament, the "messianic" interpretation of the Servant of the Lord in Deutero-Isaiah, and the connection of *Ps.* xxii with the "messianic" king. We should of course not fail to realize that the term "messianic" is understood in a sense different from the traditional Christian one, and one which has originally nothing to do with the future, but refers to the bearer of the divine kingdom envisaged in a timeless realm, and who is the bringer of luck annually in the New Year ritual. The "messiah" is thus regarded here in the context of a "cyclic" form of thought which is entirely contrary to any *unique fulfilment* of messianic expectation. The question is whether the theory is satisfactory and tenable, and whether we have the means to test its correctness and tenability. This we must now proceed to examine with all possible impartiality.

We are offered an intuitive view of the mental approach and mode of thought which characterized both the ancient Near Eastern world and that of the Old Testament which, if it is correct, must be of fundamental importance for the understanding of the traditions preserved to us from this world. It is a scholarly conception which with impressive boldness seeks to integrate a wide range of phenomena into thought patterns of really remarkable simplicity. Clearly this scholarly conception has not materialised out of thin air, but is firmly based on the precise interpretation of specific texts.

The above brief mention of the studies dealing with this subject can give only the main outlines without adducing details of their arguments or showing the whole complexity of the interrelationships in which the multitude of historico-religious

[16] Cf. Engnell, in B.J.R.L., xxxi (1948), pp. 40ff.

phenomena are brought within the pattern. Nevertheless we are dealing with a conception which is not simply to be gathered from the available traditions; it can be deduced only from a consistent interpretation along an identical line of what seem at first sight very different traditional events. Whoever wishes to pursue the question of the viability of this conception could begin with testing the individual arguments. In the present context this is not possible, nor is it the only, or perhaps indeed the most relevant way; for with regard to many existing texts there can well be differences of interpretation, since they are frequently ambiguous, without on that account giving rise to any really essential conclusion about the total conception, since this could well be maintained although various details in any particular instance might have to be differently explained. Consequently we must try to keep the whole before our eyes, and at the same time seek to test the general foundations of this whole.

In the following pages we shall deal most particularly with the Old Testament and the question of its religio-historical connection with the world of the ancient Near East, which in this theory is regarded in a very definite manner. The question of divine kingship will be given special attention, since it plays a decisive role in the Myth and Ritual scheme, and since the Old Testament tradition has something very definite to say on the subject. But we must go fairly far back, since only in this way can the comprehensive Myth and Ritual view be given justice.

It is beyond question that in the ancient Near East the conception of a divine king did exist, and that in his own person he personified the whole body politic as it was there and then envisaged, and bore in himself the life of this whole through his ritual activity. The classical land of this conception was Egypt, which led such a virtually secluded life in ancient times that during the millennia of its history it changed remarkably little, and even caught up intruding foreigners into its own way of life. Pharaoh was the godhead incarnate, and at the same time the actual priest; he was the sun and the life of his land. Engnell is therefore on sound lines when he begins his *Studies in Divine Kingship* with a description of the Egyptian kingdom.

In Mesopotamia, the other great Near Eastern riverine oasis which was also a region of very early settlement and culture, the conception of a divine king also appears to have been not entirely strange, though whether there was a general dissemination of this conception is quite doubtful. There are not really many witnesses for it, and history here was so full of vicissitudes, with so many changes of population and new rulers and different forms of government, that it must first be established that it is permissible to speak of *the* kingship in Mesopotamia at all. Was the same conception of the essence of kingship current in the ancient Sumerian city-kingdoms, on the lower banks of the Euphrates and Tigris, as was held among such later rulers as the first dynasty of Babylon, or the Assyrian warrior state, not to mention the occasional foreign conqueror from the Iranian plateau? It is possible that here too an original territorial concept of divine kingship was preserved throughout all historical changes, but this is by no means as self-evident. Mesopotamia had a very mixed population and varied forms of government; but even if a fairly uniform conception of kingship continued as a living force throughout its history, that does not mean that it was the same conception as held sway in Egypt.

In his comprehensive book *Kingship and the Gods*, 1948, H. Frankfort came to the conclusion—after an exhaustive survey of the available source material—that the Egyptian representation of the Pharaoh as the incarnate god was quite different from the conception of the king as "the elect servant" of the deity, which was the dominant theory in Mesopotamia.[17] Without pursuing this question in further detail, we must re-affirm that the general validity of the divine kingship pattern over the widespread and historically important territory of Mesopotamia is at least doubtful, even if it be permissible to regard the land as a unity.

Of more immediate significance for the Old Testament than the ancient centres of culture on the Nile, Euphrates, and Tigris, we have the interlying land of Syria and Palestine, the realm which the Israelite tribes entered and occupied. Should we want to know what conception of the essence of kingship was held in pre-Israelite (Bronze Age) Syria and Palestine, we must bear in mind that there were many small monarchies all over this region for as far back as we have any records. We now know the history of the second millennium B.C. well enough to say that movements

---

[17] C. J. Gadd, *Ideas of Divine Rule in the Ancient East*, 1948, p. 34, takes a similar view.

of very varied peoples took place across this territory, so we must investigate whether the different ethnic elements and systems of rule in this area had in any way the same ideas about kingship.

Syria and Palestine experienced at various times strong influences from the direction of both Egypt and Mesopotamia. The extent of this influence is not clear, and we cannot be absolutely certain that the concepts current in those two centres of civilization were widespread throughout Syria and Palestine as well. The theory that the same ideas had been preserved over the whole of the ancient Near East from a "primitive period" common to the whole of it is more than doubtful. The conception "early Semitic", with which the Myth and Ritual school make play (and particularly its leader S. H. Hooke), and in which Syria and Palestine are included with Mesopotamia, is a conception no longer applicable in view of modern knowledge about the manifold ethnic migrations during the oldest periods known to us. We cannot safely speak of "early Semitic" (meaning "original Semitic") with reference to Mesopotamia, where the non-Semitic Sumerians exercised a lasting and pervasive influence, and where incursions of non-Semitic elements from the Iranian highlands were always taking place.

Similarly in Syria and Palestine, during the period in which our source material allows a fairly close view of the situation, numerous non-Semitic racial elements had already begun to play a not inconsiderable role. Even the more specific concept "north-western Semitic religion",[18] which is used to refer to the whole cultic background in Syria and Palestine during the Bronze Age, can be used only with great caution in view of the motley ethnic composition of the population in Syria and Palestine during the second millennium B.C.

The sources available for the fourteenth century in Syria and Palestine do allow us, however, to make some deductions about the conception of kingship. These sources are from the period of Egyptian domination over Syria and Palestine, so that we might question whether it is not the Egyptian conception of divine kingship that finds expression here. This applies particularly to the Amarna tablets. In them the vassal princelings of the land address their royal overlord the Pharaoh as the Divine

[18] So in Engnell, *Studies in Divine Kingship*, p. 71.

Son, the Universal Giver of Life, the Omnipresent Lord, etc.[19] In these phrases Engnell finds expressions of a divine king ideology native to Syria and Palestine[20]; but if we weigh the matter with more caution we should regard these remarks addressed to the Pharaoh by governors of territory within the domain of the Egyptian hegemony as examples of Egyptian "court style", and an Egyptian attitude to the king. Even so it is clear that in the late Bronze Age in Syria and Palestine the conception of a divine king was known in the numerous city states scattered throughout the country, and if it was not directly applied to native rulers, it was at all events applied to the Egyptian overlord.

The Ras Shamra tablets go still further. They are roughly contemporary with the Amarna tablets, and so they too were written during the period of Egyptian supremacy. Their content, however, is probably older and may go back to very old traditions in which we may even discern something of aboriginal forms and thoughts. In spite of all uncertainties in the understanding of these texts it can be said that the dying and rising fertility god does play a quite substantial role; and the thoroughgoing researches of Engnell, particularly on the *Krt* text, have shown that we must reckon here with the idea that this divinity was thought of as incarnate in the king.

How much of this applies to the whole of Syria and Palestine is another matter. The city of Ugarit, whose remains are covered by Ras esh-Shamra, had a quite strongly non-Semitic, Hurrian ruling class in the fourteenth century.[21] The name of the king, during whose reign the tablets were written, may also be non-Semitic.[22] But it may be accepted as probable that the main substance of the Ras Shamra texts derives from native Canaanite tradition which was current in Syria and Palestine to an extent of which we are ignorant. We would therefore conclude that in the Syrian and Palestinian region which the Israelite tribes entered shortly after the fourteenth century a divine king ideology may not have been unknown, whether based on ancient native tradition or on the direct influence of the Egyptian

---

[19] Engnell, *op, cit.*, pp. 84ff., esp. 91ff., has gathered the most important of them.
[20] *Op. cit.*, p. 206.
[21] Cf. *Z.D.P.V.*, LXV (1942), pp. 58ff., 147ff.; also my *History*, 1960, pp. 25ff.
[22] Cf. Z. D. P. V., LXV, pp. 161ff.

overlordship. But we know very little about its distribution or development.

What relationship has the Old Testament to this ancient Near Eastern and Canaanite fund of ideas? The divine kingship school maintains without reserve that Israel (as a member of the ancient Near Eastern world) shared these ideas from the very start, and that many clear traces of this are to be found in the Old Testament. In Israel, however, there was a disintegration and democratization of the material, and within the bounds of Old Testament faith in course of time a certain caution grew up with regard to it. But before we proceed to investigate in detail the existence of divine kingship in ancient Israel, we must state some more general conclusions.

The Israelites completed their occupation of Canaan as part of a greater movement, which brought into the Syrian and Palestinian terrain Israel's neighbours—the Edomites, Moabites and Ammonites—and all those other associated elements included under the general description "Aramaeans". This general occupation of the land coincides with a break in the history of Syria and Palestine, the transition from the Bronze to the Iron Age; and the new elements in their new settlements developed a life different in various ways from the city culture of the Bronze Age. The ancient traditions of the settled region of Syria and Palestine were influenced on many points by Egyptian and Mesopotamian civilization, and it is quite clear that these traditions exercised considerable influence on the "younger peoples" who had entered their domain. But we cannot simply take it for granted that everything to be found by way of institutions and ideas in ancient Syria and Palestine was to find acceptance among later populations; still less can we assume that the later populations—even before coming into the land—shared the conceptions which existed in those cultural milieux from of old. It must first be shown that they were acquainted with a divine kingship concerned with and moulded by the New Year ritual.

Unfortunately we know next to nothing of the cultic life current among these peoples. The few inscriptions from this region do not tell us much. K. F. Euler took up this question, and came to the conclusion that there is nothing in them about either a divine origin of the king or a deification of the king

even after death, or any presentation of the king as a representative of the deity.[23] Euler holds that, on the contrary, the king
appears here as the servant of the god. Engnell may not be
altogether wrong when he points out[24] that the inscriptional
material utilized is too meagre to permit far-reaching conclusions,
but in no instance do these inscriptions contain any positive
reference to the conception of a divine kingship. Euler's study
also included the newly found inscription of King Bar Hadad (Old
Testament Ben Hadad) I of Damascus, in which the King refers
to the god Melkart as "his lord", to whom he has devoted a stele
because he has "hearkened unto his cry" (i.e. his petition).[25]
The Aramaic royal name Bar Hadad ("Son of the god Hadad")
cannot however be adduced in argument against this, for the
father/son relationship between god and king can be understood
in several ways.

Finally, the sole Moabite royal inscription which has been
preserved—the well-known Mesha inscription—again provides
no evidence of the presence of a divine king ideology.[26] Until
there is evidence to the contrary, therefore, we must assume
that a divine kingship pattern may have become known in
Syria and Palestine, through their association with the cultures
of the Nile and the Euphrates-Tigris lands, yet that the "younger
peoples" settling in Syria and Palestine around the transition
from the Bronze to the Iron Age had no knowledge of a divine
kingship.

Israel belonged to these "younger peoples", and in the Old
Testament we have such a rich tradition concerning Israel, and
indeed concerning the history of kingship in Israel, that we are
now at last on safer ground. Of course, the proponents of the
theory of divine kingship have themselves made full appeal to the
Old Testament, and sought to prove from it that Israel knew
about the ritually active divine king along with the rest of the

[23] "Königtum und Götterwelt in den altaramäischen Inschriften Nordsyriens",
in Z.A.W., N.F. xv (1938), pp. 272-313.
[24] Engnell, Studies, p. 205.
[25] On this passage, see my History, pp 240f.
[26] It is remarkable that Engnell (Studies, p. 80) says that Mesha describes himself
in the first line of the inscription as "Son of [the god] Chemosh", whereas a space
occurs in the text after the letters of the name Chemosh, so that we must presume
that it was not the name of the god Chemosh which stood here, but a personal
name formed with this divine name as its first element, and giving us the name of
King Mesha's human father.

ancient Near East—at least during the earliest period of her history.

Before discussing these arguments, we must first lay down a general principal of methodology. If we wish to make a statement about kingship in Israel, we cannot start with individual references such as are found especially in the Psalter, and thereby overlook the whole massive historical tradition of the Old Testament about kingship and its various developments. Firstly we must consider the clear and unambiguous circumstances of the case, and only then shall we seek to interpret what is uncertain and problematical. It would be folly to proceed the other way round, nor could we justify such an approach by claiming that original elements have been preponderantly preserved in the cultic texts of the Psalter, while the narrative historical tradition has been so "weeded" and transplanted that the idea of a divine kingship has been eliminated in favour of a later tendency to separate the divine and the human spheres sharply from one another. However correct it may be that original traits in cultic forms tend to be preserved with marked tenacity, and that the narrative parts of the Old Testament have suffered secondary redactions, we cannot deny any historical value to what we are told in the narratives of the Old Testament. On the contrary, the meticulous literary-critical study of the Old Testament has had not only the destructive effect of casting doubt on the traditional beliefs concerning the authorship of the Old Testament writings, it sought also to separate out the ancient material from the later redactoral editings and framework, and has led to firmly grounded results. Consequently it is no longer left to subjective standards to decide whether any passage within the Old Testament is to be regarded as ancient and original, or as late and secondary.

The most striking historical fact concerning kingship in Israel is that Israel only got around to it very late. In a country which had reckoned innumerable city monarchies since the Bronze Age, and had as neighbours those related "younger peoples" who went over to monarchy more or less upon adopting settled life, Israel lived for at least two centuries without having a king. So it does not look as if the idea of the vital importance of a divine kingship were alive in earliest Israel, nor as if Israel had brought this idea with her from the period before the occupation. It seems much more probable that Israel hesitated about establishing a monarchy, and this hesitation may well have arisen just because, in the regions of Syria and Palestine, there was bound up with the political institutions of the monarchy precisely such a cult-ritual function of a divinely conceived king as was unacceptable to Israel. Nor does Israel in its earliest stages provide any evidence for A. Bentzen's suggested derivation[27] of the "divine king" from the more general figure of a "divine primeval man" who could be envisaged as a prince, king, priest, or prophet.

In Israel's pre-monarchic period we know of no figure who could represent the whole community, cultically and ritually. To attribute this lack to the paucity of material handed down would be merely a *petitio principii* such as can hardly be justified. The charismatic leaders of the pre-monarchic period who appear now and then—the so-called "Major Judges"—had (as the old unredacted material clearly shows) limited significance only, within the bounds of individual tribes or groups of tribes, and never represented or embodied Israel as a whole. It is a later re-editing, probably during the monarchic period, which endowed them with a significance for Israel as a whole.[28] The individual tribes never had any "prince", much less the Israelite twelve-tribe confederacy as a whole; the individual tribes were represented by a gathering of the elders.

The ancient Israelite "amphictyony" had indeed a cultic focus and a common cult, but in the really ancient tradition—as distinct from the later post-exilic tradition about Aaron and his descendants—there is no definite trace of a perpetual or hereditary priesthood at the central sanctuary. In the pre-monarchic period we know of only a single permanent office for all Israel, the office of "Judge over Israel", which comes to light in the unverifiable tradition about the so-called "Minor Judges" (*Judges* x.1-5, xii.7-15).[29] Now if we simply suppose that this office carried with it the observance and exposition of a "divine law" incumbent upon Israel, the tradition provides no handle

[27] *King and Messiah*, pp. 45ff., 63ff.

[28] Still later, in deuteronomistic historical writing at the earliest, a status *vis-à-vis* all Israel is attributed to each, on account of the theory of a continuing office.

[29] Cf. my essay in *Festschrift Alfred Bertholet*, 1950, pp. 404ff. Perhaps Joshua too belongs really in the context of "minor judges".

for attaching to it any cult-ritual role in the sense of a divine king ideology.

The "patriarchs" received promises of purely local importance, so there remains only the figure of Moses, who appears with wide-reaching functions in a mediatorial position between God and people. But here we have the difficult problem of deciding how much of the Moses narrative has been added in process of time to the original nucleus, and whether the universal significance for the history of his time attributed to Moses in the final Pentateuchal narrative is not really secondary. In any case, even if the picture of Moses given in the pentateuchal narrative is to be retained, he is such a unique and isolated figure, without predecessor or follower, that he alone cannot uphold the theory of the presence of a divine kingship pattern in early Israel. It seems, therefore, that there are good grounds for claiming that premonarchic Israel had no knowledge of any kind of divine king figure, and that this ideology cannot have belonged to the original mind and imagination of Israel.

Israel continued without a king for centuries, even longer than her neighbours, but at length she too changed over to settled government with a monarchy. In the Old Testament we have such detailed and excellent ancient traditions concerning the progress of bringing the state into being on Israelite soil, that we cannot speak of the establishment of monarchy in Israel without referring first of all to these traditions. Their content has been so thoroughly examined[30] that it would be folly to by-pass the results of these investigations, for it is remarkable how clearly it is stated that the monarchy was created by human agency in a particular historical eventuality. When Saul had been seized by the "spirit of God" like any one of the charismatic leaders of the "Judges' period", and subsequently conquered the Ammonites in Transjordan, the "whole people" went to Gilgal and in the sanctuary there "made Saul king" (*I Sam.* XI.15). Naturally elevation to the monarchy was a sacral act which took place "before Yahweh" in the sanctuary; but it is "the people" who appear as the "king-makers".[31]

[30] Cf. the various histories of Israel, and especially A. Alt, "Die Staatenbildung der Israeliten in Palästina", in *K.S.*, VOL. II, pp. 1ff.

[31] It is not quite apparent what role was played here by Samuel who (according to *I Sam.* XI.14) had summoned "the people" to Gilgal. But in any case even he could only have urged "the people" on to "make Saul king".

After Saul's downfall "the men of Judah" came to David in
Hebron and anointed him there "as king over the house of
Judah" (*II Sam.* II.4a)³²; and again when Saul's son Ishbaal,
whom the army commander Abner "had made king" (*II Sam.*
II.9) was murdered, "all the elders of Israel came to the king
[David] to Hebron, and king David made with them a covenant
before Yahweh, and they anointed David king over Israel"
(*II Sam.* v.3). In this last instance mention is expressly made of a
"covenant", or agreement. It could hardly have been stated
more clearly that the Davidic monarchy rested on human
arrangements with the elders as the representatives of the
Israelite tribes. Solomon became king and successor to David
due to the human decision of his father, instigated by influential
circles at court, as is visibly and patently depicted in *I Kings*
I.IIff. After Solomon's death "all Israel" came together to
Shechem to "make" Rehoboam the son of Solomon "king"
(*I Kings* XII.I). But since the accompanying negotiations
towards this end misfired, Israel separated themselves off from
the Davidic dynasty, fetched Jeroboam and "made him king
over all Israel" (*I Kings* XII.20).

These details of the tradition are widely accepted and quite
clear as to their content; and we may not bypass them in a
question concerning the basis of Israelite kingship. It is important to remember not only that we here have very dependable
information about the actual incidents accompanying the
setting up of the state, but that these precedents were retained
and handed on. The information about Saul, David, Solomon,
and others finally arrived via numerous redactions in the great
deuteronomic history. Although we may no longer exactly
know in which circles the historical traditions about the first
kings were first gathered and then passed on, it is clear at least
that in Israel knowledge of the historical outcome was retained,
as well as knowledge that the institution of monarchy had not
been an original part of Israel's existence, but had occurred at
a quite late stage in the history of Israel, and through the
initiative of the "people" or its elders. But such knowledge hardly
allows us to accept a concept of the monarchy as an element in a

³² This must be a shortened form of expression; the anointing must certainly
have been carried out by priests, but the actual subject of the whole transaction
was still "the men of Judah".

timeless divine ordering of the world such as the divine king ideology necessarily presupposes.

The life of the monarchy in Israel was relatively short. A mere two centuries and a half after the founding of the Davidic state—that is, after a time scarcely longer than the preceding kingless period of Israel's existence in Palestine—an independent monarchy was a thing of the past for the greater part of the Israelite tribes. Even the monarchy which continued to exist for another century and a half amongst the narrower circle of southern tribes was no more than a vassal kingship within the framework of a foreign empire. Following upon the end of this petty vassal kingdom there stretched for almost half a millennium another kingless period, i.e. a period of subjection to the ruler of a foreign empire. It is true that, after the end of the Davidic monarchy, the programme for the future in *Ezekiel* XLVIII considered the cultic function of the king to be so important that it provided for these functions a future "prince". There never was such a prince, however, and his cultic functions were taken over partly by the High Priest of the post-exilic period, though of course the High Priest was not actually king.

After Israel had spent a long time without any king or divine king ideology, therefore, it is obvious that memory of the events which accompanied the establishment of the monarchy, together with the later history of the monarchy, would not greatly favour the adoption of an oriental divine-king ideology at a later date.

It is therefore not surprising that the Old Testament account of the monarchy, even where it does not in so many words reject this ideology,[33] still generally recognizes its "mundane" character, and regards all kings as mortals bound to obey their God. This is the conclusion to which C. R. North comes in his study "The Religious Aspects of Hebrew Kingship"[34]; H. Frankfort too, in the short epilogue to *Kingship and the Gods*, stresses the secular character of the monarchy in Israel. The

---

[33] Polemic against the monarchy is a comparatively recent literary phenomenon in the Old Testament, even though we may surmise that the hostile attitude itself is much earlier. The fact that this attitude—not towards individual kings but towards the institution of monarchy as such—arose at all and could show itself, tells against any general or widespread conception of the divinity of the monarchy in Israel.

[34] In *Z.A.W.*, N.F. IX (1932), pp. 8ff., esp. pp. 36ff.

relationship of God and people, which forms the basis of the substantially pre-monarchic Pentateuchal tradition, and which consists of Israel's bond with God within the framework of the divine plan of salvation, does not require the mediatorial office of a cult-ritually active divine king.

This, of course, is not the end of the story. The divine kingship school can point to passages in the Old Testament which express some indication of a divine character of the monarchy. The most striking passages are, first of all, *Ps.* XLV.7 where, according to the accepted text—which should not without due cause be changed—the king is addressed as "God"; then there is *II Sam.* VII.14; and *Ps.* II.7 (perhaps also *Ps.* CX.3) where the Davidic king is designated as "Son" of God. Even though it be established that Israel did not originally have or recognize a "divine king", these references must be given due attention. It cannot be denied that Israel, after the occupation, later adopted elements from the conceptions and modes of thought of the native Canaanite tradition in Palestine. This happened particularly in the cultic field, even though not indiscriminately. The cultic agricultural festivals of Palestine were celebrated in Israel; the rhythm of agrarian life was very closely bound up with them, and it was in connection with them that the "cyclical thinking" of the ancient East found entry into Israel at that point where these festivals changed from their direct relationship to the simple annually recurring activities of harvest and in-gathering to the constantly repeated actualization of one-time historical events.[35]

According to the statements in *Deut.* XVI and *Lev.* XXIII it was not a matter of an annually repeated cult-ritual re-creation of the world—as we find in other ancient Oriental rites of the New Year—but a "remembrance" (*Deut.* XVI.3, 12) of the great and fundamental divine act of deliverance out of Egypt. However, the deuteronomic "remembrance" may really indicate a watering down and rationalizing of a much earlier cultic realism, for which these festivals were not simply commemorative days, but ever-new, current, actualizations of the fundamental act of salvation. Even though we may have reservations about the widely accepted view that a New Year and Enthrone-

---

[35] Cf. my "Die Vergegenwärtigung des Alten Testaments in der Verkündigung", in *Ev. Th.*, XII (1952-53), pp. 6-17.

ment festival (according to common ancient Oriental pattern and content) was adopted into its cult by ancient Israel, yet we must recognize an infiltration of ancient Oriental "cyclical thinking" in the definitely proven linking of cultic annual festivals with a one-time fundamental occasion in Israel's past. This must certainly have been transmitted through the medium of the traditions of the Syro-Palestinian cultural region; and in this context we find the specifically Israelite reference to the deliverance from Egypt taking the place of the ancient Oriental recapitulation of the creation. By means of the festival calendar of Israel this ancient Oriental pattern of thought and concept finally worked its way into the formulation of the Christian church calendar.

These points seem to me of real importance. It is possible to study many sides of this question of the adoption by the tribes of Israel of cultic traditions from the agricultural parts of the land, and of the thoughts and ideas which went along with them; but this would necessitate working out in detail the complicated relationship of repulsion and receptivity on the part of Israel towards things Canaanite. It will suffice here to establish that the possibility of Israel having taken over elements of an "agricultural" ideology bound up with the establishment of the monarchy cannot *a priori* be ruled out. We merely need to prove the existence of one such adoption.

We should never speak of "the monarchy" on Israelite soil. The Old Testament tradition plainly shows—and recent studies[36] have confirmed—that in Israel we are dealing with several monarchies, which are separate from one another not only geographically but also in type. Anyone wishing to make any statement about the nature of "the monarchy" in Israel should not overlook this point; and anyone seeking to trace any adoption of an ancient Oriental divine king ideology in Israel must try to define more closely the point at which such an adoption might have come in.

After the brief interlude of Saul's military monarchy (exercised over the confederacy of the twelve tribes of Israel), from David on we have mainly the two monarchies ruling the neighbouring kingdoms of Israel and Judah. As is shown by the later history of its monarchy, a leading idea in Israel was that only a man who

[36] Cf. especially Alt, *K.S.*, VOL. II, pp. 1ff.

had previously been singled out by the utterance of a prophet as the one called by Yahweh[37] could be elevated from amongst the people or elders to be king. This is what happened with Saul. And on occasions in Israel when a person so designated was lacking, and the natural bias towards founding a dynasty expressed itself, it always happened eventually that a newly-called individual appeared to take over the monarchy.[38] This would scarcely provide a point of attachment for Canaanite ideas of kingship. This kingship over a larger number of tribes had no native tradition behind it.[39] It rested basically on the willingness of the people or of its elders; and the divine call—as in the case of the so-called "(major) judges" of the pre-monarchic period—in no way conferred divinity on the kings—it implied a commission.

Alongside of the above, there existed since the time of David a kingship over the southern group of Israelite tribes in Judah. This differed from the one in the kingdom of Israel mainly in that here the house of David continuously retained possession of ruling power. But here too the monarchy was founded on the will of the people. The "men of Judah" had once "anointed [David] king" (cf. above, p. 164). After the downfall of Athaliah who, with her usurpation of rule, had been the only one to interrupt the sequence of Davidic descendants on the throne of Judah, the people in their congregation[40] "made him [the surviving Davidic prince Joash] king, and anointed him[41]; and they clapped their hands, and said, God save the king" (*II Kings* XI.12).

On occasion the '*am hā'āreṣ*, i.e. the whole Judaean citizenry,[42] would rise to ensure the legitimate succession to the throne amongst the house of David (*II Kings* XXI.24) and to "anoint and to make king" the rightful successor (*II Kings* XXIII.30); but this kingship over the group of southern states linked up with no

---

[37] This is so in the story of the raising of Jeroboam I to the kingship, according to *I Kings* XI.29-39, XII.1ff.

[38] Cf. *I Kings* XVI.2, and especially *II Kings* IX.1ff.

[39] The most likely city to consider would be Shechem. Jeroboam I did actually live there to begin with (*I Kings* XII.25), but soon abandoned this seat, and the Israelite kings did not thereafter return to Shechem.

[40] This subject is not expressly named, but the indefinite third person plural can scarcely be understood in any other sense.

[41] Cf. n. 32 above.

[42] Cf. E. Würthwein, *Der 'Am Ha'arez im Alten Testament*, 1936.

native tradition of the settled land. The ancient Judaean royal city of Hebron had indeed been a Canaanite city-state at one time, but had been taken over by the Calebites as early as the time of the occupation, and so had no longer any Canaanite royal tradition. Furthermore, dominion over a number of tribes in the Judaean hills was no Canaanite monarchy. What is true of the monarchy in the state of Israel must therefore be true in essence for this monarchy also.

Another monarchy of a different sort existed within the Israelite realm, however—the monarchy of the Davidic line in the city-state of Jerusalem. David and his warlike following had once conquered this former Canaanite city and made it his capital. It belonged to neither Israel nor Judah. It was indeed as a "neutral" city lying *between* the territories of these two states that it had been chosen by David. Consequently the city kingship over Jerusalem was an institution of its own alongside the kingships over Israel and Judah, and this city kingship over Jerusalem did indeed have a direct Canaanite tradition. When he conquered the city David joined the succession of hitherto Canaanite city-kings; it is consequently feasible to suppose that he adopted too their cult-ritual role within the local cult of Jerusalem. We do not, however, know much about the previous history of the monarchy in Canaanite Jerusalem.

Preserved in the Tell el-Amarna archives there are six letters from Abdi-ḥepa, King of the city-state of Jerusalem, addressed to the Egyptian Pharaoh.[43] When Abdi-ḥepa addresses his Egyptian overlord in these words, that he has "set his name at the rising of the sun and setting of the sun",[44] this merely tells us something about the Egyptian king, probably in the sense of his being an incarnation of the sun god, but not about the monarchy at Jerusalem.[45] But the Old Testament gives us the figure of

[43] Cf. J. A. Knudtzon, *Die El-Amarna Tafeln*, 1915, Nos. 285-290; *T.G.I.*, pp. 23-9, *A.N.E.T.*, pp. 487-9.

[44] Knudtzon, *op. cit.*, No. 288, 5-7; *T.G.I.*, p. 26; *A.N.E.T.*, p. 488.

[45] Cf. above, p. 157. Abdi-ḥepa frequently refers to himself by an Egyptian loan-word as an *u.e.u.* of the king (Knudtzon, *op. cit.*, Nos. 285,6; 287,69; 288,10; [*T.G.I.*, pp. 23ff.; *A.N.E.T.*, pp. 487ff.]). In this word Engnell (*Studies*, p. 86) finds an Egyptian priestly title, and so evidence for the sacral role of the king of the Jerusalem city-state. This, however, is probably wrong, since we have here the Egyptian word *wsw* which signifies a minor officer, and in the context of the texts must be an expression of the submissiveness of the Jerusalemite governor *vis-à-vis* the Egyptian overlord. In spite of Engnell's argument (*Studies*, p. 86, n. 7), the

Melchizedek, who is clearly a Canaanite king of the city-state of Jerusalem who lived on in the tradition of Jerusalem,[46] and of whom it is specifically said that he combined priesthood (in the Jerusalem cult) with the monarchy (*Gen.* xiv.18; *Ps.* cx.4). This combination clearly represented the Jerusalem tradition, but scarcely implied any unusual practice, and it may even have been usual in other Canaanite city-states. This combination does, however, appear to be remarkable in so far as the tribes of Israel are concerned. This is suggested at least by the solemn declaration in *Ps.* cx.4, in which the example of Melchizedek the Canaanite king of Jerusalem is affirmed for the combination of priestly functions with the monarchy. These priestly functions, of course, are no proof of the "divine" character of the king. The descendants of David appear in these priestly functions clearly as kings of Jerusalem, and priestly activities on the part of the king are confined in the Old Testament mainly to the Davidic kings of Jerusalem.

An important point in the discussion of this problem would be to know whether the Canaanite kingship of the city-state of Jerusalem was founded on a divine king ideology of the myth and ritual pattern. We have shown above (pp. 157ff.) that this could not be assumed in any Syro-Palestinian city-state, and there is no proof one way or the other for Jerusalem. What significance would it have had for the tribes of Israel, and for David's descendants as kings of Jerusalem, if kingship of Jerusalem *had* been founded on a divine king ideology? One could argue that for the Israelites it was of little moment, since the tribes were politically linked with the city-state of Jerusalem and its affairs only through the medium of the ruling Davidic king, and it might be left to him whether he considered that, as king of the city-state of Jerusalem, he could adopt the role of a "divine king"—though of course the question did not arise with respect to him as king of Israel or of Judah. We could ask whether the Davidic king was in a position to adopt even in

---

meaning of the word *ru-ḥi*, which occurs in the same context in No. 288, line 11 (*T.G.I.*, p. 26; *A.N.E.T.*, p. 488) appears to me uncertain; even if it were the Canaanite word for "shepherd", far-reaching consequences could scarcely be drawn from it, for the metaphorical expression "I am a shepherd of the king" is susceptible of various meanings.

[46] The commonly accepted view, that in the "Salem" of *Gen.* xiv.18 we should see Jerusalem, is most probably correct.

Jerusalem such a role, which did not accord with Israelite tradition.

There was another reason, however, why the nature of the Jerusalem monarchy was of importance for the Israelite tribes. In the royal sanctuary of this city stood the sacred Ark, which had been and remained the ancient cultic focus of the tribes, and which David had transferred to his city of Jerusalem. It could by no means be immaterial for "Israel" whether here before the Ark the king did or did not appear and act in the ritual as god incarnate. Furthermore, the personal union between the city-state of Jerusalem and at least the kingdom of Judah under Davidic overlordship endured so long that the cultic situation of the kings in Jerusalem must in the long run have been decisive for the kingship in the Judaean state.

It has been maintained that the kingship of the Davidic monarchs in Jerusalem supplied the crucial point at which the ancient oriental divine king ideology in its normative Syro-Palestinian development gained entrance into the Israelite domain. And furthermore that in spite of the special position of the city-state kingship, the role of the royal sanctuary in Jerusalem as the cultic focus of the tribes served to transmit this ideology to the wider tribal circle. Can the adoption of elements from a divine king ideology be demonstrated from the Old Testament? The firm, plain tradition of the historically conditioned monarchy does not really support it. To this may be added that the important historical narratives about David, which state so clearly that David "was made king" in Judah as well as in Israel by the representatives of the tribes, and that the conquest of Jerusalem was an act of war without any sacral inauguration, in all probability arose from among the court circles of David and Solomon in Jerusalem, and were then transmitted in Jerusalem also. The divinity of the monarchy, on this showing, was clearly not something widely accepted at the Jerusalem court.

If we consider next the positive arguments put forward in favour of the divine kingship theory, we shall have to exclude all those which merely say something about the priestly functions of the king. For although these mainly refer to Jerusalem, since this is a matter of pre-Israelite observance and the kings of Israel and Judah (so far as is known) hardly served as priests,[47] yet they do not in any way prove anything about the divinity of the king-ship; on the contrary, they merely show that the king stood at the head of his subjects in the sacred sphere also.

The declaration of the king as "Son of God" presents a different problem. This relates to the Davidic king in Jerusalem, and is attested above all by *Ps.* II.7, and may also have stood in the original form of the textually corrupt passage *Ps.* CX.3. In *Ps.* II.7 there occurs a formula of adoption—also possibly in *Ps.* CX.3. This is important, for it means that the king was not by nature a "son" of God, nor did he by natural necessity enter the sphere of divinity through his enthronement, but was *declared* to be a "son" by a deliberate decision of Israel's God at his accession. Yet here the Davidic kings approached to a very close relationship with the sphere of the divine, and at this point, in all probability, we *do* have the influence of ancient Near Eastern divine king ideology.

From this point on we may perhaps indirectly conclude that the Canaanite royal tradition in Jerusalem was aware of the conception of the divinity of the person of the king; for that is the only ground from which we can understand the remarkable expressions about the Davidic kings in Jerusalem, which differ so greatly from the conceptions about the nature of the mon-archies in the realms of Israel and Judah. At all events we find a very characteristic and important modification of the trans-ferred divine king ideology if we do accept such an assumption with respect to pre-Davidic Jerusalem. The use of the formula of adoption shows that the Davidic king in Jerusalem was not god incarnate, was not of divine origin or nature, but is designated "son" by a gracious assent of his God. In this modification, there-

---

[47] King Jeroboam I of Israel appears indeed once with priestly function in his new royal sanctuary of Bethel (*I Kings* XII.33), though admittedly only in the late, post-Josianic prophetic legend *I Kings* XII.32-XIII.32 and *II Kings* XXIII.16-18, whose historical reliability is scarcely great. Furthermore we might here have nothing more than an imitation of the role of the Davidic dynasty in Jerusalem. Nor have we in any case any certain evidence that Saul had any experience of priestly office. The late insertion *I Sam.* XIII.7b-15a however is hardly to be regarded as historical. It is written from the standpoint that it was *not* permissible for the king to take on priestly functions, and seeks to make the quarrel between Saul and Samuel a secondary matter. Accordingly Saul offered sacrifice unjustifiably and with an evil conscience. It is not probable that any ancient historical tradition of Saul having actually offered sacrifice underlies this interpolation.

fore, we have less a proof of a Davidic divine king in Jerusalem than indeed an indication of a *rejection* of real divine king ideology, even though a certain concession is made to an existing royal tradition in Jerusalem. The ambiguous "sit thou at my right hand" in *Ps.* cx.1 must be interpreted accordingly. Even though this formula may derive from some pre-Davidic royal ritual in Jerusalem in the context of *Ps.* cx it has to be understood simply in the sense of a peculiar honouring of the king on the part of his God, not as setting the king on a par with God.

The formula of adoption—in a form differing from *Ps.* ii.7, and yet still clearly a formula of adoption—appears again in *II Sam.* vii.14. Probably this verse does not belong to the original form of the so-called prophecy of Nathan in *II Sam.* vii,[48] but has been taken in (not without relevance) in the later expansion of this passage. For the Nathan oracle, too, clearly concerns the Davidic monarchy of Jerusalem specifically. The "prophet" Nathan is met with in *II Sam.* xii.1ff., and especially *II Sam.* xii.25 and *I Kings* 1.8, 10ff., at the court of Jerusalem in David's close circle. In the original Nathan oracle David is promised that Yahweh will "build him a house", i.e. found a dynasty for him (vs. 11*b*), and that this house will endure "for ever" (vs. 16). We are not told in detail what is the envisaged extent of the Davidic kingdom. The whole extent of the full kingdom of David is meant, but from the viewpoint of the Jerusalem circle. The author of the great historical work concerning the question of David's successors on the throne records this oracle of Nathan and proceeds from there, because the burning question as to David's immediate successor is so far illumined that only one of David's sons is to be considered for the succession. Nathan's oracle in itself scarcely envisaged such a directly practical aim, but, as its wording shows, it deals with the Davidic monarchical institution and its future on a broad scale. It contains the promise of permanence which, in view of the historical and personal circumstances of the monarchy's establishment, is almost unbelievable.

Is it mistaken to suppose here once again a deviating from a conception of the divinity of the monarchy as was expressed in

---

[48] Following the literary critical analysis of L. Rost: *Die Überlieferung von der Thronnachfolge Davids*, (henceforth cited as *Thronnachfolge*) B.W.A.N.T., 1926, pp. 47ff., *Ps.* lxxxix.27ff. may be dependent on *II Sam.* vii.14.

the Jerusalem tradition of the monarchy? According to this oracle, the monarchy was not divine, nor the king a god incarnate; but the promise of unlimited continuation did indeed raise the institution of this monarchy out of the realm of the vicissitudes of human history and brought it close to the sphere of the divine. This again does entail that the royal ideology of pre-Davidic Jerusalem was not adopted, but that it did exercise an indirect influence.

It is recognized that the substance of Nathan's oracle has had a strong influence. Messianic expectation links up with it. It certainly has its origin in the Davidic monarchy of Jerusalem, but in all probability envisaged the whole kingdom ruled by David. This is the sense, too, in which it is understood in messianic pronouncements. Although these are found exclusively in the prophets of Judah, after Solomon's death only the state of Judah remained in alliance with the Davidic dynasty resident in Jerusalem. The substance of messianic pronouncements likewise remained "Magna-Israelitish" in outlook; and the connection between the ancient tribal sanctuary containing the Ark and the Davidic capital may also have lifted the eyes of the tribes beyond the narrow confines of the state of Judah to the Davidic house, and the promise partially fulfilled for it. What link, then, connected the promises to the house of David and the expectations of the older tradition of Israel as a whole?

In his *Sinaibund und Davidsbund*,[49] L. Rost attacked this complex of questions and drew attention to the problem that lies before us here. He comes to the conclusion that there was for the time being a simultaneity of validity in "Sinai covenant" and "Davidic covenant", which spread to the states of Israel and Judah. *Vis-à-vis* the local connection of the Ark with David's capital, this solution is perhaps too simple; and we must rather consider that, within the tradition held by Israel as a whole, the expectations bound up with the promises to David's house presented themselves in the ancient traditional relationship of God and people as a particular element referring more and more to the future, wherever and whenever adopted in Israelite tribal circles.

We still need to maintain, therefore, that divinity was never accorded to the Jerusalem kingship, let alone the monarchy in

---

[49] In *Th. Lz.*, LXXII (1947), cols. 129-34.

Israel and Judah. If that is proved, it means that the king is not to be thought of as being addressed as "God" in *Ps.* xlv.7, although here, in the middle of a psalm the first half of which addresses the king, there does occur the phrase whose simplest rendering would be, "Thy throne, O God, is for ever and ever". But it is questionable whether this phrase should be so understood,[50] as it appears to be unique in the whole of the Old Testament. There is a possible textual emendation recommended by many commentators, but I feel reluctant to accept it, since it is not really likely that such an extraordinary and objectionable expression would be introduced into the text by inadvertence. But we may indeed enquire whether we are not dealing with a shortened form of expression such as may be paralleled in the Old Testament,[51] so that the phrase should be interpreted, "Thy throne is (like) God's (throne), that is, enduring for ever and ever". In that case what we have here is the promise of the permanence of the monarchy, known from Nathan's oracle, and this would then connect *Ps.* xlv also in our minds with the Jerusalem kingship of David's line. In no case can the phrase in *Ps.* xlv.7*a* bear the whole burden of the thesis of a *divine* kingship in Israel.

The fact that we appear to have deviations from conceptions of a divine king ideology, applied in the Old Testament to the Jerusalem monarchy, is stronger evidence that this ideology itself was really not accepted on Israelite soil, and that it could not be accepted on the basis of Old Testament belief. This then makes it unnecessary to suppose that the king in the ritual specifically embodied the dying and rising god, and actually enacted his death and renewed life. Consequently there is no need to understand the laments in the *Book of Psalms* as royal psalms presenting the king in a situation of cultic ritual surrender to the power of death. The wording of the laments themselves scarcely provides support for any such application to the king.

It is as well, therefore, not to regard the hypothesis of the divinity of the monarchy in the ancient Near East or in Israel as a self-evident assumption of Old Testament exegesis. On the contrary indeed this appears to be a field in which the Old

[50] A very thorough investigation of this passage by C. R. North is to be found in *Z.A.W.*, N.F. ix (1932), pp. 27ff.

[51] Cf. North, *op. cit.*, p. 30.

Testament did not take over views which were current, though possibly not everywhere prevalent, in the lands of Near Eastern civilization. This may have been an attitude shared with all those "younger nations" which moved into the Syro-Palestinian sphere of culture at the beginning of the Iron Age, though it might equally have proceeded from the particular conditions typified in the Old Testament. It is certain that the ancient Oriental world in general possessed common mental attitudes and modes of thought such as are no longer self-explanatory to us today so that we need first to ascertain them scientifically if we wish to understand their forms of expression. But in the historical diversity of human life it is most unlikely that a developed cultic ritual scheme, such as the Myth and Ritual school suppose, should through many centuries have spread across the whole of the ancient Near East. It is more important to apprehend the specific characteristics of kingship as they appear, than it is to seek for any uniform beliefs and practices. Only in this way can we do justice to the Old Testament within the ancient Near Eastern world.

There is one final question, which cannot be answered here but which arises from the matters discussed, and which needs a thorough investigation. When we read the massive book by H. Riesenfeld—*Jésus transfiguré* (1947)—in which the revelation of Jesus in a messianic sense is interpreted against the background of ancient Near Eastern divine king ideology, we are strongly impressed by the almost overpowering amount of material which the learned author is able to adduce from post-canonical Jewish and rabbinic literature to support the thesis that this literature was aware of and presupposes all the cultic ritual content of that ideology, in worship and thought-mode and concept. Riesenfeld was convinced that all that survived was known to Israel, and held in common with the whole of the ancient Near East. He rejected the idea, therefore, that this material might have found its way into the post-canonical writings only at a later date. He may well be correct in this rejection, for there is not much to be said for the supposition of a mechanical acceptance of foreign ideas, since there must at least be points of contact presumed from which the assimilation of foreign views and customs may proceed. Some, however, may not think it right to maintain an early date for concepts with late provenance, unless there is definite verification; those who are unable to find in the Old Testament the idea of a divine kingship, with all its functions and ramifications, will not be able to accept Riesenfeld's arguments. They would particularly question that the late Jewish allusions and forms of expression go back to a close-knit system of concepts and ideas, or that they are "disintegrated" elements of an older system. They will therefore have to seek an explanation for the late emergence of numerous (and in some instances quite weighty) customs and opinions.

It will be recalled in this connection that in other cases the appearance of comparatively ancient ideas, not known to the Old Testament, may be observed in post-canonical Jewish writings—as, for example, in the sphere of angelology and demonology. Here it is clearly not a matter simply of late growths, but rather of further development and transformations of ancient material belonging to the ancient Near Eastern world of thought.[52] Are we here dealing with vestiges of a mass of popular beliefs which existed in Israel, but had officially been rejected by the Israelite confederacy of tribes, until they eventually found their way into post-canonical Judaism? Should we perhaps bear in mind that, on the score of faith, ancient Israel stood in opposition and aversion to ancient Oriental ideas, but that this attitude relaxed during times of decadence? Did the Old Testament faith so entrench itself with the passage of time, did it feel so secure on account of its canonical scripture, that it was able to display a readier toleration toward many popular concepts? Should we perhaps infer that the ancient secluded Israel of the twelve tribes knew how to guard its uniqueness and distinctiveness, and that it was only the disintegration of this ancient Israel and the rise of a widely distributed Diaspora which favoured the acceptance of current popular concepts of the ancient Near Eastern world?[53]

Such questions as these must here be left open. Indeed there may be no clear single answer, since life is always many-sided

---

[52] Aage Bentzen (*King and Messiah*) has studied this matter under the heading " 'Renaissance of Mythology' in later Judaism"; though indeed, by giving it this heading, he has imparted to it a definite bias which should not be lightly accepted.

[53] In this case it should be borne in mind that these concepts might not have been adopted unchanged. Riesenfeld speaks (*Jésus transfiguré*, Copenhagen 1947, pp. 239ff.), not without justification, of a spiritualizing and eschatologizing of ancient cult-ritual *motifs* in late Judaism.

and complex. But the importance of the questions becomes clear if we cease to accept the hypothesis of a general pre-established scheme of concepts and ideas, which continued on and on in an essentially changeless form, and which Israel shared with the whole ancient Near Eastern world. Earlier I have tried to show briefly that such a scheme cannot be taken for granted. Even the inclusion of post-canonical writings can hardly salvage the assumption that an obvious divine king ideology was current in Israel from the very beginning.

VI

History and Word of God in the Old Testament

In 1819, when the Protestant theological faculty in Bonn was being built up step by step, Johannes Christian Wilhelm Augusti was appointed, as the first Professor of Old Testament Studies. He was elected Rector of the University in the same year, and was the first member of the teaching body ever to be elected to that post.[1] Like all the evangelical Protestant theological faculties of that time he took the role of mediator in all the differences of opinion and conflicting standpoints of the time. He wholly supported the literary criticism of the books of the Old Testament that was then developing, but on the other hand he clearly disavowed the customary rationalistic approach, and worked along the lines of the tradition of the Christian Church. In his many published works we are faced with a conception of the Old Testament which, opposed to all extreme one-sided views, can be seen as a popular middle-of-the road conception, even if it is not particularly original.

Already in his work *Grundriss einer historisch-kritischen Einleitung in's Alte Testament*, published in 1806, he had formulated especially clearly his concept of the historical position of the Old Testament, which could scarcely have been improved in those times. In his view the Old Testament arose from a civilization belonging to the prehistory of mankind, of which nothing else is known apart from what is learnt from the Old Testament:

> The Old Testament is the oldest record of the human spirit.
> Here the annals of literature have their beginning, and here
> for the first time we glimpse also the genesis of literary
> culture in the rest of the world (*Para.* 10).

[1] Concerning him cf. Fr. von Bezold: *Geschichte der rheinischen Friedrich-Wilhelms Universität von der Gründung bis zum Jahre 1870* (1920), pp. 183ff.; O. Ritschl: *Die evangelisch-theologische Fakultät zu Bonn im ersten Jahrhundert ihrer Geschichte*, 1819-1919 (1919). pp. 7ff., 88.

A vague historical world looms on the very fringe of the Old Testament, but it is only known to us through what the Old Testament itself actually tells us about it. Augusti continues:

> The Old Testament provides us with a most agreeably diverse picture of the manners and customs of the ancient world. It does this by revealing in an instructive manner the national characteristics of the most prominent Asiatic peoples beyond the borders of Palestine (*Para.* 12).

Nevertheless the people of the Old Testament remain the most ancient of all known peoples. This is shown by the following observation concerning language: "The Ebrew or Hebrew language . . . is the oldest of all known languages", though it has to be admitted that "the language, for so long thought to be the mother of all, was after all only the eldest sister" (*Para.* 19). At this point indeed this learned Orientalist, who had started as a university lecturer in Oriental languages in Jena at the age of twenty-six, turns against the then popular conception of Hebrew as the original language, and examines the relationship between Hebrew and the other Semitic languages. Indeed, he is quite convinced of a historical development of Hebrew, and recognizes that attention must be given to "the variations of linguistic usage, and to archaic, Syriac, Arabic, and Persian turns of expression...".[2] But in accordance with what was known at the time, it was inevitable that Hebrew should still appear to him as the oldest of all languages.

All this serves to show how completely our ideas have changed as a result of the rapid expansion of our historical knowledge. Ancient Oriental scholarship, in many cases admittedly spurred on by interest in the Old Testament though in the main independent of the data given there, has been able to develop its many branches of study on the basis of numerous original discoveries and documents. In this context the Old Testament is seen to have arisen only at a relatively late stage of the long troubled history of the ancient Orient; the history of Israel emerges as continually dependent on the various situations and movements in the history of the ancient Near East, and the language and literature of the Old Testament are revealed as genuine ancient Oriental material.

[2] See *Versuch einer historisch-dogmatischen Einleitung in die Heilige Schrift*, 1832, p. 69.

The origins of the Israelite people must now be sought in the history of the ancient Near East in the second millennium B.C., a period which is gradually becoming quite well known. Discoveries of written documents have helped to illuminate these origins. Towards the end of the last century the clay tablets of Tell el-Amarna in Egypt—letters of different Near Eastern kings and, most important, of numerous Palestinian and Syrian vassal-princes of the Pharaoh—threw a great deal of light on the political situation in Palestine and Syria at the time immediately before the occupation of territory in this region by the Israelite tribes, a situation which is of the utmost significance with regard to this occupation, and even beyond this to the whole of Israelite history. In this way the external framework for the earliest history of Israel becomes plain.

More closely connected with the content of the Old Testament was the discovery in 1929 of numerous clay tablets, bearing alphabetical cuneiform characters, at the ruins of Ras Shamra on the north Syrian coast. These cultic mythological texts from Ras Shamra revealed for the first time original historical material from the Canaanite world, from a time immediately before the occupation by the Israelites. These discoveries also confirmed in many details that Israel had not only adopted the Canaanite language of the land and culture which it entered, but also had opposed the cultic traditions of this culture only at certain very specific points, while taking over a great deal in Canaanite worship. These texts take us right to the heart of the environment of the Old Testament but there is one still more recent discovery of written materials which, I believe, leads us right back to the prehistory of the people of Israel.

There appears to have been some sort of relationship between the Israelite tribes and those ruling classes which established the first dynasty of Babylon in Mesopotamia. Both groups have the same characteristic way of forming proper names.[3] Mesopotamian rulers clearly came from the steppe and desert region along the middle Euphrates, for along the middle Euphrates at that time we find the same characteristic proper names occurring in large numbers.[4] At first, however, the distance in space and time

---

[3] Cf. my *Die israelitischen Personennamen im Rahmen der gemeinsemitischen Namengeburg*, B.W.A.N.T. III, No. 10, pp. 27ff., 43ff.

[4] For more exact details cf. Th. Bauer: *Die Ostkanaanäer*, 1926.

separating these ruling classes in Mesopotamia from the
Israelite tribes seemed to be so great that any historical connection was hard to envisage. Recently, however, some important connecting links have been found. The so-called Egyptian
execration texts of the period of the Egyptian twelfth dynasty
showed that in the nineteenth and eighteenth centuries B.C.
relatives of this same Babylonian upper class—who again bear
these highly characteristic proper names—also appeared in
Syria and Palestine as a new element of the population. This
seems to show that at that time both Mesopotamia in the east
and Syria and Palestine in the west were populated by tribes
which originated from the same region.[5] Clearly it is in this
region therefore that the prehistory of the Israelite tribes must
be sought.

In 1933 French excavations were begun at some ruins on a
hill overlooking the middle Euphrates, which today has the
name of Tell Ḥarīri. It appeared that this hill covered the
remains of the city of Mari, which for a time was the royal
residence and state capital. The remains of the state archives
here were discovered with over 20,000 cuneiform tablets. The
publication and study of this most surprising and unusually
extensive discovery of public records will still take a great deal
of time, but it is clear that these tablets (particularly those containing the official correspondence of the different kings of
Mari), not only shed considerable light on the general historical
situation of that time, but also provide us with more precise
evidence about the relationship between the Mari invaders and
the later Israelite tribes. In particular, the Mari texts show that
the difference in time separating them is considerably shorter
than was formerly imagined. It has been proved from these texts
that the first Babylonian dynasty must be dated centuries later
than had formerly been supposed, and this of course brings the
historical events of the second millennium before Christ much
closer together. The Mari texts belong to the end of the eighteenth
century B.C. They show that the kings and upper classes of Mari
on the middle Euphrates, as well as the neighbouring tribes in
the Syro-Arabian desert, belonged to the same circles as the
first Babylonian dynasty, and those contemporary elements in

---

[5] Cf. my *Die syrisch-palästinische Bevölkerung des zweiten Jahrtausends vor Christi, im
Lichte neuer Quellen*, in *Z.D.P.V.*, LXV (1942), pp. 20ff.

Syria and Palestine which appear in the Egyptian execration texts.

The Mari texts also show certain very striking connections with the world of the Old Testament. Names and words occur in them which are otherwise encountered only in the Old Testament. Here they seem to be in quite common use.[6] A large group of tribes bordering on the state of Mari is mentioned frequently in the texts under the name "Benjaminites" (banū-yaminā).[7] This is not to suggest that they are probably the ancestors of the later Israelite tribe of Benjamin; but the use of Benjamin as a tribal name, meaning really "those living in the south",[8] is common to both. To signify a military chief, the word dāwidūm* is found in the Mari manuscripts. This must certainly be the same word that is known from the Old Testament as a proper name, and as the name of King David[9]. The name Noah is met in its phonetically more original form nāḥ. A closer examination of the actual nature of these relationships is still necessary, but it can hardly be doubted that there are definite connections.

Over and above these very noteworthy (though not very conclusive) comparisons of names, the Mari texts also mention prophecy, which obviously cannot be separated from that very significant element of the Old Testament. This phenomenon must now be considered more closely, with particular reference to three of the published texts.

In the first of these texts,[10] Itur-asdu (the governor of the royal city of Mari) sends the following information to his king, who is apparently away at war. A man, whose name and homeland are given, has come to him and informed him that he has had a dream, and in this dream he has seen himself in the sanctuary

[6] For general information concerning the Mari texts cf. W. von Soden, "Das altbabylonische Briefarchiv von Mari", in Die Welt des Orients III (1948), pp. 187ff.; also my "Mari und Israel" in Geschichte und Altes Testament (Bei H.Th. 16, 1953).

[7] Cf. G. Dossin in Mélanges syriens offerts à René Dussaud, VOL. II, 1939, pp. 981ff.

[8] This long-standing interpretation of the name is borne out in the Mari texts in so far as the corresponding tribal name "those living in the north" also occurs in them.

[9] This interpretation of davidum is now known to be false; so the proposed identification with the name David cannot stand. See H. Tadmor in Journal of Near Eastern Studies XVII (1958), pp. 129ff.—Tr.

[10] Published and discussed by G. Dossin, in Revue d'Assyriologie, XLII (1948), pp. 125ff.

* Now proved to be a non-existent word, mis-transliterated by Assyriologists.

of the god Dagan in the city of Tirka. This god asked him a question, which he answered, and then charged him as follows: "Now go! I am sending you to Zimri-lim [the king of Mari] and you yourself shall say to him: 'Send your messengers to me and submit all your affairs to me'. Then shall the god Dagan give the King victory over the hostile Benjaminites."

By the side of this must be placed a second shorter text which I will give in translation in its entirety, in order to convey some idea of the nature of these texts:

> Say to my lord [i.e. to King Zimri-lim]: Thy slave Kibri-Dagan [has said] the following: The god Dagan and the god Ikrub-il are both safe and sound. The city of Tirka and all around [it] are safe and sound. Furthermore: On the day when I was bringing this my tablet to my lord, a *muḫḫûm-man* of the god Dagan came and said a word to me as follows: the god has sent me [charging me thus]: inform the King quickly, sacrifices of the dead shall be made to the shade of Yaḫdun-lim. Thus hath this *muḫḫûm*-man spoken to me. I am thus informing my lord. May my lord do as he thinks fit.[11]

Finally this same Kibri-Dagan informs the King, in what is unfortunately only a very fragmentary text,[12] that a man of the god Dagan[13] has come to him and said: "The god Dagan has sent me [charging me thus]: Send to your lord . . .", and here again follows a definite command.[14]

In these texts therefore we meet the figure of a messenger of

---

[11] Cf. *Archives royales de Mari III*, 1948, No. 40. In transcription the text runs as follows:

¹[a-n]a be-lí-ia ²ḳí-bí-ma ³um-ma Ki-ib-ri-ᵈDa-gan ⁴warad-ka-a-ma ⁵ᵈDa-gan ù ᵈIk-ru-ub-il [ša]-al-mu ⁶a-lum Ti[r-ḳ]aki ù ḫa-al-ṣú-(um) ša-lim ⁷ša-ni-tam ûmum ṭup-pí an-ni-e-im ⁸a-na [ṣ]i-ir be-lí-ia ú-ša-bi-lam ⁹awîlum mu-uḫ-ḫu-um ša ᵈDa-gan ¹⁰il-li-[i]k-ma ¹¹a-wa-tam ki-a-am iḳ-bi-[e-im] ¹²um-ma-a-mi ¹³ilumlum iš-pu-ra-an-[ni] ¹⁴ḫu-mu-uṭ a-na šar[rim] ¹⁵šu-pu-ur-ma ¹⁶ki-is-pí a-na i-te₄-im-m[i-im] ¹⁷ša Ia-aḫ-du-un-li-[im] ¹⁸li-ik-ru-bu ¹⁹an-ni-tam awîlum mu-uḫ-ḫu-um šu-ú ²⁰iḳ-bi-e-im-ma a-na be-lí-ia ²¹aš-ta-ap-ra-am ²²be-lí ša e-li-šu ṭà-ba-at ²³li-pu-úš.

[12] *Archives Royales de Mari II*, Paris 1941, No. 90.

[13] Here unfortunately the text has been very poorly preserved. It could be that in front of the words *saᵈ Da-gan* (l. 17) was perhaps *awilum muhhum* as in the previous text (l. 9).

[14] The text reads in lines 19-20: "ᵈDa-gan iš-pu-[ra-an-ni] a-na be-lí-ka šu-pu-ur-ma. The complete texts with translation can be found in W. v. Soden: "Verkündung des Gotteswillens durch prophetisches Wort in den altbabylonischen Briefen aus Mari", in *Die Welt des Orients*, 1950, pp. 397-403.

God, who, without being either questioned or requested, suddenly appears with some specific divine charge. In the whole of the ancient Near East there is not, as far as I can see, any other exact parallel to this phenomenon. There is that scene in the Phoenician city of Byblos on the sea-coast where the Egyptian Wen-Amon, describing his voyage along the Palestine-Syrian coast, says:

> While he [i.e. the king of Byblos] was offering sacrifices to his gods, the god himself seized one of his noble youths, making him frenzied, and he said: "Bring the god up to me; bring the messenger who has of him! It is Amon who has sent him, he it is who has brought him!"[15]

Here also we seem to have a divine message announced spontaneously. This report by Wen-Amon, however, is only from the time around 1,100 B.C. and the events revealed in it seem to us to be somewhat isolated. It is not impossible that they have some distant historical connection with the phenomena in the Mari texts, since relatives of the population in and around Mari also went to Syria and Palestine. Nevertheless the emergence of this man in Byblos is not wholly clear, and thus observations cannot be made with any certainty.

The similarity between these messengers of God in the middle Euphrates with the Old Testament prophets cannot be denied. They, too, categorically state that they are the messengers of God; they too proclaim the prophecy with which they have been charged, without being asked or requested. The usual introduction to their prophecy—"Thus saith the Lord"—is the traditional formula by which a messenger is represented as a man charged to give a verbal message.[16] The agreement between the two even extends to the actual wording of the statements to be made. When the man in the first Mari text hears the god Dagan speaking to him in the vision in the following words: "Go, I am sending you to Zimri-lim, as follows shalt thou say", then we are reminded of the command which the prophet Jeremiah hears when he is called in a vision: ". . . for thou shalt go to all that I shall send thee and whatsoever I command thee thou shalt speak" (*Jer.* 1.7), or of the command which the prophet Ezekiel

---

[15] Translated in *A.O.T.* p. 72; *T.G.I.*, p. 381; A.N.E.T., p. 26.
[16] Cf. L. Köhler: *Deuterojesaja stilkritisch untersucht*, Bei *Z.A.W.*, No. 37, 1923, pp. 102ff.

receives: "I do send thee unto them [i.e. the Israelites]; and thou shalt say unto them, Thus saith the Lord God" (*Ezek.* 11.4).

When in the second and third Mari texts the messenger of the god proves his authenticity to the royal officials, stressing that he was called, by saying: "God has sent me" or "The god Dagan has sent me", we are reminded that the Old Testament prophets used almost the same words in stressing the nature of their calling, or when their authenticity was doubted, or whenever their hard words provoked bitter opposition. There is a striking example of this in *Jer.* XXVI. The harsh judgment of Jeremiah against the Temple of Jerusalem so aroused the priests and the cult ecstatics of the sanctuary that they wanted to take his life. In the ensuing discussion before the royal officials all Jeremiah says in his defence is: "The Lord sent me" (vs. 12), and then again: "for, of a truth, the Lord hath sent me unto you to speak all these words in your ears" (vs. 15).

These can hardly be chance agreements, particularly as nothing comparable has been found anywhere else in the whole of the ancient Near East. Thus it can hardly be doubted that the figure of the messenger of God now made known to us in the Mari texts reappears in the prophets of the Old Testament. These messengers of God are not merely parallel figures to the Old Testament prophets, they actually form a part of the pre-history to prophecy. We must therefore consider here a historical connection, particularly as there exist such striking links between the Mari texts and the Old Testament. It is not possible to fix the exact nature of this historical connection, for the difference in time between the two is still relatively large, but future discoveries may bring further enlightenment. For the time being we shall have to be satisfied with the more general fact that in all probability the origins of the Israelite tribes are to be found in those circles which clearly emerge for the first time in history at the time of the first dynasty of Babylon, in the lands situated around the edges of the Syro-Arabian desert. It is clear, therefore, that the figure of the prophet who plays such a central part in the Old Testament has some sort of prehistory and is conditioned by historical events. Thus the great significance of the discovery of the Mari texts is clearly that it has not only brought to light more knowledge of the historical and religious civilizations

surrounding the Old Testament, but also begins to throw light
on the origins of Israel and significant elements of Israelite life
and belief.

As soon as we accept a historical connection between this
messenger of God and the Old Testament prophet, the great
difference between the two figures immediately becomes
manifest. This difference does not lie in the way in which they
actually appear, but in the content of what is announced as a
divine message. The Mari texts deal with political and cultic
matters of very limited and ephemeral significance. The command of the god Dagan imparted in the vision is intended to
bring about fuller recognition of the god's sanctuary in the city
of Tirka, where apparently it had not received enough attention
from the King. The King is to lay everything before the god
Dagan, and keep messengers constantly in his sanctuary who can
pass on to him any information given by the oracle in the sanctuary. The editor[17] has suggested that this text is a purely
fictitious decree, by which the priests of Dagan in Tirka hoped
to push their sanctuary into a more prominent position. There is
no plausible reason for accepting this, but even if there were, this
"pious deception" could still only have had the desired effect if
the people of those days accepted it as a possibility that a man
could be so charged by God in a dream. In the second of the
texts, the divine message demands that sacrifices for the dead be
brought for the shade of a former king of Mari, Yaḥdun-lim, who
had been murdered. No reason is given for this, though we may
suspect that perhaps some calamity had been traced back to the
damaging intervention of the shade of Yaḥdun-lim, who must
therefore be appeased with sacrifices.

At all events we can still compare this with the divine messages
of the two men, who according to the Old Testament appeared
occasionally before David as "prophets", turning to the King
just as the divine messengers of Mari had done. Following the
census which David had ordained in his realm of Israel and
Judah, the prophet Gad had appeared before him in the name of
his God, in order that he should choose from three different
calamities a punishment for impiously undertaking this census.
Shortly afterwards God appeared again before the King to
charge him with the erection of an altar in a particular place,

[17] Cf. above, p. 183, note 10.

in order to halt the plague (*II Sam.* xxiv.11ff., 18ff.). Then according to the traditional text of *II Sam.* vii.4ff., the "prophet" Nathan was instructed one night (i.e. in a dream) to pass on a divine message to King David that a temple which he proposed to erect for the Ark in Jerusalem did not have God's approval. The fact that the "prophet" Nathan was sent to David after his adultery with the wife of one of his subordinates, to reveal his guilt before God in very serious words (*II Sam.* xii.1ff.), shows a depth and earnestness which go far beyond anything we know about the divine messengers of Mari. The same is true of the punitive words of Elijah against the infidelity and law-breaking of King Ahab of Israel.

The words of the Old Testament "writing prophets", in particular, can in no way be compared with the statements of the Mari divine messengers. They deal with guilt and punishment, being and non-being, the present and the future of the Israelite people as a people chosen for a special service by God; they also seek to explain the present great and stirring world events as taking place according to the will of God, leading to a future goal which is itself also the will of God. Even where the prophets impart instructions for practical activity in some definite contemporary situation, they still keep this wider connection in mind. Since in general they do not speak of fundamentals or in comprehensive generalizations, but bring some definite message concerning one particular situation, their decrees generally deal with some specific announcement conditioned by the historical situation; nevertheless these particular decrees do have some connection with the larger field of God's planned intervention in history. Whether they are predicting and interpreting the coming events at the time of the emergence of the Assyrian power in Syria and Palestine, or whether they are demanding a particular course of action in face of the attacks of the Neo-Babylonian King Nebuchadnezzar, they always speak in the name of God, who alone controls the great powers of world history, and on whose will all the forces and movements of history are dependent.

These prophets stand on an incomparably higher plane than Mari's divine messengers.[18] Yet a fundamental question arises

[18] Cf. H. W. Wolff, "Hauptprobleme alttestamentlicher Prophetie", in *Ev.Th.* xv (1955), pp. 448ff.

here which crops up repeatedly with the increasing knowledge of the historical environment of the Old Testament. The history of Israel has shown itself as completely dependent at any given moment on the general situation in the ancient Near East. As we now know for certain, the language of the Old Testament was neither a holy language nor an original language of mankind, nor was it even the eldest sister in the family of Oriental languages. In fact it appeared relatively late amongst the Semitic dialects, quite apart from other ancient non-Semitic languages of the ancient Near East. It has been shown that the forms of divine worship in Israel, with all its institutions and activities, for the most part go back to old (pre-Israelite) Syrian or Palestinian tradition.

It now appears that this historical dependence had a still more profound effect on the essential content of the Old Testament, and that even the figure of the prophet as the central agent of the word of God in the Old Testament had its prehistory outside Israel. For a long time we have been able to point to different religious phenomena such as soothsayers, oracles, seers, and ecstatics in any comparison with Old Testament prophecy, thereby explaining certain elements in our picture of this prophecy; the very essence of the question, however, is that the prophets saw themselves as messengers of God and formulated their decrees accordingly. In the Mari texts the figure clearly emerges of a divine messenger, in a realm which seems to have a historical connection with later Israel. Merely to say that the words of the Old Testament prophets are very much richer and deeper and have a higher significance than the words of the divine messengers of the Mari texts, in no way overcomes the fundamental problem that, in this connection between the divine messengers and the prophets, the qualitative difference between the Old Testament and its historical and religious environment is removed. According to biblical tradition, however, where there is only an Either-Or, a Yes or No, Divine Truth or Human Error, the true direct word of God is independent of all human factors, and seems completely incapable of having any human or historical dependence.

The question arises therefore whether, seen from this point of view, there can possibly be any union between the word of God and history, i.e. historical development with all its changing features; and if the content of the Old Testament is historical in most important details, the question again arises whether this does not mean that the claim of the Old Testament to speak the true word of God is a false claim.

Seen from the point of view of biblical revelation, however, this question is not wholly relevant. God announces himself in history, which is seen as the stage upon which human life on earth is played out, and he provides figures and phenomena which fit in with the human, historical world. The fact that in the figure of the prophet there reappears the traditional figure of the divine messenger (who is known in the historical environment of Israel) is relevant in this context, and helps to clarify the matter at a very important point. For in this way Man is confronted in the world in which he lives by the biblical word of God, and is directly addressed as a human being. He does not have to cut himself off from life in this world, he does not have to rise above his own world in order to find the way to God. He could not even hope to do this. Biblical faith is completely without mysticism, though experiences of mystic ecstasy are not unknown in the Old Testament world, and even the prophets had such experiences. But it is significant that they did not have to call upon such events in order to prove their authenticity. Indeed they tended to suspect ecstatics of being false prophets. Whenever their authenticity was questioned, they replied simply that they were "sent" as messengers of God.

The Bible does not actually recognise any special sphere of holiness separate from the rest of the world. Admittedly the concept "holy" is applied many times in the Old Testament with regard to cultic matters. Holy places, holy days, holy ornaments, and holy sacrifices are all mentioned. The gravity and inviolability of the "holy" is recognized, but this is essentially traditional material from the ancient cultic civilizations, and despite the numerous cultic enactments occurring in the Old Testament, cultic activities do not appear to be of first importance. It is very clear in the Old Testament that other nations too worshipped their gods in a similar fashion. Thus we are faced with a general historical religious phenomenon of which worship in Israel was part. Most often the adjective "holy" in its original sense refers to God; only relatively rarely does it refer to human beings, and then not in the sense of inherent holiness, but in the sense of a union with God granted to them, or asked of them.

According to biblical tradition, God confronts Man in the midst of the unholy (non-divine) world, and also makes use of the historical events of this world. This emerges very clearly in the Old Testament. If we are right in saying that the history of Israel is the true sphere of divine activity in the Old Testament,[19] the field of activity of the word of God is made up of those events here which are historically conditioned in every respect, even in the most subtle expressions about life. Thus the Old Testament clearly stresses the truly historical nature of Israel, which had not always existed, but evolved from among the ancient Oriental tribes. It was not from the very beginning in possession of the land which it later occupied, but only acquired this land at a particular point in its history by dispossessing the former occupants. It was never considered as the centre of world events around which all other nations merely revolved on the periphery.

From the human standpoint it had a much less brilliant past. Its ancestors, the patriarchs, had once been semi-nomads who, as wandering herdsmen without possessions, had been dependent upon the superior power of landowners; and their descendants had lived for some time in a humiliating position as foreigners in Egypt. At one point in the Old Testament it is actually said that Israel was smaller and weaker than the peoples who had lived in the land before her, and considerably smaller and weaker than the powerful nations in the broader field of the ancient Near East. It is even stated that Israel was not more righteous than all the other races (*Deut.* ix.1, 4ff.). The Old Testament wholly maintains that Israel was one of the junior, smaller, and least significant peoples in world history. This sober historical judgment in the Old Testament forms the basis of the conviction that within this insignificant piece of history God once intervened and spoke, that he used the available historical unit of the tribes of Israel as a means of revealing himself.

On the more specific level he made use of the historical institutions available at the time. Here there was a traditional cultic system which had been clearly determined by ancient cultic tradition of the land. This cultic system had to serve to give the worship of God a definite form, the content of which was fully developed from the word of God in the Old Testament. This system of worship therefore constantly ran the risk of being

[19] Cf. G. Mensching: *Vergleichende Religionswissenschaft*, 2nd edn. 1949, p. 66.

practised in the sense of human idolatry. Quite late, at one particular point in the history of Israel, the institution of the kingship was established on the pattern of other races. This is noted in *I Sam.* viii.5. In the Old Testament this kingship is not regarded (as it is amongst other ancient Oriental peoples) as the divinely eternal element in a timeless world order, but is understood as something that has developed historically. According to the Old Testament, God made use of this kingship in order to carry out his plans within the history of Israel; and, as the messianic proclamation tells us, he will make use of this institution of the kingship yet again in the future in some decisive act.

It is within this context that the phenomenon of the messenger of God, which is so significant within the history of religion, takes its place. According to the Mari texts, this phenomenon was known in early pre-Israelite times in those circles from which it is believed the tribes of Israel once came. According to the Old Testament, God made use of these messengers in order to proclaim, in some definite decisive historical period, the word of God which announced some imminent event, and revealed at the same time a part of his planned intervention. This in no way hindered the appearance in the same way, by the side of God's true prophets, of false prophets who set themselves up as God's messengers, but displayed only human wilfulness. For all historical phenomena, if they are really to belong to human history, must be ambiguous; and it does not become easy to differentiate between the true and the false by applying merely superficial criteria.

This then is a brief outline of what the Old Testament has to say about the connection between history and the word of God. This does not prove that the Old Testament method of divine revelation, making use as it does of given historical phenomena, stands on a higher plane than other methods of divine revelation. It only shows that it is addressed to man in the world in which he really lives—in the world of history. Naturally it cannot be proved that the Old Testament, indeed the New, deals with real divine revelation, or the real word of God.

The words of the Old Testament prophet are significant, as he sets down his task:

. . . and thou shalt say unto them, Thus saith the Lord God.
And they, whether they will hear, or whether they will for-
bear, . . . yet shall know that there hath been a prophet
among them.   (*Ezek.* II.4f.)

Significant also are St. Luke's words that it can be "given" to a
person "to know the secrets of the kingdom of God (*Luke* VIII.10).

VII

The Understanding of History in Old Testament Apocalyptic

The life of a human being on earth runs its course on a plane which we call history, conditioned by what is at times a unique constellation of scarcely comprehensible historical circumstances, which in their turn are determined by the actions and sufferings of human beings, and which moreover share and influence the further course of historical events. It is therefore natural that the question whether there are any *laws* of history, should crop up again and again. What is the *meaning* of history? Indeed we are well justified in characterising the problem of history as "our most pressing, our most extensive and our most difficult problem".[1]

In our western civilization, one of the very roots of our understanding of the essential significance of history for life on earth lies in the Christian Bible, and, above all in the Old Testament. "A truly historical literature within the area of 'Near Eastern and European' civilization" has been created "only among the Israelites and the Greeks"; and "particularly among the Israelites, who occupy a special place among all the civilized peoples of the Orient, this literature arose at a surprisingly early time, and began with some highly significant creations"[2] which are quite considerably older than the earliest productions of Greek historiography. It is indeed noteworthy that the Old Testament contains an abundance of historical traditions of various types and dates which differ wholly from the documents relating to the cultural and religious environment to which the Old Testament belonged. Here without doubt we are decisively involved in the Old Testament belief in God, for obviously so much of the history of Israel and also of the nations is frequently

[1] From G. Krüger, *Die Geschichte im Denken der Gegenwart*, 1947, p. 5.
[2] E. Meyer, *Geschichte des Altertums*, vol. i. Pt. i, 6th edn. 1953, p. 227.

narrated in the Old Testament not just for its own sake, but rather because within this history the hand of God was experienced at work. It is precisely in this special respect that the Old Testament differs fundamentally from its environment.

In the religions of the ancient Oriental world we have a constantly recurring play of mythical forces, in which the superhuman control by the divine is observed and admired, whether it be in matters concerning heaven and earth, or the stars and the elements of life and death, whereas in the Old Testament it is chiefly the once-occurring event which is understood as a divine manifestation. This Old Testament conception has exercised within the Christian sphere a considerable influence, which is still to be felt in our own times.

We have still not said anything about what the Old Testament understood by the idea of *history* and whether there can be found in it any definite idea of the nature of history. Just how problematic this question actually is can be seen by the fact that a leading expert on the Old Testament was able, in spite of the existence of Old Testament historiography, to pass the judgment that an "outstanding characteristic feature of the Hebrew spirit is" that "the conception of history. hardly plays any role at all".[3] There is little significance in the fact that the Old Testament does not have a word for *history*, for we rarely come across conscious discussions and definitions there, although we very often find the very essence of things discussed without any definite verbal concept being used for them.

As far as the question of the understanding of history in the Old Testament is concerned, however, a quick and easy answer cannot be found. Perhaps there is no single answer, for the Old Testament in its narrative and historical literature speaks in one way about history as the sphere within which the planned activity of God takes place, but it speaks quite differently in its classical prophecy, which sees the decisive intervention of God concentrated on the present and immediate future; and different again is that late phenomenon, the so-called apocalyptical writing in the Old Testament, in which some of the divine mysteries are to be revealed through visions and auditions. In view of this it is expedient to examine this question of the understanding of history in the light of just one of these phenomena

[3] From L. Köhler, *Hebrew Man*, tr. Ackroyd, 1956, p. 136.

within the Old Testament. Let us consider the Old Testament Apocalyptic.

Apocalyptic is found in the Old Testament above all in the *Book of Daniel.* The two visions of world history in *Dan.* II and VII in particular deserve further examination with respect to their understanding of history. The vision of *Dan.* II is told as a story within a story. According to this the neo-Babylonian King Nebuchadnezzar had a very disturbing dream which none of his soothsayers could interpret, mainly because they could not comply with the King's demand that they should inform him of the very content of his dream without him telling them. It was only Daniel, one of those Judaeans deported to Babylon by Nebuchadnezzar, who was able to interpret it on the strength of the divine wisdom given to him.

In his dream the King had seen a colossal statue of a human figure, composed of different materials: the head of gold, the chest and arms of silver, the belly of bronze, and the legs of iron, while finally the feet were composed of iron and clay. In the vision a stone—apparently from a rock or mountain which had risen up alongside the image of the statue—is cast down in a most strange manner without human agency, hitting the feet of the statue and crushing them so that the whole image was destroyed and every trace of it disappeared, while the stone became an enormous mountain filling the whole earth. The interpretation revealed the different parts of the statue to be "kingdoms" which were to follow one another, and the first and the third of which were specifically intended to represent a universal power.

The vision therefore deals with a succession of empires, actually four in number; the statue indeed has five parts, but because the iron legs and the iron and clay feet in reality represent only the lower half of one single part, it is expressly assumed in the interpretation that the feet of iron and clay are also included in the phrase "the fourth kingdom."[4] The stone which destroys the statue is interpreted as the eternal kingdom of God which will one day replace all human kingdoms.

Quite a clear and simple idea of the course of world history

[4] The "toes" in vs. 41 and vss. 42, 43 represent a late addition, which is meant to have a special historical bearing but does not specifically change the content and meaning of the vision.

appears to be put forward here; events on earth take place in a succession of world dominions replacing each other, following a downward path, getting more and more inferior until finally the coming of the Kingdom of God on earth suddenly brings the succession of human kingdoms to an end. A closer study, however, reveals some difficulties. It appears doubtful whether the seer was really deeply impressed by the idea of decline in world history. This idea is indeed raised incidentally in the interpretation, but is in no way expanded. It must also be remembered that old traditional ideas are evidently incorporated in the dream and interpretation, and we must therefore check how far this traditional material was significant in itself for the apocalyptic writer, and how far it only served him as a means of arriving at what he really wanted to say. We must therefore go more deeply into the different elements of the dream and its interpretation, and in so doing our field of study will quickly extend far beyond the *Book of Daniel*.

The vision of the statue of the human figure may perhaps need no particular explanation. That the whole of the world is depicted—here with special reference to world history—in the "microcosm" of a human figure[5] is an obvious idea used many times before, though here we can see it arising quite spontaneously. That a statue could be composed of different materials may be clearly shown from many examples of the plastic arts from the earliest times in the ancient Orient—even though the statue in the vision would be a little impractical! In this vision, however, we have the new concept of a definite series of metals which represent certain successive periods of time. We may suppose that this idea is connected with the notion that as each new metal was discovered it inaugurated a new epoch in everyday life; we must then think of the transition from the Bronze to the Iron Age, which ended a "period of bronze" and inaugurated a "period of iron" in ancient Oriental civilization.

This experience would then have been the starting-point for the further development of this idea, though the seer in *Dan.* II could scarcely have been aware of a definite connection with this hypothetical source of the theory of metal periods, which had occurred almost a thousand years before his own age. He probably took over the traditional view (recorded in a developed

[5] Cf. A. Bentzen, *Daniel* in Hb. A.T., 2nd edn. 1952, p. 27.

form in Hesiod) of four world epochs characterised by gold, silver, bronze, and iron. There was a similar Iranian tradition.[6] Where this idea of the four Metal Ages arose,[7] where and how it was passed on and developed, and by what paths it succeeded in reaching the period in which the *Book of Daniel* arose, are questions which cannot readily be answered. It can, however, be safely asserted that the idea does not stem from among ancient Israelite Old Testament tradition, for before Daniel there is no trace of it in the Old Testament, nor indeed is there any trace of a teaching concerning the different World Epochs which could have developed from this idea. It has therefore come down to the author of the *Book of Daniel* from somewhere or other outside his own circles.

The interpretation of the dream in *Dan.* II does not relate the four metal parts of the statue to different world epochs, but to world empires—to historical and political manifestations of greatness. That is something quite different. We may wonder whether the notion of the world epochs is connected with the idea (popular in the ancient Orient) of a cycle of life on earth which went on repeating itself, and therefore whether it originally incorporated the idea of a new beginning, with the repetition of the same cycle, after the ending of each period of four ages. *Dan.* II in no way shares such an idea, which would render history most unhistorical, indeed mythical. But if the teaching of the world epochs is not[8] to be understood in the cyclic sense, the world epochs in *Dan.* II would be given a new interpretation as world empires. The four metals as symbols of four consecutive epochs were therefore incorporated in the vision of *Dan.* II only as traditional material, without taking over with it the theory originally linked with this material.

The interpretation of the vision as a series of successive world empires at first appears to be an idea original to the *Book of Daniel*, and easily explained if we keep in mind the Old Testament appreciation of history as the essential sphere of human life on earth. But the matter is not quite so simple, nor is the historical basis of the interpretation quite clear. The golden head of the

[6] The list of references is to be found in all commentaries on *Daniel*.

[7] W. Baumgartner, *Th. R.*, N.F. XI, 1939, p. 212, suggests a Babylonian source, but gives no definite proof.

[8] In Iranian circles at any rate a teaching of "world epochs" may be understood not in the cyclic but in the linear sense.

statue is expressly and solemnly interpreted as Nebuchadnezzar, who is thus signified as the ruler chosen by God over the whole of the inhabited world and all living beings in it, just as he had been the God-willed ruler of the world for the prophet Jeremiah in his day (*Jer.* xxvii.6ff.).[9] Since a second "kingdom" following Nebuchadnezzar is discussed, and then a third and a fourth "kingdom", then obviously the whole of the Neo-Babylonian kingdom is represented in the person of Nebuchadnezzar—and he was indeed its most significant ruler. The other kingdoms are not named in the interpretation, but are indicated by hints.

Since Daniel's story in chap. ii, as well as the rest of his stories in chaps. i-vi[10] are set during the period of Neo-Babylonian rule, and thus the dream and interpretation are related to a period in the future still far beyond his own age, the real names could not be given. It is clear, however, that the fourth kingdom is meant to represent the Macedonian Empire of Alexander the Great and the Diadochi. Recent commentators on the *Book of Daniel* are more or less in agreement about this.[11] As candidates for the second and third kingdoms, only the "Medes and Persians" need be considered, to whom, according to *Dan.* v.28, the "kingdom . . . is given" after the end of the Neo-Babylonian Empire.

In a later chapter also, in *Dan.* viii, the "kings of Media and Persia" are mentioned (vs. 20), who one day are going to be overthrown by the "king of Ionia" (= Greece)—and undoubtedly Alexander the Great is meant. These formulations do not, it is true, sound quite as if the Median Empire and the Persian Empire are thought of as two quite different phenomena. But in his interpretation of the dream in *Dan.* ii the seer seems nevertheless to have in mind a Median as the second Empire and a Persian as the third.[12] This admittedly introduces some

[9] The reference to this passage in *Jeremiah* makes unnecessary the consideration whether in *Dan.* ii.37, 38 certain themes around an idea of primitive men and kings might not be incorporated (cf. Bentzen, *Daniel*, p. 29).

[10] Only the last of these stories (*Dan.* vi) is set in the period of the kingdom of "Darius the Mede".

[11] This belief is supported by the particularly thorough study by H. H. Rowley, *Darius the Mede and the Four World Empires in the Book of Daniel*, 1935, pp. 70ff.

[12] It remains uncertain whether the references made in the frame-work to the story in the *Book of Daniel*—which in *Dan.* vi.1, ix.1 mention the "Mede Darius" and in *Dan.* x.1 "Cyrus, King of Persia"—presuppose completely separate Persian and Median Empires, or whether we have merely a rather vague formulation of a "Medo-Persian Empire", especially as, possibly in vi.1 and definitely in ix.1, the concept "Median" is only meant to indicate the personal origin of Darius.

historical difficulties, for the Median Empire was not the successor to the Neo-Babylonian Empire, but existed concurrently with it. One would therefore have to accept that in the stories of Daniel, which were probably written during the course of the third century B.C., the great names which arose some centuries before this date were misplaced, in the wrong relationship.

This becomes particularly understandable when one remembers that the idea of four consecutive world empires did not arise spontaneously in the *Book of Daniel* as a result of historical reflection, nor did it stem from ancient Old Testament tradition, but was taken over in ready-made form as a traditional pattern. The idea of four world empires has been fully verified in the Roman world.[13] At first this would seem to have nothing at all to do with the circle in which the *Book of Daniel* arose, and yet it can be shown to stand in a historical relationship to it. In numerous passages, apparently from the second century B.C. right up to the late Roman era, we can trace the idea that a series of four great world empires preceded the Roman domination. This idea is applied, varied, and modified in many different ways, which do not need to be elaborated here; its basic form, however, was quite clearly that it was the world empires of the Assyrians, the Medes, the Persians, and the Macedonians that had preceded the Roman domination of the world. We need only give one example of the many that can be found. Appian, the Roman historian of the second century A.D., tells in his book on Punic history of an incident which, he expressly states, Polybius actually saw and heard.[14] The younger Scipio had apparently wept on seeing the destruction he had wrought on Carthage, and had thought that all the empires on earth were laid open to destruction and that "the empire of the Assyrians and the Medes, and that empire—so great in its day—of the Persians, and also that empire of the Macedonians which had only recently emerged so brilliantly"[15] had suffered the same fate.

[13] Cf. J. W. Swain, "The Theory of the Four Monarchies. Opposition History under the Roman Empire", in *Classical Philology*, XXXV (1940), pp. 1-12; also W. Baumgartner, "Zu den vier Reichen von *Daniel* 2", in *Th. Z.* I (1945), pp. 17-22; and the very full list of references by H. Fuchs in *Basler Zeitschrift für Geschichte und Altertumskunde* XLII (1943), p. 50, n. 37 (and in addition the quotation from Rutilius Namatianus on p. 49).   [14] Cf. Polybius, *History* XXXVIII.22.

[15] The mention of Ilion which precedes this derives from a completely different tradition. It is moreover mentioned in a special sentence of its own, whereas the above quotation belongs to a second quite complete sentence.

It is obvious that this idea of a series of predominantly Oriental empires was not formed within the Roman horizon of ideas—nor can it have derived from the historical horizon of the Greeks. It must beyond doubt stem from the Orient, and in all probability came down to the Romans during that period when they came into close contact with the Oriental world, i.e. the first half of the second century B.C.[16] This brings us close in time and space to the *Book of Daniel*. Factually the relationship is also close. In its last three members, the succession of world empires mentioned by Appian agrees with the historical ideas put forward in the interpretation of the dream in *Dan*. II. As regards the first member, Daniel is inaccurate, whereas the Roman idea of a series in which the Assyrians, Medes, Persians, and Macedonians succeeded each other corresponds to the historical truth. Factual priority therefore must obviously rest with the tradition passed on to the Romans, and it can in no way be said that this whole complex of ideas has its source in the Old Testament apocalyptic of the *Book of Daniel*, which must have appropriated its material from elsewhere.

It seems to me that we are now in the fortunate position of being able to ascertain with a fair degree of certainty the origin and earliest development of this recurring pattern of four world empires. There must have been a period in world history when the idea was brought home to men that events on earth were characterized by a succession of world empires following upon one another; and indeed there was, as far as we are informed, only one such occasion in early antiquity. This was the time when within the possible span of a single human life the change from one great dominion to another occurred twice. In the year 612 B.C. the Assyrian Empire came to an unexpected and sudden end. It had been a universal empire in the eyes of the ancient Oriental world, and the very first empire of this type; for only shortly before it was itself defeated, Assyria had succeeded in subjugating its old opponent Egypt.

[16] Swain, in *Classical Philology*, XXXV (1940), p. 2, works from a quotation culled from Velleius Paterculus I.6, 6 by the otherwise unknown Aemilius Sura, whose statement, on the basis that the Diadochic names Philippus and Antiochus are mentioned, he dates as somewhere around the time between 189 and 171 B.C. It is questionable whether this exact dating and the specific derivation from Asia Minor are as well founded as Swain believes. Nevertheless he may well be on the right track. (Cf. Baumgartner in *Th. Z.* (1945), pp. 20f.).

The Neo-Babylonians and the Medes had together brought the Assyrian Empire to an end, and they shared out the spoils between them. After only sixty to seventy years, however, the Persians put an end to the Neo-Babylonian—Median rule when they replaced first the Median Empire in 553 B.C.[17], the Neo-Babylonian Empire in 539 B.C.; and then the Persians themselves set up what, in the ancient Oriental view, was again a universal dominion, soon afterwards successfully subjugating Egypt once more. Here was the example of successive world empires. The idea grew from the historical events of a definite period, and it could well have arisen at the time of the Persian Empire—in the first instance limited to three world empires. For the first time in history we find an actual sequence of world empires.

The Greek Ctesias, who as physician to King Artaxerxes II lived at the Persian court, divided his study of the history of Persia—a work of which only fragments are preserved—so that it dealt firstly with the history of the Assyrian Empire, then the Median; only after those did he turn to the history of the Persian Empire.[18] Here, therefore, we already have the first three members of that succession of four which finally came down to the Romans as a well-developed tradition. We can also say something about the space of time during which this idea was formed and took shape. Between the period of universal Assyrian dominion and the universal Persian Empire came the period of the co-existence of the Neo-Babylonian and Median Empires, quite apart from Egypt, which was then (for the time being) once again independent. The succession of Assyrians, Medes, and Persians can only have been visualized somewhere within the ambit of former Median rule which included the Iranian and Armenian mountains and the Assyrian homeland, and was not therefore within the Old Testament sphere—whether by this one thinks of Palestine itself, or of the areas inhabited by those who were deported and dispersed after the catastrophes which marked the beginning of the sixth century B.C.; within this particular sphere the sequence would have to read: Assyrians—Babylonians—Persians. But this sequence is nowhere documented.

The further development of the idea of a succession of world empires can only be reconstructed hypothetically—yet neverthe-

---

[17] With regard to this date, cf. K. Galling in *Z.D.P.V.*, LXIX (1953), p. 49.
[18] Cf. Swain, *op, cit.*, pp. 6f.

less with a good degree of probability. With the fall of the Persian empire and the establishment of Macedonian rule under Alexander the Great the fourth member in the succession emerged—the Macedonian Empire. One would immediately imagine, therefore, that in Alexander's empire this idea, stemming from the Persian era, of a course of history which saw the successive formation of world empires was diligently taken up with the present empire being seen as the fourth in the series, thus making up the round figure of four, which approximated roughly to the completed whole, possibly as the four quadrants of the world. In this way the empire of Alexander was presented as the completion of the series of world empires. The Romans may well have got to know the pattern in this particular form. This pattern could not, admittedly, represent for them a completely rounded-off picture of world history—they would see it rather as a neat summary of the history leading up to their own rule.

Let us return to the apocalyptic writing of the *Book of Daniel*. We must ask whether this pattern of world empires corresponds to the idea with which the apocalyptic writers were themselves acquainted. It is very possible that this idea was so transformed during the period of the rule of the Diadochi over the subject peoples of the Orient, where there was growing opposition to the foreign Macedonian domination, that the world empires were seen to be following a declining path and would eventually reach their lowest point, and perhaps their end. The idea might have developed from this to become an element in the spiritual opposition to existing rule; and then, working from the very origins of the idea, the Seleucid state might be seen as the one towards which this further development might have been directed.[19] Then, however, the question arises whether this idea of four world empires has not even at this stage already become linked with the conception of four world epochs characterised by four different metals, and therefore interpreted in the sense of a continual downward development. Since the teaching of world epochs is also documented in Iranian tradition, such a combination might well lie within the bounds of historical possibility. What was expected to happen when the series of world empires reached the end of its course would then remain an open

---

[19] Cf. Swain, *op. cit.*, p. 8.

question. If this had been considered, the beginning of a new series of world empires might possibly have been hoped for.[20] Yet these reflections can only remain guesses as long as there continues to be a lack of adequate documentary proof. One thing only is certain—that the author of the stories in *Daniel* took over, in the dream and its interpretation in *Dan*. ii, material which had already been well developed and given meaning.

In what sense and with what intention did the author take this material over? He obviously had no precise knowledge of the actual course of events, and so could not say that events must have happened definitely in one particular way and in no other. Otherwise it would have been difficult for him to be able to insert the Neo-Babylonian king Nebuchadnezzar with such surprising freedom at the beginning of the four-power succession, in place of the Assyrian Empire which actually holds this position, thereby clashing most conspicuously with historical reality. For all probability suggests that the introduction of Nebuchadnezzar into the traditional pattern must be laid at the door of the author of the *Daniel* stories. By this means he adapted the dream and interpretation to fit within the framework of these stories which "Daniel" sets in Neo-Babylonian times, among those Judaeans who had been deported to Babylon. A dream which on correct interpretation was meant to disclose the future (as is expressly stated in vss. 29, 45), could not very well (in the era to which Daniel is assumed to belong) refer to the Assyrian empire, which by then already belonged to the past. Therefore a change in the pattern suggested itself, and this change could more easily be put forward if the historical sequence of empires was not taken to be essential.

Even the idea of a sequence of metals composing the statue to represent world history, and showing historical epochs becoming increasingly inferior, does not seem to have been considered very important by the author of the *Book of Daniel*. It is given only a very minor place in the interpretation, which stresses most pointedly that Nebuchadnezzar represents the first world empire, though this is done mainly for the sake of the story. The whole story takes place in contemporary times and at the court

[20] It is very uncertain that an eschatological end of history was already being thought of (as E. Meyer suggests in *Ursprung und Anfänge des Christentums*, VOL. ii, 1921, pp. 197f.; also Swain: *op. cit.*, p. 9; Baumgartner: *op. cit.*, pp. 21f.)

of Nebuchadnezzar. He it was who had the dream, and the interpretation is addressed to him. He is highly praised by Daniel, who is one of his subjects—as was then customary in such cases in ancient Oriental empires—and in addition this praise was closely connected with an ancient oracle of the prophet Jeremiah. None of this could take into consideration the fact that it was Nebuchadnezzar *himself* who had caused Jerusalem to be destroyed and many Judaeans to be deported. After the Neo-Babylonian Empire of Nebuchadnezzar there will follow, according to the interpretation, a period of decline, for the second empire will be "inferior" to that of Nebuchadnezzar. Here therefore, for a moment at least, the interpretation follows the idea contained in the sequence of metals of a descending line, but even this is used only for other special reasons.

If the interpreter had at this point happened to think of a Median Empire, according to the traditional pattern which he had taken up, he would undoubtedly have been caused some embarrassment. There had never been complete Median supremacy in the history of Israel, and the Median Empire could consequently never have been an empire of universal significance—a fact which is historically most striking; this made the depreciatory estimate of the second empire suggest itself. Beyond this, however, the idea of a descending line is pursued no further.

The empire placed in the third position is again expressly formulated as a universal world dominion. The same is said of this empire as was said of the Neo-Babylonian Empire of Nebuchadnezzar—though the form is shorter. This is quite understandable, for the interpreter must have had the Persian Empire in mind.

Finally, the interpretation of the last world empire almost seems to hint at an upward gradation when it says that this empire will not only rule everywhere, but will crush and destroy everything. It is only at the end of the interpretation of this last empire that a decline is once more mentioned, when it is said in explanation of the iron and clay feet of the statue that it will be a divided empire; although still "there shall be in it of the strength of the iron", it will nevertheless only partially possess this power and strength. This last point brings up a special circumstance which must be considered.

That we are not really dealing in *Dan.* II with the representation of a definite course of history, nor a definite historical development, is shown by a set of circumstances which have always been difficult to explain. At the end of the dream and interpretation it almost seems as if the interpreter did not see a series of world empires following one another, but a group existing together in time. In the dream the falling stone destroyed the whole statue at once. One might well say that this could not very well have been otherwise given the actual image that was chosen, since indeed the statue made up of different parts had suddenly appeared before the dreamer in its complete form. Nevertheless it is expressly pointed out that after the stone had struck and destroyed the iron and clay feet, then "was the iron, the clay, the brass, the silver and the gold broken to pieces *together*" (vs. 35).

Decisive, however, is the fact that also in the interpretation, which was not so restricted as the vision itself, it is carefully explained at the end that "in the days of these kings" the eternal empire of God is to be set up, just as if the four world empires were all still there together in the present. This circumstance has incidentally given rise to the contention that the story in *Dan.* II is not meant to suggest successive empires, but empires which exist side by side. That cannot possibly be so if we follow the clear wording of the interpretation; for our author took over a four-world-empire pattern which was aware of a historical series. It does seem quite obvious, however, that in the eyes of the author of the *Daniel* stories the whole course of history faced by the coming kingdom of God was simply condensed to one single compact phenomenon.

The question arises why have these traditions been taken up at all in *Dan.* II when the essential ideas connected with them had no significance whatsoever for the dream and interpretation. There was here, nevertheless, at least one important thing in the traditions—the notion of four as an ultimate number which led to the expected termination of the course of history; and this was the end towards which the dream and interpretation in *Dan.* II was aiming. This is shown by the fact that the fourth and last empire is given special consideration. In the vision, with the description of the iron legs and iron and clay feet, the prerequisites have already been created for the interpretation, which is then so clear as to enable the identification of this fourth and last empire to be made incontestably, and without any names being mentioned.

That strong and all-consuming empire, which is however to be a divided empire with only partial power, is evidently the Macedonian Empire which was eventually divided after the death of Alexander between the Diadochi, of whom mainly the Seleucids and the Ptolemies come into consideration as far as Old Testament civilization is concerned.[21] On this point the dream and interpretation are so transparently clear, that there can really be no serious doubt about the historical connection. This must have been equally clear for the contemporaries of the Daniel stories, for it can scarcely be doubted that the story in *Dan.* II, and indeed all the stories in *Dan.* I-VI, were written at the time of the Diadochi, or rather—more exactly—during the course of the third century B.C. The visionary dream of world history in *Dan.* II and its interpretation are intended to make clear to the people of those times, in that strange way characteristic of apocalyptic, and by the use of traditional material, that the present constitutes the time of the last empire which will be followed by the eternal Kingdom of God. This kingdom might now come at any time and bring human history to an end. The whole therefore obviously seeks to foretell the imminent arrival of the Kingdom of God.

Two further points must be noted. First, it is not due to the particular nature of the Macedonian Empire—which certainly did not differ basically from the other empires—that the eschatological end of history is to follow it; nor does the sequence of four world empires logically lead on to this end because it follows a particular succession of events in history, since no such succession is traced out in *Dan.* II. Essentially the whole of world history must be included in this expectation of the imminent arrival of the kingdom of God. In *Dan.* II the whole of world history is represented—for reasons grounded in the author's own times—under the guise of a series of successive world empires. But these world empires, as has been shown, appear all together in opposition to God's rule just at the point in the interpretation where the establishment of the Kingdom of God is mentioned;

---

[21] The addition mentioned above, n. 4, has a special significance with regard to the relationship between the Seleucid and the Ptolemaic kingdoms.

just as if, at the decisive final moment, all of world history had come together contemporaneously. Basically, therefore, the dream and interpretation seek to say—admittedly with special reference to their own epoch—that the coming of the Kingdom of God is always a matter for the whole of world history.

Second, it is worthy of note that in *Dan*. ii the question of the actual point in time for the ending of history is left open. Nothing is said about whether the last empire is to have a long or short period of respite. All that is said is that men must be constantly prepared for this end. This is expressly confirmed in *Dan*. vii.

Most of what has been said about *Dan*. ii is valid for *Dan*. vii, which provides a visual image and interpretation not set in a narrative framework, but with short accompanying notes in which Daniel himself is described as the receiver of the vision and audition. *Dan*. vii stems from a later period than *Dan*. ii, and has been added later to the *Daniel* stories.[22] In the vision the seer looks upon "the great sea" which the four winds had stirred up, and from which four fantastic beasts arise. The first of these is like a lion with eagle's wings, but then its wings are plucked off and it is lifted up from the ground, made to stand on two feet like a man, and given a man's heart.[23] The second beast is like a bear, which however is raised up on one side and has three ribs in its mouth. This bear receives a command from an unknown party to "devour much flesh". The third beast looks like a panther, but has four wings of a bird and four heads. Finally the fourth beast is not compared with any creature of the terrestrial animal world but is depicted as a particular horror, with its iron teeth and claws, its voracity and its destructive rage. We shall have to come back to this beast later.

Now the seer looks upon a scene of the heavenly assize, after which the fourth beast is slain and then burnt, dominion is taken away from the other animals, and they are given a definite, limited, span of life. In the interpretation the four beasts

---

[22] I should like to point out that I am not convinced of the literary "unity" of the *Book of Daniel* (as is H. H. Rowley, in *Hebrew Union College Annual* xxiii (1950-1951), pp. 233-273).

[23] I cannot see that the proposed adaptations of the traditional text which are suggested by H. L. Ginsberg in *Studies in Daniel*, 1948, pp. 14f., are either well-founded or indeed necessary.

are explained as "kings" (or kingdoms)[24] which hold sway on earth until finally the kingly rule of the "saints of the most high" takes their place.

The similarity in the conception to that of *Dan.* II is immediately noticeable. The basis again is the idea of the four successive world empires by which world history is characterized. The last empire is again meant to signify the Macedonian, as we shall see later. As far as the three preceding empires are concerned—and these are only given a .very summary interpretation—it can be asked whether the interpreter is dependent on the idea in *Dan.* II and thinks therefore of the Babylonians, Medes, and Persians, or of the Assyrians, Medes, and Persians, in the traditional pattern. This question cannot be answered decisively, nor is it important for the actual understanding of *Dan.* VII. More important is the fact which emerges very clearly from *Dan.* VII that with the reference to the four world empires the approximate course of history is represented; but obviously the whole course of world history is not meant to be comprehended and explained here. Whereas in the dream and interpretation in *Dan.* II it seems as if world history is to be viewed only from the period of the Neo-Babylonian King Nebuchadnezzar, this second vision in *Dan.* VII goes back right to the very beginnings of history. The fact that in the preamble to the story a date from the period of the Neo-Babylonian Empire is mentioned is of no significance at all with regard to *Dan.* VII. The seer looks upon the sea which the four winds had stirred up; here undoubtedly he has in mind the primeval sea of chaos of the ancient Oriental stories of creation, and therefore the beginnings of all history. Then immediately the beasts which represent the world empires rise up.

The fact that no comprehensive theory of the course of history can be developed here is quite evident if one keeps Old Testament prerequisites in mind. For the rich Old Testament historical tradition speaks only of historical periods in which events on earth were not yet determined by any world empire; and even if some great and powerful empire had existed at a very early period, the Old Testament would have remembered only Egypt, which could scarcely have been the empire in mind in *Dan.* VII.

---

[24] It seems possible that in the original text the word "kingdoms" (instead of "kings") was used. Cf. *Biblia Hebraica*, by R. Kittel, 3rd edn., Stuttgart 1937, and Ginsberg, *op. cit.*, p. 65, n. 8.

Nor does *Dan.* VII appear to be set on revealing a comprehensive idea of the actual course of history.

The question remains whether a definite line of development is meant to be represented. The answer to this question depends on the specific interpretations of the fantastic beasts. There have been attempts to see a declining tendency[25] here also, but this is an error. The specific characteristics given in the description of the beasts can hardly be interpreted as allegorical. The illustrative material for these beasts was provided by the ancient Oriental plastic arts with their abundance of grotesque monsters, the only difference being that in the vision the combination of fantastic elements is even more grotesque than was possible in the plastic arts.

The first beast appears in two forms. Firstly it is a winged lion, such as was depicted a great many times in Mesopotamia both in the round and in relief. Then a change takes place, and it becomes a lion without wings standing upright on its two hind legs, bearing itself like a human being (this is what is meant when it is stated that the beast was given a man's heart). We meet this figure frequently in Mesopotamian art.[26] What is the meaning of this metamorphosis of the lion? Perhaps only that in this way two different depictions of lions familiar at that time are combined together into the image in this vision. Perhaps, however, an allusion is made to one of the older Daniel stories (*Dan.* III.31-IV.34), according to which King Nebuchadnezzar was once turned into an animal with the heart of an animal instead of a man, but after a long time was changed back again, when he regained his human heart. If this assumption is correct, the first beast in *Dan.* VII (as in *Dan.* II) would be meant to represent the Neo-Babylonian Empire. There is no suggestion that the details of the lion image and the process of the metamorphosis have a historical significance. The graphic depiction of the lion symbolizes simply a powerful empire, just as do the two following beasts.

Observation also underlies the depiction of the bear, though this animal is but rarely depicted in the plastic arts of the

---

[25] E.g. J. A. Montgomery, *The Book of Daniel*, 1927, pp. 286, 288, and H. Junker, *Untersuchungen über literarische und exegetische Probleme des Buches Daniel*, 1932, p. 37.

[26] We can take as examples the seal-engravings reproduced in Otto Weber, *Altorientalische Siegelsbilder*, 1920, Nos. 15, 17, 64, 101, 117ff., and others.

ancient Orient,[27] for it is not exactly at home in the riparian oases which were the centres of development of the ancient Oriental civilizations. It was seen only in the mountains, and the few reproductions of bears that are known come therefore from the Iranian mountains and their immediate vicinity. The description in *Dan.* VII is reminiscent of bears pictured standing ready to attack, with their front paws raised.[28] The rest of the details are meant only to depict its voracity, and can hardly have a special historical significance.

The third beast, the panther with four wings and four heads, is reminiscent of the ancient Oriental depictions of irregular beasts with pairs of wings and several heads. The image as it stands, however, is not authenticated among examples of the ancient Oriental plastic arts; here the seer's power of imagination is given full rein. The panther nowhere plays a very important role in the ancient Orient. In Egypt it appears occasionally in figurative speech and representational art as a particularly fearsome beast; it appears once prominently in Asia Minor, in the great rocky shrine of Yazilikaya in the vicinity of the Hittite royal city, in high relief, supporting the chief Hittite goddess with her young companion. It is possible to suppose, therefore, that certain definite animals were valid as symbols for different lands of the ancient Orient, that the seer in *Dan.* VII knew of only three of these symbolic beasts, and was hence able to depict the first three beasts, not having any definite model for the last beast. This hypothesis, however, cannot be proved. The only thing that seems quite certain to me is that the seer is working with traditional ancient Oriental illustrative material, that the particular details in the description of the beasts are not especially important in the interpretation of the whole, and that in the particular sequence of beasts the intention is not to depict a particular line of development.

The fourth beast is quite different. In this beast an intensification can definitely be seen, as in *Dan.* II. It is expressly stated that it was both more dangerous and more frightful than the beasts

---

[27] Cf. M. Hilzheimer, *Reallexikon der Assyriologie*, VOL. I, 1932, pp. 398f.

[28] As in the seal engraving (Persian) No. 511 in Weber, *op. cit.*, and on an Assyrian vessel in Sir A. Layard, *The Monuments of Nineveh II*, 1853, p. 66, and Perrot and Chipiez, *Histoire de l'art dans l'antiquité*, VOL. II, Paris 1884, p. 751, fig. 408. A running bear is depicted on an Elamite *Kudurru*; cf. Morgan, *Mémoires de la délégation en Perse* 12 (1911), p. 227, fig. 464.

that have gone before. The emphasis on this beast rests on the fact that the fourth and last empire symbolized by this beast was the actual ruling empire at the time when *Dan.* VII was composed. In the form of *Dan.* VII which has come down to us[29] particular details are added to the general description of this beast, which are meant to be understood as indications of historical manifestations. The interpretation of the vision refers back in detail to these when it gives a similar historical explanation.

It is stated that the fourth beast has ten horns, just as in the plastic arts of Mesopotamia many gods in human form—and also many daemonic monsters—wore a crown of horns with several pairs of bulls' horns arranged one above the other.[30] These ten horns are explained in the interpretation as ten kings of the last empire. Perhaps with this use of symbolic horns an allusion is made to the Seleucid state and its kings, since the first Seleucids had their coins decorated with horns.[31] When, therefore, a small eleventh horn appears in the vision between the other pairs of horns and plucks out three of the other horns, this detail should probably be connected with the interpretation itself, which mentions an eleventh king who will bring defeat to three preceding kings. What is then said of this eleventh king leaves us in no doubt that the interpreter has the Seleucid Antiochus IV in mind. The vision along with its interpretation should be placed, therefore, within a definite, narrowly limited period of time when *Dan.* VII was written in its present form. From this point in time the end of world history and the coming of the kingdom of God is awaited.

The whole of world history is seen together, as if it were all happening in the present. For in *Dan.* VII just as in *Dan.* II we have that hovering between the idea of successive empires and contemporary empires, which has led many interpreters to think of empires which did not follow one another but which existed

---

[29] I refrain from discussing the question of the literary prehistory of *Dan.* VII. It is not important here, because even if there has existed an older form which did not contain this special reference to Antiochus IV, we should be led to the same results in the main, as far as the questions under discussion here are concerned.

[30] Gods in human form with crowns of horns have been so frequently depicted that it hardly seems necessary to produce a list of examples. Monsters with crowns of horns are shown, for example, in the reproductions in *Altorientalische Bilder zum Alten Testament*, ed. H. Gressmann, 2nd edn., 1927, Nos. 378, 381.

[31] Cf. S. Morenz, in *Z.A.W.*, LXIII (1951), pp. 151-4.

together. But the text testifies clearly (in *Dan.* VII) to a chronological succession of empires. Even if the interpretation explains the four beasts summarily in one sentence as four empires, it nevertheless mentions clearly in the vision itself that the four beasts appeared in succession (vss. 6, 7). But we still have at the beginning of the vision the statement that four beasts emerged from the sea—as if it were all one single event.

In *Dan.* VII the four empires appear just at the end as if they were all still present together. There follows the discussion of the annihilation of the fourth beast; then immediately the three remaining beasts are discussed, and we are told that their dominion is taken away and they are assigned a definite span of life. One would at least expect these statements to come in the opposite order, for one would think that their life-span and their period of rule were identical. When the stipulated span of life has run its course, the end of the actual period of rule takes place; and after the first three beasts have had their stipulated time the fourth beast, which is the most important of all, is also destroyed. This is all stated as if the most decisive moment in the whole course of events had actually been reached at that particular time; and thus the particular assertions can be made in an order which is actually opposed to the chronological order. In *Dan.* VII we are not, therefore, dealing either with the depiction of historical events following their course according to this or that definite law, but with the mutual confrontation of world history as a whole and the kingdom of God.

Dan. VII admittedly goes further than *Dan.* II in that the actual point of time for the end of history is fixed as the period of the eleventh king in the last empire, i.e. the period of Antiochus IV, and even the actual days of grace still left to the king are defined by intimations which are admittedly mysterious but nevertheless transparent (vs. 25). In the form which has come down to us, *Dan.* VII actually dates from the time of Antiochus IV. We have before us, therefore, an eschatological expectation about the immediate future. This is explained by the oppressed and persecuted state in which the body of worshippers in Jerusalem found themselves, owing to the assaults of Antiochus. The way out of this situation—and also the period of time right up to this expected end of world history—has been depicted in great detail in the visions of the last chapter which was added at that time to the Daniel stories.

In concentrating on this new decisive epoch expected after the short interval of a few years, and in trying to determine the actual detailed future course of history within contemporaneous limits, the historical outlook of the apocalyptic writing in the second half of the *Book of Daniel* has deviated from its own sound starting-point, and wandered off on a very dangerous false track. Here the words of the New Testament are very apt: "But of that day or that hour no one knows, not even the angels in heaven, nor the Son, but only the Father" (*Mark* XIII.32).

The apocalyptic writings absorbed all sorts of material current at that time concerning the idea of world epochs and world empires, and perhaps too all sorts of material concerning symbols for historical manifestations and powers. But they considerably depleted this material and robbed it of its original content and real value by merely applying it to make the motley colouring and changeable nature of world history more vivid. The notion of once-and-for-all happenings of history as the true sphere of human life is nevertheless an idea which is seriously accepted along with this material. The apocalyptic writings, however, do not recognize definite laws in the development of history. Taken as a whole the judgment concerning history is a negative one. History did not seem to show the writer either a constantly heightening development of the power of evil, or a positive advance towards an ideal goal. History takes its course in a series of changing phenomena, and God lets it happen in just this way.

History is seen wholly in the light of the present and offers a similar picture to every era. The historical past is not considered with the conscious detachment which is so natural in our historical outlook. We must accept the judgment that "the concept of history [in our sense] scarcely plays any marked role" for the apocalyptic writings.[32] What (according to apocalyptic) gives world history its final unity amidst all its variety of different phenomena, and indeed its significance, is the fact that it stands face to face with the kingship of God, which is to pronounce judgment upon the whole of history.

[32] Cf. p. 195 above.

VIII

The Holy Ones of the Most High

Sigmund Mowinckel, to whom this essay is dedicated[1] as a token of gratitude and respect, has observed in his book *Religion og Kultus* that in the Old Testament the concept of "the holy ones" usually signifies "divine beings", and he has also expressly maintained that "the holy ones" (defined no more closely than this in the Old Testament itself) are "supernatural" beings.[2] Let us consider this question in greater detail, for Mowinckel's definition may be an important contribution in the interpretation of the expression "the holy ones of the Most High", which plays such an important role in the interpretation of the vision in *Dan.* VII, characterizing as it does the eschatological kingdom expected after the end of world history.

There hardly seems to be any problem in understanding the expression "the holy ones of the Most High", which seems to refer to the chosen people of Israel in the Old Testament in a real or ideal sense[3]; and it cannot be denied that at first sight the statements in *Dan.* VII concerning "the holy ones of the Most High" seem to confirm this interpretation. Procksch, however, referring to the general use in the *Book of Daniel* of the word "holy", has put forward the thesis that in *Dan.* VII divine beings must have been meant by the expression "the holy ones of the Most High".[4] This idea has met with very little approval, and

---

[1] The *Festschrift* for S. Mowinckel actually appeared in 1955, but contributions had been submitted for publication in January 1954. Thus in the above essay it was impossible to take into account the complete publication of the fragments of MSS. from Cave I of Khirbet Qumran which were in the possession of the Hebrew University of Jerusalem.

[2] In the German translation *Religion und Kultus*, Göttingen 1953, p. 35, and p. 142 n. 47.

[3] Cf. S. Mowinckel, *He that Cometh*, trans. G. W. Anderson, Oxford 1956, p. 350.

[4] O. Procksch, in *Christentum und Wissenschaft*, III 1927, p. 429; in *Neue Kirchliche Zeitschrift*, XLIV 1933, p. 80; *Theologie des Alten Testaments*, 1950, p. 537.

possibly only E. Sellin has agreed with him.[5] Otherwise his thesis has been hurriedly glossed over[6] or even ignored completely.[7] It seems to me that the argument put forward by Procksch deserves our attention, and that it should be examined again more closely in connection with Mowinckel's statement. Perhaps we had better first take note of the expression "the holy ones of the Most High" on its own, and then examine the contexts in which this expression appears in *Dan.* VII.

Procksch has observed that, excluding ch. VII, the word "holy" is used throughout the *Book of Daniel* (in both the Aramaic and Hebrew parts) only of God himself or of divine beings.[8] But the *Book of Daniel*—particularly as it hardly represents a literary unity or completely unified linguistic usage—is too narrow a basis upon which to build an argument. The whole of the Old Testament must therefore be taken into consideration.[9] There we find that there is no question of the concept "holy" being applied chiefly to God and divine beings; it can also be used of human beings in so far as it deals with their special relationship to God. In the Old Testament Israel is spoken of as a "holy people". The Israelites are told that they should be "holy". Specifically, cultic personnel can be characterised as "holy" in the widest sense. The High Priest Aaron is described as "the holy one of the Lord" (*Ps.* CVI.16); the priests are described predicatively as "holy" (*Lev.* XXI.6-8); the whole congregation may be given the predicate "holy" when their right to act as a cultic community is claimed (*Num.* XVI.3); the Levites are addressed attributively as "holy to the Lord" (*II Chron.* XXXV.3); a Nazirite is characterized predicatively as "holy" (*Num.*

---

[5] E. Sellin, *Israelitisch-jüdische Religionsgeschichte, Alttestamentliche Theologie auf religionsgeschichtlicher Grundlage* VOL. I, Leipzig 1933, pp. 129f.

[6] As in H. Junker, *Untersuchungen über literarische und exegetische Probleme des Buches Daniel* 1932, p. 56, n. 1. W. Baumgartner, in *Theologische Rundschau*, N.F. XI (1939), pp. 215ff.

[7] Cf. R. H. Charles. *A Critical and Exegetical Commentary on the Book of Daniel*, London 1929; A. Bentzen, *Daniel*.

[8] We need not here consider that textually most uncertain passage in *Dan.* VIII.24.

[9] Cf. the explanation of the concept of "holiness" by O. Procksch, in *Theologisches Wörterbuch zum Neuen Testament*, (hereafter *T.W.Z.N.T.*) ed. Kittel VOL. I 1933, pp. 88ff.; A. J. Festugière: *La Sainteté* 1942, pp. 72ff.; O. Procksch: *Theologie des Alten Testaments*, 1955, pp. 533ff. In these expositions the necessary references are given to passages dealing with matters which cannot be specially handled in the above essay.

vi.5, 8); a prophet is spoken of as "a holy man of God" (*II Kings* iv.9). It matters little whether the word "holy" is used predicatively, attributively, or in apposition. It is much more important to take note of the occasions when the *adjective* "holy" crops up.

These occasions are nearly all in quite late passages in the Old Testament, and are therefore fairly close in time to the *Book of Daniel*. There is a succession of quite clear instances in which the expression "the holy ones" means heavenly beings close to God. In *Ps.* LXXXIX.6, 8, the expressions "the congregation of the holy ones" or "the assembly of the holy ones" run parallel to, or are connected with the expressions "heaven", "clouds", "sons of the mighty", "all them that are about him" [God]. In *Job* xv.15 "his [God's] holy ones" are mentioned in parallel with the word "heaven", and to contrast with "man" and "he which is born of a woman". In *Job.* v.1 Eliphaz asks Job to "which of the holy ones" he will turn, since the divine world will still deny him an answer. In *Prov.* IX.10 "the knowledge of the holy" stands parallel to "the fear of the Lord"; and in *Prov.* XXX.3 the same expression "the knowledge of the holy" occurs again obviously in the sense of "supernatural knowledge".[10] Furthermore according to one very probable conjecture, which is also supported by the Septuagint, in *Exod.* xv.11 the "holy ones" were originally mentioned parallel with "the gods". In *Deut.* XXXIII.3 [2] and *Zech.* XIV.5 "the holy ones" appear as the heavenly companions of the coming God.[11] In *Sirach*, which stands very close in time to the *Book of Daniel* and particularly to *Dan.* VII, "the holy ones of God" appear and are identical with "the [heavenly] hosts of God" mentioned immediately after them (XLII.17). In *Tobit* VIII.15 are mentioned "all thy [God's] holy ones and all thy

[10] Usually we accept for these two passages in *Proverbs* a sort of "*pluralis maiestatis*" (Knowledge about the Holy One) cf. Gemser: *Sprüche Salomos*, 1937. Yet this seems a little forced. Does not this indefinite plural rather signify the heavenly world in a broader sense?

[11] In neither of these passages has the text come down to us intact, and therefore we cannot be certain about this. A plausible reconstruction of the text of *Deut.* XXXIII.2, 3 is offered by F. M. Cross and D. N. Freedman in *J.B.L.* LXVII (1948), pp. 193, 199. For the text of *Zech.* XIV.5, cf. Fr. Horst in Robinson and Horst: *Die zwölf kleinen Propheten*, 2nd edn., 1954. The uncertainties concerning these texts, however, are of very little importance here. Owing to the complete corruption of the text, which scarcely allows us to get any idea of what the original was actually like, I shall pass over *Hos.* XII.1 and *Ps.*XVI.3, where "the Holy Ones" appears in the current text.

creatures . . . all thy angels and thy chosen people"—here again it seems fairly likely that divine beings are again meant.[12]

The only certain example where "the holy ones" is used with a different meaning is in *Ps.* xxxiv.10[9] where the pious must be meant when "his [God's] holy ones" are mentioned. Only in the Hellenistic literature of the Diaspora does an occasional similar example occur (cf. *Wisd.* xviii.9).[13] According to this we must conclude that "the holy ones", used as a noun to which a genitive can be joined ("the holy ones of God", "his holy ones", "thy holy ones"), generally refers to divine beings—even if some connection with the pious congregation cannot be wholly excluded.

Apart from the Old Testament, we still have to take into account the writings of those groups which have become known to us through the manuscript discoveries in the caves around Khirbet Qumran, to which the "Damascus Document" must be added. For it is very probable that these groups have their roots in the religious tensions of the second century B.C., i.e. close in time and material to the visions of the *Book of Daniel*. Above all the expression "the holy ones of the Most High", which in *Dan.* vii appears in its Aramaic formulation, occurs in *Dam.* B20, 8 in its original Hebrew form. Of course interpreters of the *Book of Daniel*, even though for some strange reason they seem to have generally overlooked the well-known passage in the Damascus Document,[14] have long shown that the expression "the holy ones of the Most High" in the Aramaic text of *Dan.* vii must go back to a Hebrew original, since we find in *qaddîšê 'elyônîn* the Hebraism *'elyôn*. The Damascus Document in fact gives this Hebrew original. This proves that the translation "the holy ones of the

---

[12] The passages in *I Macc.* x.39, 44 do not here come under consideration (as Procksch suggests they do in *T.W.Z.N.T.* VOL. I (1933), p. 95, for here τοῖς ἁγίοις and τῶν ἁγίων lead back to a neuter τά ἅγια (cf. F. M. Abel: *Les Livres des Maccabées*, 1949, pp. 188ff.)

[13] I shall only mention here passages which touch on the issue under discussion. In *Num.* xvi.5, 7, by using the phrase "he who is holy", the question who is "holy" is answered in the sense of one who is a cultic participant qualified to carry out cultic action; here therefore we have a very special use of the word "holy". In *Isa.* iv.3 it is said that "he that remaineth in Jerusalem" at the end "shall be called holy"; the predicative use of the word "holy" is not to be compared to these instances where the word "holy" occurs above.

[14] I can only find one reference to this passage in J. A. Montgomery, *The Book of Daniel*, 1927, p. 307.

Most High" is correct, and that therefore the plural ending on the dependent genitive does not refer to this particular genitive, but to the whole phrase, which is quite possible linguistically.

This rules out the possibility discussed by Procksch[15] that in *Dan.* VII there occurs a partitive genitive ("the holy ones among the high (heavenly) beings") or an epexegetic genitive ("the high holy ones"), for although this possibility is linguistically justifiable, it cannot be considered if in *Dam.* B20, 8 we actually have the Hebrew original in front of us. This has become very probable in the light of research into the age and origin of the Damascus Document. Unfortunately the passage in the Damascus Document does not give an absolutely certain answer to the question whether we are meant to understand "the holy ones of the Most High" as divine beings, or as pious folk in the sense that is found in the Damascus Document; for the passage only says that evil doers are cursed by all the holy ones of the Most High, which leaves room for both interpretations.[16]

In other passages of the Damascus Document the adjective "holy" does not occur at all.[17] A few passages in other parts of the writings to which the Damascus Document belongs go a little further. The adjective "holy" only occurs very rarely in them,[18] but these passages do at least have some bearing on the problem. In one of the poetic passages at the end of the list of "community rules" (D.S.D.) the following occurs:

> He [God] has given them a share in the inheritance of the holy ones and has joined their community with the heavenly ones [literally: the sons of heaven] (IX. 7ff.).

The parallelism leaves no doubt that "the holy ones" here are meant to signify heavenly beings close to God. In addi-

---

[15] *Christentum und Wissenschaft*, III (1927), p. 429.

[16] R. H. Charles in *The Apocrypha and Pseudepigrapha of the Old Testament*, VOL. II, refrains from any note on the expression "all the saints of the most High". L. Rost, who translates and deals with the passage in *Th. Lz.*, LXXVIII (1953), cols. 144, 146, leaves the question open whether "people of perfect holiness" or "angelic powers" are meant.

[17] The conjecture made by R. H. Charles, *loc. cit.*, concerning Dam. A. 6, 4, whereby the expression "the earlier saints" is used, must remain a very uncertain hypothesis which does not allow any very far-reaching conclusions to be drawn.

[18] Apart from the passages now to be discussed it only occurs elsewhere in DSD 3.7, where a "holy spirit" is mentioned.

tion there is a passage from the "Songs of Thanksgiving" (D.S.T.):

> To join the garrison of the host of the army of the holy ones
> and to enter into the union of the host of the congregation
> of the heavenly ones [literally: the sons of heaven].[19]

Here also it clearly follows from the parallelism that when "the holy ones" are mentioned, divine beings are meant. The occurrence of the same parallel twice serves to show that it was not unusual in the culture from which these writings stem to use the concepts "the holy ones" and "the heavenly" as synonyms. Finally there is in the "Songs of Thanksgiving" a further passage which is unfortunately rather obscure, but which does mention "the community of holy ones",[20] though there is no clear indication as to what the expression means. As far as I can see, there are no further passages with the substantive adjective "holy"—above all there is no evidence to show that human beings were characterized by this adjective.[21]

Our examination therefore has gone beyond the relatively narrow bounds of Procksch's arguments and now has a much broader basis. Taking the whole of the Old Testament—though noting that the later parts are the most important here—and including the writings of those groups that have become known to us by the manuscript discoveries of Khirbet Qumran, we now have enough material to understand the questions which arise in a comparison with *Dan.* VII. It will be seen that quite a consistent picture emerges, if we keep in mind the independent substantive usage of the concept "holy". There is an important distinction when, following the pattern in *Deuteronomy*, a "holy

---

[19] For the text see E. L. Sukenik, *The Dead Sea Scrolls of the Hebrew University*, Jerusalem 1955, col. III, lines 21ff. (Pl. XXXVII). English translations are in T. H. Gaster, *The Scriptures of the Dead Sea Sect in English Translation*, with Introduction and Notes, 1956; S. Holm-Nielsen, *Hodayot, Psalms from Qumran*, Aarhus 1960, p. 64; G. Vermes, *The Dead Sea Scrolls in English*, 1962, p. 158.

[20] Text in Sukenik, *The Dead Sea Scrolls*, col. IV, line 25 (Pl. XXXVIII).

[21] W. H. Brownlee, in a note to his translation of D.S.D. (*B.A.S.O.R. Suppl.*, 1951, sections 10-12) refers, in connection with the passage 11, 7ff., to *Test. Levi* III.3 and *Ps. Sol.* XVII.43 for "the holy ones" used in the sense of heavenly beings. And he is quite right, because in *Test. Levi* III.3 the inhabitants of the fourth heaven are referred to as "holy", and in *Ps. Sol.* XVII.43 heavenly beings must be intended by the expression "the holy ones". It is moreover important to note that the Testaments of the Twelve Patriarchs, and the *Testament of Levi* in particular, are very closely related to the writings of Khirbet Qumran (cf. A. Dupont-Sommer, *The Jewish Sect of Qumran and the Essenes*, 1954.

people"[22] is mentioned or even "holy men"[23], or when Israel is told to be "holy", or when on the other hand "the holy ones" are mentioned, employing a sort of technical term which can claim to be clearly understandable without further explanation. The expression "the holy ones of the most High" goes back to the independent usage of the concept "the holy ones", and only such passages where it is used in similar ways can be taken as direct comparative material.

What Procksch has deduced about the meaning of the word "holy" from the different parts of the *Book of Daniel* with its tales and visions does not completely satisfy this stipulation; only the passages *Dan.* IV.10, 14, 20 and VIII.13 (twice), where the word "holy" occurs, are really suitable to explain the expression "the holy ones of the Most High". But Procksch's argument has been proved basically correct after more extensive research. Only the one passage *Ps.* XXXIV.10 shows a meaning of the expression "the holy ones" standing alone which agrees with the traditional interpretation of "the holy ones of the Most High" in *Dan.* VII. If the interpretation of this concept in *Dan.* VII is open to debate at all, and if the interpretation as God's people Israel does not seem to be proved incontestably already by the words in *Dan.* VII about "the holy ones of the Most High"—in which case it would be necessary to adduce *Ps.* XXXIV.10—then we must give serious consideration to the comparative material which has been put forward. Indeed this comparative material adds such weight to the interpretation of "the holy ones of the Most High" as heavenly beings that this interpretation must be regarded as extremely probable, so that the only question is whether the content of the statements in *Dan.* VII concerning "the holy ones of the Most High" is such that we must nevertheless finally decide against this probability.

It is therefore necessary to examine whether *Dan.* VII decisively

[22] Something like this occurs in the text of the "Struggle of the Children of Light against the Children of Darkness", where the phrase is, "We are thy holy people" (E. L. Sukenik, *The Dead Sea Scrolls*, Pl. XXIX.12; H. Bardtke in *Th. Lz.* LXXX (1955), col. 415, translating col. XIV.12). Elsewhere the word "holy" occurs in the parts of the manuscript originally published only in the short section reproduced on the title page of E. L. Sukenik, *Meghillôth Genûzôth*, VOL. I, Jerusalem, 1948. However, see Sukenik, *The Dead Sea Scrolls*, Pl. XXVII, 1-8 and the translation by Bardtke in *Th. Lz.* LXXX (1955), col. 412 of col. XII.1-8.

[23] Cf. the expression "men of holiness" in *D.S.D.* 5.13; 8.17, 23, and similar expressions.

excludes the possibility that we are meant to understand heavenly beings by this phrase "the holy ones of the Most High". For this purpose we need only refer to the interpretation in vss. 15-28. It would be an error in method to bring in the vision itself and take that element in the vision of "a Son of Man" as part of the argument. For the individual parts of the vision—especially the scenes of the heavenly courts of justice and the appearance of the one who looked "like a man"—have their own antecedents and are not directly connected with the interpretation. Of course the "Son of man", who is to obtain world dominion for all time, points to "the holy ones of the Most High" who are to receive the eternal kingdom (vs. 18). But the coming of "the Son of man" "with the clouds of heaven" still by no means proves that "the holy ones of the Most High" must also have belonged to a heavenly world (as Procksch believes): for there may well be a special reason for the coming with the clouds of heaven, and we should beware of trying to expound this in the light of the interpretation which we are given.

If we look at the interpretation alone, the first passage where "the holy ones of the Most High" occurs (vs. 18) states nothing about their actual nature. This is not surprising, for it is merely a general observation that the four world empires symbolized by the beasts in the vision will be followed by the eschatological eternal rule of "the holy ones of the most High". Keeping in mind the dream and interpretation of *Dan.* 11.31-45, according to which the history of the world empires terminates in the eternal "kingdom" to be set up by "the God of heaven" (vs. 44), it seems natural to expect the prospect of an eschatological empire of "heaven" in *Dan.* vii.18 also. We cannot exclude the possibility of such an idea in *Dan.* vii also, in which the heavenly powers take over rule on God's behalf in place of the earthly world empires at the end of their time. But of course *Dan.* vii proves nothing at all merely by pointing to *Dan.* 11.31-45, since in all probability *Dan.* vii is somewhat later in date than *Dan.* 11 and was written by a different author,[24] so that it may have had a quite different idea of what was expected at the end.

Since the literary unity of *Dan.* vii.15-28 is questionable, and especially as vss. 21-22 pose literary problems, it is best to proceed without considering the actual successive series of occasions

[24] See pp. 208ff.

where "the holy ones of the Most High" occur. At the end of the separate interpretation about the fourth beast there appears once more—and this time in greater detail—the statement which has already been anticipated in the summary interpretation of vss. 17-18, that finally the "kingdom" is to be given "to the people of the holy ones of the Most High" (vs. 27). Here now the concept "the people" stands side by side with the concept "the holy ones of the Most High". Now the question should surely arise—and even the most detailed commentaries pass it over—how is this genitive relationship between "the people" and "the holy ones of the Most High" to be understood? Generally we think immediately of an epexegetic genitive,[25] though we might also consider a possessive genitive differentiating between "the people of the holy ones of the most High" and "the holy ones of the Most High", so allowing God's people Israel to imply a people belonging to the heavenly world.

The natural assumption, however, that in vs. 27 nothing is meant to be essentially different from vs. 18, and that therefore "the people of the holy ones of the Most High" in vs. 27 means the same as "the holy ones of the Most High" in vs. 18, tells against the idea of such a possessive genitive, and makes an epexegetic genitive seem more probable. Does not this inclusion of the concept "the holy ones of the Most High" with the general concept "the people" prove that the interpretation of "the holy ones of the Most High" as a definite earthly people, i.e. God's people Israel, is the only one possible? By no means. Again the Khirbet Qumran texts show this. In the passage from D.S.T. quoted above on p. 220, the "host of the army of the holy ones" and the "host of the congregation of the heavenly ones" are mentioned. The word translated as "host" is the same Hebrew word *'am* ("people") which also stands in *Dan.* VII.27.[26] We

---

[25] I cannot quite understand why J. A. Montgomery, *The Book of Daniel*, p. 316, in rejecting this interpretation still fails to give any other positive suggestion.

[26] This passage has indeed been translated in many different ways: some translators see in *'m* the preposition "with" (Hempel, *loc. cit.*, Schubert, *loc. cit.*, even Wallenstein, *Hymns from Judaean Scrolls*, p. 15, where admittedly the translation is too free to give us a clear idea of the translator's conception); also Bardtke, in *Th. Lz.*, 1956, col. 593). Yet that does not seem possible to me, since the word "garrison" says too little if it is not more closely explained by some following genitive. We can refer to DAM. B9, 32, where the same word "garrison" is clearly more closely defined by a following genitive ("in order to stand at the garrison of the men of holy perfection"). Bardtke: *Die Handschriftenfunde am Toten Meer,*

should therefore translate *Dan.* VII.27 as: "And the kingdom . . . shall be given to the *host* of the holy ones of the Most High, their kingdom shall be an everlasting kingdom, and all dominions shall serve and obey them". Then, however, there is nothing in this passage to help us to decide the question whether in *Dan.* VII "the holy ones of the Most High" are to be understood as earthly or heavenly beings.

In the interpretation of the fourth beast, and especially of the eleventh horn, mention is made of the action by the king represented by this eleventh horn (Antiochus IV) in opposing "the Most High" and "the holy ones of the Most High"; he "shall speak great words against the Most High" and shall also inflict some violence on "the holy ones of the Most High" (vs. 25a). Here the parallelism between "the Most High" and "the holy ones of the Most High" supports the idea of a connection between the latter and heavenly beings.[27] If the "holy ones of the Most High" are to be understood here too as God's people Israel, as has been accepted as completely self-evident—it is because only a human, earthly object seems to fit in with the following verb. As far as can be gathered from the traditional text,[28] the intensive form of B L' which stands here is derived from a stem known to all Semitic languages and dialects and means "to be consumed", "to be worn out", "to be used up", "to dwindle away", and is used mainly of articles of clothing.[29] Now, quite apart from the question of the correct interpretation of "the holy ones of the Most High", it is very questionable whether

---

p. 153, translates correctly when he reproduces '*m* as "people", but then again makes the error of conceiving what follows as being in apposition to "people" (instead of as a dependent genitive) which is hardly possible, since the indeterminate "people" requires a closer definition. All these more or less forced translations proceed from the impression that one cannot have genitive relationships made up of a chain of perhaps three or four members. Yet there is nothing in Hebrew to prevent an even longer chain of genitive associations; it is undoubtedly just such a chain which occurs in the passage just mentioned in DAM. B9, 32 (cf. Sukenik: *Dead Sea Scrolls*, pl. XXVII.5, 8).

[27] The word "the Most High" here has its genuine Aramaic form, whereas in the compound "the holy ones of the Most High" it appears in that form of Hebraism which was mentioned on pp. 218f. of this essay.

[28] F. Perles (quoted in W. Gesenius, *Hebräisches und aramäisches Handwörterbuch über das alte Testament*, 1921, proposed a modification of the text which would make it much more simple to connect "the saints of the Most High" with heavenly beings—but this modification has no certain basis.

[29] In Akkadian the verb is used of hair falling out, of smoke drifting about, of fires dying out, etc.

an intensive of this stem could have had a *personal* object. We might have to consider a *figurative* usage of the verb which would produce an acceptable sense in a more or less forced manner.

The question arises, however, whether the intensive with a personal object is really derived from the stem mentioned. Arabic has two different verbs which are phonetically relevant. The first is the verb *baliya*, used to denote clothes being worn out, and belonging to the common Semitic stem just mentioned; the second is the verb *balā* which means "to test", "to handle roughly", "to torment", "to offend". I hardly need point out that in this stem the idea of a personal object immediately suggests itself. It would therefore seem more correct to translate *Dan.* VII.25*a* as: "And he shall speak great words against the Most High, and shall *greatly offend*[30] the holy ones of the Most High".

Even if this *is* correct, however, it still cannot be proved from vs. 25 that "the holy ones of the Most High" must have meant God's people Israel. On the contrary, the parallelism in this verse positively supports the interpretation of "the holy ones of the Most High" as heavenly beings, and when it is said that the godless king shall seek "to change the times and the laws", we are meant to understand from the whole context that this is an attack on the divine world and the divine order of things.

There still remains the difficult passage in vss. 21-22. Verse 22, however, is of little help, for it only states that "the holy ones of the Most High" or "the holy ones" shall receive the kingdom, as is also stated in vss. 18 and 27 which we have already discussed. But this verse poses certain literary problems of its own. After the statement that "judgment was given to the holy ones of the Most High",[31] the following assertion that "the time came when the saints received the kingdom" has a remarkably weak effect, and suggests a clumsy imitation. We may wonder whether this ending to the verse is not a quite meaningless addition, which is detectable because instead of the whole expression "the holy ones of the Most High" we have simply "the holy ones", an

[30] By this means we can roughly convey the use of the intensive form of the stem.

[31] The above translation presupposes an acquaintance with that supplement to the traditional text proposed by Ewald, who guessed that it might be defective as a result of "homoiteleuton". Ewald's proposal has since been accepted by many interpreters of the *Book of Daniel*.

abbreviated style although there is obviously no difference in the interpretation.

The same expression "the holy ones" occurs also in vs. 21; quite obviously in this verse we are to understand human beings by "the holy ones", specifically the chosen people of Israel, or rather that part of the people remaining true to God's beliefs and traditions. For even if we still read the statement that "this same horn" (i.e. the eleventh horn of the fourth beast) waged war "with the holy ones" in the same sense as vs. 25*a*, and see in it a battle against the heavenly world, then the next observation, that it (the eleventh horn) "prevailed against them" (the holy ones) can only refer to the victorious struggle of Antiochus IV against the worshipping congregation in Jerusalem. The question arises, however, whether we can decide the meaning of the phrase "the holy ones of the Most High" for the whole of *Dan*. VII from vs. 21 alone.

It can of course hardly be doubted that vss. 21-22 are a later addition from the literary point of view. Even if we accept a basic literary unity, not perhaps for the whole of the *Book of Daniel*[32] but at least for ch. VII, we can scarcely help feeling that in vss. 20-22 there is a secondary augmentation—anyone who believes that we have to envisage a more or less complex literary pre-history for *Dan*. VII will see in this passage a secondary insertion that was only added after the greater part of the traditional literary form of ch. VII had already emerged. For the special concern (beginning in vs. 19) with the meaning of the fourth beast with all its peculiarities loses all its continuity and is thrown out of connection by vs. 20*b*. Indeed, although vs. 20*b* has no apparent relevance, a conjectural emendation of the text[33] might connect it a little more smoothly to the context that precedes it. In vs. 21, however, this is not possible; here the sudden reappearance of the style used in describing the vision—which is completely un-motivated and out of place in dealing with the particular point at issue—clearly indicates a not very well considered addition. Moreover, by naming merely "the holy ones", the removal of one of the elements of the interpretation is so out of place that we must conclude that a secondary hand has been at work here,

---

[32] Cf. recently H. H. Rowley: "The Unity of the Book of Daniel", in *Hebrew Union College Annual*, XXIII, No. 1 (1950-51), pp. 233ff.

[33] Cf. *Biblia Hebraica*, ed. R. Kittel, 7th edn., 1951.

who ignored the organic construction of the chapter as a whole.

The same goes for vs. 22 also. Indeed vs. 22 can scarcely be separated from vs. 21 at all, especially as the beginning of vs. 22 can hardly be connected with anything but the first words of vs. 21. However the present form of vss. 21-22 may be explained, vs. 21 at any rate can clearly be seen as a secondary element. A. Bentzen, who regards *Daniel* as a "unified composition" and feels there is no cause to try a critical literary analysis of this chapter, nevertheless regards vs. 21 as an addition: "The only verse which I find difficult to consider original is vs. 21".[34] From the same basic starting-point J. A. Montgomery[35] reaches the same conclusion. R. H. Charles, who asks no such critical literary questions with regard to *Dan.* VII and sees only a few textual corruptions which can be overcome by means of textual criticism, nevertheless recognizes that at least in vs. 21*b* there is a later addition, although he finds very little to object to in the passage vss. 21-22.[36] We may therefore quite legitimately consider that the necessity of understanding "the holy ones" as earthly human beings in vs. 21 arises acutely only in this second half of the verse.

The facts are as follows: in the traditional form of *Dan.* VII it is clear that "the holy ones of the Most High" refers to the chosen people of Israel. This conception is of very early date, for even if a complex literary growth for *Dan.* VII is accepted, and the very latest addition demonstrable in the chapter as a whole is seen in the decisive vs. 21, it is still probable that *Dan.* VII with all its secondary additions was completed not very long after the time of Antiochus IV, i.e. the time in which the traditional ideas of the dream and interpretation received their basic and lasting form. But this conception rests solely on one single verse, and perhaps even only on a half verse. We need not agree with Procksch, who regards the main part of the interpretation with its special reference to the fourth empire as secondary, in order to maintain that the interpretation of "the holy ones of the Most High" refers in its original meaning to divine beings; nor need we agree with

---

[34] Aage Bentzen, *Daniel*, 1952, pp. 57-58.

[35] J. A. Montgomery, *The Book of Daniel*, 1927, pp. 95, 312.

[36] R. H. Charles, *A Critical and Exegetical Commentary on the Book of Daniel*, 1929, pp. 164ff., 192.

Sellin,[37] who eliminates as later additions those elements of the interpretation which especially connect the eleventh horn with Antiochus IV, in order to consider as primary the placing of "the holy ones of the Most High" in the heavenly world. We need only accept that the small and evidently secondary element in the interpretation—the passage in vss. 21-22, and possibly only 21*b*—has introduced a later change in the meaning of "the holy ones" so as to refer to the chosen people of Israel.

But is such a late change in meaning probable? Or can such a small element in the interpretation carry the burden of proof against the relatively rich comparative material, which makes it seem at least extremely probable that originally "the holy ones of the Most High" referred to heavenly beings? The older sections of *Dan.* VII at least (especially vs. 25*a*) seem to suggest this. By carefully considering the pros and cons, it does seem that in the main part of *Dan.* VII "the holy ones of the Most High" are thought of as the heavenly associates of God, and that only subsequently did a change in meaning take place, so that Mowinckel's assertion that "the holy ones" in the Old Testament are divine beings is confirmed in *Dan.* VII, and therefore, just as the basis of the dream in *Dan.* II is the expectation of an eschatological "kingdom of God", the vision of *Dan.* VII amounts basically to a proclamation of the imminent "heavenly kingdom".

[37] E. Sellin: *Alttestamentliche Theologie auf religionsgeschichtlicher Grundlage*, VOL. I, 1933, pp. 129f.

IX

Office and Vocation in the Old Testament

The whole of human history is full of examples of tension between tradition and inspiration, the reflective and the spontaneous, between institutions and direct action, the conventional and creative innovation. On both sides there are dangers whenever one aspect predominates. On the side of tradition there is the danger of paralysis and lifelessness, on the side of inspiration the danger of instability, of slipping into the fantastic and the fanciful. Particularly in the history of religious communities we find this simultaneous co-existence and opposition between the holy order and direct experience of God, of ecclesiastical duty and direct vocation.[1] This complex relationship has played its part in the history of Christianity—especially in the early days of the Church.[2] It is also to be found in the Old Testament, and I should like to outline a few important points with regard to this particular sphere.

The Old Testament, like the ancient Oriental world from which it stems, has no clearly defined idea of "office". There is no single word in the languages concerned to signify exactly what we ourselves understand by the word. In the Old Testament community, which had far outgrown the rudimentary and simple stage, there are indeed special functions which were looked after continuously by individually chosen people either in the service of a particular group or community, or in the service of some particular superior. In such cases we are entitled to speak of "offices", but still without definitely fixing the concept "office". In the ancient Near East, however—and this is

---

[1] Cf. for example: G. van der Leeuw, *Phänomenologie der Religion,* 1933, pp. 196ff. (Eng. trans.: *Religion in Essence and Manifestation,* 1938).

[2] Cf. H. von Campenhausen, *Kirchliches Amt und geistliche Vollmacht in den ersten drei Jahrhunderten,* 1953.

especially true of the Old Testament—the spheres of the sacred
and the profane, the spiritual and the worldly, the divine and
the human, were not separated off from one another. A separate
set of laws for "worldly" institutions and offices could not have
existed. This is particularly true since Old Testament belief
recognizes no order or events on earth which are not created by
God, and over whose history God has not stood as Lord. In Old
Testament belief one had to be constantly aware of God's direct
and unexpected action.

Direct intervention by God could be expected above all in
that office which was specially concerned with communication
between God and Man—the office of priest, but according to
Old Testament tradition it is just here that such directness is
completely lacking. The Old Testament priesthood is completely
without any charismatic element.[3] In the older, so-called pre-
exilic literature there is not much said at all about priests; where
priests are mentioned they appear simply as persons who, in
specific holy places, are authorized to undertake cultic activities
and also to look after the holy sphere along with everything in it.
Indeed the priest had to act on behalf of everybody who belonged
to the holy place, whether as community or individual.

In the earliest times the presence of a priest was by no means
essential for carrying out cultic activities, for every fully authorized Israelite—especially the *pater familias*—had the right to
carry out sacrifices. But with the development and consolidation
of cults in Palestine it became customary for priests to be
employed, especially at the larger and more important sanctuaries, and also for the priestly office to remain in the same family;
the office of priest, in practice, became hereditary.[4] There were
apparently no special laws laid down concerning the assumption
and exercising of the office of priest, except perhaps lack of
physical disability, and cultic, ritual purity.[5] Thus for example
a man who set up and equipped a private sanctuary on his own

---

[3] It is a unique note in *II Chron.* xxiv.20 when the "Spirit of God" takes hold
of a priest, or rather a priest's son. The Chronicler, to whom we must attribute this
note, here lets a priest's son appear in the role of a prophet. He is hardly seeking
to characterize the office of the priest by this; the giving of the spirit is shared by
many different men (cf. for example *I Chron.* xii.19).

[4] This general development is well known and needs no further detailed
documentation.

[5] Cf. individual examples in *Lev.* xxi.1-xxii.16 and *Ezek.* xliv.15-27.

land could appoint one of his own sons as priest in this sanctuary (*Judges* XVII.5); on a higher plane, at a later date David was able to appoint his sons as priests in the royal shrine (*II Sam.* VIII.18b). The more ancient Old Testament tradition never once recognizes a special act in the conferring of the priestly office, for the traditional expression used (from the most ancient to the most recent Old Testament times) as a technical term for the appointment of a priest obviously does not signify a consecrating act. The expression used is "to fill the hand".[6]

With what is "the hand" of the newly appointed priest "filled"? This expression appears in no other context in the Old Testament.[7] The question therefore is whether it is to be understood in a literal sense,[8] or with some figurative meaning. Since there is no comparative Old Testament material, if we look for the derivation and meaning of this old expression (which may well have been taken over from pre-Israelite tradition) in the ancient environment of the Old Testament, we can find only one passage where the phrase "hand-filling" is used, and that is in the cuneiform texts from Mari on the central Euphrates, which date from the time around 1700 B.C. It is scarcely possible to see this as mere coincidence, since connections have already been

---

[6] The oldest literary documentation occurs in *Judges* XVII.5, 12. It is hard to determine the age of *Exod.* XXXII.29. *I Kings* XIII.33 belongs to the literary framework of the historical work in *Deuteronomy*. Then the expression occurs in the ritual of *Lev.* XVI (vs. 32) in the Holiness Code (*Lev.* XXI.10) as well as several times in Priestly Source narrative (*Exod.* XXVIII.41, XXIX.9, 29, 33, 35; *Lev.* VIII, 33; *Num.* III.3); then there is in P the use of the shortened expression the "filling" for the appointment of the priest in *Exod.* XXIX.22, 26, 27, 31, 34; *Lev.* VII.37, VIII.22, 28ff. In *Chronicles* the expression is still used in its technical sense in *II Chron.* XIII.9, but on the other hand in *I Chron.* XXIX.5 and *II Chron.* XXIX.31 in a vague sense, apparently with the meaning "to offer cultic gifts"—from which it can be seen that the Chronicler no longer knew the actual meaning and has therefore appropriated a more contemporary meaning). Highly significant and unique is the use of the expression with regard to the altar in *Ezek.* XLIII.26; in this probably secondary section of the *Book of Ezekiel* the expression has possibly been understood in the general sense of cultic service.

[7] In exactly the same formulation the expression otherwise only occurs in *II Kings* IX.24 but in quite a different sense: Jehu "filled his hand" with a bow, i.e. he took it in his hand; *Lev.* IX.17 and *Ps.* CXXIX.7 can be compared to this (with a slightly varied form). Worthy of note is *Ps.* XXVI.10, where it is said that the "right hand" of the enemies of the worshipper is "full of bribes"; here is meant the receiving of money (the same formulation is found in the traditional meaning in *Ps.* XLVIII.11).

[8] The original concrete meaning is still quite clear in those passages mentioned in the previous note.

established at different points between the Mari texts and the Old Testament, especially the earlier Old Testament tradition: so we must accept that there existed definite historical connections between the ruling class of Mari and the beginnings of Israel, though these are admittedly rather obscure.

In the Mari texts the expression "hand-filling" occurs in the same way as a technical term, though in a totally different connection. Here it signifies the exactly determined share of the spoils of war which is due to an officer, or a definite category of officers.[9] It seems to mean the allotment of a share in return for some definite activity, and indeed as recompense for carrying out this activity. The application of this expression to priestly activity was natural; for the priest, as we learn from numerous passages in the Old Testament, used to receive a clearly defined share of the sacrificial offerings brought to the shrine. Therefore the "hand-filling" of the priest in the Old Testament will have to be understood quite simply in the sense of acceptance of a definite share commissioned to him of the sacrifices. It can no longer be ascertained, however, whether this original—still fairly concrete—meaning of "hand-filling" was maintained, or whether in the course of time the expression continued to be preserved merely as a misconstrued technical term, or was interpreted in some other figurative sense.[10]

We learn nothing from the older traditional material, except

[9] The most important documentary passage is in A.R.M. vol. II (1950), 13, 17; it is treated by Ch.-F. Jean, here on pp. 36ff. The letter A.R.M. II.13 deals with the fact that on a certain occasion officers "in order to increase their handful" (*ana mil kātišunu šumūdim*) appropriated more of the spoils (*šallutum*) than was their due, and indeed apparently at the cost of the king, the letter-writer, and the soldiers. From this the expression "hand-filling" can be interpreted also in the fragmentary and therefore rather vague passage *A.R.M.* 1.103, 20 (cf. A. Finet, A.R.M. xv, 1954, p. 220). We must however differentiate the expression, which though similar is not exactly the same, "to fill somebody's hand with something" which has been documented many times in Akkadian, and also occurs in the Akkadian of the Mari texts (A.R.M. v.2, 7, *Revue d'Assyrologie*, XLII (1948), pp. 128ff.; *Rev.* 1.31); it means "to leave, to entrust, to deliver something to someone" (cf. Fr. Delitzsch, *Assyrisches Handwörterbuch*, 1894, p. 409b and W. Müss-Arnolt, *Assyrisch-englisch-deutsches Handwörterbuch*, 1905, p. 542). Quite different is the usage of *malûm* D and Dt with a personal object and an expression with *ana*, which signifies a class or profession or something similar; the meaning is "to order or to detail somebody" (cf. A. Ungnad, *Babylonische Briefe aus der Zeit der Hammurapi-Dynastie*, 1914, p. 334; also A.R.M. vi.40, 7f., 24f.).

[10] Cf. however some points of connection at least with regard to this in the passages mentioned above at the end of note 6.

that a priest is appointed in return for a definite sum of money by anyone who possesses a shrine. The apparently very early story in *Judges* XVII-XVIII, which contains the most comprehensive information about the appointment of a priest to be found anywhere in the Old Testament, uses a very significant word in one passage which says that the priest is "hired" (*Judges* XVIII.4). This word is only used otherwise with regard to labourers who are taken into employment for a specified wage. *Judges* XVII.10 also expressly reports just such an agreement; in order to obtain a man as a priest, the owner of the sanctuary offers gifts of gold and other valuables[11]—quite apart from the usual "hand-filling"—which are to be allotted to the priest he has in mind. A definite rank is, of course, thereby given to the priest along with his new appointment. He becomes a "father" (*Judges* XVII.10) and is perhaps even addressed by this title. This is equally valid even if the person in question is a young man, as in *Judges* XVII and XVIII. Thus the priest takes over a task which originally had been the responsibility of the *pater familias*.[12]

From all this, a picture emerges of the oldest priesthood in Israel which is not noticeably different from the picture which can be obtained from existing sources of the beginnings of the priesthood in other ancient Oriental religions.[13]

What is striking is that, over and above these beginnings, the priesthood with its basis in Old Testament belief could not have developed and changed in the same way as the definitely cultic religions. The divine service in the Old Testament knew—at least in its legitimate form—no divine image of a god which would have to be looked after. Exorcism and the discussion of omens lay outside the priest's control, and were also alien to Old Testament belief. Admittedly the earliest Old Testament

[11] Unfortunately it is not quite clear how we are to understand in *Judges* XVII.10 the reference to time with regard to the "ten shekels of silver" offered to the priest.

[12] There is no reason at all why we should conclude from the incongruity between the age of the "young man" and the rank of "father" which he obtains as a priest that there is a lack of literary unity in the story. This conclusion has been drawn by G. R. Driver, "Glosses in the Hebrew Text of the Old Testament", in *Orientalia et Biblica Lovaniensia*, I, 1957, p. 143. The rank of "father" is obviously only related to the office of priest as such and has nothing whatsoever to do with the bearer of the title himself.

[13] Cf. H. Bonnet, *Reallexikon der ägyptischen Religionsgeschichte*, 1952, pp. 596ff.; B. Meissner, *Babylonien und Assyrien*, VOL. II, 1925, pp. 52ff.

tradition recognizes the right of the priest to act as an oracle; the technical oracle by lot, the so-called "Urim and Thummim" in the Old Testament, was in the hands of the priests. But this aspect of priestly activity, far from being gradually extended, in time came to be curtailed.[14] In striking contrast to the priests in the surrounding areas who at certain times and places were very powerful and influential, the priests in ancient Israel hardly had a very important historical or even political role. One solitary example is the decisive intervention of the Jerusalem priest, Jehoiada, in removing Queen Athaliah (who had usurped the throne of David in Jerusalem after the death of her son King Ahaziah), and in establishing Joash, legitimate heir to the throne. In this case the priest had a particular reason for intervening, since Athaliah—as a woman who did not even belong to the house of David—must have seemed intolerable to the priest of the Jerusalem shrine over which she ruled.

The Old Testament priesthood had limited cultic tasks to perform in each shrine. One of these tasks was the management of the old oracle by lot, the "Urim and Thummim"; another, perhaps the most important task of all, was to impart information and instruction concerning cultic and ritual matters, which mainly arose from inquiries by those taking part in cultic activities.[15] This simple role of the priest, together with the basic form of the cultic divine service, may date from the time of the earliest pre-Canaanite beginnings of Israel. There is positive support for this in the clearly technical expression for the appointment of a priest in the language of the Mari texts, which must have taken form during the very early days of Israel's origins, about which we are still so much in the dark.

The process of infiltration of the Levites into the priesthood in the early days of Old Testament priesthood was of great significance. This process is difficult to explain, mainly because it is not easy to say who the Levites basically were. The ancient

[14] The "Urim and Thummim" of the post-exilic High Priest are obviously only a piece of tradition.

[15] To give tôrâ ("instruction") seems especially in certain prophets to have been the most important task of the priest; cf. *Hos.* iv.6; *Zeph.* iii.4; *Mic.*iii.11; *Jer.* ii.8, viii.18. In this the prophets evidently presume that the content of the priestly tôrâ goes beyond a narrow cultic ritual framework to encompass the teaching of a correct way of life. The tôrâ of the priest did in fact with time develop further in this direction, in accordance with the instructions which the priest had to give regarding the prerequisites for participating in the cult.

story in *Judges* XVII-XVIII shows that even at a very early date a Levite was favoured as a priest above all others. Later the Levites claimed—apparently in face of considerable opposition— that the office of priest (or at least certain definite priestly functions) was theirs alone.[16] Finally, as the law in *Deuteronomy* shows, they carried through their claim to the exclusive exercise of the office. This, however, did not bring about any essential change in the significance and tasks of the actual office.

An important change in the priesthood did occur with the end of the monarchy in Israel, and especially with the end of the rule of the house of David in Jerusalem. As a result of this the priesthood achieved an importance which had been denied to it hitherto—especially the High Priest of the Jerusalem shrine. As a result of the so-called cult reform by the late Judaean King Josiah on the basis of the deuteronomic law, the original royal temple in Jerusalem became the only legitimate shrine, after the removal of all other shrines in the land. The position of the first priest of this sanctuary, to whom evidently a part of the cultic functions of the king were now transferred, became quite different from what it had been when the priests of Jerusalem were mere employees in the royal shrine, for he now became a "High Priest".

It is well known that the costume of the High Priest of the post-exilic period, as it is described in detail in *Exod.* XXVIII and XXXIX, has certain ornamentation which is obviously of royal origin. This is particularly true of the headgear. The special headband which the High Priest wore is designated by a special word (*miṣnepheth*), which otherwise only occurs in *Ezek.* XXI.31, where it designates a part of the official robes of a "prince" (i.e. a Judaean king), which is so important that its removal designates

---

[16] Documentary evidence of this is found above all in the Levi saying in the so-called Blessing of Moses in *Deut.* XXXIII.8-11. Here the claim of Levi—whose name was mentioned at the beginning of the saying in the original text—to control the oracle by lot (the "Urim and Thummim") is granted (vs. 8), and he receives divine support against his later opponents (vs. 11). In the central part of the decree—which is in the plural in contrast to the passages at the beginning and end, which are in the singular, the right to imparting of *tôrâ* and offering of sacrifices are counted among the tasks of Levi (vs. 10). The question arises whether this middle section is secondary, incorporating a later extension to the basic form of Levi's claims. Then the Levites would have claimed the sole right to give an oracle. The Levite priest in *Judges* XVII and XVIII gives an oracle though we are admittedly not informed how he does this (XVIII.5, 6).

his dismissal from office. The same can be said of the "flower" which the High Priest wore at the front of the headband; this insignia was considered life-giving and potent to avert ill-luck,[17] and when worn in earlier times by the king was such an important piece of regalia that in *II Kings* xi.12 the giving of this "flower" at the investiture of a king is expressly mentioned.[18]

The breast-plate of the High Priest should probably be interpreted within the same context. It is described as a pouch in which the High Priest is to carry on his breast the stones of "Urim and Thummim"—which at this late period were not used at all, merely representing an ancient traditional part of the priest's raiment. This purpose alone, however, fails to explain either the rectangular shape of the pouch, or why it is set with twelve precious stones arranged in rows. The whole thing is a composite mixture, in which one original element is clearly a royal breast decoration, similar to a rectangular pectoral trimmed with precious stones, which formed part of the royal costume as worn in pre-Israelite Syria and Palestine. Such an article was presumably also worn by Israelite kings.[19]

Just how conscious of this royal element in the costume of the High Priest people were—even at a quite late time—is shown by some very remarkable evidence. At one point on the famous murals from the Jewish synagogue of Dura-Europos on the central Euphrates, Aaron is depicted as a High Priest; there is no doubt that this is the correct identification,[20] for his name is attached, but the costume in which he is portrayed in no way

---

[17] Cf. A. de Buck, "La fleur au front du grand-prêtre," in *Oudtestamentische Studïen*, IX (1951), pp. 18-29; here mainly Egyptian documentary evidence is used to interpret the life-giving flower.

[18] The word *nēzer* is mostly translated by "diadem": it only means "consecration, inauguration", however, and is used interchangeably with *sîs* ("flower") in explanations of the costume of the High Priest. (Cf. *Exod.* xxviii.36 with xxix.6 and xxxix.30 as well as *Lev.* viii.9, where both words are linked). Most important of all is *Ps.* cxxxii.18 where it is said that upon the king (upon his head) "shall his *nēzer* flourish". Also therefore in *II Sam.* 1.10; *II Kings* xi.12; *Ps.* lxxxix.40 the *nēzer* of the king is to be understood as the "consecration" which exists in the life-giving flower.

[19] Cf. chiefly G. Widengren, *Sakrales Königtum im Alten Testament und im Judentum*, 1955, pp. 26ff., with the examples given in n. 57.

[20] Cf. the coloured reproduction of this picture in the large final publication, *The Excavations at Dura-Europas, Final Report*, vol. vii, Pt. i: *The Synagogue*, by C. H. Kraeling, 1956, Pl. lx.

corresponds to the description of the dress of the High Priest in the Old Testament[21]; it resembles rather the Iranian costume.[22] The tradition that the royal costume belongs to the Old Testament High Priest was so firmly rooted in Judaism, even at the beginning of the third century A.D., that depictions of Old Testament history—such as these murals—anachronistically represent the dress of the High Priest as the King's dress at the same place and time.[23] Dura-Europos belonged at that time to the Parthian civilization, and as a result the Old Testament High Priest was depicted without reference to the description of his finery as given in the Old Testament. It was considered only right and proper that royal insignia should belong to the High Priest in this post-exilic period. The costume of the rest of the priests is briefly described in *Exod.* xxviii and xxxix. It is very much simpler, and—what is most important—it lacks all those elements which originate in royal insignia. For the royal tradition within the cult could of course only be represented, after the downfall of the kingdom, by the single paramount priest at the time.

There is still, however, another most important element of the royal tradition which was carried over in the post-exilic office of High Priest. This is the anointing which took place when the actual transfer of office was carried out. It is clear that the act of anointing was transferred from the kingship to the high priesthood, because in the Old Testament tradition of the earlier period only the anointing of kings is mentioned—not of priests; this anointing only recurs afterwards with respect to the post-exilic High Priest. Initially the anointing was intended for the High Priest alone, and not for the rest of the priests as well. Only later, in the course of making the office more "democratic", were they included in the circle of the anointed. Thus the act of anointing did not originally belong to the office of priest, for then every priest would have been anointed. Initially, therefore, this

[21] C. H. Kraeling's efforts, *op. cit.*, pp. 127f., to show at least that there are partial elements in the costume of Aaron that agree with the description in *Exod.* xxviii are not very convincing.

[22] C. H. Kraeling, *op. cit.*, has also pointed out this connection with the Iranian royal costume; but more important is G. Widengren, in V.T. Suppl. iv, 1957, pp. 212ff. and Pl. iv.v.

[23] For the rest these murals of the synagogue also show Iranian-Parthian costume in the persons they depict; cf. the details in Widengren in V.T. Suppl. iv (1957), pp. 209ff.

anointing appertained only to the special royal status of the post-exilic High Priest.[24]

This, however, brings up the whole question of the nature and significance of the office of the king in the Old Testament, for anointing enters the Old Testament tradition with the monarchy. With the very first kings—Saul, David, and Solomon—anointing of the king is mentioned as if it were the normal practice. It was, however, not quite so normal, for we know that kings were anointed in neither Egypt nor in Mesopotamia.[25]

What does anointing signify, and from where does it come? We shall see the point of this question when we remember that it is from the anointed king of the Old Testament that the word "Messiah" derives, and also—in its Greek translation—the word "Christ", and that therefore our designation as Christians goes back to this practice of anointing kings. The Hebrew word for "to anoint" is of common Semitic stock and means originally "to embrocate, to rub in, to smear". It occurs occasionally with this original meaning in the Old Testament. In its more sacred sense it was known apparently even in pre-Israelite Syria and Palestine. In one of the Ugaritic texts it is stated that a cultic object is anointed; even the Old Testament mentions the anointing of cultic objects which are thereby consecrated,[26] and

[24] This is clear in the Holiness Code in *Lev.* xxi.10, 12 and in the P- narrative in *Exod.* xxix.7; *Lev.* viii.12; cf. also *Num.* xxxv.25. Also in the sacrificial *tôrâ* the most senior priest is meant by "the anointed priest" (*Lev.* iv.3, 5, 16, vi.15—this latter passage shows this most clearly of all). *Exod.* xxix.29, in mentioning "the sons of Aaron," is dealing with the question of Aaron's successor in the office of High Priest (cf. also *Lev.* xvi.32). In comparison with this, those passages which mention the anointing of those sons of Aaron who are not High Priests are most certainly secondary; cf. *Exod.* xxviii.41, xxix.21, xxx.30, xl.13-15 (here vs. 15 is obviously a later addition which adds the anointing of Aaron's sons, whereas in vs.13 only the anointing of Aaron is reported); *Lev.*vi.13 (here either the mention of the sons of Aaron or of the anointing is secondary), vii.36 (here, if the reference to the anointing is original at all, possibly the sequence of his successors as High Priest is meant by the sons of Aaron), viii.30, x.7; *Num.* iii.3.

[25] Cf. H. Bonnet, *Reallexikon der ägyptischen Religionsgeschichte*, 1952, p. 649, where it is indeed accepted as probable that the king was anointed when appointed to take office, but nevertheless the concession has to be made that in the rich Egyptian tradition nothing is known concerning the anointing of kings. Nothing certain concerning the anointing of kings has come down to us either from Mesopotamia; cf. B. Meissner, *Babylonien und Assyrien*, vol. i, 1920, pp. 46ff. (that anointing with oil was part of the King's toilet—Meissner, *op. cit.*, p. 64—is a quite different matter).

[26] The Ugaritic text is 76 ii, 22.23 (Gordon); cf. G. R. Driver: *Canaanite Myths and Legends*, 1956, p. 117 (Baal iv, Col. ii, 22.23); the translation "to anoint" is not

it is expressly stated that the anointing is done by oil being poured over the object to be consecrated.[27] The anointing of the king is carried out in the same manner—oil is poured on to his head from a horn. This way of anointing the king was not known over the whole of the ancient Orient, but it must have been known in pre-Israelite Syria and Palestine. In one of the Amarna letters it is said that Pharaoh Thutmose III (supreme ruler in north Syria in the fifteenth century B.C.) "appointed a king" and "had oil poured on his head"[28]: in this he was following the general practice—not in Egypt, but in Syria and Palestine. If such a practice existed in Syria and Palestine during the late Bronze Age, but is found neither in Egypt nor in Mesopotamia, then we are inclined to search for its origins in the Hurrian or Hittite civilizations, unless we accept that it arose spontaneously in Syria and Palestine. There is even some evidence that the anointing of kings was known to the Hittites.[29]

The meaning of the act, however, provides really no problem. According to the ancient oriental conception, oil contained vital energy; it is "life-giving oil".[30] This divine life-giving power is carried over to the anointing itself. The anointed person is given permanent additional vital energy, so that he stands out from the ordinary run of mortals. The statements concerning the anointing of a High Priest give the stereotyped explanation of the effect of anointing as "to make holy", i.e. impart an exalted state above the everyday sphere of the profane. In these later assertions the original meaning of the anointing is doubtless understood in the same sense as it was formerly with reference to

---

absolutely certain, but is highly probable. With regard to objects anointed in the Old Testament see G. Lisowsky, *Konkordanz zum hebräischen Alten Testament*, 1958, pp. 87of.

[27] Cf. *Gen.* XXVIII.18: Jacob pours oil on the stone set up as a *maṣṣēbâ* in Bethel whereby he "anoints" it (the word "anoint" is not expressly mentioned, but it is obvious that anointing is meant).

[28] Cf. J. A. Knudtzon, *Die El-Amarna-Tafeln*, No. 51, 4ff.

[29] This is in a text dealing with the appointment of a substitute king which nevertheless reports a ceremony which was primarily just the same as that carried out at the appointment of a normal king. According to this text the king was anointed "with the fine oil of the kingdom" and then ceremoniously proclaimed king; cf. A. Götze in *Kulturgeschichte des alten Orients*, Ser. III, PT. I, 1933, p. 84, n. 2. The anointing of priests furthermore was not unknown to the Hittites; cf. the passage quoted in *Archiv für Orientforschung*, XVIII, No. 1 (1957), p. 127, from KUB XXXVI.90, 15-18.

[30] As is stated in an Akkadian text; cf. B. Meissner, *Babylonien und Assyrien* VOL. I, 1920, p. 243.

the king. The earliest stories about the beginnings of the monarchy in Israel reveal the anointed man to be untouchable.[31] The anointing is therefore a means of consecrating the office, and the bearer of the office is thereby given increased power on his appointment.

When kingship emerged in Israel the act of anointing was taken over from the royal tradition of pre-Israelite Syria and Palestine. The fact that there is no anointing of the king in other civilizations of the ancient Near East may be explained by saying that this act was not necessary where kingship itself was regarded as divine; a king who was considered divine by the very nature of his office did not need consecration by being anointed. At all events anointing belonged to Syria and Palestine, later to Israel in respect of the fully developed institution of kingship, from there it was passed on to the post-exilic High Priest, and finally it was extended to include the priesthood as a whole.

There was yet another aspect of kingship in Israel, however, from which we can learn much, although nothing of it lives on in the later conception of the High Priest. This was the direct divine calling of each particular king. In this most complex phenomenon of kingship in Israel the ideas of office and divine calling stand from the very beginning unharmonized, side by side. The career of Saul began, according to *I Sam.* xi., while he was still a farmer like other Israelites, in a situation where Israel was sorely oppressed from outside; suddenly "the spirit of God came upon Saul", so inspiring him that he set himself at the head of the military levy of the tribes of Israel and led them to a quick victory. Only then did the tribes make him their first king. A more recent tradition that has come down to us adds that all this had been preceded by an incident which had taken place in secret, when Saul was directly called to be the future king by the divinely prompted words of the prophet Samuel (*I Sam.* ix.1-10, 16), and was then and there anointed by him.

Just how deeply "the Spirit" of God, i.e. the direct influence of God, is rooted in this conception of the kingdom is shown by the beginning of the Davidic tradition, according to which the end of the rule of Saul was sealed by the fact that this "spirit" was taken away from him (*I Sam.* xvi.14). Direct call, however, arises not only at the very beginning of kingship in Israel. Jeroboam,

---

[31] *I Sam.* xxiv.7, 11, xxvi.9, 11, 16, 23; *II Sam.* i.14, 16, xix.22.

the first king of the later independent state of Israel, after the death of Solomon, was personally called through the mouth of the prophet Ahijah (*I Kings* xi.29ff.); in Israel particularly the idea was kept alive that basically only he who was personally called could legitimately be king. King Baasha of Israel was called to office by the words of a prophet, but then his calling was taken away from him, and the rule of his house brought to an end by other words of a prophet (*I Kings* xvi.1-4). A prophecy spoken directly in the name of God brought Jehu to the throne of Israel (*II Kings* ix.1ff.). Shortly before the end of the state of Israel the prophet Hosea proclaimed that the appointment to the office of king must proceed directly from God, and that it was a sign of complete decline when this no longer happened (*Hos.* viii.4).[32]

In contrast with this, the tendency to rigidity and institutionalism inevitably made itself felt. Those who were personally called established dynasties, and the kingship then proceeded for a time by way of succession without individual calling. This was most noticeably so in the state of Judah, in which the house of David held the royal throne from beginning to end. But here also divine calling was seen as a basic prerequisite for the office of king, the only difference being that David's entire dynasty was regarded as being called. As a result of the prophecy given to David personally, not only he himself but all of his successors were directly entrusted with the kingship by God (*II Sam.* vii).

How did this variance in the nature of kingship come about in the land of Israel, producing as it did (especially in northern Israel) a more unstable kingdom than usual? How did it come about that in the fairly late story of the anointing of David by Samuel the sudden coming upon David of the spirit of God, could be reported as resulting from this act of anointing (*I Sam.* xvi.13), thereby making it seem that the independent authority of the spirit of God is bound up with the institutional act of consecrating the office? Obviously kingship in ancient Israel

---

[32] For an insight into the varied nature of the kingdom in the Old Testament we must be grateful most of all for the work of A. Alt.; cf. latterly A. Alt, "Das Königtum in den Reichen Israel und Juda", *V.T.* i, 1951, pp. 2-22, *K.S.* ii, 1953, pp. 116-34. Even the "law of the king" in *Deuteronomy* seeks in vain to unite these opposites by, on the one hand, demanding that God "shall choose" the individual king, and, on the other, by leaving Israel free within certain limits to appoint a king for herself (*Deut.* xvii.15).

had many different roots. After it had once emerged under the pressure of a particular historical situation, quite late in the history of Israel, it absorbed certain basic elements of the royal tradition of pre-Israelite Syria and Palestine, which were to act as stabilizers to this institution, and which were incorporated almost out of necessity into an institution which was still new in Israel.[33]

On the other hand kingship had had its own prehistory in Israel itself, as becomes eminently clear immediately Saul is made the first king. His emergence was the result of the spirit of God acting directly upon him, placing him at the head of the Israelite tribes; only after this was he made king. Saul was not the first to act promptly in the face of a dangerous situation, as a result of a direct divine calling. There had been others before him who, likewise inspired, had emerged without office or preparation to take over leadership. These are the figures who appear in the traditional material in those major stories in the *Book of Judges*: they are the so-called charismatic leaders in the pre-monarchic age in Israel. They were called to act, whether by a direct experience of God, or by a prophecy, and they stepped into the background once more after they had carried out the deed to which they felt themselves called; for they were not bearers of office but were chosen and called to act on one single occasion.

Following them, kingship appears in Israel with Saul. This had to follow other laws, but it never completely lost this charismatic element. The later tradition has strangely enough finally made even these charismatic leaders of the pre-monarchic period into office-bearers, and describes them as "judges", whose task should have been to "judge Israel" in continuous succession after performing their own exploit. This is a secondary construction, which goes back to the deuteronomic historian[34], but it is not entirely distinct from the ancient institution of kingship.

It is worth noting that according to the Old Testament tradition the charismatic element may have played an even

---

[33] It can hardly be a mere chance that this form developed in the kingdom of Judah. For the Judaic royal city of Jerusalem was a Canaanite city until it was captured by David, and it most certainly still had a living Canaanite royal tradition even if it no longer had a king in the period immediately before David, having been ruled aristocratically.

[34] Cf. my *Überl. Studien*, i, pp. 47ff.

greater part in the field of the law, although this is a field in which we expect to find a firm existent order, and little direct intervention of the spirit. In the collection of judgments in the so-called *Holiness Code*, which mainly contains a list of instructions concerning the sacred and profane prescriptive law, a passage has been incorporated which does not fit in with the general pattern (*Lev.* xxiv.10ff.). An account is given of an offence on which it was felt that it was impossible to come to any decision in Israel, evidently because the case was not provided for in any of the legal maxims. The delinquent is therefore put in prison until an oracle is obtained to decide the matter. The relatively late *Holiness Code* is set in the time of Moses, and Moses appears in this passage as receiving the divine decree, though we are never told how he obtained this direct divine decision. But this is rather exceptional. Normally the elders of the tribes or villages in the community[35] would pass judgment, following a verbal tradition which later became a codified prescriptive law. Nevertheless the possibility was evidently accepted of a directly inspired legal judgment, which was then incorporated in the stock of traditional legal maxims. The *Holiness Code* most certainly incorporated the episode mentioned above from an older tradition, as can be seen from the contents of the *Holiness Code* itself, and by the fact that it gives a few ancient accounts of charismatic, inspired, legal judgments.

In *Judges* iv.4f. we are told that a prophetess, Deborah, at that time "judged Israel" and used to sit at a special place to pass judgment upon the Israelites who came to her. This information is not amplified any further, and is used only to characterize this woman, who is mentioned in the tradition because she summoned one of the charismatic leaders to action by a divine prophecy in the era before the monarchy.

In addition to this we have what is possibly a very old piece of information concerning Samuel (*I Sam.* vii.16, 17), which states that Samuel from year to year used to stop at certain specific places and "judged Israel" there; Samuel, however, was regarded outside the old tradition as a seer, a prophet, and it is at least possible that his power to judge belonged to his nature as a

[35] Cf. the rectoral address by L. Köhler: *Die hebräische Rechtsgemeinde* Zürich 1931, later incorporated in *Der hebräische Mensch* 1953, pp. 143-171 [Eng. trans: *Hebrew Man*, 1956, p.149ff.]

charismatic. But with Samuel the question immediately arises whether he was not at the same time the holder of a definite office. There was in Israel before the time of the monarchy the office of "judge of Israel".[36] The scanty and probably incomplete accounts we have only refer to some sort of uninterrupted succession of bearers of this office, which was held by one individual at any given time. We are told of the origins of these officers and how long they stayed in office, but unfortunately we learn nothing of the special tasks connected with the office. At any rate (leaving on one side the rather uncertain case of Samuel[37]) it is clear that there were inspired charismatics among those who held this office. One of them was Jephthah, who is certainly the same person as the charismatic leader dealt with in the long Jephthah narrative. Now this does not mean that the spirit of God, which had inspired Jephthah to lead in battle against the Ammonites, also possessed him during the six years up to his death in which he held the office of judge of Israel. But it is highly probable, to say the least of it, that he became the judge of Israel[38] solely because he had shown that he was endowed with the spirit. The deuteronomic historian who, on the basis of the Jephthah tradition, combined the charismatic leaders of the time before the monarchy with the office of judge of Israel, is not therefore entirely wrong.[39]

Now the passing of judgment was also the concern of subsequent

[36] Cf. my "Das Amt des 'Richters Israels' " in *Festschrift für A. Bertholet*, 1950, pp. 404-17.

[37] The list given in *Judges* x.1-5, xii.7-15 of the "Judges of Israel" is presumably incomplete both at the beginning and at the end. It might be possible that Samuel held the office of "Judge of Israel". The most important indication of this is the statement in *I Sam.* vii.16 that he "judged Israel". This statement is made in connection with an apparently old tradition and most often characterizes the "Judges of Israel". The same statement, however, is made of Deborah in *Judges* iv.4 and in this case it is much more difficult to accept that she also might have been the holder of this office of "Judge of Israel" (at some time or other before the "Judges of Israel" mentioned in *Judges* x.1-5, xii.7-15). The deuteronomic historian counted Samuel among the "Judges" (cf. my *Überl. Studien*, pp. 54ff.)—but not in the sense of the "Judges of Israel" in *Judges* x.1-5, xii.7-15, but in the sense of the major stories of the "Judges" in the *Book of Judges*.

[38] Unfortunately we know nothing of how the "Judges of Israel" were created and appointed to office.

[39] As far as charismatic judgments are concerned, cf. H. J. Kraus, *Gottesdienst in Israel*, 1954, pp. 64ff.; G. v. Rad, *Old Testament Theology*, trans. D. M. G. Stalker, vol. i, Edinburgh, 1962, pp. 93ff. It is not easy to say how far Moses can be understood as the prototype of the charismatic judge. (Cf. Kraus, *op. cit.*, pp. 61ff. and pp. 247ff. of this study with regard to *Deut.* xviii.15ff.).

kings. We have no exact knowledge of what became of the office of "judge of Israel" once the monarchy had appeared.[40] From the traditional material, however, it is certain that the kings passed judgments, that they were at least considered as the highest court for legal decisions and passed sentences accordingly. We are not told that the kings of historical times, even if they were called to office by an inspired prophecy, were themselves charismatics; nor are we told that they waged their wars on the basis of a special direct call, despite the connection between kingship and charismatic rule in the era before the monarchy. But in the picture of the ruler as he appears in the proclamations of a future king to be chosen by God, that is, in the messianic promises, the charismatic right to pass judgments is characteristic.

Just as it is said in *Isa.* ix.6 that law and justice will be the bases of the promised kingdom of the future, in *Isa.* xi.1-5 the new David, who is to proceed from the stem of the house of David, is also depicted as one specially endowed with the spirit of God, who, on the basis of this gift, shall pass judgments in a perfect way. Even in the Psalms of Solomon—which are post-canonical, originating probably from the first century B.C.—the promised king is depicted as being endowed with the holy spirit of God, as a result of which he will bring justice, law, and order. The idea of the charismatic judge, together with the figure of the charismatic leader, are incorporated in the Old Testament conception of the monarchy, which above all has coloured the later picture of the promised kingdom of the future. That the messianic king will achieve his result by the spirit of God rather than through strength and violence is the post-exilic prophet Zechariah's comment on the governor Zerubbabel, who he thinks is the Messiah (*Zech.* iv.6).

Alongside the king, and on certain occasions in opposition to him, we find in the Old Testament the real charismatic—the prophet. He is personally called and chosen.[41] We generally speak of the vocation of the prophets; and although the word

---

[40] There is something in Kraus's conjecture (*op. cit.*, p. 113) that the office of the "Judge of Israel" was wholly incorporated into the office of the king. Then however we must remember the Kingdom of David in its "amphictyonic" role. Cf. below, pp. 250-259.

[41] We are only dealing here with the individual prophets quite apart from the guilds of ecstatic "prophets" and the so-called cult-prophecy connected with them.

"called" is never used in the Old Testament to describe the authorization of the prophets,[42] this formulation is quite appropriate. Without delving into the difficult question of the origins of prophecy,[43] we can at least say that the prophet in the Old Testament appears (generally without being sought or desired) as a messenger who is commissioned to pass on a message directly entrusted to him by God.

As far as prophecy itself is concerned, which shows in essence the direct independent intervention of God, there are a few indications that there was a definite tendency towards an official status for prophets. A pointer towards this is the fact that by the side of the kings appear prophets who are not royal officials, but who nevertheless appear to have a definite connection with the king; thus on one occasion the prophet Gad is referred to as David's "seer" (*II Sam.* xxiv. 11), just as if he possessed some sort of permanent position at court.

Above all, however, the relationship of the prophets Elijah and Elisha to each other points to a succession which might well suggest the existence of prophetic office, passed on from prophet to prophet. According to *I Kings* xix.15, 16, Elijah received instructions to anoint Elisha as a prophet in his place, as his successor; to instal him in his office as a prophet, even carrying out the official consecration by anointing him. This is the only passage where the anointing of a prophet is mentioned. Perhaps we cannot attach too much weight to this, since the expression "to anoint" is possibly here only carried over mechanically to the appointment of a prophet, following the anointing of two kings which is mentioned directly before. We are, however, definitely dealing with a question of succession from Elijah to Elisha. This relationship is presupposed in the note in *I Kings* xix.19-21 which originates from another source,[44] and above all in the story in *II Kings* ii.1-18. Here even the conferring of the spirit on Elisha by Elijah is mentioned, and indeed Elisha as

[42] The servant of Yahweh in *Deutero-Isaiah* says of himself that he was "called" by God (*Isa.* xlix.1)

[43] Concerning the prehistory of prophecy as it emerges in the Mari texts, cf. above, pp. 179ff.

[44] In this passage the mantle of Elijah plays the important role of bearing the power which is passed over from Elijah. Other passages are known where the mantle has a similar significance, e.g. in the Mari texts (cf. my article in *Journal of Semitic Studies*, 1 (1956), pp. 327ff.). In a somewhat different role the mantle of Elijah crops up also in *II Kings* ii.8, 13, 14.

Elijah's heir receives the first-born's share of the spirit of Elijah.

This conferring of the spirit, however, can of course not take place just like any other heritage being conferred on an heir. Indeed the spirit appears in a most unusual manner as a possession of Elijah's, and Elisha asks for the share due to a first-born. But neither Elijah nor Elisha have it in their power to transfer this inheritance from one to the other. It happens in a most astounding manner; and from the sense of the story it can only be assumed that the actual conferring of the spirit remains dependent on the direct intervention of God; this again, therefore, rules out and surpasses the idea of a simple succession of office.

Finally the deuteronomic law recognizes that the prophet was exercising an office, linked to the treatment of the offices of judge, king, and priest (*Deut.* xviii.15-22); and it seems to be taken for granted that a holder of this office existed continuously in a succession which went back to Moses himself. Whereas the other officers were accorded limited but nevertheless very definite powers,[45] the prophet must always prove himself genuine by the full power of authority of his prophecy. Thus we see that even the deuteronomic law cannot really place the prophets in the series of office-bearers.[46] Indeed the phenomenon of Old Testament prophecy cannot be understood in the sense of an office. Its basis is an independent divine calling, which cannot be bound to any order of a worldly nature. The relationship between Elisha and Elijah needs to be studied as a single special case, from which it is difficult to generalize.

If we make a general survey of the complex relationship between the ideas of office and divine calling in the Old Testament, it is quite clear that everything that is peculiar to the Old Testament is to be found on the side of divine calling. The various offices go back to very ancient Oriental tradition, but the charismatic leader and the charismatic judge of Israelite early history

---

[45] O. Plöger in *Z.A.W.* LXIII (1951), p. 179, points out this difference.

[46] The question arises whether at this point there is any definite reality behind the deuteronomic law, or whether the legislator has not merely tried from an ideological standpoint to fit the phenomenon of prophecy within the scheme of offices in general. The formulation of "the law of the prophets" in *Deut.* xviii leaves the question open whether there is considered to be an unbroken succession in the "office" of prophet. The uncertainty makes it difficult to argue from *Deut.* xviii.15ff. (cf. H. J. Kraus, *Gottesdienst in Israel*, 1954, pp. 62ff.).

are unique phenomena in the Old Testament. An element in the nature of kingship is inherited from them, and alongside the kingship we find charismatic prophecy. Thus king and prophet appear together in some very noteworthy passages. In the admittedly late *Ps.* cv the patriarchal ancestors of Israel are referred to as the "anointed (i.e. kings) and the prophets" of God, obviously thereby being characterized as those among the peoples specially called by God (vs. 15); in this way the concepts "anointed" and "prophet" appear to be "democratized" in a most striking manner.[47]

Above all, however, both king and prophet play a part in the Old Testament proclamations about the future. In one of the appendices of the *Book of Deutero-Isaiah*[48] we find at the beginning of a prophecy of future happiness: "The Spirit of the Lord God is upon me, because the Lord has anointed me to preach good tidings to the afflicted" (*Isa.* LXI.1). Who is speaking here? Is it a prophet, or is the prophet here allowing a king of the future to speak? The statements made seem to come partly from a king, partly from a prophet. The mention of anointing indicates a king, and the proclamation that follows concerning "liberty" and the opening of prisons (i.e. an amnesty) deals with the sovereign right of kings. On the other hand the idea of being "sent" is characteristic of a prophet, and it is also the task of a prophet to bear tidings. There can, therefore, be no clear-cut conclusion to this question "king or prophet". The speaker is both, at one and the same time, a prophetic king and a royal prophet; but in this dual role he is endowed with the spirit, and therefore is one who has been called and chosen, a charismatic.[49]

[47] A similar generalization occurs in the unusual statement that the whole of Israel is a "kingdom of priests" (*Exod.* XIX.6; cf. also *Isa.* LXI.6). Now that is indeed meant to signify that Israel is singled out from the "profane" races of the world (in the immediate context Israel is characterized as a "holy race") and then perhaps also that Israel is to take care of "divine service" for the whole of the world.

[48] We cannot here go into the complicated problem of the Servant of Yahweh in *Deutero-Isaiah*; in this figure also we have the apparent mixture of both royal and prophetic characteristics. But this raises a host of other matters.

[49] In passing, perhaps the speaker in *Isa.* LXI.1ff. also appears with the function of a priest; for the proclamation of "the acceptable year of the Lord" (vs. 2) could, if we remember the institutions of the Sabbatical and Jubilee year, be seen as a cultic task of the priest, but perhaps after all we have a function of the king who is decreeing a year of remission.

The formulation is of course markedly cultic, and thus the question could be

With these qualities he is to be the centre of the future period of happiness. Here in this figure we find concentrated everything which is essential of what the Old Testament can tell us about direct divine calling. And this passage from the *Book of Isaiah* is quoted in the New Testament (*Luke* IV.18, 19) with the comment that the promise made in it is now fulfilled (vs. 21).

asked whether some old royal privilege has not been later transferred to the priest. Another matter is the mention of the priests in *Isa.* LXI.6 (cf. above, n. 47) which stands in a passage (vss. 5, 6) which, since it deviates from the general formulation, must be seen as secondary (cf. W. Kessler, *Studie zur religiösen Situation im ersten nachexilischen Jahrhundert, und zur Auslegung von Jesaja* 56-66, 1956, p. 55).

X

David and Israel in II Samuel VII

The important Chapter VII of *II Samuel* gives the impression of being neatly rounded off and complete in itself. Even though it has come down to us as part of a larger literary context it seems, within this context, to have an individuality of its own both in nature and contents. It soon becomes obvious that this chapter contains many difficulties. One of these is the fact that in certain passages the original text has apparently suffered corruption; this is true perhaps in vs. 11, probably in vs. 19*b*, and most certainly in vs. 23—i.e. in passages which are not entirely unimportant in answering questions concerning the construction and train of thought in the chapter. Nevertheless textual questions are not those of paramount importance in this chapter. We are concerned, however, with the literary unity and the unity of content of the chapter. There is not much need for a critical literary analysis, though the obviously new insertion in vs. 8, and the occurrence of Yahweh in the third person in vs. 11*b* do give rise to literary-critical questions. The main question is the unity of content, and attempts to analyse this chapter generally turn on the question of the content, no matter what conclusions are reached, and however much they rely in detail on matters of style and form.

The subject-matter of the chapter is threefold: the building of a temple for the Ark, the divine steering of the history of Israel, and the promise of lasting rule for the House of David. It is not certain whether these matters were originally related to one another, or whether they were only put together more or less by chance within the framework of a divine message from the prophet Nathan to David. Literary criticism may show that they were only brought together as a result of secondary editing. By closely relating the references to the history of Israel with the

promise given to the dynasty of David, many have found the
decisive pivot of the whole chapter and the key to the whole
content in the contrast between the two sentences: "Thus says
the Lord; would you build me a house to dwell in?" (vs. 5), and:
"Moreover the Lord declares to you that the Lord will make you
a house" (vs. 11b).[1] But there is not the slightest indication that
the author intended to contrast these two sentences which stand
so far apart, and so convey the idea: "*You* will not build *me* a
house, but *I* will build *you* a house." Apart from the use of two
different verbs in the two sentences, in vs. 5b a stressed "you" is
surely taken for granted, whereas in vs. 11b it is not the subject
that is stressed but the predicate ("house"), as if the concept
"house" is now introduced as a new element in the train of
thought—in the traditional meaning of "dynasty". On the basis
of the text, therefore, it would seem that W. Caspari[2] is right in
suggesting that the sentence in vs. 13a is to be seen as a counterpart to vs. 5b; for in vs. 13a ("He will build a house for my
name") not only is the same verb used as in vs. 5b, but also the
subject is in a stressed position, so that we might well agree with
Caspari that the stressed "you" in vs. 5b demands the statement
in vs. 13a as its counterpart. That, however, is also impossible.
The reason given in vss. 6, 7 for the question in vs. 5b, which
suggests that a refusal will be given, does not leave open the
possibility that somebody *other* than David is to build a house for
the Lord. In addition, vs. 13a[3] has been regarded by most
interpreters as a deuteronomic addition.[4] The question therefore
remains how the stressed "you" in vs. 5b is to be explained, and
the most probable explanation is that David is shown as a human
being, even though he is the king.[5] Only God himself could order
the building of such a house if he wanted it (cf. vs. 7).

[1] Cf. R. de Vaux, *Les livres de Samuel, La Sainte Bible de Jérusalem*, Paris, 1953,
p. 160, n.c.

[2] Caspari, *Die Samuelbücher*, Kommentar zum Alten Testament VOL. VII, 1926,
p. 482.

[3] Vs. 12b may be taken along with vs. 13a as the point where the deuteronomic
addition is introduced (not vs. 13b).

[4] The formulation in vs. 13a that the house is to be built "for the name" of the
Lord is quite rightly seen as deuteronomic, whereas in vs. 5b it is said that it was
to be "a house" for the Lord (cf. the ancient saying used for blessing the temple in
I Kings VIII.13).

[5] As M. Simon rightly suggests in *Revue d'histoire et de philosophie religieuses*,
XXXII (1952), p. 50.

If this makes it difficult to consider the idea of "building a house" to be the central idea in *II Sam.* vii, and one which includes the whole content of the chapter, then the unity of content in the chapter appears to be very questionable. Indeed L. Rost, who has written a very comprehensive analysis of *II Sam.* vii, has come to the conclusion that the chapter is made up of different elements which are partly of separate origin, and partly represent secondary additions to a more ancient basic form.[6] Many others have agreed with his very acute proposals,[7] yet his conclusions are not entirely satisfactory. He makes very fine stylistic differentiations which are not wholly convincing, because the basis for his stylistic examination is far too narrow. His literary-critical analysis leads to a discussion of single independent sections, which are left hanging in the air because they cannot wholly be placed within broader literary contexts; and behind his stylistic and literary criticisms there is the presupposition that the whole *does* lack literary unity. Let us look a little more closely at this idea.

Rost's starting point is the prayer of David in vss. 18-29, which seems to be relatively complete and consistent.[8] He judges the first half of the chapter from the standpoint that it must be attributed to the original narrative, which has a definite technical connection with the prayer. It is indeed possible to use the prayer of David as a starting-point. The sentence in vs. 27a is most striking, with its particularly ceremonious form of address "Thou, O Lord of hosts, the God of Israel . . .". Thus is the God addressed who has promised David a lasting rule for his dynasty. Rost sees this sentence as part of the original form. He calls it "the very kernel of the prayer of David",[9] because it harks back to the real subject of the divine promise. Directly preceding this in vs. 26, the originality of which is not questioned by Rost, the name of God is "The Lord of hosts [is] God over Israel"—and side by side with the wish that this name shall be magnified for ever is the wish that the house of his servant David

---

[6] Rost, in *Thronnachfolge*, pp. 47-74.

[7] Cf. my *Überl. Studien*, pp. 64f.

[8] It is quite probable that there are deuteronomic extensions in vss. 22-4 or at least in vss. 23-4; nevertheless this passage does contain also non-deuteronomic, probably more ancient material but this, however, can no longer be determined with any certainty because of the bad condition of our text of vs. 23.

[9] Cf. Rost, *Thronnachfolge*, p. 48.

be established before him. This juxtaposition is particularly worthy of note, for in itself it is not necessary, and can only be understood if we presuppose that a definite relationship between the promise to David and his dynasty and the name of the God of Israel was important in the author's eyes. In this it is perfectly clear that the concept "Israel" in vss. 26 and 27 is used in the old sacral sense of a union of tribes, which had in the past been the object of great acts of salvation. The promise to David, therefore, is counted along with these blessings of the past.

Considered from this point of view it does not seem mere chance that in other passages of *II Sam.* VII the name of Israel as the people of God is emphasized. In the prayer to God in vss. 23 and 24, the expression "thy people Israel" occurs twice. These verses, however, are suspected to be of deuteronomistic origin, and have at least been expanded deuteronomistically. Since, however, the deuteronomic material cannot be singled out with any certainty, it remains at least possible that the sentences with the expression "thy people Israel" do belong to the original form. Verse 11 looks back to the time when judges were placed "over my people Israel". But it seems very doubtful whether the passage in vs. 11*a* is original, for it fits badly into the context. In vss. 8 and 10 mention is made of "my people Israel". In vs. 8 it is said that God has made David *nāghîdh* over his people Israel, and in vs. 10 that God has appointed a fixed place for his people Israel.[10]

I do not think it is correct to separate the references to the history of God's dealings with "his" people Israel from the matter of the promise to David, seeing in it some secondary addition to the original story of the promise made concerning David's dynasty. The ceremonious pronouncement of the name of the God of Israel in vss. 26-27 suggest a previous reference to the history of this God with his people, so we must see certain basic statements concerning the history of Israel before and during the time of David as part of the original text of the chapter. Above all, this brings in for consideration the passage in vss. 8-10. The

---

[10] Like W. Caspari, *Die Samuelbücher*, p. 489, one is tempted, following the popular usage in the Old Testament, to understand by *māqom* in vs. 10 a "place for divine service," a cultic place, thinking of Jerusalem. The statements which follow in vs. 10, however, clearly prohibit this interpretation; from them it is clear that *māqôm* refers to the land given to Israel.

connection between the history of Israel and the history of David and his dynasty is made most clear in the sentence where it is said that it was determined by God that David was "to be *nāghîdh* over my people, over Israel" (vs. 8). Without going into the difficult question of the actual meaning of the technical term *nāghîdh* on the basis of etymology and its use in this chapter[11], it is at least clear that this statement in vs. 8 connects the historical figure of David with the previous history of Israel—at any rate with the history of Saul (cf. *I Sam.* ix.16, x.1).[12] It must also be remembered that the concept *nāghîdh* in the older parts of the Old Testament is generally connected with Israel as the people of God; a *nāghîdh* is appointed by God "over [his] people Israel".[13] In *II Sam.* vii.8, therefore, a function is assigned to David in Israel as the ancient sacral tribal confederacy.[14]

This is very remarkable, for as we learn from the Old Testament tradition, David carried out his great rise to power without any consideration of the traditions of the more ancient sacral Israel. He had himself made king first over the southern group of Israelite tribes—only, therefore, over a part of ancient Israel; then when the rest of the Israelite tribes offered him their kingdom he added this second kingdom to the first, but did not make a political unity of the whole. For his royal city he chose Jerusalem, which was not an Israelite but a Canaanite city, completely without any tradition for ancient Israel[15]. Is it then pure fiction when David is declared "*nāghîdh* over Israel" in *II Sam.* vii.8, and a positive significance within the framework of traditional Israel, as the people of God, is attributed to him, to his rule, and to his dynasty? Such a fiction could date from the time of David himself, from the circle of the royal court, with the

---

[11] Cf. Albrecht Alt: *Die Staatenbildung der Israeliten in Palästina*, in *K.S.*, vol. ii, pp. 22f.

[12] The title *nāghîdh* is also used in connection with David in *I Sam.* xxv.30; *II Sam.* v.2; vi.21 (cf. also *I Sam.* xiii.14). It seems improbable to me that the statement in *II Sam.* vii.8 has a literary or traditional dependence on one of these passages. The opposite seems more probable.

[13] As is expressly stated in *I Sam.* ix.16; xiii.14; xxv.30; *II Sam.* v.2; vi.21 (here very comprehensively: "*nāghîdh* over the people of the Lord, over Israel"), vii.8. In *I Sam.* x.1, the meaning is technically the same when it is formulated that the *nāghîdh* is appointed over the "inheritance" of the Lord.

[14] This assertion would stand even if the sentence in vs. 8b were not original, for it does not rest alone on the occurrence of the word *nāghîdh* but on all the references to "God's people Israel" in *II Sam.* vii.

[15] Cf. above, pp. 132-144.

intention of legitimating the new institution of his kingdom
vis-à-vis the traditions of Israel. It could also have been added at
some later date, in order to give some continuity to the history
of Israel by bridging the gap which had really been caused by the
emergence of David and the establishment of his kingdom.

It is however neither necessary nor probable that this was a
fiction, for we know of an act of King David by which he put
himself and his kingdom into direct relationship with the history
of Israel as the people of God. This is the transfer of the Ark,
the ancient shrine of the tribes, into his royal city of Jerusalem
(*II Sam.* vi). It is the only act of this nature known to us from the
time of David's rule, and it immediately sets the technical
relationship between the promise to David and his dynasty within the history of Israel and the theme of the Ark shrine, just as it
is to be found in *II Sam.* vii. We would have to accept the shrine
of the Ark in Jerusalem as the setting for the promise to David
and his dynasty as formulated in *II Sam.* vii.8-29, even if this
shrine had not been mentioned earlier. The matter of the Ark
at the beginning of *II Sam.* vii cannot therefore be regarded as
foreign to the whole of the chapter.[16]

The unity of content in *II Sam.* vii lies in the fact that everything in the chapter is seen from the standpoint of the shrine of
the Ark in Jerusalem. We cannot here follow up the significance
of this for the historical understanding of the person of the
"prophet" Nathan. It seems important to indicate, however,
that from what has been said we can also learn something about
the basis and significance of the "kingdom", which David is
promised will endure for his successors. Indeed we must ask what
"kingdom" is actually meant in *II Sam.* vii.8-29. For David
united many kingdoms under his hand—the kingdoms of Judah,
of Israel (in the limited political sense), of the city-state of
Jerusalem, indeed even of Ammon (according to *II Sam.* xii.30).
It is obvious that none of these kingdoms will fit the text here,
but only a single "kingdom"—the ancient, sacral "Israel" whose

[16] W. Caspari, *Die Samuelbücher*, p. 478, has seen the unity of *II Sam.* vii in the
fact of the significance of a state sanctuary for the existence and permanence of a
dynasty and has explained the dynasty-promise to David as a sort of substitute for
the plan to build a temple which was rejected. This conception is not wholly mis-
guided but it is a too one-sided view of the whole to see it from the standpoint of
reasons of state whereas in fact in *II Sam.* vii it is less the state sanctuary as such that
comes into consideration than the Ark with its ancient tradition.

God was "Lord of hosts" (vs. 27).[17] If this kingdom of David and his successors was to exist as any more than a dream, then it had to have some focal point, and it seems that only the shrine of the Ark in Jerusalem could provide this. On the other hand, David could not be the royal master of the shrine of the Ark in Jerusalem in his capacity as king of Judah or Israel in the narrower sense. He could and did hold this position as king of the city of Jerusalem, in so far as the Ark shrine was a sanctuary belonging to the territory ruled by the city of Jerusalem. But by virtue of the Ark being in this sanctuary, he had also to be king among God's people of Israel in the old sense. It is in this capacity that his rule and the rule of his successors is promised permanence in *II Sam.* vii.8-29.[18]

From all this it emerges that the whole of *II Sam.* vii deals with David as master of the sanctuary of the Ark in Jerusalem. He is addressed as master, and utters his prayer as master—even when the scene changes, for according to vs. 1 the first conversation between the king and his prophet (vss. 1-3) and even the reception of the divine message of Nathan (vss. 4-17) takes place in the "house" of David, whereas his prayer (vss. 18-29) takes place "before the Lord", i.e. certainly in the sanctuary of the Ark.

This unity of content in *II Sam.* vii does not, however, guarantee its form-critical or literary unity. The probability has arisen from quite another source that this chapter belongs in its entirety to a very definite *genre*, which can be defined by parallels drawn from Egypt. It has been shown in various ways that the kingdom of David was in many respects formed on an Egyptian pattern. Egyptian influence appears in the shaping of the royal civil service,[19] in certain details of the royal ritual,[20] in the use of

---

[17] There are reasons which suggest that the ceremonious cultic name "Lord of hosts" has special connections with the Ark (cf. Otto Eissfeldt: "Jahwe Zebaoth," in *Miscellania Academica Berlinensia*, Berlin 1950, pp. 128-150). The twofold appearance of this ceremonious cultic name in *II Sam.* vii.26, 27 (cf. also vs.8) is related to the sanctuary of the Ark in Jerusalem.

[18] This is also to be kept in mind with regard to the later effect of *II Sam.* vii which has been generally accepted as one of the messianic anticipations in Old Testament prophecy.

[19] Cf. R. de Vaux, in *Revue biblique*, XLVIII (1939) pp. 394-405; Joachim Begrich in *Z.A.W.*, LVIII (1940-41), pp. 1-29.

[20] Cf. Gerhard von Rad: "The Jewish kingly ritual" in *The Problem of the Hexateuch*.

certain forms in official language.[21] It is therefore not surprising that a part of *II Sam.* VII can be explained from the institution of the kingdom in Egypt.[22] S. Herrmann has shown that *II Sam.* VII can be compared with a certain element of the Egyptian royal tradition which has numerous documentary examples, and which Egyptologists have generally described not very happily as the *Königsnovelle* or "King's Letter".[23] It traces certain arrangements and orders back to royal decisions, which came either as a result of divine revelation, or directly from the king on the strength of his own divinity, and were made known to his dignitaries at an audience. Herrmann has been able to carry the comparison between *II Sam.* VII and the Egyptian "King's Letter" right down to many striking details, and these details concern the form of *II Sam.* VII as a whole and not only individual sections, so that we may add that not only does it have unity of content but also unity of genre.[24]

Verses 1-7 of this chapter deal with the king's consultation with a prominent local man, concerning the question of building a temple for the Ark, and the divine rejection, passed on by a "prophetic" revelation, of the plan to build a temple.[25] I see no reason to dispute the unity of this section, for the fact that the narrator refers to "the King" whereas the divine message that follows speaks of "my servant David" is hardly a basis for critical literary differentiation. Nathan's statement in vs. 3 is hardly a decision (in the narrator's sense) on the question of building a temple, but is a polite formality customary before the king, which is only then followed by the divine decision which the

---

[21] Particularly important here is the expression in *II Sam.* VII.9 "to make a great name" which refers to the full title of the King. G. von Rad, *op. cit.*, refers to this. Cf. especially Siegfried Morenz, "Aegyptische und davidsche Königstitulatur" in *Zeitschrift für Aegyptische Sprache und Altertumskunde*, LXXIX, pp. 73ff.

[22] It can be seen, above all, that Egyptian influence was certainly present in the traditions of the city-kingdom of Jerusalem which had stood for centuries under Egyptian overlordship.

[23] Siegfried Hermann, "Die Königsnovelle in Aegypten und in Israel", in *Wissenschaftliche Zeitschrift der Karl-Marx-Universität, Leipzig, Gesellschafts—und sprachwissenschaftliche Reihe*, III, 1953-54, Heft I, pp. 51-62.

[24] These details can be found in S. Herrmann's essay, which quite correctly not only shows the positive relationship, but also the changes which the Egyptian tradition underwent on Israelite soil.

[25] M. Simon, in *Revue d'histoire et de philosophie religieuses*, XXXII (1952), p. 41, quite rightly opposes Mowinckel and others in stressing that it is a question of a basic refusal.

"prophet" had received.[26] The addition in vs. 8, which is open to literary criticism, cannot be given too much weight from the standpoint of form criticism; for Herrmann has shown that the "building of the temple and the theology of the king [are] the main themes of the Egyptian King's Letter"; thus this addition must denote only the transition from one theme to another within the same unity.

Verse 11b raises considerable difficulties with the abrupt change from God's direct speech to speech about God in the third person. Rost has singled out vs. 11b (together with vs. 16) from the section vss. 8-17 as belonging to older material. It nevertheless remains strange that Rost's postulated later revisor of the older material did not insert it into this context a little better. On the other hand, textual criticism of vs. 11b is faced with serious problems of method. We wonder whether the passage in its traditional form does not after all indicate the beginning of the promise to the dynasty, to be put on a level with the *kh 'mr yhwh ṣb' wt* of vs. 8, so that we might suppose a *l' mr* after vs. 11b, that would have produced the transition to the text of the dynastic promise announced there. There are, of course, changes and additions,[27] and the original text of the chapter can no longer be reconstructed in every detail with absolute certainty.

In the "King's Letter" in *II Sam.* VII, questions are decided which must have arisen as a result of transporting the tribal shrine of the Ark to Jerusalem. The question of building a temple for this shrine in Jerusalem is decided, as is the question of the position of the kingdom of David with regard to the traditions of ancient Israel represented by the Ark. Both questions are decided permanently. For the rejection of the plan to build a temple is certainly meant as fundamental; and the position of the kingdom of David within "Israel" is clarified with regard not only to David's person but also his whole dynasty after him. Not only is the duration of the dynasty in itself dealt with, but also the

[26] The space after vs. 4a found in a series of Massoretic manuscripts cannot be brought into the argument. This is certainly not the original form of the manuscript but is a Massoretic addition, the possible reasons for which need not be discussed here.

[27] The most obvious addition is, as mentioned already, the passage in vss. (12b)13a. Vs.1b also could be a deuteronomic addition, as is shown by the formulation of the language used.

relationship of the reigning Davidic monarch to the God of Israel (vss. 14-16).[28]

It seems difficult *not* to regard the original form of *II Sam.* VII as pre-Solomonic. Only the sanctuary of the Ark can be seen as the setting for the tradition in *II Sam.* VII. Here this traditional material was most certainly first formulated, and it was here also that it was preserved.

Does all this not suggest a new standpoint? May there not have been a larger literary context, into which the originally independent unit *II Sam.* VII was fitted before it was taken up into the general complex of the Davidic tradition in the Old Testament?

[28] In vs. 16 "before me" (not "before thee") may have been the original, which would again refer to the relationship of the kingdom of David to God.

XI

The Jerusalem Catastrophe of 587 B.C., and its significance for Israel

Considered from the standpoint of world history, the event which took place in Jerusalem in the summer of the year 587 B.C. was no more than the ordinary fate of a small centre of government, within the sphere of influence of a great ancient Oriental power. For those directly concerned, however—in this case the dynasty of David, the circle of royal officials, the priests of the royal sanctuary, and the inhabitants of Jerusalem and of the state of Judah—it signified the end of a way of life and all that it represented. For them the event was therefore of decisive importance.

What was its significance for "Israel", i.e. for that entity (so difficult to define exactly) which looms behind the Old Testament, and which is the proper subject of the "history of Israel"? The Old Testament tells us that "Israel" was the symbol of a special divine intervention, she received the "promised land" and lived there as an association of twelve traditional tribes. Did the year 587 B.C. signify the end of the history of Israel, or was it the final act of a long tragedy which had begun one and a half centuries earlier with the direct intervention of the Assyrian power, which had wrought the destruction of the northern state of Israel and the subjugation of the southern state of Judah, and —with the elimination of the state of Judah—culminated in the end of "Israel"?

It could be asked whether the national and political independence that was removed in 587 B.C. from what remained of "Israel" was really part of its original character. It could be shown that Israel had existed for long enough without the institution of kingship, without a royal palace or royal sanctuary, that Jerusalem had remained a non-Israelite city right in the middle

of Israel for some centuries before David conquered it and
Solomon rebuilt it sumptuously as the royal residence. What was
destroyed in the year 587 B.C., therefore, was the last vestiges of
institutions which Israel had certainly not possessed from the very
beginning, but had arisen only during the course of its history.
Was it therefore merely the end of an *episode* in the history of
Israel, which had only lasted about four centuries? In answering
this question in the affirmative, we must bear in mind that
history never returns to a past state of things, to reproduce a
former situation after the conclusion of a definite episode.

After all that had happened during the time of the kings in
Israel, the event which took place in 587 B.C., concluding a long
series of catastrophes, signified a very decisive step in the history
of Israel, even if it by no means brought "Israel" to an end. In
the ancient tradition of the Pentateuch a very important place
is given to the promise by Israel's God to give them possession
of the land and its fruits, and its subsequent materialisation; but
this did not include the idea that any particular *national* organiza-
tions should be established in the land taken over, although
indeed unfettered occupation of the land was intended, without any domination by foreign powers. The Canaanites (who
had previously lived in the land, but had not so completely
possessed it that the Israelite tribes could not have co-existed
with them) had to be "driven out", as we learn expressly
from the narrative comment in the deuteronomic law, so
that Israel could really have complete freedom to occupy its
land.

This freedom was now over, and the disappearance of the last
vestiges of national independence in 587 B.C. has an important
significance. The reign of King Josiah, which did not after all lie
very far back, had shown that the small state of Judah (with its
capital city Jerusalem) could, under favourable circumstances,
become the starting point of an attempt at restoration. Josiah
had taken advantage of the decline and collapse of the mighty
Assyria to strive for the restoration of the rule of the Davidic
dynasty over the whole of "Israel"; he had been well on the way
to this goal when his sudden death in the Battle of Megiddo
(609 B.C.) brought an end to his political work. The fall of
Jerusalem in 587 B.C. crushed all hope of winning back political
independence for "Israel" within a reasonable space of time,

and the free occupation of the promised land. Now the lamentation was fully justified: "Our inheritance has been turned over to strangers, our homes to aliens" (*Lam.* v.2).

"Israel" had not always had a monarchy; it had gone over to this form of government very much later than its neighbours. But it could not really maintain its independence within the concomity of national states in Syria and Palestine except by the institution of a monarchy, once the older form of organization of the sacral union of tribes had faded into the background. Thus it came about that the Davidic monarchy in Jerusalem received a promise (*II Sam.* vii) which was apparently not generally recognized throughout "Israel", but which was at any rate regarded as valid by the southern tribes and perhaps others. For all those who had believed in this pledge, the deposition of the last ruler of the house of David in Jerusalem signified the end of this divine promise.

Jerusalem itself, although brought so late into relation with Israel, had ever since the days of David and Solomon gained a most important significance in the eyes of Israel as the city of the central sanctuary, a significance which went even beyond the circle of supporters of the Davidic dynasty.[1] The Ark, the last historical reference to which is in *I Kings* viii.3-9, had (as the traditional tribal sanctuary) handed on its central importance for the whole of Israel to the Temple in Jerusalem. Strangely its loss is mentioned nowhere in the Old Testament, for it must have perished in 587 B.C. when the Temple was destroyed. Perhaps the reason is that in the meantime its unifying role had been taken over by the holy place itself. Thus the deuteronomic law in a stereotyped expression speaks of one central cultic *place*, "the place that the Lord will choose to cause his name to dwell there". This place was retained, but it became a ruined sanctuary where the arrangements for the cult were more or less destroyed.

From the historical point of view, therefore, the year 587 B.C. was a very deep cut into the history of Israel, signifying not only the final act, but the climax of God's judgment on Israel as it had been proclaimed by the prophets. How did "Israel" take the events of 587 B.C.? First we must try to put ourselves in their position and see things through contemporary eyes, we must be prepared to adopt a variety of attitudes, according to the

[1] For details cf. above, pp. 132-44.

situation in which the individual parts of the larger unit of Israel found themselves at that time.

Of the tribes of the former state of Israel the upper classes had been deported a century and a half earlier by the Assyrians (*II Kings* XVII.6). These upper classes disappear, and it seems improbable that they took any further part in the events in the "land of Israel". On the other hand, the remainder of the settled peasant population in the former state of Israel was still there. They lived under a foreign upper class (*II Kings* XVII.24) in the Assyrian and Neo-Babylonian provinces of Samaria, Dor, Megiddo, and Gilead, each of which had a separate political and cultic life (cf. *II Kings* XVII.29-31), particularly in the "cities" (*II Kings* XVII.24, 29). The events in Jerusalem and Judah were not without importance for the Israelite population in these provinces. It is true that the loss of political independence and of an independent monarchy in Judah may have had little effect on them. Judah itself was now experiencing what they had experienced a century and a half earlier, and had long accustomed themselves to. Their short-lived partial "freedom" under Josiah would hardly have left any lasting effect on them, and it is doubtful whether there were still many amongst them who clung to the promise given to the dynasty of David.

The situation in cultic matters, however, was quite different. Naturally we know hardly anything about cultic arrangements at the beginning of the sixth century B.C. among the Israelite population of the former state of Israel, but it seems probable that the cultic connection with the central sanctuary in Jerusalem did not disappear, despite the political separation after the death of Solomon. It may be that the cultic union with Jerusalem had become weaker as time passed, especially among those at a greater distance, as for centuries—ever since the time of David and Solomon—there had existed many local sanctuaries side by side with the central place of worship. But the connection certainly had not been broken altogether. Then towards the end of the seventh century the deuteronomic injunction of a single place of worship was implemented by Josiah in favour of Jerusalem, not only in Jerusalem and Judah but also in the province of Samaria annexed by him (*II Kings* XXIII.15, 19); it seems unlikely that these local Samaritan sanctuaries which had been desecrated by Josiah were brought back into cultic use after his death. Thus for the Israelites in the province of Samaria at least Jerusalem was the real sanctuary in 587 B.C. Even if, therefore, the local cult was prominent in the provinces of Dor, Megiddo, and Gilead (which were situated at some distance from Jerusalem and therefore had only a slight cultic relationship with the city), nevertheless in the province of Samaria, directly neighbouring upon Jerusalem, a strong if not wholly exclusive union existed with the Jerusalem cult.

Some evidence of this is to be found in the one passage in the Old Testament which has any significant bearing on this question. According to *Jer.* XLI.5, soon after the catastrophe that had overtaken Jerusalem, eighty men from Shechem, Shiloh, and Samaria—i.e. from cities of the province of Samaria— arrived with all the usual signs of mourning, and bringing "offerings" and "incense" to the "house of the Lord". By "the house of the Lord" we are certainly meant to understand the sanctuary in Jerusalem, and there is evidence for this in the fact that the men passed by Mizpah, which in all probability is to be sought at the present-day Tell en-Nasbe on the road from the Samarian mountains to Jerusalem. They brought sacrificial offerings; therefore in their eyes the place of worship in Jerusalem was still a holy place, even though in ruins. Might it not be concluded that the holy place even now could still give opportunity to people to present "offerings" in the usual simple manner, and to burn "incense"—even though it was no longer possible to bring animal sacrifices after the equipment of the sanctuary had been destroyed? In short, can it not be concluded that after the catastrophe cultic activities still took place at the traditional spot, even though they could only take place to a limited extent? What was the significance of the signs of mourning? Surely they were mourning the desolate sanctuary just as one would mourn a dead man. This surely implies that even before the catastrophe it had been the custom among the descendants of the ancient tribes of Israel, in the former state of Israel—at least in the province of Samaria, but probably even beyond—to participate in the Jerusalem cult and to consider the Jerusalem sanctuary as the official central sanctuary. After the events of 587 B.C. all that remained was resigned mourning, whilst maintaining what was left of cultic activity.

The same can surely be said of the citizens of Jerusalem and

Judah, who were more directly concerned. As for those who had been deported to Babylon, all that remained to them was a sad longing for Zion (cf. *Ps.* cxxxvii); those who had remained in the land could only sing lamentations for the dead (cf. *Lamentations*) and undertake a few cultic activities on the site of the sanctuary. But they had lost far more than the Israelites of the former state of Israel. They had lost the last vestiges of political independence, even if it had already previously been limited by the rule of a foreign overlord; they had lost their monarchy, the dynasty of David which had been specially singled out as a result of the promise given to it and to the whole of Israel. They had lost the hope that the restoration of "Israel", which Josiah had sought only a short time before, would come about under Davidic rule.

Did they really lose this hope completely? We must remember that Jerusalem had already been conquered eleven years earlier, in 597 B.C., and Jehoiachin, who was then the ruling member of the house of David, had been deported to Babylon by Nebuchadnezzar with members of the upper classes of Jerusalem and Judah.

Between 597 and 587 B.C. there had been *two* "Kings of Judah" of the house of David. One was Zedekiah, appointed by Nebuchadnezzar in Jerusalem as a vassal king of the tributary state of Judah, which had been left with a limited independence; he was the son of the famous Josiah. The other was Jehoiachin, a grandchild of Josiah's, who shortly before the fall of Jerusalem in 597 B.C. had followed his father Jehoiakim to the throne as king, and had had to pay for Judah's infidelity as a tributary state not only by being deported along with the other members of the upper classes, but also by being made a state prisoner in Babylon while, strangely enough for a man in his position, retaining the title King of Judah. We know this from the cuneiform documents which E. F. Weidner[2] has published, and which originate from Babylon in the period between 597 and 587 B.C.[3] These deal with the giving of oil to "King Jehoiachin of Judah" and to five "royal sons of Judah" (i.e. probably princes of the house of David) as well as to a few other Judaeans, all of whom therefore

---

[2] Cf. E. F. Weidner: "Jojachin, König von Juda, in babylonischen Keilschrifttexten," in *Mélanges syriens offerts à M. R. Dussaud*, VOL. II, Paris 1939, pp. 923-35.

[3] Cf. Weidner: *op. cit.*, p. 925, according to which one of the dates occurring in these documents is the thirteenth year of the rule of Nebuchadnezzar (592-1 B.C.).

seem to have been treated quite tolerably despite their imprisonment. One might well ask why Nebuchadnezzar had allowed Jehoiachin his life as the defeated king of a rebellious tributary state. It could hardly have been because of his youth (according to *II Kings* xxiv.8 he was eighteen years old when taken captive), nor could it have been because of his personal innocence (he had had to take over the inheritance of his disobedient father Jehoiakim only shortly before the catastrophe of 597 B.C.). Personal, humane considerations would hardly have swayed Nebuchadnezzar. Did he perhaps have political reasons for not killing Jehoiachin, and allowing him to be called King of Judah even in Babylon? He may have seen him as a possible counterpawn to Zedekiah, to be used when the opportunity arose. We cannot be sure, but the fact remains that between 597 and 587 B.C. there were two representatives of the house of David, both of whom had the title King of Judah.

It is natural to expect that among the people of Jerusalem and Judah there were circles which supported Zedekiah as the actual ruling king, and on the other hand circles who saw in Jehoiachin the legitimate king who had been wrongfully displaced.[4] We can accept this possibility, even though we are not expressly told so in the books of the prophets Jeremiah and Ezekiel. Indeed certain oracles of the prophets (particularly of Jeremiah) only become really comprehensible when viewed against this background. Jeremiah himself belonged without doubt to those who supported Zedekiah; for he was the king in Jerusalem appointed by Nebuchadnezzar, and in the eyes of Jeremiah, Nebuchadnezzar was the all-powerful legitimate overlord chosen by God to be world ruler (cf. *Jer.* xxvii.6ff.), to whom all peoples and princes must show obedience. Jeremiah therefore called Zedekiah to submit to Nebuchadnezzar, and finally ordered him to capitulate when the Babylonian troops sent to put down the revolt were standing outside Jerusalem; in this way Jeremiah hoped to maintain the *status quo* (*Jer.* xxxviii.14ff.). The higher royal officials and certainly large parts of the population of Jerusalem and Judah also supported Zedekiah. The higher officials did not like the close relationship between king and prophet (cf. *Jer.* xxxviii.25), for they wanted Zedekiah to revolt against

---

[4] Cf. with regard to this and to the following, A. Malamat, in *Palestine Exploration Quarterly*, LXXXIII, 1951, pp. 81-7.

Nebuchadnezzar and fight to the end against the Babylonians, in order to re-establish the political independence of the Davidic monarchy. Their motto was: "with Zedekiah against Nebuchadnezzar". They succeeded eventually, and the outcome of their endeavours was the catastrophe of 587 B.C.

In that period between 597 and 587 B.C. there were, however, also circles in Jerusalem and Judah who supported the deported Jehoiachin, and hoped that through him the re-establishment of the old independence might be achieved. This trend is represented by the prophet Hananiah who, according to *Jer.* xxviii.2ff., proclaimed the return of Jehoiachin in the near future, along with the Judaeans deported with him and the costly vessels of the Temple which had been taken away as booty. It was he who proclaimed: "I will break the yoke of the king of Babylon" right in the middle of the reign of Zedekiah,[5] just as if there were no such king as Zedekiah at all!

Jeremiah answered—and it is perhaps significant that the name Jehoiachin is passed over in silence—that he also wanted to see the return of those deported, and the stolen treasures, but that it was improbable that Hananiah's proclamation was correct. After receiving a further message from the Lord, he categorically gave the lie to the words of Hananiah. The very harsh words of Jeremiah about Jehoiachin can only be really understood in the light of the hopes which were placed on Jehoiachin. In *Jer.* xxii.24 the complete rejection of Jehoiachin is announced in a divine prophecy. Even if Jehoiachin were something as costly as a signet ring upon the right hand of God, he would still "pluck it off".[6]

The prophecy in *Jer.* xxii.28-30 tells us still more. When questioned (possibly by the people in Jerusalem and Judah) whether Jehoiachin was a worthless clay vessel which had been thrown out and cast into a foreign land, the divine judgment is announced with the unusually ceremonious introduction "O

---

[5] The date which now stands in *Jer.* xxviii.1 is the result of a textual distortion. Originally the "fourth year of King Zedekiah of Judah" was mentioned (cf. W. Rudolph: *Jeremia, Hb.A.T.*, 2nd edn., 1958, p. 162).

[6] Vss. 25-7 are probably an addition to this short prophetic saying, which relates the saying to the surrender of Jehoiachin to Nebuchadnezzar, and which purposefully stresses that Jehoiachin will never return again from the land into which he has been thrown. Perhaps the shorter prophetic oracle is thereby more correctly interpreted.

earth, earth, earth, hear the word of the Lord". "This man" (Jehoiachin) is to be written (in the genealogical register) as "childless" since no descendant of his shall ever again sit on the throne of David and rule Judah. Therefore even if Jehoiachin has, or shall have, descendants[7] he will still officially be regarded as childless. Divine decree therefore has ruled that the line of Jehoiachin shall have no claim to the throne of David in Jerusalem. This prophecy is only completely understandable if it is seen as directed against certain hopes linked with Jehoiachin and his successors.

With this differing attitude towards Zedekiah and Jehoiachin there naturally went a varying judgment of the relative worth of those deported and those left behind in 597 B.C. Where was the "remnant" of the true "Israel" to be found? Each of the two groups would be inclined to consider itself the superior. The deported upper classes may well have seen in the fact that Jehoiachin was still alive a sign of his and their future significance, and have linked the hope of a restoration with their own existence. Hananiah is an example to show that there were still circles in the homeland who did not acquiesce. On the other hand, it was natural for Zedekiah and those who had been left behind to draw a distinction between their own fate and that of the deportees, in such a way that they were absolved from the divine judgment on Israel and therefore carried with them the future of "Israel". Jeremiah disputed this idea decisively. Although he saw in Zedekiah the then legitimate King of Judah, and although he tried right to the last possible moment to make Zedekiah bow to the rule of Nebuchadnezzar and so maintain the *status quo*, he nevertheless had to announce the end of the rule of Zedekiah and the remnant of the Judaean state, thereby extinguishing any hope of a restoration from that quarter. He gave warning against those prophets who proclaimed that the treasures of the Temple, stolen in 597 B.C., would be returned (cf. *Jer.* XXVIII.2ff.) and announced that even what remained of the Temple vessels would be taken to Babylon as booty (*Jer.* XXVII.16-21).

[7] The incontestable tradition in *I Chron.* III.17. is that Jehoiachin did in fact have sons. Some of them might already have been born at the time of the above prophecy of Jeremiah. It cannot be said with certainty whether the "royal sons of Judah" mentioned in the cuneiform documents were really the sons of Jehoiachin or of some other member of the house of David.

In the vision of the two baskets of figs (*Jer.* xxiv), which had a definite significance for the people remaining in Jerusalem and Judah, he equated these people with the bad inedible figs—as compared with the deportees—and thereby proclaimed their downfall. He expressly warned those who had been deported against having hope in the "king that sitteth upon the throne of David" (Zedekiah) and the "brethren that are not gone forth . . . into captivity" but remained in the old homeland (*Jer.* xxix.16). Neither on the other hand did he come out on the side of those deported. It was not only that he decisively rejected all the expectations linked with Jehoiachin, who was still living amongst them. He also attacked the fact that *human* hopes were being placed on the deported upper classes. Admittedly in *Jer.* xxiv the "good" figs are interpreted as those who were deported—not, however, because they were "good" in themselves, but because God would once more "give them a heart to know me that I am the Lord" and in that way "they shall return". Admittedly there is no mention in this context (vss. 6, 7) of Jehoiachin and the dynasty of David. The famous letter of Jeremiah to the deportees, which dates from the period between 597 and 587 B.C., shows that this interpretation did not signify the fulfilment of frivolous hopes in the near future. Here again of course it is said that God "will visit" those deported, and in their prayers they will "find" God, and then he "will turn away [their] captivity" and "will gather" them together again (*Jer.* xxix.10-14). But the more direct concern of the letter is to warn them against false prophets who were foretelling a speedy restoration, and to call upon the deported to make their home in the foreign land, for the "turning away of their captivity" would only come after seventy years (vs. 10), which meant that scarcely any of them would live to share this event, except for the little children. That this negative side of the letter was seen by the exiles as Jeremiah's chief concern is shown by the complaint made by an unknown spokesman against Jeremiah to the High Priest of Jerusalem (*Jer.* xxix.24ff.), alleging that he had set himself against their hopes.

Jeremiah told both sides that the message of God was "No". Human hopes of a "restoration" could be based neither on Zedekiah and those left behind, nor on Jehoiachin and those deported. There was no region which the judgment of God over Israel did not reach or would not reach in the future. There remained nothing to which their contemporaries might cling hopefully. If God should decide to create something new at some time in the future, which those living would not live to see, he would one day gather the descendants of those deported together again; but it would be a new beginning, having no connection with the past. And if one day a "righteous Branch" of the house of David should rule again as the true "king" over "Judah and Israel" (*Jer.* XXIII.5, 6), God would raise him up without any connection with Jehoiachin and his descendants, and indeed without any necessary connection with Zedekiah and his house.[8]

In *Ezekiel* the situation is the same, though with slightly different nuances here and there.[9] Ezekiel turns categorically against Zedekiah and those left behind in 597 B.C. The threats and the symbolic actions in *Ezek.* I-XXIV proclaiming disaster vividly depict the imminent end of the remnant of the state of Judah which was left in 598 B.C.; and even if in the coming catastrophe in Jerusalem a few individuals who have not taken part in the "abominations" are to be spared (*Ezek.* IX.4, 6; cf. XIV.14-20), nothing will remain of the former situation which could serve as a starting-point for a future restoration. Ezekiel particularly attacks the opinion of those left behind that they, not those who were deported, constituted the remnant of "Israel". When those people of Jerusalem who were not deported consider themselves as rightful inheritors of the promise of a land given to "Israel", saying "to us this land is given for a possession" whereas the deported are "far from the Lord", then Ezekiel proclaims that God will cause a future revival to be brought about by those who were deported, by "gathering" them together again and by giving them a new spirit and a new heart (*Ezek.* XI.14-21). And when those left behind compare themselves with Abraham and console themselves with the thought that he received the divine promise of a land though he was but a single individual, whereas they (though much reduced) are still

---

[8] The name of the future king "The Lord Our Righteousness" (vs. 6) has readily been seen as an allusion to the name "Zedekiah". That may be quite correct. Yet it does not contain the idea of a historical connection with Zedekiah, but rather the idea that this "Zedekiah" will be replaced by a king who will rightly be able to bear the name "The Lord Our Righteousness".

[9] Since the opinions about Zedekiah and Jehoiachin were shared by those who were left behind and those who were deported (cf. above, with regard to Jeremiah), none of the following statements help to tell us whether Ezekiel lived in Jerusalem or in Babylon before 587 B.C.

numerous, and claim the promise for themselves again with the words: "the land is surely given to us to possess", then Ezekiel answers them by proclaiming the total destruction of all that remains after the former catastrophe (*Ezek.* XXXIII.23-29)[10]. Deportation and death in Babylon are prophesied for King Zedekiah in the extensive allegory in *Ezek.* XVII.1-21 (cf. especially vs. 16).

In *Ezekiel* we do not, as in *Jeremiah*, find similar words against unjustified hopes among the deportees. We might conclude from this—and from the passage in *Ezek.* XI.14-21—that Ezekiel supported King Jehoiachin and those who had been deported, and founded his hopes for the future of "Israel" on this group. In this connection the statements of Ezekiel about the members of the house of David must be more closely examined. It is of little importance here that the *Book of Ezekiel* is dated according to the years of "King Jehoiachin's captivity", for this probably applies to the editing of the book, which the prophet is not likely to have done himself. Thus it can be accepted that such a dating system was customary among those deported to Babylon, since Nebuchadnezzar had let Jehoiachin live and even go on being called King. If those who had been deported did not want to date their years according to the years of the Babylonian King's rule then it was quite natural for them to adopt this method of dating in their internal affairs, without committing us to any far-reaching idea about the significance of Jehoiachin himself.

An important passage for Ezekiel's appreciation of Jehoiachin is the "lamentation for the princes of Israel" in ch. XIX, which is divided into three stanzas with the customary 3-2 rhythm of the lament (with 2+2 at the end of the stanza). Since the text and meaning of this lamentation are doubtful in many respects, a closer analysis is necessary. This reveals that the first stanza forms quite an appropriate starting-point, since it has come down to us fairly complete. No doubts can be raised about its meaning. It reads:

> 2. What a lioness was your mother
>   among lions!
>   She lay there among young lions,
>   she nourished her whelps.

---

[10] As its content shows this passage must belong to the period before the fall of Jerusalem in 587 B.C. It must therefore not be connected with the two previous verses.

3. And she brought up one of her whelps,
    he became a young lion.
  He learned to catch the prey,
    he devoured men.

4. Nations were roused against him,[11]
    he was taken in their pit.
  He was brought with thorns
    to the land of Egypt.

Generally these stanzas are regarded as referring to King Jehoahaz of Judah, the son and successor of King Josiah; for he was the only one of the "princes of Israel" (i.e. the Judaean kings) who fits the last line of the stanza. According to *II Kings* XXIII.33-34, soon after he had ascended the throne he was taken "to Egypt" by Pharaoh Necho, and died there.

The connection is uncertain, however, in the second stanza which reads:

5. When she saw that she had been deceived,[12]
    and her hope was vanished,
  she took (another of) her whelps
    and made him a young lion.

6. [He went up and down among the lions,
    he became a young lion.
  He learned to catch prey,
    and devoured men]

7. He made palaces quake
    and terrified cities,[13]
  so that the land and all in it was struck with amazement
    by the noise of his roaring.

[11] The verbal form at the beginning of the verse must be vocalized as Hiphil (without changing the traditional form of the consonants).

[12] The meaning of *YHL* (Niphal) in this context is not clear; the above translation is pure guesswork.

[13] This line in its traditional form is incomprehensible and is surely a textual distortion. I would guess, taking into consideration the continuation in vs. 7*b*, that the two verbal statements in this line originally read: *wayyar'ēdh* (Hiphil is not documented anywhere else with a causative meaning) and *heḥĕrîdh*. The form *'almānôth* stands instead of *'armānôth*, as in *Is.* XIII.22. The suffixes of both nouns in this line must have referred to the *'ādhām* of the previous line, but the unmotivated juxtaposition of a singular and plural suffix clearly shows that the text here is not in order. The "palaces" and "cities" of course refer to the inhabitants.

8. [Then the nations were set against him
   on every side out of the provinces.]
   They spread their net over him,
   he was taken in their pit.

9. They set him in a 'cage'[14]
   brought[15] him into 'custody'[16];
   [That his voice should no more be heard
   upon the mountains of Israel].[17]

These stanzas have been interpreted as referring to Zedekiah.[18]
Yet it is hardly adequate proof for this assertion that Jehoahaz
and Zedekiah had not only the same father (Josiah) but also the
same mother (Hamutal) (cf. *II Kings*, XXIII.31, XXIV.18), who
therefore must be meant in *Ezek.* XIX by the lioness who nurtured
her whelps. It is even less probable that the Queen Mother
Hamutal played such an important role that she was incorporated as a special figure in the lion image in *Ezekiel*; moreover the
description in the second stanza of the young lion spreading
terror all around hardly fits the weak and fearful Zedekiah. The
lioness-mother in *Ezek.* XIX could much rather symbolize Judah
or the Judaean kingdom (cf. *Gen.* XLIX.9f.), and then the second
stanza must surely refer to Jehoiakim, the successor of Jehoahaz.
According to *Jer.* XXII.13-19 he was a brutal ruler (cf. also
II Kings XXIV.4); he died in Jerusalem, just as Nebuchadnezzar
had sent troops into his land to punish his infidelity (*II Kings*
XXIV.2). The mention of the capture and imprisonment of the

[14] The word *baḥaḥîm* is secondary, taken over from vs. 4*b*; in contrast to vs. 4*b*,
however, it has no real sense in this context.
[15] The note "And they brought him to the king of Babylon" is obviously an
explanatory gloss, which completely destroys the rhythmic measure of the line.
[16] The last word of vs. 9*a* could be retained in the meaning "ropes, nets"; yet
perhaps we are to read *mĕṣûrôth* as "confinements" if, parallel to the previous
sûgār, we do not read *maṣṣereth* (stem *nṣr*) which finds no other documentation in
Hebrew but occurs in Akkadian as *maṣṣartu*, in the meaning "custody, prison".
[17] Since vs. 9*a* in its original form seems to be the closing 2+2 line, vs. 9*b* can
certainly be reckoned a secondary addition. It is problematical whether certain
other lines are not secondary, and whether perhaps the second stanza did not
originally have as many lines as the first. In this case, chiefly the two lines of vs. 6
would have to be considered as additions, since verse 3 is here repeated verbally,
and the statement of vs. 6*aβ* clashes with vs. 5*bβ*. If perhaps one of the two lines of
vs. 8 were an addition, then there would be the same number of lines as in the first
stanza. The lines in parentheses in the above translation are those which in the
original are doubtful.
[18] Cf. J. Herrmann, *Ezechiel* (*Kommentar zum Alten Testament*), 1924, pp. 116ff.

second young lion in *Ezek*. xix.8*b*, 9*a* refers to this situation.[19]

What now is the significance of the third stanza in *Ezek*. xix, where the image of the lion is replaced by the image of the vine, which must also surely refer to the kingdom of Judah? The change of image must be seen as the free touch of poetic art, and it is therefore unnecessary to search for a deeper, more significant reason for it. This third stanza reads:

10. Your mother was like a vine 'in the vineyard',[20]
    planted by the waters:
she was fruitful and full of branches
    by reason of many waters.

11. And she had strong rods
    for the sceptres of them that bare rule.
[And her stature was exalted
    among the thick branches][21]
She looked proudly upon her height,
    upon the multitude of her branches.[22]

12. But she was plucked up,
    she was cast down to the ground.[23]
The east wind dried her up,
    her fruit dropped.
[Her strong rods were broken and withered;
    the fire consumed them.]

[19] There is not much to say for the interpretation of the second stanza as referring to Jehoiachin (cf. A. Bertholet: *Hesekiel* (1936), p. 71). Only the secondary addition in vs. 9*a* mentions that the prince was taken away to Babylon. For the rest the image of a particularly fearsome lion is as inappropriate for Jehoiachin, who only ruled for such a short time, as it is for the timid Zedekiah. Moreover, it would be strange if Ezekiel had completely passed over Jehoiakim in this context after beginning with the scarcely important Jehoahaz.

[20] The phrase "in thy blood" which stands in the traditional text cannot be original; on the basis of the consonantal text I read—although "simplifying"— *bakkerem*.

[21] This means branches of other trees up which the grape vines creep.

[22] In the two lines of vs. 11*aβb* the unexpected 2 + 2 metre is striking—as also is the masculine form which has no connection with what has gone before and from vs. 12 onwards is replaced by a feminine which points back to *gephen*. In order to support a masculine, one would have to read *matteh* instead of *mattôth* in vs. 11*aβ*. But even if *matteh* in vs. 11*aα* is original—which seems quite possible (in the second half of this line the singular *šēbet* would then have to be accepted as original)—then the statements in vs. 11*aβb* refer more to the "vine" than to the "branch". I consider that vs. 11*aβb* is a secondary addition.

[23] There is a beat missing in the first half of vs. 12*a* also. Since this line is indispensable in this context one might well ask if Bertholet: *Hesekiel*, p. 68 is not perfectly right in reading *wĕhî huttĕšâ* at the beginning of the line.

13. And now she is planted in the wilderness,
     in a dry ground.[24]

14. [Fire is gone out of a rod,
     has devoured her branches and her fruit.
     So has she no strong rod
     to be a sceptre to rule.]

This stanza is mostly understood to refer to Zedekiah.[25] But the fact that in *Ezek.* XVII Zedekiah is actually referred to under the image of a vine is inadequate proof of this. *Ezek.* XVII and XIX are completely independent units; the prophet was free to use whatever images he wished, and the interpretation of each unit must be sought quite independently. The content of the third stanza of *Ezek.* XIX does not fit Zedekiah very well. The vine is to be transplanted from a well-watered vineyard to a "dry and thirsty ground". If *Ezek.* XIX belongs to the period before 587 B.C., it would have to end with a threat to Zedekiah. This would be a very weak interpretation.[26] If, however, *Ezek.* XIX is not a lamentation in anticipation of the future, but a lamentation over what is already past, to regard the contents of this third stanza as referring to Zedekiah would be far too weak an interpretation, remembering his terrible fate after the fall of Jerusalem. Moreover, in the third stanza a second person is addressed, whose mother is likened to a vine, and then the fate of the vine itself is discussed,[27] whereas actually the fate of this second person is

[24] The last word of this line is perhaps to be omitted with the Septuagint. The question arises again here whether the original form of the third stanza did not have the same reduced number of lines as the first stanza. At any rate the line vs. 14aα may well be secondary as a 3+3 line (if *piryâ* is not omitted with the Septuagint). Then the last line (vs. 14aβ) might also be regarded as secondary. This would make vs. 13 the concluding line where, in accordance with the other two stanzas, one would expect to find a 2+2 line (perhaps *bammidhbār* is an explanatory addition). Otherwise perhaps the third line of vs. 12 could be considered a later expansion.

[25] Cf., for example, Herrmann: *Ezechiel*, pp. 116ff. Bertholet: *Hesekiel*, pp. 69ff.

[26] Admittedly in *Ezek.* XVII (vs. 9), just as in *Ezek.* XIX.12ff., mention is made of the destruction of a vine; and clearly, in *Ezek.* XVII, the reference is to Zedekiah. Nevertheless in *Ezek.* XVII.9 the complete destruction of the vine is stressed even more: and in *Ezek.* XIX especially the statement of the transplantation of the vine into dry ground is added, and shows that previously (vs. 12) the complete destruction of the vine was not in mind. This is quite different in *Ezek.* XVII, here it is obviously meant that the vine met a wretched total end.

[27] The lines in vs. 11aβb, where we pass over from the feminine of the vine to a masculine cannot really be used as proof that now the discussion passes from the mother-vine to some quite different person (depicted perhaps in the "branch"

meant.[28] We may wonder whether the vine, which undoubtedly meant Judah and its kingdom, did not at the same time include the idea of a real queen mother, whose fate could have been considered along with the fate of the second person who is addressed. This would lead us to Jehoiachin who, as is expressly stated in *II Kings* XXIV.12 (cf. *Jer.* XXII.26), was deported with his mother, the Queen Mother Nehushta.

This may seem debatable, but even apart from this it seems highly probable to me that the third stanza refers to Jehoiachin. Ezekiel did not necessarily have to follow the exact historical succession of Judaean kings from Jehoahaz onwards in his lament, but it remains highly probable that he did deal in correct sequence with those kings whose rule he had actually experienced himself. A definite pointer to Jehoiachin is the statement that the vine was transplanted from rich to dry ground. Only Jehoiachin, who was deported, had a personal fate which was as relatively tolerable as this—not Zedekiah. It cannot be said against the Jehoiachin interpretation that the image of a sumptuously growing vine does not fit the three-month rule of the young Jehoiachin; for we also have the same full poetic image in the first young lion of the first stanza of *Ezek.* XIX, which (it is generally agreed) refers to Jehoahaz, who likewise was king for a bare three months. Thus the lament obviously refers to past events. The *wĕʿattâ* at the beginning of vs. 13—which originally was quite possibly the concluding line of the whole lament— must, stressed as it is, be taken literally. So the prophet with this stressed "now" is speaking of the situation in his own day; and, as a statement referring to the present, vs. 13 can hardly refer to Zedekiah, but could very well refer to the deported Jehoiachin.

If this interpretation of *Ezek.* XIX is correct, it would be significant that Ezekiel simply ignores Zedekiah in the sequence of the *nĕśîʾê yiśrāʾēl* (princes of Israel) in his lament, which was probably

---

of vs. 11aα) thereby differentiating one individual king from the general manifestation of the monarchy. For since the feminine crops up again in vs. 12, the lines of vs. 11aβb can only be considered an addition (cf. above, n. 22). The author of this addition must surely have thought of an individual king when he formulated this gloss.

[28] The question remains who this second person addressed in the lament actually was. The writer obviously has in mind the king mentioned in the last stanza, even though he is mentioned in the third person in the image of the vine.

written during the rule of Zedekiah or at any rate sometime after 587 B.C. He simply does not count Zedekiah. This would fit in very well with his other statements concerning Zedekiah and those left behind in 597 B.C. Did Ezekiel, however, still have hope in Jehoiachin? *Ezek.* XIX implies not, for a lament presupposes an immutable end, and Jehoiachin is to be lamented as a dead man is lamented.

Finally, our understanding of *Ezek.* XIX must guide our interpretation of the passage in *Ezek.* XVII.22-24. Firstly, in XVII the Judaean kingdom is spoken of figuratively as a powerful cedar. The top of the cedar is one day torn off by a great eagle and taken to a land of merchants. This signifies the deportation of Jehoiachin by Nebuchadnezzar. Then a lowly vine is mentioned which is transplanted, by which we are to understand Zedekiah. This vine is one day to be torn up. Then however—as vss. 22-24 tell us—the Lord will one day take a tender shoot from the top of the cedar and will plant it on a high mountain in Israel. This goes beyond the image of the vine, and is linked again with the first image of the cedar. Is this not a hope for the future based upon Jehoiachin or his descendants? Not necessarily, for the cedar is not meant to represent Jehoiachin, but the Davidic monarchy, which is to be restored in the future by an act of God, and we are not told that Jehoiachin and his family will have any significance in this event. It is after all presupposed that the Judaean monarchy has come to an end with Jehoiachin. Zedekiah is only a lowly vine, which was planted as a substitute for the once mighty cedar tree, thereby asserting the legitimacy of Jehoiachin against Zedekiah, even if the final hope for the future is not linked with the presence of Jehoiachin, but with a new act of God in the future. Over and above this we must question the originality of the final paragraph of *Ezek.* XVII. It has been judged as a later addition by Ezekiel himself,[29] for whom, at least after 587 B.C., Jehoiachin would have been the last legitimate ruler of the house of David. It would be difficult to disprove, however, that an "unauthentic" addition by another hand altogether is to be seen in *Ezek.* XVII.22-24.

We can now return to the question what remained for "Israel" after the catastrophe of 587 B.C. Jeremiah and probably also Ezekiel had already disputed that there was anything left, or that

[29] Cf. for example, Herrmann: *Ezechiel*, p. 107, Bertholet: *Heskeiel*, p. 65.

anything would remain which could form a starting-point for a new Israel of the future. Despite their serious words, however, it would have been humanly very strange if, after the downfall and defeat of Zedekiah and the liquidation of the independent state of Judah, King Jehoiachin of Judah, who was still alive, had not immediately become the object of all kinds of vague hopes, especially as he was already considered the legitimate king by many, both deportees and those left behind. This is particularly true of those deported with him in 597 B.C., but also of those more recently deported in 587 B.C. Otherwise there was not very much, apart from memories of past times, which could have kept them linked with the traditions of "Israel". The popular belief that they had taken with them important sections of pre-exilic Old Testament literature cannot be verified, and seems quite improbable. There is just as little documentary evidence to show that there were any beginnings of synagogue worship amongst them as a substitute for the Jerusalem cult. Possibly a more or less regular intercourse was maintained with the ancient homeland.

But there was not much left even for the descendants of the ancient tribes in the "land of Israel". A considerably reduced cult at the holy place of worship probably still continued (cf. above p. 263ff.). They must have had those pre-exilic traditions of Israel which had been written down, such as the ancient records from the narrative material of the Pentateuch, the earlier historical records, the written law-books, and a few collections of sayings of the prophets, etc.[30] But their present life was miserable enough. Did they also look to Jehoiachin? That would be easier to accept if perhaps the name of Jehoiachin had been linked in some way or other with the "land of Israel". In Tell Beit Mirsim and er-Rumēle (Beth-Shemesh) impressions of a seal have been found with the inscription "[Belonging] to Eliakim, the administrator of Jaukin", which according to the archaeological and historical evidence can only date from the period between 597 and 587 B.C. It seems highly probable that "Jaukin" is the name of the King, Jehoiachin, and the owner

[30] The deuteronomic history was based on numerous more ancient historical sources, and probably written down in Palestine (cf. my *Überl: Studien*, p. 97, n. 6; p. 140, n. 1). The thesis is hardly probable that there were only verbal traditions in Israel right up to the time of the exile and that the whole fixed written tradition only followed in the post-exilic period.

of the seal was presumably the administrator of his property.[31]

This seems to show that Jehoiachin still owned property in Judah even after his deportation, that this was looked after for him by a deputy, and that therefore the Babylonians legally allowed the deported "King Jehoiachin of Judah" at least a part of the royal landed possessions, and they may have allotted another part to Zedekiah, whom they had appointed. That may have suited the ambiguity which they possibly intended in the relationship between Jehoiachin and Zedekiah. What happened then in 587 B.C. to the crown lands of the king of Judah? We do not know. Zedekiah and his sons were removed, and with them the reigning Davidic dynasty in Jerusalem. The Babylonians had no valid reason for keeping Jehoiachin in reserve as a possibly useful counter claimant to Zedekiah any longer. Did they leave Jehoiachin still legally in possession of the crown lands of Judah or at least a part of them, and continue to have them supervised for him? If so, Jehoiachin would still have had some significance for the ancient homeland and those left behind in it. But we must be very careful of drawing hasty conclusions from the inscription on Eliakim's seal. It is quite possible that Eliakim's official status, and the fact that a seal was made for him, dates from the very short period of Jehoiachin's rule in Jerusalem, that the vessels with the impressions of the seal go back to this period, and that the seal of Eliakim was used later. This may be improbable, but we dare not overlook any possibility.[32]

[31] The word *na'ar* must probably be interpreted according to II *Sam.* IX.9, XVI.1, XIX.18. Cf. W. F. Albright: "The Seal of Eliakim and the latest pre-exilic history of Judah, with some observations on Ezekiel", J.B.L. 51, 1932, pp. 77-106.

[32] I do not consider well-founded the explanations given by H. G. May in "Three Hebrew seals and the status of exiled Jehoiakin", in *American Journal of Semitic Languages*, LVI (1939), pp. 146-8. The Seal of Jaazaniah found at Tell en-Nasbeh (cf. C. C. McCown: *Tell en-Nasbeh*, VOL. I, (1947), p. 163, pl. 57.4, 5) with the inscription "(Belonging) to Jaazaniah, the Servant of the King", which was found in Grave 19 and cannot be given an exact date, tells us here nothing certain since the name Jaazaniah is documented far too frequently in the seventh and sixth centuries B.C. to be able to identify the Jaazaniah of the seal satisfactorily with the Jaazaniah of II *Kings* xxv.23. Even if correct it would still not prove that the sign of office and the seal of Jaazaniah only date from the period after 587 B.C., and that therefore even after the catastrophe of Jerusalem there was still an official of "the King" in the ancient state of Judah. Even less significant here is the seal of Gedaliah from Tell ed-Duweir with the inscription "(Belonging) to Gedaliah who (is placed) over the House", which May brings into the argument, since neither the name nor the sign of office are historically unequivocal in this seal inscription.

Whether Jehoiachin was still the legal owner of the crown lands of Judah or not, it is at any rate probable that even after 587 B.C. he was not wholly forgotten in what was then the province of Judah; and possibly here and there even further afield, where there were descendants of the ancient tribes of Israel, he would be remembered with all sorts of illusions concerning his future return and some sort of "restoration". We find some justification for this view in the fact that after the catastrophe of 587 B.C. the Babylonians in many respects only created a provisional *régime*. Once again they removed or deported the prominent people of Judah (*II Kings* xxv.18-21); and, according to *Jer.* LII.30, some years later an even greater number of Judaeans were deported for reasons which we do not know. But the Babylonians did not instal foreign upper classes in the province of Judah, and therefore left a vacuum there. On the other hand they left alive, among the deportees, the former King of Judah, who continued to be considered the legitimate king by many. We might well suppose that this state of affairs kept alive all kinds of hopes of a "restoration". Indeed it is not improbable that the living Jehoiachin, and the hopes placed on him, held together large circles of those Judaeans deported to Babylon after 587 B.C., and preserved them from tamely accepting assimilation into their new environment.

Admittedly these hopes were illusory. Jeremiah and Ezekiel had long since rejected any false hope that anything would remain after the divine judgment on Israel. Israel had to bear the divine judgment in full, without any human hope of some starting-point for a new future—and history proved the prophets right, for eventually Jehoiachin died in Babylon, freed from prison when Amel-Marduk (the son and successor of Nebuchadnezzar) ascended the throne, but nevertheless by no means rehabilitated. There had certainly been no intimation of a return of Jehoiachin to the throne of his forefathers in Jerusalem (cf. *II Kings* xxv.27-30).

Only after Israel had completely accepted the ordained divine judgment could she be told in *Deutero-Isaiah* that God would now create something new.

INDEX OF HEBREW AND ARAMAIC TERMS

GENERAL INDEX